Management Accounting Handbook

C I *m* A

Published in association with
the Chartered Institute of
Management Accountants

Books in the CIMA Professional Handbook series

Series Editor: Rob Dixon

Strategic Management Handbook
Edited by John L. Thompson

Management Accounting Handbook

Second Edition
Edited by Colin Drury

Butterworth-Heinemann
Linacre House, Jordan Hill, Oxford OX2 8DP
A division of Reed Educational and Professional Publishing

℞ A member of the Reed Elsevier plc group

OXFORD   BOSTON   JOHANNESBURG
MELBOURNE   NEW DELHI   SINGAPORE

First published 1992
Second edition 1996

British Library Cataloguing in Publication Data

Management accounting handbook – 2nd ed – (CIMA professional handbook series)
1   Managerial accounting
I   Drury, Colin   II   Chartered Institute of Management Accountants
658.1′511

ISBN 0 7506 2191 5

Typeset by Datix International Limited, Bungay, Suffolk

Printed in Great Britain by Clays Ltd, St Ives plc

Contents

Contributors

Robin Bellis-Jones, MBA, FCMA, BSc, BComm, is a Director of Management Consultants Develin and Partners who specialize in helping companies improve their business performance. He has been instrumental in the development and introduction of the 'new' approaches to management accounting such as Activity Based Cost Management and Customer Profitability Analysis in a wide range of companies. Robin is also a member of the CIMA Council, Chairman of the CIMA Activity Based Costing Forum and lectures widely on Activity Based Cost Management. He has also authored a short book on *ABCM* and has made a direct contribution to Kaplan and Cooper's recently published book, *The Design of Cost Management Systems*.

Al Bhimani is a lecturer in Accounting and Finance at the London School of Economics. He was educated at King's College (London), Cornell University and the LSE, and qualified as a certified management accountant in Canada. He has previously held teaching positions at the universities of York and Western Ontario in Canada. His current research interests include the relationship between technology and management accounting practices and more generally, the social analysis of accounting change in different organizational contexts. He is co-author of *Management Accounting: Evolution not Revolution*.

T. J. ('Stan') Brignall spent ten years in industry as a management accountant and has been a lecturer in accounting and finance at Warwick University Business School for 12 years. He has published research in the form of books or articles on the Steel Industry, Industrial Policy and Shadow Planning, Inflation Accounting, the Coal Industry and Performance Measurement in Service Businesses. His current research interests include Strategic Management Accounting, Performance Measurement and Management Accounting in Service Organizations.

Jim Brimson, MBA, is a Partner of Coopers and Lybrand Deloitte (C & LD). Prior to C & LD, Jim worked for CAM-I, an international consortium conducting research and development in advanced manufacturing technology, where he originated the cost management project. He is editor of *Activity Accounting – An Activity-Based Costing Approach* and co-editor of *Cost Management in an Advanced Manufacturing Environment*. He has a BS from Auburn University and an MBA in quantitative science from Arizona State University.

Michael Bromwich is the Chartered Institute of Management Accountants' Professor of Accounting and Financial Management at the London School of Economics. He was Convener of the Department of Accounting and Finance from 1985 to 1989. He has served on BSRC committees. He is active in the accounting profession, has served a term on the Accounting Standards Committee and is a Past President of the Chartered Institute of Management Accountants. His most recent book is *Management Accounting: Evolution not Revolution.*

Ian Cobb spent nineteen years in industry, mainly with multi-national companies. Most of his experience is in management accounting, though he has also spent some time at the 'sharp ends' as a buyer and as a salesman. He has been a lecturer at Dundee University for seven years. His main current research interests are the management accounting implications of Just-in-Time, and data warehousing.

Nigel Coulthurst, BA ACAM CertEd, is a Management Accountant with The Boots Company Plc. He was employed previously by H J Heinz Co Ltd, the Rank Organization and Beecham Group and, prior to joining Boots was a lecturer in Financial Management at Loughborough University. He is the author of a number of books and articles on aspects of management accounting.

Colin Drury is Professor in Accountancy and Finance at Huddersfield Polytechnic. His best known publication is *Management and Cost Accounting* which is the UK's consistently most successful text on management accounting. He has published articles in academic and professional journals in the field of management accounting.

David Dugdale, ACMA, gained his PhD in Operational Research from the University of Hull in 1971. He then spent sixteen years in industry gaining experience as an Operational Research Analyst, Production Control Manager, Corporate Planner and Management Accountant before joining Bristol Polytechnic as a Senior Lecturer in Management Accounting in 1987. He would like to acknowledge the support of the

Management Control Association and the Bristol Business School in funding his research into the costing systems used in UK manufacturing industry.

Lin Fitzgerald currently lectures in Management Accounting on Undergraduate, Postgraduate and Executive courses at Warwick University Business School. She gained considerable industrial experience and completed her CIMA qualifications while working for British Telecom. Her research interests and publications are in the areas of performance measurement and cost information for management decision making.

John Innes is a Professor of Accountancy at the University of Dundee and **Falconer Mitchell** is a Professor of Accounting at the University of Edinburgh and is also a Canon Foundation Visiting Fellow. They have completed three British activity-based costing (ABC) case studies and in 1990 CIMA published the results entitled *ABC – A review with Case Studies*. In 1991 they conducted a survey of the use of ABC and also finished a case study of the development and implementation of an ABC system over a period of two years. They have contributed to a number of ABC courses organized by CIMA and they are both members of CIMA's ABC Working Party.

Robert Johnston has held several line management and senior management posts in a number of service organizations both in the public and private sector. He moved into academe in 1980 and is now a Senior Lecturer in Operations Management in the Warwick University Business School. He is the Director of the School's Consortium MBA programme. Robert has written extensively on the service management and has contributed many articles to journals and chapters to books. He is the editor of the *International Journal of Service Industry Management* and maintains active links with many organizations through his research and consultancy activities.

T. Colwyn Jones is Principal Lecturer in Sociology at the University of the West of England, Bristol. He is the author of *Accounting and the Enterprise: A social analysis* and (with David Dugdale) *Accounting for Throughput*. His research interests are centred on the relationship between management accounting, the development of advanced manufacturing technology, and organizational change. Much of this has been conducted jointly with David Dugdale.

Laurie McAulay is a Lecturer in Accountancy in the School of Management at the University of Bath. He joined the University of Bath in 1988 with experience both as a teacher and as a management accountant in large organizations. His current research interests are mainly concerned with the interface between management accounting and information technology, with particular reference to expert systems.

Graham Motteram is Financial Controller, Trent Engines at Rolls-Royce. Prior to this appointment he held senior financial posts within Rolls-Royce manufacturing group, involving considerable work on advanced manufacturing technology.

Bill Neale is a Lecturer in Finance and Accounting at Bradford University Management Centre. His research interests are in capital budgeting systems and international trade and marketing, areas in which he has published extensively, and delivered numerous conference papers. He is co-author of a book on investment post-auditing recently published by Longmans. In addition, he contributes to the CIMA mastercourse 'Post Auditing of Capital Investment Projects'.

Maurice Pendlebury is Professor of Accounting at Cardiff Business School, University of Wales College of Cardiff. He has previously worked for several public sector organizations and has had extensive experience, both in the UK and overseas, as a lecturer, researcher and consultant in public sector accounting topics.

Richard Pike is Provident Financial Professor of Finance and Accounting at the University of Bradford Management Centre. After qualifying as a chartered accountant he spent a number of years as planning controller for a major company. His main research interests lie in the capital investment area.

Rhian Silvestro, BA, MBA, teaches service operations management in Warwick University Business School. She spent three years on a research project in the field of performance measurement in service organizations and is co-author of *Performance Measurement in Service Businesses* which is being published by the research sponsor, The Chartered Institute of Management Accountants. She was formerly production manager in Mitaka, a Far East translation and typesetting company.

John Sizer, CBE, DLitt, BA, FCMA, is Chief Executive at the Scottish Higher Education Funding Council. Prior to this he was Professor of

Financial Management and Director of the Loughborough University Business School. His best-known publication is *An Insight into Management Accounting* and he has published extensively in the fields of management accounting and higher education policy and institutional management.

Cyril Tomkins, Professor of Accounting and Finance, School of Management, University of Bath. He has published about 100 book, articles, reports on a range of matters relating to financial management in both the private and public sector. His current funded research projects include work on devolved management within the FMI/Next Steps Initiative in Central Government, Investment Behaviour in UK and West German car components manufacturers, investment behaviour in an investment bank and development of accounting in Middle East institutions. His latest book is *Corporate Resource Allocation: Financial, strategic and organizational perspectives* (Blackwell, 1991).

Keith Ward, MA, FCA, FCMA, is currently at the Cranfield School of Management. Prior to going to Cranfield in 1981 he worked both in the city and abroad as a consultant, and held senior financial positions in manufacturing and trading companies (the last being as group financial director of Sterling International). His research interests are primarily in the fields of financial strategy, strategic management accounting, and accounting for marketing activities. He is the author of *Financial Aspects of Marketing, Management Accounting for Financial Decisions*, and *Strategic Management Accounting*, as well as publishing numerous articles.

Mohamed Zairi holds the SABIC chair in Best Practice Management at the University of Bradford Management Centre. Professor Zairi holds a PhD in The Management of Advanced Manufacturing Technology, an MSc in Safety Technology and a BSc (hons) in Polymer Science and Technology. He has written numerous books on benchmarking and performance measurement and has acted as advisor to large corporations all over the world and to various governments.

1

Introduction
Colin Drury

A considerable amount of attention has been focused recently on the relevance of contemporary management accounting practices. During the past ten years there has probably been more written on this topic than the combined writings of the previous fifty years. Much of this recent attention has resulted from the impact of the changing manufacturing and competitive environment. Opinions seem to differ as to whether or not significant changes in management accounting are necessary, but some commentators do believe that management accounting is in a crisis situation and that fundamental changes in practice are required.

There is a need for practitioners to be well informed on the current debate relating to the relevance of management accounting practices and also for them to update their knowledge on the key developments which are taking place. This book aims to meet this need. It contains seventeen chapters and includes contributions from leading academics and practitioners. Each chapter focuses on an important contemporary issue. It is hoped that a greater awareness of the issues and problems which are currently being discussed will aid and stimulate readers to improve future management accounting practice. This chapter briefly discusses some of the major criticisms which have been the subject of debate in recent years.

It was during the 1980s that criticisms of current management accounting practices began to appear in the professional and academic accounting literature. The most prominent critic was Robert Kaplan, from Harvard Business School, who, in a series of articles in the mid-1980s, questioned the relevance of current practices. In 1987 Kaplan co-authored a book with Thomas Johnson called *Relevance Lost: The Rise and Fall of Management Accounting*. An enormous amount of publicity was generated from this book as a result of the authors' claims that firms were still using 30-year-old management accounting practices which were obsolete and no longer relevant to today's competitive and manufacturing environment.

The principal criticisms of current management accounting practices can be summarized under the following headings:

1   Conventional management accounting does not meet the needs of today's manufacturing and competitive environment.
2   Traditional product costing systems provide misleading information for decision-making purposes.
3   Management accounting practices follow, and have become subservient to, financial accounting requirements.
4   Management accounting focuses almost entirely on internal activities and relatively little attention is given to the external environment in which the business operates.

Failure to respond to changes in the manufacturing and competitive environment

In the 1980s advanced manufacturing technologies such as computer-aided manufacturing and just-in-time manufacturing techniques dramatically changed the production processes in many organizations. In order to compete successfully it was necessary to produce innovative products of high quality at a relatively low cost and also provide a first-class customer service. Many companies responded to these competitive demands by investing in AMTs, implementing JIT manufacturing philosophies and emphasizing in their corporate objectives quality, delivery innovation and a flexibility to meet customers' needs.

Investing in advanced manufacturing technologies has caused many problems such as how to appraise the capital investments, how to compute product costs and how to modify control systems and performance measures so that they motivate managers to meet the new strategic manufacturing and competitive goals of their organizations. Some organizations have reported that their existing cost systems have hindered, rather than helped, the required changes to come about. This has resulted in claims by some writers that current management accounting systems are obsolete and that a revolution in management accounting is required to match the revolution in manufacturing technology.

The apparent inability of capital investment appraisal techniques to justify AMTs is frequently cited as a major reason for underinvestment in new manufacturing technology. A proposed remedy is that the financial appraisal of investments in AMTs should be abandoned and the investment should be based solely on strategic considerations. Most of the criticisms, however, relate to incorrect applications of the techniques, rather than weaknesses of the financial appraisal system. For example, critics claim that benefits which are difficult to quantify in monetary terms are often ignored, excessive discount rates are used, inflation is dealt with incorrectly, and a comparison of the investment is often made against the status quo. That is, investments are compared against an alternative that assumes a continuation of the current market share, selling prices and costs. However, this status quo alternative is unlikely to apply as competitors are also likely to invest in the new technology. In this situation investment should be compared with the alternative of not investing, based on assuming a situation of declining cash flows. A further criticism is that the financial appraisal focuses excessively on short-term results and, since investments in AMTs tend to yield longer term benefits, investment is being thwarted.

Investment in AMTs is extremely difficult to evaluate because many of the benefits cannot be easily measured in monetary terms. Nevertheless the financial appraisal is still important and should not be abandoned. Financial managers should resist calls for investments in AMTs to be made on faith alone because the financial appraisal is too restrictive. The challenge is for accountants to seek ways of avoiding the pitfalls and ensure that financial appraisal techniques are wisely applied when evaluating AMT investments. In particular, sensitivity analysis should be used and top management presented with a complete picture of the range of possible outcomes. This would not require alterations to the investment appraisal system which is outlined in most textbooks.

There is, however, a growing recognition that traditional cost control and performance management systems do not provide the appropriate information to control the activities of companies which operate in an advanced manufacturing environment. Investment in AMTs dramatically changes cost behaviour patterns. Computer technicians, software programmers and engineers replace direct labour, and variable costs tend to consist of only direct materials and energy costs to operate the machinery. More of the firm's costs become fixed (and sunk) and direct labour costs represent only a small percentage of total manufacturing cost. Overhead costs are a much higher fraction of total manufacturing cost and consequently need to be understood and controlled much more carefully than in the past.

JIT manufacturing is best described as a philosophy of management dedicated to the elimination of waste. Waste is defined as anything which does not add customer-perceived value to the product. The lead time involved in manufacturing and selling a product consists of process time, inspection time, move time, queue time and storage time. Of these five steps, only process time actually adds value to the product. All the other activities add cost but no value to the product. JIT manufacturing aims to substantially reduce non-value added activities. In particular the emphasis is on high quality and inventory reduction. Inventory reduction is achieved by rearranging the production process and closely co-ordinating suppliers' delivery schedules with production so that the delivery of materials immediately precedes their use.

The production process is rearranged by changing from a batch production functional layout to a product layout using flow lines. With a functional plant layout products pass through a number of specialist departments which normally contain a group of similar machines. Products are processed in large batches so as to minimize the set-up times when machine settings are changed between processing batches of different products. Batches move via different and complex routes through the various departments, travelling over much of the factory floor before they are completed. Each process normally involves a considerable amount of waiting time. In addition much time is taken transporting items from one process to another. The consequences of this complex routeing process are high work in progress levels and long manufacturing lead times.

The JIT solution is to reorganize the production process by grouping the products into families of similar products. All of the products in a particular group will have similar production requirements and routeings. Production is rearranged so that each product family is manufactured on a flow line. In a product line flow, specialist departments containing similar machines no longer exist. Instead, groups of dissimilar machines are organized into product family flow lines that function like an assembly line. For each product line the machines are placed close together in the order in which they are required by the group of products to be processed. Items in each product family can now move from process to process more easily thereby reducing work in progress and lead times. The aim is to produce products from start to finish without returning to the stock room.

Conventional cost control and performance measurement systems were designed to meet the requirements of a traditional manufacturing system. Sometimes they can motivate behaviour which is not consistent with the requirements of a JIT philosophy. For example, traditional manufacturing measures, such as volume variances, can lead to excessive inventories because they emphasize maximizing output. Absorption costing systems are extensively used for internal monthly profit computations. Profit centre managers might, therefore, seek to increase inventories so as to reduce the impact of the fixed cost charged against the current period. When JIT is implemented stocks are continuously reduced over several months. This has a detrimental effect on monthly profits when absorption costing systems are used. In these situations the performance measurement system is pushing in the opposite direction to the JIT philosophy. Standard costing, variance analysis, labour efficiency and overhead absorption measures were developed to meet the needs of a traditional manufacturing environment. It is doubtful whether calculating variances in monetary terms for resources such as direct labour and the so-called fixed overheads, where spending is not aligned with consumption, provides useful information for short-term operational control purposes.

With JIT there is a need to move towards greater use of simplified non-financial measures which are directly related to manufacturing strategy and which provide fast and effective feedback. In addition greater emphasis is placed on control through direct observation, by training the workers to monitor quality, production flow and set-up times continuously. Workers will have pinpointed variances by direct observation long before they have been calculated for financial reporting purposes. Variance analysis will not therefore be particularly useful for operational control purposes. However, standard costs and variance analysis will continue to be useful for financial accounting purposes, preparing monthly profit statements and as an input to the budgeting process.

Surveys of firms operating in an advanced manufacturing environment indicate that direct labour costs account for less than 15 per cent of total manufacturing cost. However, traditional management accounting systems tend to place a far greater emphasis on reporting direct labour cost and efficiency while relatively little attention is given to reporting and controlling direct materials and overhead costs. Many firms which operate in an advanced manufacturing environment still recover overheads on a direct labour basis. Consequently the attention of management is directed to reducing direct labour by trivial amounts. To reduce their allocated costs managers are motivated to reduce direct labour since this is the basis by which all other costs are attached to their cost centres and products. This process overstates the importance of direct labour and directs attention away from controlling escalating overhead costs.

Traditional management accounting systems have also been criticized because they fail to report on such issues as quality, reliability, lead times, flexibility and customer satisfaction, despite the fact that they represent the strategic goals of world-class manufacturing companies. Traditionally, management accounting reports have tended to focus on costs. Consequently there is a danger that if the non-financial measures which are necessary to compete successfully in today's worldwide competitive environment are not emphasized, managers and employees will be motivated to focus exclusively on cost and ignore other important marketing, managerial and strategic considerations.

Limitations of traditional product costing systems

In the late 1980s a considerable amount of publicity was given to product cost measurement and profitability analysis. In a series of articles in the late 1980s Cooper and Kaplan drew attention to the limitations of traditional product costing systems. Their criticisms relate to the methods of allocating overheads to products.

Full product costs must be computed in order to meet financial accounting requirements. The management accounting literature advocates that full product costs, using financial accounting principles, are not suitable for decision-making purposes. Instead, the literature states that decisions should be based on incremental/avoidable costs. With this approach, decisions such as introducing new products, discontinuing products and product pricing should be based on a study of only those incremental expenses and revenues which will vary with respect to the particular decision. This approach implies that special studies should be undertaken when the need arises.

The limited amount of empirical evidence on the use of product costs for decision-making, however, suggests that managers use full product costs for decision-making purposes. For example, on the basis of observations of 150 costs systems over the past seven years in the USA, Cooper (1990) claims that traditional full product costs were used by all of the companies as a basis for decision-making. A survey by Drury *et al.* (1993) also reports the widespread use by UK companies of traditional full product costs for decision-making purposes. The evidence suggests that managers require periodic estimates of long-run variable costs for each product and traditional product costs are used to provide an approximation of these costs.

The deficiencies of traditional product costs for decision-making purposes has been widely publicized, most notably by Cooper and Kaplan. Traditional product costing systems were designed decades ago, when most companies manufactured a narrow range of products and direct labour and materials were the dominant factory costs. Overhead costs were relatively small and the distortions arising from inappropriate overhead allocations were not significant. Information processing costs were high and it was, therefore, difficult to justify more sophisticated overhead allocation methods.

Today, companies produce a wide range of products, direct labour represents only a small fraction of total costs and overhead costs are of considerable importance. Simplistic overhead allocations using a declining direct labour base cannot be justified, particularly when information processing costs are no longer a barrier to introducing more sophisticated systems. Furthermore the intense global competition of the 1980s created a need by managers for more accurate information on how product mix, introduction an abandonment decisions affect their organization's profitability.

It is against this background that activity-based costing (ABC) emerged. ABC systems differ from traditional product costing systems in the treatment of non-volume-related resources. Traditional systems measure accurately volume-related resources that are consumed in proportion to the number of units produced of individual products. Such resources include direct labour, materials, machine time and energy. However, many organizational resources exist for non-volume-related activities that are unrelated to physical volume. Consequently, traditional product cost systems which assume that products consume resources in proportion to their production volumes will report distorted product costs.

Non-volume-related activities consist of support activities such as material handling, material procurement, set-ups, production scheduling and first-item inspection activities. Resources are consumed by activities that are performed each time a batch of products is produced. Consider, for example, activities such as setting up a machine to produce a different product. When the machine is changed from one product to another, set-up resources are consumed according to the number of set-ups performed and are independent of the number of units produced after completing the set-up.

In order to illustrate the differences between traditional systems and ABC systems let us assume that the cost of resources consumed by set-up activities is £120,000 and only two products are produced – product L (a low volume product) and product H (a high volume product). Production for the period was 5,000 units of product L and 45,000 units of product H. The low volume product is produced in batches of 500 units whereas the high volume product is produced in batches of 9,000 units. Thus product L requires 10 set-ups and product H, 5 set-ups.

With the traditional product costing system the set-up costs would be allocated to the production departments and then charged to products using volume-related bases such as machine hours or direct labour hours. Assuming that both products required the same number of machine or direct labour hours per unit then the traditional system would allocate 10 per cent (5,000/50,000) of the set-up costs to product L and 90 per cent (45,000/50,000) to product H. Thus set-up costs of £12,000 (10% × £120,000) would be allocated to product L and £108,000 (90% × £120,000) would be allocated to product H. The overall outcome is that a set-up cost of £2.40 would be attributed to each product (£12,000/5,000 units for product L and £108,000/45,000 units for product H).

With the ABC system costs are traced to products according to the products' demands for activities. Product L has consumed two-thirds (10 out of 15 set-ups) and product H has consumed one-third (5 out of 15 set-ups) of the set-up resources. Thus set-up costs of £80,000 would be traced to product L and £40,000 would be traced to product H. The set-up cost per unit is £16 for product L (£80,000/5,000 units) and £0.89 (£40,000/45,000 units) for product H. Cooper and Kaplan argue that traditional cost systems report distorted product costs whenever the cost of non-volume-related activities is significant. In particular low-volume products tend to be undercosted and high-volume products overcosted. Assuming that the selling price for product L was marginally higher than product H the message from the traditional cost system is to de-emphasize product H and focus on more profitable speciality low volume products similar to product L. In reality this strategy would be disastrous since product H is cheaper to make and replacing the lost output with low-volume speciality products will further increase the overheads relating to support activities.

Practitioners have shown an enormous amount of interest in ABC. There has been a surge in the number of delegates attending courses and conferences on this topic and much publicity has been generated by articles which have been published in professional accountancy literature. This would seem to suggest that practitioners are dissatisfied with traditional product costing systems and are not convinced that the incremental approach advocated by academics provides the product cost information which they require for the decisions which they face in the real world.

ABC has attracted a considerable amount of interest because it not only provides a basis for calculating more accurate product costs, but it also provides a mechanism for managing overhead costs. An ABC system focuses management's attention on the underlying causes of costs. It assumes that resource-consuming activities cause costs and that products incur costs through the activities they require for design, engineering, manufacturing, marketing, delivering, invoicing and servicing. By collecting and reporting on the significant activities a business engages in it is possible to understand and manage costs more effectively.

With an ABC system costs are managed in the long term by controlling the activities which drive them. In other words the aim is to manage the activities rather than costs. By managing the forces that cause the activities (that is, the cost drivers) costs will be managed in the long term. Examples of cost drivers include number of set-ups, set-up costs, number of pur-

chase orders for material procurement activities and number of production orders for production and scheduling activities.

ABC is in its infancy and it remains to be seen whether it turns out to be
the 'fad' of the 1990s or a mechanism which provides more meaningful
information to help managers make better decisions and manage overhead
costs more effectively.

Management accounting has become subservient to financial accounting

Johnson and Kaplan claim that management accounting practices follow,
and have become subservient to, financial accounting requirements. They
justify their claim by asserting that product costs which are computed for
financial accounting purposes are also being used for decision-making
purposes. Such costs include arbitrary overhead allocations and provide a
poor estimate of the resources consumed by products. Costs based on the
principles of financial accounting provide a satisfactory approximation for
allocating costs between costs of sales and inventories for external financial reporting purposes but distort *individual* product costs through
cross-subsidization arising from the misallocation of overhead costs. Consequently strategic decisions are subordinated to financial accounting
requirements.

Most academics have been surprised by these criticisms. Textbooks do
not advocate that management accounting practice should be dictated by
financial accounting practices. Indeed, they go to great lengths to indicate
that information prepared for financial accounting purposes ought not to
be used for management accounting purposes. Therefore, if management
accounting practices have been driven by financial accounting requirements it must have happened despite the recommendations advocated in
the literature. Johnson and Kaplan's criticism implies that senior management accountants and top management have blindly allowed external
financial accounting to determine internal management information
requirements.

The fact that information prepared for management is not inherently
different from the information which is produced for external financial
reporting does not by itself indicate that management accounting is subservient to financial accounting. Perhaps a plausible explanation is that
advocated by Holzer and Norreklit (1991). They suggest that, until
recently, many companies have considered that the benefits of sophisticated cost systems have not been sufficient to outweigh their additional
cost. Information processing costs are considerably less today than they

were twenty years ago and the change to a more competitive climate over the years has made decision errors due to poor cost information more probable and more costly. Holzer and Norreklit conclude that over the years the increased opportunity cost of having poor cost information, and the decreased cost of operating more sophisticated cost systems has increased the demand for more accurate product costs. Thus some companies may have responded to the changing environment by developing activity-based costing systems.

Johnson and Kaplan reject the above argument. Without any supporting empirical evidence their claim cannot be accepted as generally valid. Nevertheless, their controversial assertions have stimulated both academics and practitioners to question whether or not current cost management systems are merely a by-product of the financial accounting requirements or have been designed to help managers make better decisions.

Relatively little attention is given to the external environment

Recently, management accounting has been criticized because it has been heavily biased towards the internal comparisons of costs and revenues and relatively little attention has been given to the external environment in which the business operates. Critics argue that there is a need for management accounting to adopt a more strategic perspective by reporting information relating to the firm's markets and its competitors.

A successful business strategy requires the development and maintenance of some form of sustainable relative competitive advantage. It is therefore argued that management accounting information should highlight the relative competitive positioning of the organization. In order to protect an organization's strategic position managers require information which indicates by whom, by how much and why they are gaining or being beaten. Conventional measures of profits do not provide the required information. Instead, more strategic indicators of performance are required which provide advance warning of the need for a change in competitive strategy. For example, a very simplistic indicator for many firms would be an unexpected movement in the relative market share of their major products. By monitoring movements in market share, an organization can see whether it is gaining or losing position, and an examination of relative market shares will indicate the strength of different competitors. Including market-share details in management accounting reports helps to make management accounting more strategically relevant. Ward (see Chapter 10) however, argues that very few businesses regularly incorporate such information in their internal management accounting reports.

The literature also suggests that strategic management accounting should focus on providing information on the market prospects of existing products, their position in the product life cycle and the portfolio of products produced. This analysis should not be based solely on the individual organization but on its competitive advantages relative to its competitors. Using externally based comparisons helps to explain the relative current changes in sales revenues, profits and cash flows and can add considerable value to the accounting system in its function of supporting financially based strategic decisions.

During the 1980s academics, consultants and senior managers have highlighted the need to focus on developing and implementing competitive strategies. Conventional management accounting does not provide the financial information required to monitor existing strategies or support strategy formulation. Strategic management accounting seeks to remedy this situation by providing the financial analysis to support the formulation of successful competitive strategies.

Outline of the book

This chapter has discussed the principal criticisms of management accounting practices. In the light of the criticisms the Chartered Institute of Management Accountants (CIMA) commissioned an investigation to identify:

> the criticisms being made, the way in which management accounting techniques already exist to meet them, the findings of research in this field and any gaps that might initiate further research.

The results of this investigation were published in 1989 in a report entitled *Management Accounting: Evolution not Revolution* (Bromwich and Bhimani, 1989). Five years later Bromwich and Bhimani (1994) updated their report with a second report entitled *Management Accounting: Pathways to Progress*. The second report reviewed the literature and research in the intervening years and focused on the wider array of opportunities now facing the management accountant. The report concluded that in the UK no one school of opinion yet dominates views on the nature of reforms which might be appropriate for management accounting. The case for wholesale reform has not been accepted in practice.

In Chapter 2 Bromwich and Bhimani, the authors of the CIMA reports summarize and briefly update the findings of their second report. This is followed by three chapters on activity-based costing (ABC). Innes and Mitchell, the authors of the ABC case studies published by CIMA, describe in Chapter 3 how an operational ABC system can be created. This is followed by an evaluation of ABC systems. In the following two chapters Brimson and Bellis-Jones describe practical aspects of ABC based on their experience of implementing activity costing systems.

Chapters 6 and 7 deal with the changing manufacturing environment. In Chapter 6 Cobb describes the changes that are necessary when accounting for a just-in-time manufacturing philosophy and in Chapter 7 Dugdale and Jones describe throughput accounting theory and techniques. This is followed by a chapter by Zairi on the role of non-financial performance assessment.

Chapters 9–10 focus on strategic management accounting. In Chapter 9 Bromwich outlines its essential characteristics and reviews the literature. This is followed by an examination of the role of strategic cost analysis in costing the value of product attributes. Chapter 10 is entitled 'Accounting for marketing strategies'. In this chapter Ward discusses the decision support information which is required to develop and implement specific competitive strategies.

Most of the management accounting literature has tended to focus on the application of management accounting techniques within the manufacturing sector. This book seeks to redress this situation by including three chapters which are concerned solely with management accounting in a non-manufacturing environment. Chapter 11 focuses on performance measurement in service organizations. In particular the authors pursue the links between performance measures and competitive strategies. They present three case studies and examine the extent to which strategies are supported with appropriate performance measurement systems. In Chapter 12 Coulthurst describes various aspects of management accounting within the Boots Company Plc. He discusses the difficulties that arise in satisfying management's accounting information requirements and describes how developments in information technology have provided an opportunity to overcome some of these difficulties. In the final chapter relating to the non-manufacturing sector Pendlebury describes the nature and role of local government management accounting practices.

Chapters 14 and 15 are concerned with capital budgeting and investment appraisal. In Chapter 14 Pike and Neale focus on the role of management accounting within the capital budgeting process. They demonstrate that capital budgeting is far more than just appraising individual investments and stress that it should be viewed within the context of strategic planning. They also discuss the post-auditing review of capital projects. The problems associated with appraising capital investments in advanced manufacturing technologies are discussed by Sizer and Motteram in Chapter 15. In this chapter the authors describe and examine eight major sequential steps involved in successfully evaluating and controlling proposed investments in advanced manufacturing technologies.

Transfer pricing has been one of the most widely debated topics in the management accounting literature. The literature is confusing, and complex solutions, some of which are highly mathematical and difficult to implement in practice, have been advocated. In Chapter 16 Tomkins and McAulay briefly review the literature and identify those situations where clear, simple and practical advice can be given. In particular the authors present a case for basing transfer prices on long-run variable costs which, they suggest, can be approximated by setting transfer prices to recover full cost. They then provide practical guidance on how a fair profit element to add to full cost can be derived.

In Chapter 17 Drury and Dugdale examine differences between the theory and practice of management accounting. They review the published empirical studies on management accounting practice and discuss some of the observed differences between theory and practice.

References

Bromwich, M. and Bhimani, A. (1989). *Management Accounting: Evolution not Revolution*, Chartered Institute of Management Accountants.

Bromwich, M. and Bhimani, A. (1994). *Management Accounting: Pathways to Progress*, Chartered Institute of Management Accountants.

Cooper, R. (1990). Explicating the logic of ABC. *Management Accounting*, November 1990, 58–60.

Cooper, R. and Kaplan, R. S. (1988). Measure costs right: make the right decision. *Harvard Business Review*, September–October 1988, 96–103.

Drury, C., Braund, S., Osborne, P. and Tayles, M. (1993). A Survey of UK Management Accounting Practices. Chartered Association of Certified Accountants.

Holzer, H. P. and Norreklit, H. (1991). Some thoughts on cost accounting developments in the United States. *Journal of Management Accounting Research*, March 1991, 3–13.

Johnson, H. T. and Kaplan, R. S. (1987). *Relevance Lost: The Rise and Fall of Management Accounting*. Boston, USA: Harvard Business School.

2

Management accounting: emerging pathways

Al Bhimani and Michael Bromwich

During the 1980s a considerable amount of attention was given to criticisms of management accounting practice. As a result of these criticisms the Chartered Institute of Management Accountants commissioned an investigation to review the current state of development of management accounting and of the various claims being made regarding it. The findings were published in a report, entitled Management Accounting: Evolution not Revolution, *by Bromwich and Bhimani (1989).*

Five years later Bromwich and Bhimani (1994) updated their report with a second report entitled Management Accounting: Pathways to Progress. *The second report reviewed the literature and research in the intervening years and focused on the wider array of opportunities facing the management accountant. In this chapter the authors of the reports summarize and briefly update the basic findings of their second report. The first part of the chapter reviews aspects of management accounting in Japanese enterprises with special reference to target cost management practices. After discussing some arguments by advocates of management accounting reform, a brief review of expected future accounting developments is made and important aspects of the report's recommendations, including a consideration of organizational and socio-technical issues, are outlined.*

Since the 1980s, industry in Western countries has had to respond to a number of major challenges. These include the need to increase spending on R&D and the requirement to make major investment in new technology and in supply processes. International competitors have also posed the challenge of delaying cumbersome managerial structures and downsizing organizations to become leaner and thereby increase productivity to withstand competition from 'world class' firms in a recessionary global environment. Competitive challenges are also to be met by, for instance, increasing product diversity, offering higher quality, better delivery and increased flexibility to satisfy new consumer demands as well as meeting enhanced international competition.

Over the same period, accounting commentators and professional accountancy bodies particularly in North America have levelled major criticisms at management accounting practices. In part, these calls for change were tied to the environment within which 'high tech' manufacturing activities were taking place, although other factors were also responsible for these criticisms. The main arguments for supporting reforms in managerial accounting are as follows.

Competitive pressures

First, at the international level, competitive manufacturing methods used by major Japanese corporations and by those of newly industrialized countries were seen as superior to those used in the West. To an extent, this was ascribed to socio-cultural characteristics of Japanese workers from factory-floor operators to senior executives. But what was viewed as more significant, was the application of flexible manufacturing technologies by the Japanese to produce a greater diversity of high-quality, low-priced product more quickly. Specific modes of work organization, production systems and motivational incentives were seen to differ radically from those used in the West. All these factors also raised interest among accounting practitioners and academics about the implications of differences in management accounting activities and management practices generally.

New technologies

Second, the adoption of flexible technologies in manufacturing and service oriented enterprises including manufacturing and enterprise resources planning (MRP II and MRP III) systems, computer-aided design and manufacturing (CAD/CAM), robotics and other features of computer-integrated manufacturing (CIM) led to conventional accounting methods for cost allocation being questioned. In particular, whereas the manufacturing environment had become more automated, more specialized and more flexible, and consequently required larger capital investments, methods of costing products continued to operate under the past assumption that company operations were geared toward repetitive production of homogeneous products relying on labour-intensive activities which, although somewhat true of traditional manufacturing settings, was not the case for modern ones. Management accounting techniques were thus seen to be anachronistic given the new manufacturing environment. Similar problems have been raised about cost accounting methods in service industries.

Dominance of financial accounting

A third reason was also voiced in support of calls for change in management accounting. North American academics in the main viewed management accounting as initially having had a rich history of development tied to changes in business strategy. However, from the post-First World War period, progress in management accounting was seen as virtually ceasing principally as a result of the growing importance of external reporting priorities especially in the area of inventory valuation over those of internal organizational accounting. Some critics of traditional management accounting thus assert that management accounting has, for over seventy years, been subordinated to the requirements of financial statement preparation for external parties. Advocates of this school have supported calls for management accounting reforms based on the argument that the field must once again be allowed to develop in its own right, rather than remain a function secondary to financial accounting.

The diverse roles of management accounting

Finally, many commentators have made more substantive arguments focusing on the propriety of accounting practices given the roles which management accounting is intended to fulfil. In this respect, critics have questioned the usefulness of complex methods of organizational costing and pricing in the face of the belief that the price of a product must ultimately meet the expectations of the marketplace rather than those of its producers. Others have given weight to the argument that management accounting has for too long remained isolated and divorced from other enterprise functions. Conventional accounting practices have installed, within the organization, channels for information flow and routes for data-exchange which have rendered some organizations static, inflexible and excessively structured, especially in the case of firms operating in dynamic and fast moving markets. Some accounting commentators have also suggested broader functional roles of accounting as part of an all-encompassing cost management expertise which, with specialist guidance, can be made to serve enterprises in a renewed and more effective light.

In the light of these criticisms, the Chartered Institute of Management Accountants (CIMA) commissioned an investigation to identify

> ... the criticisms being made, the way in which management accounting techniques already exist to meet them, the findings of research in this field, and any gaps that might initiate further research.

The research monograph *Management Accounting: Evolution not Revolution* published by the CIMA in 1989 was the first attempt to document this research exercise. In the ensuing years, novel perspectives in management accounting approaches continued to grow. More importantly, evidence from industry as to the impact of adopting altered cost management approaches emerged. CIMA thus commissioned another large-scale study of management accounting changes and perspectives which was published in 1994 as a research monograph entitled *Management Accounting: Pathways to Progress*. The investigation retains much of the substantive material of the earlier report continuing to address the original brief but also indicates possible paths forward for accountants. It thus examines the implications for management accounting of the changes which are taking place within British firms which are adopting different forms of advanced manufacturing techniques and managerial processes. It reviews information concerning changing managerial perceptions of information requirements, the use of new communication forms and channels, and the implications of changing organizational structures so as to help the management accounting profession to react to this new environment.

The report supports its conclusions by exploring the findings of empirical investigations of British, North American and Japanese firms undertaken by various independent researchers and concentrates on documenting changes in management accounting processes in these countries.

This chapter seeks to summarize and briefly update the basic findings of this latest report. The first part of this chapter reviews aspects of management accounting in Japanese enterprises with especial reference to target cost management practices. After discussing some arguments made by advocates of management accounting reform, a brief review of expected future accounting developments is made and important aspects of the report's recommendations, including a consideration of organizational and socio-technical issues, are outlined.

Japanese management

The past success of the Japanese economy is legendary. During the 1960s an unprecedented rate of economic growth exceeding 10 per cent per year was attained. The major economic shocks of the 1970s, including two major oil crises, were weathered and the average annual economic growth in the 1970s and 1980s was 5 per cent and 4 per cent respectively. In comparison, generally economic growth in the USA has not exceeded, at most, 3 per cent over any significant period.

The Japanese share of world exports grew from about 2 per cent to well over 6 per cent per annum in a 30-year period to the mid-1980s while the world share of USA exports declined by 6 per cent to 11 per cent over the same period (McMillan, 1985). From 1985 to 1991, the Japanese gross national product rose on average by approximately 4.6 per cent per annum and exports similarly increased by 6.7 per cent per annum (*Financial Times* 14 August 1993, p. 4). Only Germany came near to matching this record of economic growth and only the USA could match the increase in exports. Even in recent years Japan has coped relatively well though the impact of recession in the 1990s is substantial with industrial output falling by over 4 per cent, with attendant redundancies and reduced earnings. It is not yet clear how the problem of the recession which some see as structural will be overcome but some commentators believe that major responses are underway.

Japanese industrial success is relatively narrowly focused on a number of industries which require a great deal of pre-production planning, can be conducted mainly as assembly operations, embody modern technology, and reward the philosophy of high quality and low costs. Japan has been especially successful in motor vehicle manufacture, electronics of all kinds, the computer industry, office machinery and optics. This portfolio of successful products changes with time. Sunrise industries are strongly encouraged by the government and industry, while sunset industries are ruthlessly rationalized.

The literature in English explaining Japanese management accounting practices has increased considerably over the past few years (see Yoshikava, Mitchell and Moyes, 1994), often concentrating on what has come to be called 'target costing' and related techniques (see, for example, Inoue, 1992; Morgan and Weerakoon, 1989; Sakurai, 1989b; Worthy, 1991; and Yoshikawa, *et al.*, 1989). Often the available literature explicitly or implicitly urges the use of Japanese practices in Western firms. For example, many authors have taken Hiromoto's suggestions that Japanese management accounting predominantly plays a behaviour influencing role to indicate that Western accounting should be re-orientated towards this perspective (Hiromoto, 1988). This tendency may have been aided and abetted by the title of the article: 'Another Hidden Edge – Japanese Management Accounting'.

Although almost every observation about Japan is controversial, there is general agreement that Japanese economic success cannot be traced just to a set of separate individual techniques and environmental factors. Rather, Japanese success is held to flow from mutually interacting institutional and cultural factors, objectives, organizational management practices and a set of interlinking techniques and practices. All of these factors build on and mutually reinforce each other.

Clearly, the Japanese 'economic miracle' is tied to many factors which cannot be linked directly to the nature of business training which Japanese companies afford their workers, nor to formal managerial practices. However, it has been argued that aspects which are central to Japanese-style management in large companies include seniority-based payment/promotion systems, enterprise unions, lifetime employment, consensus-oriented bottom-up decision-making, lifetime in-company training, recruitment of workers directly from school/university for lifetime employment, and various company incentives and perks, low interest loans, company housing and special welfare schemes (Gow, 1986; Misawa, 1987) though a number of these characteristics are now less commonly practised and may have never been generally practised as described in the Western literature. Such characteristics have implications for the ways in which accounting can regulate organizational affairs, as well as for the manner in which Japanese corporate life conditions accounting. For instance, where decision-making is based on accounting data, factors of production such as labour cannot be assumed as being fixed costs by virtue of the lifetime employment system operating in many large Japanese companies. In reality, labour costs may be variable and employees in such companies can be easily moved to other jobs, can be made redundant or face the prospect of 'forced demotions' (possibly from a principal firm to one of its subcontractors or sister companies). To an extent therefore, labour can be viewed as being variable as described by many of the traditional cost accounting conventions resorted to by Western management accountants.

Japanese management accounting

Employees in Japanese companies do not typically enter a department as juniors at the start of their career in expectation of holding a more senior post in that function at the end of their working life. Rather, a Japanese accounting manager is likely to have spent a few years in different departments gaining all-round experience in both staff and line functions, in the Western sense of the term.

It must be recognized however, that management accounting is often used with different objectives in Japan to those assumed in Western organizations (Monden and Sakurai, 1989). In some companies, the influencing role of management accounting dominates its informing function, which is often seen as taking precedence in the West. Thus, in a capital-intensive environment, preference may be given to direct labour as an allocation base because this is likely to inspire in managers and designers burdened with high overhead costs, a pro-automation attitude, motivating the further reduction of the utilization of labour. In such contexts, the utility of accurate costs is secondary. Cost distortions caused by using highly-leveraged burden rates are inconsequential since costing calculations are used in this instance, not to inform but to influence and motivate particular attitudes and behaviours.

Overwhelming characteristics of Japanese management accounting are a desire to 'keep it simple', make sure it is understood by everyone, and a wish to use accounting techniques which only further the firm's objectives (Bhimani and Bromwich, 1992). In this area, 'simple is beautiful'. The use of actual costing, and estimated costing (where cost bookkeeping is undertaken using estimated costs rather than actual costs) provides an example. Another is the use of payback for investment appraisal rather than more sophisticated discounted cash flow models. Though other reasons for this can be found in the Japanese finance system which have been argued to generate a lower cost of capital, the Japanese decision-making system does not accord primacy to numerical calculation and encourages concerns about enterprise market growth, especially in an environment of short product life cycles. Projects with a short payback period should have high market potential and are said to reduce the risk effects of short life cycles. Moreover, generally investments put into action an agreed strategy and therefore simple investment appraisal methods may be seen as quite appropriate.

Cost accuracy is sought in particular circumstances by Japanese managers though often within a set of objectives different to those of Western companies. Whereas many firms in the West are said to rely on cost accuracy in pricing products, in Japan product prices are often set according to a calculus determined primarily by the potential customer's utility for the product, the desired market positioning of the producer and internal estimates of resource inputs required to manufacture the product. What might be called 'target pricing' for instance, is based on the price which a product can command on the market, the perceived benefits of being an early market entrant and reaping the advantages of the relationship between large scale volume and experience effects, as well as the coordinated efforts of accountants, designers and engineers to obtain the predetermined target cost. Product pricing is thus a mixture of cost information, marketing factors and manufacturing capabilities. Its complexity is underlined, not by the use of sophisticated cost accounting techniques but by the extensive interflows of information between different parts of the organization. For this reason, what the West calls management accounting is valued as an important tool of enterprise management but is not held supreme in any hierarchy of management tasks and often accountants will not be in charge of what Western commentators would call accounting tasks.

Target costing

Because large Japanese firms often deal in global markets with clear market prices, target costing is market orientated. Target costing indicates for each product (and each cost element of that product) what cost reductions (over time) must be achieved by the firm and its suppliers in order to ensure that the company's strategy is realized throughout the product's life cycle, whilst maintaining a competitive market price for the product offered.

A preliminary step in this process is for the enterprise to come to a view over the whole product life cycle as to their product strategy in terms of the product attributes to be offered relative to competitors, including options, quality and after sales services, the technology to be used and the desired profit and market share. A comparison with expected prices in the market over the product life cycle determines the price at which the product with the planned characteristics can be offered in the market and be expected to obtain their target profit and target market growth.

Target profit is often phrased in terms of a target return on sales or in terms of an absolute profit amount. Both of these measures are easy to calculate in a high variety product environment.

Difficulties in pricing using the market for a relatively new product is aided by 'pricing by functions' which is used by many Japanese firms. The product is decomposed into many elements or attributes and a price for each element is determined which reflects the amount the consumer is willing to pay for each element. Aggregating these attribute prices gives the estimated selling price (Kato, 1993).

This process requires a great deal of strategic information which often is not collected in the West or is, at least, not used for pricing decisions. In order to set strategic targets, detailed information is required about competitors' strategies, their pricing policy, and likely changes over the product life cycle. This information is required in order to forecast the current state of the market and changes over time, and to estimate how successful the firm's strategy will be. Similarly, information concerning the product attributes which consumers value and for which they are willing to pay is required. Target costing thus links performance and strategy by incorporating the strategy of the organization and communicating and forcing this down the organization.

It is generally said that the contribution of target costing is in terms of cost management by planning cost reductions in the planning, design, development, purchasing and manufacturing stages of the product. It also plays an important role in satisfying consumer needs at the planning stage, in planning product quality and improving the time taken to introduce new products.

Target costing in Japan is seen as a cost reduction exercise which seeks to get 'cost down' in the pre-production stages. It seeks to force designers to reduce costs, though there is a substantial debate concerning how far target prices should seek to include strategy and how far it should be seen predominantly as a continuing cost reduction device. Such an approach may be supplemented by levying extra costs on non-standard parts, excessive tooling, non-standard or new machines and excessively long parts lists. The procedure contains a number of other lessons for at least some Western firms. One is that prices are determined in the market and reflect competitors' strategies and customers' demands. Attempting to arrive at sensible prices relying substantially on cost-plus pricing, however much these are adjusted for perceived market factors as is common in the West, is unlikely to arrive at prices which fully reflect market characteristics, however many informal adjustments are made to cost-plus prices. Target costing also requires that the firm collects and uses a great deal of information external to the organization which may not exist in Western firms, or if they are collected may not impact on the finance department. Finally, it illustrates the possibility of incorporating strategy into accounting and performance measurement more generally. Perhaps, target costing should be called in the West 'target pricing' to reflect its connections with markets and the firm's strategic objectives.

The process of target costing

There is no need to describe target costing in great detail as there are now a number of very good descriptions (see Kato, 1993; Sakurai, 1990; Tani et al., 1993, Yoshikawa et al., 1993). The stages of target costing are broadly as follows:

1 determine the target price for the product;
2 calculate the target cost of the product in manufacture after allowing for the desired profit;
3 prior to production, use value engineering teams and other techniques to reduce the expected cost of the product (so-called drifting cost) to its target cost (allowable cost), thereby determining a target cost for each component and/or function, and
4 set aggregate target costs for each production stage and monitor that these are met by using budgetary control and standard costing or a specially designed accounting system.

There are a number of ways of setting target costs. These include the following:

1 determine the difference between allowable cost (selling prices – desired profit) and forecast costs determined using current costs;
2 determine the difference between allowable cost (using planning selling price net of the required return on sales) and current costs, and
3 apply the desired cost reduction to current costs.

The above description of target costing should be seen as an ideal. There is considerable evidence that Japanese firms often fail to make the target cost at least prior to manufacture and either adjust the target costs or decide not to continue with the product at least in its existing form. Similarly many Japanese firms are adopting method 3 for setting target costs. Method 3 is also fairly common in the West, for example in vehicle production.

The role of accounting in target costing

The accounting function in Japan (which will include a substantial number of non-accountants, none of whom will be qualified accountants in the Western sense) plays a strong role in target costing and in a minority of cases is in charge of the function. It is generally more likely that this responsibility will reside with product planning, development or product engineering. Sometimes accountants are not included in the target costing team (in some 60 per cent of firms, according to Tani *et al.*, 1994). In 20 per cent of firms, the accounting department is in charge of preparing the information for target costs. However, it is generally the accounting department's job to monitor the achievement of target costs, especially at the purchasing and manufacturing stage.

Tools for target costing

In Japan, value engineering (VE) is an activity which helps to design products which meet customer needs at the lowest cost while assuring the required standard of quality and reliability. A number of tools are generally used in this activity. These include:

1   **Functional analysis**

The aim here is to determine the functions of the product and indicate how far the design of these functions will satisfy the consumer (ascertained by market research) and at what cost relative to that part of the target cost pricing by elements allocated to that function. This allows the variance between the target cost per function and its current cost to be calculated. It also allows the contribution which a function makes to consumer needs to be ascertained relative to its cost, thereby leading to redesign where two items are not well matched (see Yoshikawa *et al.*, 1993; Tanaka, 1989).

Yoshikawa *et al.* (1993) make the point that with the widespread use of functional analysis in the firm 'a logical development is to incorporate costs by functions as well as parts' (p. 69), though they indicate that ideally the system would be set up to identify variable costs associated with each function.

2   **Cost tables**

Cost tables are detailed simulated databases (generally, not yet computerized in Japan) of all the costs of producing a product, either for product functions or product components, based on a large variety of assumptions. Thus, they allow very quick answers to 'what if' questions relating to decisions to change any aspect of the product. Such tables may well include simple mathematical versions of cost functions which, for example, show how changes in the material components of products will alter cost. Thus, a cost table will show the variety of cost performances when using different types of materials for a given component. The data in cost tables will be accepted by all members of the organization, and therefore ensure common thinking throughout. There will be a cost table for each part of the product's life cycle. Yoshikawa *et al.* (1993) see cost tables as the property of accountants. However, Tani *et al.* (1994) suggest that the responsibility for these tables is spread around a number of departments in different firms, though accountants can make a substantial contribution to these tables wherever the responsibility for them is located. The use of cost tables does not seem well known in the West (Yoshikawa *et al.*, 1993).

3   VE collections
These are libraries of case studies of the detailed experience from previous VE activity, the use of which is to improve future target costing
and VE. Of course, all the other well-known techniques used in Japan,
such as JIT methods and quality circles, are utilized, where appropriate, in target costing exercises.

Simplicity in dealing with complexity

The emphasis placed on simplicity as opposed to sophistication of
accounting practices is also reflective of the different attitudes to organizational affairs taken by the Japanese. Studies have suggested that not only
do Japanese firms show a preference for less complicated accounting tools,
but often, the increased simplicity of accounting activity in the Western
sense, is a function of the rising complexity of situations within which
accounting is deployed. Thus, whereas there appears to be an inclination
on the part of Japanese managers to rely on payback and accounting rates
of return calculations as opposed to discounting cash flows when evaluating investment projects, even greater stress is placed on the former and on
other non-accounting strategic considerations, especially when the capital
projects entail large investment outlays in long-term facilities, such as CIM
(Sakurai, 1990).

The evidence from a large number of surveys and articles is that Japanese firms seem to use accounting figures much less in decision-making
than Western firms (see, for example, Inoue, 1988). Rather, the focus is on
cost management, though it should be understood that relevant accounting figures are considered in the decision-making process described earlier;
they are just not given the primacy they seem to have in decision-making in
the West.

The focus on assembly

Enterprise cost structure in Japan is such that, on average, material and
component costs account for some 60 per cent of cost, direct labour some
14 per cent and overheads some 24 per cent (Tanaka, 1993), though these
percentages vary very substantially across firms and industries. On this
evidence, it can be said that material costs are proportionally higher than
in the West and that overheads are substantially lower. Similar figures from
the USA are material and component costs 53 per cent, direct labour 15

per cent and overheads 32 per cent. In Japan, it is expected that the material and labour cost percentages will remain stable and that overheads, especially fixed overheads, may increase. The higher proportion of material costs in Japanese cost structures reflects the assembly nature of many large Japanese firms.

The final assembly stage often takes place following receipt of material and bought-in parts produced by a relatively small group of subcontractors who may at least help design the part and who in turn rely on other subcontractors lower down the chain for their inputs. In many organizations, between 80 and 90 per cent of products are already processed by subcontractors (Yoshikawa, 1988b). Material cost control thus typically entails working with contractors to achieve efficient methods monitoring the labour and other overhead costs passed through the subcontractor pyramid to the final assembly plant. The manufacturing unit which heads the pyramid reduces its dependence on the managerial abilities of subcontracting suppliers, by itself playing an active role in mutual exercises in evaluating and improving the operations, work standards, quality controls and cost containment practices of subcontracting firms. The corporate head office thus maintains planning and control 'tentacles' throughout the pyramidal chain of suppliers.

The 'crisis' in management accounting

In North America, the particular development of management accounting is viewed by influential advocates of reform in the field, to have taken place within the backdrop of the historical emergence of the modern business organization. As such, changes in accounting techniques are seen to have been closely aligned to alterations in business strategy and its attendant consequences on organizational structure (Chandler and Daems, 1979). The argument has been made that, historically, advances in accounting were accompanied by changes in the nature of the business and until the time of the First World War had demonstrated continued innovativeness, amelioration and progress. As was said earlier, some contemporary critics of management accounting have, however, argued that from that time, the field has stopped growing (Johnson and Kaplan, 1987). Kaplan (1983; 1984; 1985; 1988a; 1988b) holds that internal accounting systems are lagging behind the times,

> ... living off innovations in management accounting that were made 60, 80 and 100 years ago.
>
> (Kaplan, 1986a, p. 7)

Such criticisms of management accounting have been argued by some British accounting researchers as being country-specific and pertinent only within a narrow view of the role of management accounting in recent history (Ezzamel *et al.*, 1990).

Subservience to financial accounting

Johnson and Kaplan (1987) have argued that over the past half a century, increased demands were placed on external financial reporting resulting in financial accounting reports providing key management information in distorted form. This problem arose because the underlying generators which are said to drive costs are not recognized or revealed by financial accounts. In particular, they incorporate indirect costs which are allocated arbitrarily without being traced to their cause.

This allocation process may satisfactorily meet the objectives of financial reporting of portraying overall profit figures and provides data for inventory valuation. It is seen however, to be inappropriate for making decisions about individual product prices and sales mixes. Cost determinations based on the principles of financial cost accounting are viewed as providing a distorted picture of product costs since cross-subsidization between products results from the misallocation of overhead costs between these products. Effective strategic production decisions are consequently subordinated to financial accounting requirements. The budgeting system linking managerial rewards to return on investment or profit is said to further exacerbate the situation for enterprise segments. This problem occurs because internal decisions about product management are directly linked to financial reporting criteria which emphasize short-term results. All in all, the perceived malaise of management accounting has been attributed to its 'subservience' to financial reporting objectives (Johnson, 1988).

Activity costing

Concerns about overhead allocation have been welcomed by many managers and, perhaps more importantly, the need to account in a way that recognizes the activities which cause costs rather than using traditional methods of overhead allocation is recognized by professional accounting bodies. The published evidence on the payoffs and costs of installing activity-based cost and management information systems is not unequivocal. Partly this is because seeking an association between major changes in organizational and management structures and management accounting is a very difficult and time consuming exercise. The practising management accountant must be satisfied that the benefits likely to accrue from any change will outweigh its costs, though cost-benefit quantification is no easy exercise. Moreover, proven theoretical advances do not always succeed in obtaining implementation in organizations. To date, there is still little public evidence that any new accounting method which attempts to facilitate the management decision-making process actually increases the ability to generate greater profits, though it must be recognized that providing such evidence is very difficult. Cooper and Kaplan (1991, p. 130) see the evidence as suggesting that:

> ABC has emerged as a tremendously useful guide to management action that can translate directly into higher profits.

Ascribing increased profitability to the implementation of a costing technique such as ABC is a difficult if not foolhardy exercise. Problems arise in tracing changes in the 'bottom line' to managerial action associated with altered costing information. The inability to isolate the effects of a single change such as the adoption of ABC *ceteris paribus* and to use another company as a 'control' for comparative purposes makes any assertion of a profitability link dubious. This is especially so in that changes in organizations often come in bundles, after for example the appointment of a new managerial team. Perhaps the ultimate test of establishing whether a switch from a traditional cost system to ABC yields increased benefits is a market test which seeks to ascertain whether such a switch becomes a permanent one for a sufficiently large number of companies adopting ABC. Given the relative novelty of this costing approach, however, it is probably too early to apply this test. Moreover if, as Johnson and Kaplan have suggested, inappropriate costing approaches can become 'ingrained' (1987, p. 246) so as to prevent a better understanding of costs, then even the permanency of a switch to ABC by a large number of companies cannot be taken as conclusive of definite benefit stemming from ABC. One embedded system may be replaced by another which becomes equally ingrained.

It is significant that case studies in cost management often shed greater light on managerial perspectives and priorities than on the integrity of a costing approach. In examining the case studies supporting activity costing, it is difficult to escape the view that some of the documented problems of US companies which have been the subject of ABC case study literature are more fundamental than can be solved by reforming their accounting systems. The companies reviewed sometimes seem, for example, to be wedded to providing a full range of products using cost-dominated prices and appear to be willing to go to extraordinary lengths to provide spare parts for often long cancelled products. This may not be as sensible a policy as concentrating on a few high-volume products. The large number of products also seems to force important strategic decisions down to very low levels in the managerial structure. Similarly, routine accounting workers are used to making important decisions which, at least ideally, need a consideration of future results. Pricing seems to take up a great deal of management time and is often approached using routine methods resting largely on cost-plus calculations. In many ways, these issues relate to business policy and management style rather than the efficacy of the cost management system in use. It is also notable that early field study evidence from UK companies suggests that a switch to an ABC system triggers a wide variety of unanticipated effects (Bhimani and Pigot, 1992a; 1992b; Gietzmann, 1991; Friedman and Lyne, 1995).

Before making conclusive judgements on activity-based approaches, more evidence would be desirable. However, there are many managers who believe that these new accounting methods have changed their approach to decision-making, indirectly yielding increased profits and, more importantly, a much better understanding of their business (see Cooper and Kaplan, 1991, and Cooper et al., 1992, for case studies). Some existing problems encountered with overhead allocation where, for instance, the source of the overhead is difficult to trace or is sunk or is common to diverse activities remain without solutions. Arbitrariness and judgement will therefore continue to significantly affect overhead cost accounting. There is strong support, however, for the argument that a dynamic and changing manufacturing (and non-manufacturing) environment does render redundant, conventional cost accounting systems which emphasize information priorities other than those emerging as virtually indispensable in today's competitive marketplace. For example, strategic cost analysis, cost-benefit appraisal for long-term projects, life cycle consideration (Raffish and Turney, 1991), quality and customer satisfaction data are likely to become increasingly meaningful in service and manufacturing environments (Dale and Plunkett, 1990).

The problems encountered in viewing management accountants as being subservient to financial reporting supports the notion that management accounting must now be allowed to develop of its own accord rather than being subverted by other accounting pursuits, but it does not by itself point the direction for such developments. Revisions of management accounting practices have produced novel approaches based on information which traditional accounting practices fail to provide. Within the context of large manufacturing companies, it is principally alterations in work organization and production techniques which have paved the way for renewed creativity in the field of accounting. The acquisition and implementation of AMTs is associated with increased product diversity and complexity of operations. Such changes have necessitated, in the minds of many advocates of management accounting reforms, a more rational approach to both costing and investment appraisal (Kaplan, 1986). Thus, techniques such as activity-based costing (ABC) (Cooper, 1987; 1988; 1989; Cooper and Kaplan, 1987; Johnson, 1988), lifecycle costing (Berliner and Brimson, 1988), the balanced score card (Kaplan and Norton, 1992) backflush accounting (Horngren *et al.*, 1994; Bhimani and Bromwich, 1991) and throughput accounting (Adler, 1987; Galloway and Waldron, 1988) are appropriate reactions to the changing business and strategic elements of management accounting.

Tackling existing challenges

Many issues affecting accounting activities remain to be tackled. For instance, where a trend exists for large firms to become increasingly assembly-orientated and to subcontract the production of semi-finished components, requirements and opportunities exist for altering accounting systems to respond to this change. The accounting and control of materials and subcomponents and the appraisal and monitoring of subcontractors offers new possibilities for novel management accounting approaches, including virtual management accounting systems and inter-corporate data exchange. This is an important element of the new manufacturing environment, the accounting implications of which appear to still be neglected.

In many organizations, certain overhead costs exist which do not vary as a function of the volume or diversity of output. Accounting techniques for cost allocation relying on conventional methods of applying overhead burden or on activity-based costing do not offer appropriate means of dealing with such costs. Rather, these costs may be decision-driven overhead costs. They may leave within the enterprise, a legacy of costs which may be viewed as past or sunk but of which account must be taken. Alternatively, they may be costs which are viewed as shared by the manufacture of two or more different products or the operation of multi-processes. No fully appropriate method of dealing with such costs have been developed. Historically, such costs have been arbitrarily allocated; typically, on the basis of volume-driven denominators. ABC attempts to categorize them by investigating the root of their provenance but is ultimately forced to allocate them arbitrarily or to leave them out of manufacturing costs. Management accounting thought must continue to address such cost issues as they lie at the base of many managerial concerns.

Non-financial measures

Whereas management accounting has concentrated its efforts on providing largely financial and invariably quantified information, operational management is increasingly concerned with non-financial and often purely qualitative information of the economic consequences of operating activities. Advanced manufacturing technology enables a wider product range to be provided with more flexibility and with an emphasis on product quality. Information on quality levels, warranty returns, productivity yields, product mix sales performance, customer utility for individual product characteristics and experience curve variables are important inputs for managerial decision-making and play an increasing role in the running of modern business enterprises. Management accounting systems can integrate many such monitors as part of their scorekeeping data and attention directing reports and their less frequent special decision-making analyses; but as far as is known, such information is generally separately provided, often outside the formal information networks and only infrequently reaches top management (in contrast to Japan).

The service sector

Management accounting techniques have tended to emphasize the needs of manufacturing organizations particularly in view of the growing implementation of flexible production technologies and novel methods of work organization. Yet important changes are also taking place in service industries which in fact constitute a larger proportion of economic output than manufacturing activities in both the UK and North America. Progress in technology has enabled rapid changes in, for instance, the running of financial institutions. UK financial markets have recently undergone a massive change from their previously labour intensive systems of operational management and auxiliary administrative activities. Customers are offered novel products made possible by more modern automated electronic and communication systems. Such products have to be priced, activities costed and resources to be accounted for. Decisions to invest in the expensive technology complementing long-term strategy must also be made. Although the role of accounting is likely to be altered as marketing concerns, design implications and strategic issues come to bear on the changing service sector environment, accounting must orient itself to solving such problems with the same vigour that has been urged for addressing issues facing the changing manufacturing environment. Internal accounting for service organizations is likely to be increasingly subjected to the criticisms raised about management accounting in other areas and opportunities exists for directing efforts at tackling such concerns in a way which goes beyond the documented early attempts (Banker and Johnston, 1988; Chaffman and Talbott, 1991; Chapter 11, this volume).

Organizational concerns

A manufacturing environment which utilizes advanced manufacturing techniques may affect perceptions of cost structures because of the changes these techniques cause in the overall production process (for instance, direct labour may decrease simultaneously with increases in overhead cost). Management accounting information needs to recognize these changes and utilize its techniques for decision-making embodying these new cost structures. Constraints may, however, limit the applicability of certain management accounting techniques for decision-making in the new environment. For instance, a production manager may propose adopting a numerical control machine which replaces three conventional machines arguing that part of the financial justification for such an investment is the direct labour costs saved by utilizing only one machine operator rather than three. There may nevertheless be limits on how far the production manager can affect personnel matters and the release of two machine operators may not be possible. Likewise, it has been suggested that the installation of a NC machine, or a CAD/CAM system or some other flexible manufacturing system, cannot be considered to be an isolated event to be judged on its own merits given the wide effect on inputs, departments and products that are directly and immediately affected as a consequence. Thus it is not sufficient to consider the cost of the particular AMT *vis-à-vis* its merits (financial or otherwise). What is essential is to question whether the expected benefits are able to accrue given the specific organizational and managerial structure of the enterprise.

A more fundamental problem is whether a capital acquisition decision can be formulated in terms which embed factors at play in the utilization of the AMT in question. Effectively, what needs to be considered is whether those who stand to gain from an acquisition need to 'massage the figures' to see the decision go through.

In terms of implementing a management philosophy such as just-in time or total quality management, which have a variety of accounting implications, it is widely held that such management programmes can ultimately affect most, if not all, areas of organizational activities. Yet it is often not clear that management accounting encompasses the financial implications in such wide terms. This is of particular relevance in organizations which have a diverse product base requiring sophisticated manufacturing technologies and processes and which operate within a complex supply and marketing infrastructure. Moreover, organizations tend to develop particular characteristics over time which become an ingrained part of their functioning. Accounting changes deemed desirable cannot overlook employee attitudes and organizational culture which can in large part determine the 'success/failure' of an accounting information system implementation irrespective of technical merits.

There is evidence that in many Western organizations accounting information systems often collect and process information which is not ultimately reported or where the intended manager does not use it. Whilst such instances are not new, they ought to raise questions about whether such information should be collected and whether it addresses managerial needs. It is not implausible that organizational changes precede accounting alterations with a time lag that is unjustifiably long.

In considering the installation of AMTs or the adoption of novel work organization philosophies, it is difficult to escape the view that changing methods of production will affect the manner in which and to whom information is communicated aside from technical considerations. Altering channels of communication as well as the substance of information is likely to affect accounting information needs and uses. It is for the management accountant to understand specific enterprise situations where such changes are occurring and ideally to alter the provision of accounting information accordingly. Associated with this are the more fundamental changes in operational workers' responsibilities and controls caused by production changes. An accounting system must attempt to match controllability and responsibility, given work circumstances with the accounting information collected and reported.

Finally, accounting information intended for decision-making does not always shape the decision. Rather, in many instances, once the decision is taken, appeal is made to accounting to lend support to it. Although this is not necessarily an undesirable role for accounting, as it can facilitate the managerial process, especially its informal processes, it is essential that the management accounting professional is aware of the way in which accounting is likely to be used. This is especially significant where the organization adopts alternative accounting mechanisms since resistance to their adoption may be reflective of accounting's wider roles.

Effectively, what is evident is that only in very limited instances does a change in one aspect of the functioning of the enterprise not have consequences for others. Altering technology or work methods can be seen to implicate accounting change, though not necessarily in an isolated way.

Moreover, accounting processes affect an array of enterprise activities indirectly which cannot be disregarded in environments where a systems change is being considered. The organizational settings within which management accounting techniques are thought to be useful, may thus alter their applicability in abstracted terms because of organizational features not compatible with the assumptions underlying accounting tools (Bhimani, 1994). Thus, if management accounting techniques such as variance analysis, differential cost evaluation and break-even calculations are to continue to be of value within a rapidly changing production environment, the assumptions upon which they are based need to be reviewed in the light of organization-specific factors.

Many empirical studies now acknowledge that informal communication within firms is paramount to their effective functioning. This is also consistent with what is known about Japanese practices. Management accountants in firms may interact informally with operational managers resulting in exchanges which would, perhaps, not otherwise take place using only formal communication channels. It has also been widely reported that managers in high growth, new technology-based businesses are likely to employ a blend of symbols, signals, and data derived from an extreme range of sources which are interpreted within 'a personalized framework and result in managerial action' (Littler and Sweeting, 1988, p. 2). Informal communication therefore, appears to be advantageous in certain contexts and may be particularly important in high technology manufacturing where product markets incorporate considerable uncertainty with respect to product development, demand and profitability.

Operational factors

Management accountants should seek to become even more familiar with the language of operational activities if only because cost functions are the product of input quantities reflecting the underlying technology and input prices. This may best be achieved by there being an increased willingness to cross boundaries which have traditionally been viewed as limiting their responsibilities (for instance, by working in closer proximity to line managers and experiencing their concerns first hand). This may generate ways of providing information of significance in the organization. Such information is not strictly within the purview of the usual management accounting information categories, such as scorekeeping, attention-directing and problem-solving. Attempts to make management accounting practice fit better with the organization's operational activities can be taken one step further by identifying parts or levels of the organization within which forms of learning, control and accountability initially arise. For instance, there is evidence that important knowledge about cost relationships in production processes may be found locally rather than centrally in certain organizations (Jonsson and Gronlund, 1988). The form of cost information understood by operational managers may not be compatible with the canons of professional management accounting. It may be valuable therefore to provide managerial information which reflects processes that are specific to the firm's operations.

The future of management accounting

The new CIMA report has covered a wide literature stemming from theory, practice and learned commentaries. It has addressed both technical and organizational and wider managerial issues in exploring existing concerns and challenges in management accounting. Any attempt to distil the variety of issues covered into a set of techniques giving surefire success cannot be fruitful. What is sought, however, is to indicate possible ways in which the management accountant can assess specific enterprise situations in the context of current developments in the field. The following are suggested as offering potential for enhancing accounting's advance toward becoming involved in, if not tackling, certain enterprise concerns, which directly or indirectly impinge on management accounting activities:

1 The ensemble of emerging work organization philosophies and advanced manufacturing technologies affect ways in which cost management can take place. The implementation of JIT, TQM or MRP as well as the installation of AMTs have been accompanied in many enterprises by the adoption or consideration of novel accounting perspectives. These include activity-based costing, target costing, throughput accounting, lifecycle costing, backflush accounting and others. There is no recorded instance of any of these techniques fully resolving the problems they set out to tackle. But likewise, many companies using such approaches decidedly continue to do so. Clearly certain benefits are perceived and learning about accounting's potential continues to take place. Ultimately, few cost management approaches can be deemed good or bad in generalized terms. Organizational context and managerial ethos play a large part in determining the worthwhileness of accounting approaches. What is clear is that many companies are experimenting with novel accounting approaches and others are well beyond that stage. Novelty has become convention in some cases and the change is irreversible. One cannot therefore

dwell on assessing go/no-go judgements on particular techniques and approaches, but must highlight what has been learned. What can be said is that any one novel technique or even a combination of such techniques can neither shore up a poorly managed organization or convert badly managed firms into leading edge firms. Such problems require more than a change in accounting technique. By the same token, one lesson has been that experimenting with novel approaches in management accounting can be of much value as long as more traditional accounting tools are not jettisoned prematurely.

2   The evidence suggests that accounting mechanisms do not operate in isolation of organizational or managerial factors. Thus in exploring the potential of novel techniques in management accounting, attention must be paid to interrelationships between accounting activities and other enterprise processes. Moreover, innovative cost management techniques often create novel communication channels and information links between accountants and operational line managers. Such changes in the organizational infrastructure cannot be ignored and must comprise part of any effort to redesign an accounting information system.

3   Trends in altering management philosophy in the functioning of organizations affect cost management systems. Accounting can thus be viewed as reactive to enterprise changes. However, it is not always clear what potential an innovation in management accounting has for enhancing the managerial process until it is in phase and experience with its workings has been gained. The management accountant has a duty to go beyond a watchdog function and positively to develop mechanisms of likely use to the manager or management team. The fast pace of developments in the field allows him or her to satisfy such a role more so than ever before. Ultimately, management accounting can seek to proactively mobilize managerial attention and action in ways which may be neglected in the absence of the accountant's initiative.

4   More focused pathways must entail some technical issues, including the following:
    a Accounting's role is expanding as enterprise activities grow. For example, manufacturer–supplier relationships are in many industries becoming more intricate and purchasers and suppliers interface to a more significant extent. This requires an expansion of the role of accounting in channelling information effectively and in ways seen as relevant to managers. Certainly, extending a system of backflush accounting may be appropriate if just-in-time approaches are in place. But, likewise, where activity-based costing is utilized,

monitoring trends in cost driver measures can offer insights on experience effects.

b   It is clear that activity-based costing offers attractions to some companies and not to others which have considered its permanent adoption. Certainly, ABC's organizational 'fit' is an issue. But more generally, it remains to be more fully acknowledged that ABC requires certain quite stringent preconditions to be met. It is largely a technique which depends on the ability to trace costs to the point where they become incremental *vis-à-vis* the product or the enterprise's hierarchy. Such traceability is not always conceptually, let alone operationally, possible for some processes and therefore for some costs which may represent a substantial part of traditional overheads. Problems exist with the manner in which costs are shared by different facilities or departments or products. It has been suggested that the incremental contribution table approach offers one avenue to resolving some of the problems. Again, the extent to which such an approach can provide a viable solution is associated with the managerial ethos of the company.

c   It has been pointed out that a financial evaluation of managerial options is appropriate in different contexts but has its limits. It is sometimes desirable to quantify in non-financial terms the specifics of a project or the priorities for the organization. For example, in considering strategy as a relevant issue in appraising investments, quantification of significant variables may be possible. It remains a reality of managerial decision-making, nevertheless, that decisions cannot and need not take place purely on the basis of numbers. Not all organizational complexities are amenable to expression within a quantified frame of reference. For this reason, it is not undesirable for a company to consider financial and non-financial means of performance in tandem with qualitative information. Cost management innovations must therefore not be seen as precluding the worthwhileness of unquantified information.

d   Ultimately, enterprise problems entailing the use of accounting information can be aided by a particular technique such as ABC or target costing or lifecycle costing depending on circumstances. But no enterprise can tackle all its accounting challenges through any one such technique. ABC or any other such accounting tool cannot be a universal panacea for enterprise ills.

5   It is clear that certain management accounting techniques may seem so innocuous as not to assume a specific cultural context. For instance, activity-based costing, throughput accounting and lifecycle costing

may at first appear to be able to yield anticipated effects in whatever cultural context in which they are applied. Conversely, target costing, benchmarking and backflush accounting might be expected to be dependent on an acceptance of their cultural underpinnings. Yet it has been suggested that different countries focus on very different technical accounting approaches and use common approaches differently. Thought must be given to the array of organizational practices which are in some sense reflective of wider cultural characteristics before any attempt is made to transplant these mechanisms into a foreign environment. No doubt attempts can be made to mould any technique or philosophy to a given context, but expectations as to what they might contribute must likewise be reassessed. It is not suggested here that the Japanese approach to cost tables, or the French 'tableau de bord' or the German capacity usage focus is not to be adopted outside these countries, but that emphasis on these practices may rely on a variety of factors which may not be present in all contexts. Thus, experimentation is desirable so long as an awareness of enterprise-specific complexities and possibly relevant socio-cultural factors is present.

Conclusion

This chapter has reported on the findings of the second CIMA-commissioned study on the challenges confronting management accounting practice. The caution that management accounting reforms on a wholesale scale have not yet been justified at this juncture is qualified by stressing the need to encourage experimentation with novel techniques, in particular organizational settings. No universal solution can be offered to deal with what has been viewed as the crisis in management accounting by some commentators. Rather, the perception that reforms are needed is the result of many interacting factors which individually represent different origins and which need to take account of inter-relationships with other suggested routes for action. The approach to management accounting progress needs to be cognisant of the uniqueness of an enterprise. No single universally generalizable technique is potentially available within management accounting. Change is evidently a necessary part of maintaining management accounting's integrity in facing and resolving particular organizational situations caused by the fast changing business environment of the 1990s. The perception by enterprise managers that management accounting must become more outward-orientated and emphasize strategic information is to be addressed. Likewise, the recognition that complexities of altering man-

agement accounting methods brings about many unexpected consequences must also be dealt with. Thus, the changing nature of information exchange, both informal and formal, as well as emerging facets of the
politicization of management accounting and the renewed alliance
between conception and execution of tasks informed by management
accounting are all issues which the practising management accountant
cannot ignore. The evidence is overwhelming that management accounting
can play a part in providing novel and creative approaches in organizations
but its interrelationships with other functional areas is not negligible and
cannot be overlooked.

As new tools for costing output, pricing products, appraising new
investments, reporting non-financial monitors and managing financial
resource allocation within companies come to be further implemented, the
relevance of much of management accounting's rich past is not necessarily
negated and its methods should therefore not be jettisoned. The constancy
of change in the business environment presupposes the need to adapt and
to develop new pathways to progress. This does not require shedding past
achievements in management accounting but building on them, in different directions.

References

Adler, P. S. (1987). A plant productivity measure for 'hi-tech' manufacturing,
   Interfaces, November/December, 75–85.
Banker, R. D. and Johnston, H. H. (1988). Cost driver analysis in the service
   sector: an empirical study of US airlines. Carnegie-Mellon University Working
   Paper.
Berliner, C. and Brimson, J. (1988). *Cost Management in Today's Advanced
   Manufacturing: The CAM-I Conceptual Design*. Boston: Harvard Business
   School Press.
Bhimani, A. (1994). Modern cost management: putting the organisation before the
   technique, *International Journal of Production Economics*, 29–37.
Bhimani, A. and Bromwich, M. (1992). Advanced manufacturing technology and
   accounting: a renewed alliance, *Computer Integrated Manufacturing Systems*,
   199–207.
Bhimani, A. and Bromwich, M. (1991). Accounting for just-in-time manufacturing
   systems, *CMA: The Management Accountants' Magazine*, 31–34.
Bhimani, A. and Pigott, D. (1992a). ABC in a pharmaceutical company: a remedy?
   Management Accounting (UK), December, 18–21.
Bhimani, A. and Pigott, D. (1992b). Implementing ABC: a case study of
   organisational and behavioural consequences, *Management Accounting
   Research*, June, 119–32.

Bromwich, M. and Bhimani, A. (1989). *Management Accounting: Evolution not Revolution*, London: CIMA.

Chaffman, B. M. and Talbott J. (1991). Activity-based costing in service based companies, CMA: *The MA Magazine*, Dec./Jan., 15–21.

Chandler, A. and Daems, H. (1979). Administrative coordination, allocation and monitoring: a comparative analysis of the emergences of accounting and organisation in the USA and Europe. *Accounting, Organizations and Society*, pp. 3–20.

Cooper, R. (1987). The two-stage procedure in cost accounting – part 2, *Journal of Cost Management for the Manufacturing Industry*, Summer, 39–45.

Cooper, R. and Kaplan, R. S. (1987). How cost accounting systematically distorts product costs, in *Accounting and Management: Field Study Perspectives*. (eds. W. J. Bruns and R. S. Kaplan), Boston: Harvard Business School Press.

Cooper, R. and Kaplan, R. S. (1991). Profit priorities from activity-based costing, *Harvard Business Review*, May/June.

Dale, B. G. and Plunkett, J. J. (1990). Epilogue, *Management Quality*, London: Philip Allen.

Ezzamel, M., Hoskin, K. and Macve, R. (1990). Managing it all by numbers: a review of Johnson and Kaplan's 'Relevance Lost', *Accounting and Business Research*, 153–66.

Friedman, A. and Lyne, S. (1995). *Implementing Activity-Based Techniques*. London: CIMA.

Galloway, D. and Waldron, D. (1988). Throughput accounting, *Management Accounting (UK)*, November, 34–35.

Gietzmann, M. (1991). Implementation issues associated with the construction of an activity-based costing system in an engineering components manufacturer, *Management Accounting Research*, 2(3), 161–225.

Gow, I. (1986). Raiders, invaders or simply good traders?, *Accountancy*, March, 66–73.

Hiromoto, T. (1988). Another hidden edge – Japanese management accounting, *Harvard Business Review*, July/August, 22–6.

Horngren, C. T., Foster G. and Datar, S. (1994). *Cost Accounting: A Managerial Emphasis*. Englewood Cliffs, N. J.: Prentice-Hall.

Inoue, S. (1988). Recent development of cost management problems under technological change in Japan, *Research Paper No. 30*, Department of Information Science, Kawaga University.

Inoue, S. (1992). A comparative study of cost management problems: JUSs (Japanese affiliates in the USA) and JUKs (Japanese affiliates in the UK), *Research Paper No. 46*, Department of Information Science, Kawaga University.

Johnson, H. T. (1988). Activity-based information: a blueprint for world-class management accounting, *Management Accounting*, June, 23–30.

Johnson, H. T. and Kaplan, R. S. (1987). *Relevance Lost: The Rise and Fall of Management Accounting*. Boston, Mass.: Harvard Business School Press.

Jonsson, S. and Gronlund, A. (1988). Life with a subcontractor: new technology and management accounting, *Accounting, Organization and Society*, 513–34.

Kaplan, R. S. (1983). Measuring manufacturing performance: a new challenge for managerial accounting research, *The Accounting Review*, 686–705.

Kaplan, R. S. (1984). Yesterday's accounting undermines production, *Harvard Business Review*, July/August, 95–101.

Kaplan, R. S. (1985). Accounting lag: the obsolescence of cost accounting systems, (eds K. Clark and C. Lorenze) in *Technology and Productivity: The Uneasy Alliance*. Boston: Harvard Business School Press pp. 195–226.

Kaplan, R. S. (1986a). Introduction, *Cost Accounting for the 90s: The Challenge of Technological Change Proceedings*. Montvale, New Jersey: National Association of Accountants, pp. 7–10.

Kaplan, R. S. (1986b). Must CIM be justified by faith alone?, *Harvard Business Review*, March/April, 87–95.

Kaplan, R. S. (1988a). Relevance regained, *Management Accounting (UK)*, September, 38–42.

Kaplan, R. S. (1988b). One cost system isn't enough, *Harvard Business Review*, January/February, 61–6.

Kaplan, R. S. and Norton, D. P. (1992). The balanced scorecard: Measures that drive performance, *Harvard Business Review*, Jan–Feb., 71–79.

Kato, Y. (1993). Target costing support systems: lessons from leading Japanese companies, *Management Accounting Research*, March.

Littler, D. A. and Sweeting, R. C. (1987). *Growth Business in High Technology Growth Companies – CIMA Report*. London: CIMA.

McMillan, C. J. (1985). *The Japanese Industrial System*. Berlin: de Gruyter, 2nd revised edition.

Misawa, M. (1987). New Japanese style management in a changing era, *Columbia Journal of World Business*, Winter.

Monden, Y. and Sakurai, M. (eds) (1989). *Japanese Management Accounting: A World Class Approach to Profit Management*, Cambridge, MA: Productivity Press.

Morgan, M. J. and Weerakoon, P. S. H. (1989). Japanese management accounting: its contribution to the Japanese economic miracle, *Management Accounting (UK)*, June.

Raffish, N. and Turney, P. B. B. (1991). Glossary of activity-based management, *Journal of Cost Management for the Manufacturing Industry*, Autumn.

Sakurai, M. (1990). The influence of factory automation on management accounting practices: a study of Japanese companies. In *Measures for Manufacturing Excellence*, (ed. R. S. Kaplan) Mass. US.: Harvard Business School Press.

Schonberger, R. I. (1982). The transfer of Japanese manufacturing management approaches to US industry, *Academy of Management Review*, 479–87.

Seddon, J. and Jackson, S. (1990). TQM and culture change, *The TQM Magazine*, August, 213–16.

Seed, A. H. (1988). Adopting Management Accounting Practice to an Advanced Manufacturing Environment, Montrale, New Jersey: NAA.

Shank, J. K. and Govindarajan, V. (1988). Transaction-based costing for the complex product line: a field study, *Journal of Cost Management for the Manufacturing Industry*, Summer, 31–8.

Shields, M. D. and Young, S. M. (1991). Managing product life cycle costs: an organisational model, *Journal of Cost Management for the Manufacturing Industry*, Fall, 39–52.

Shields, M. D. and Young, S. M. (1989). A behavioural model for implementing cost management systems, *Journal of Cost Management for the Manufacturing Industry*, Winter, 17–27.

Singhal, K. (1987). Introduction: the design and implementation of automated manufacturing systems, *Interfaces*, November/December, 1–4.

Spicer, B. H. (in press) The resurgence of cost and management accounting: a review of some recent developments in practice, theories and case research methods, *Management Accounting Research*.

Stamm, C. L. and Golbar, D. Y. (1991). Customer and supplier linkages for small JIT manufacturing firms, *Journal of Small Business Management*, July, 43–9.

Stanbus, G. J. (1990). Activity costing: twenty years on, *Management Accounting Research*, 249–64.

Stec, S. (1989). Costing for the '90s, *Management Accounting (USA)*, September, 59.

Stokes, C. R. (1989). JIT: Will suppliers embrace their new roles? *Business*, June, 37–40.

Tagushi, G. (1986). *Introduction to Quality Engineering*, New York: Asian Productivity Organization.

Tanaka, M. (1989). Cost planning and control in the design phase of a product, in *Japanese Management Accounting: A World Class Approach to Profit Management*, (eds Y. Monden and M. Sakurai), Cambridge, Mass.: Productivity Press.

Tanaka, Y. (1993). *Problems in Manufacturing and Cost Managment in Japan. The Situation in 1990*, Working Paper, Kagawa University.

Tani, A. (1992). Diffusion of numerically controlled machine tools in Japan and the USA, in *Computer Integrated Manufacturing (Volume III): Models, Case Studies and Forecasts of Diffusion*, (eds R. U. Ayres, W. Haywood and I. Tchijov), London: Chapman and Hall, pp. 85–99.

Tani, T., Okano, H., Shimizu, N., Iwabuchi, Y., Fukuda, J. and Corray, S. (1994). Target cost management in Japanese firms: current state of the art, *Management Accounting Research*, 5, 67–84.

Tatikonda, L. U. and Tatikonda, R. J. (1989) *Success in MRP*, Management Accounting (US), May, 34.

Tatikonda, M. V. (1988). Just-in-time and modern manufacturing environments: implications for cost accounting, *Production and Inventory Management*, 1–5.

Tchijov, I. (1992). International diffusion forecasts, in *Computer Integrated Manufacturing (Volume III): Models, Case Studies and Forecasts of Diffusion*, (eds. R. U. Ayres, W. Haywood and I. Tchijov) London: Chapman and Hall, pp. 287–318.

Thackray, P. (1990). The issue is quality, *Management Accounting (UK)*, September, 43.

Tsurumi, Y. and Tsurumi, H. (1985). Value-added maximising behaviour of Japanese firms and roles of corporate investment and finance, *Columbia Journal of World Business*, Spring, 29–35.

Turney P. B. B. (1990). Ten myths about implementing an activity-based cost system, *Journal of Cost Management for the Manufacturing Industry*, Spring, 5–13.

Vangermeersh, R. (1986). Milestone in the history of management accounting, in *Cost Accounting for the 90s: The Challenge of Technological Change Proceedings*, Montrale, New Jersey: NAA, pp. 7–10.

Vor, J. A., Saraph, J. V. and Petersen, D. L. (1990) JIT implementation practices, *Production and Inventory Management Journal*, 57–9.

Walkin, L. (1991). ABC-key players and their tools, *Management Accounting (USA), February, 18*.

Wilson, G. E. (1983). Theory: implications for management accountants, *Management Accounting (US)*, November, 2–5.

Wilson, R. M. S. (1991). Strategic management accounting, in *Issues in Management Accounting*, (eds D. Ashton, T. Hopper and R. W. Scapens) London: Prentice Hall, pp. 82–105.

Woods, M., Pokorny, M., Lintner, V. and Blinkhorn, M. (1985). Appraising investment in new technology: the approach in practice, *Management Accountant (UK)*, October, 42–3.

Woods, M. D. (1989). How we changed our accounting, *Management Accounting (USA)*, February, 42–5.

Worthy, F. S. (1991) Japan's . . . secret weapon, *Fortune*, August 12.

Yamamoto, M. (1988) Private correspondence, 28 December.

Yoshikawa, T. (1988a). Report of Meeting on March 14, Edinburgh University.

Yoshikawa, T. (1988b). Characteristics of cost accounting systems and their practical applications in Japan, unpublished paper, Yokohama University.

Yoshikawa, T., Innes, J. and Mitchell, F. (1989). Japanese management accounting: a comparative study, *Management Accounting (UK)*, November.

Yoshikawa, T., Mitchell, F. and Moyes, J. (1994). *A Review of Japanese Management Accounting Literature and Bibliography*, Chartered Institute of Managment Accountants.

Yoshikawa, T., Innes, J., Mitchell, F. and Tanaka, M. (1993). *Contemporary Cost Management*. London: Chapman and Hall.

3

A review of activity-based costing practice

John Innes and Falconer Mitchell

In this chapter John Innes and Falconer Mitchell review activity-based costing (ABC) practice. They begin by discussing some of the factors which have contributed to the dissatisfaction with conventional costing systems. Then they illustrate how traditional costing methods can undercost highly automated and low volume products and overcost labour intensive and high volume products.

Having identified the limitations of traditional costing systems Innes and Mitchell proceed to describe ABC systems. First they describe in some detail five major steps which must be achieved in order to create an operational ABC system. The authors then discuss some of the variations which have been identified arising from empirical observations of ABC systems.

In the final section of the chapter Innes and Mitchell evaluate ABC systems. In particular they stress that ABC more accurately captures the resources consumed by products and enhances the understanding of cost behaviour. They also discuss some of the other claimed advantages of ABC and then describe some of its limitations. Finally they identify three factors which are necessary for the successful implementation of ABC.

Introduction

Although the concept of activity-based costing (ABC) has been established for the best part of twenty years (e.g. Staubus, 1971) its current popularity and form can be traced to the development of practical systems in a small number of US companies in the mid-1980s. Their experiences have received wide publicity particularly through a series of Harvard Business School cases and publications authored by Professors Cooper and Kaplan (Cooper, 1988/9; Kaplan, 1988; Cooper and Kaplan, 1988). ABC emerged in these companies in response to a recognition by both their managers and management accountants that conventional costing systems produced product cost information which was often so inaccurate as to seriously mislead managerial policy-makers. The problem was caused by three compounding factors. First, the structure of product cost in many contemporary businesses had changed substantially, with production and non-production overhead costs growing in relative size and importance while direct labour, due to increased automation, had shrunk dramatically. For example, in many electronics companies it has fallen to well under 5 per cent of production cost. Second, direct labour and machine hours have persisted as major bases of production overhead absorption by products. Both of these bases relate fairly closely to production volume and their use therefore rests on the assumption that overhead incurrence is output driven. In addition the frequent attachment of non-production overheads to products in proportion to their production cost remains a widely used unitization method. Again the validity of this practice is questionable as their incurrence may often bear no close relationship to their production cost. Third, there is the gradual alteration in the nature of production overhead cost to reflect predominantly costs which are influenced by the diversity and complexity of output rather than simply by the volume of output. Production overheads of this type have been concisely summarized by Miller and Vollman (1985) as falling within four transaction type categories:

1 *Logistical transactions* concerned with organizing the flow of materials and other resources throughout the production process.
2 *Balancing transactions* concerned with matching the supply of resources with demand for them.
3 *Quality transactions* concerned with the validation that outputs are in accordance with specifications.
4 *Change transactions* concerned with providing the ability to cope with changes to orders, product design, etc.

It is notable that the major focus of all of the above factors is on one element of cost – overhead. Their combined effect has been to generate business situations where overheads (a) are a major portion of cost, (b) are attached to products by historically convenient, primarily volume-related bases, and (c) have major cost components which are not primarily influenced by output volume. The combination of these circumstances can cause the serious systematic distortion of reported product costs. For example, Illustration 1 demonstrates how the use of a traditional approach to overhead absorption (which is perpetuated after a change in circumstances renders it inappropriate) will result in a misleading allocation of overhead between a highly automated and a labour intensive product. Illustration 2 shows the effect of using a traditional overhead absorption basis where production involves both a high-volume batch product and a low-volume batch product. In these illustrations the use of traditional costing methods means that the highly automated product and the low-volume batch product are consistently subsidized respectively by the labour intensive product and the high-volume product cost. These examples show how resultant product information based on the perpetuation of inappropriate methods will provide management with a consistently inaccurate view of the relative costs of the items in their product range. The use of such flawed information will clearly be dysfunctional in production performance assessment, product profitability measurement and in strategic policy decisions.

Illustration 1

Assume two products are manufactured with the same direct material content and in identical volumes of 1,000 units. Each product is marketed, distributed and sold in the same way. One product is produced in a labour intensive manner, the other by a capital intensive process. An equal cost substitution of capital for labour exists, i.e., the replacement of labour by capital equipment does not alter the total product cost. Most of the firm's overhead relate to the automation of the latter product's production process.

Total costs

	£
Direct material	200,000
Direct labour	100,000
Production overhead	100,000 (100% of direct labour)
Non-production overhead	200,000 (50% of production cost)
	600,000

Product costs

	'Labour intensive' product £	'Capital intensive' product £
Conventional costing		
Direct material	100	100
Direct labour	80	20
Production overhead (100% direct labour)	80	20
Non-production overhead (50% of production cost)	130	70
	390	210
'Real' costing		
Direct material	100	100
Direct labour	80	20
Production overhead [equal capital/labour) substitution]	20	80
Non-production overhead [identical sales and marketing]	100	100
	300	300

Illustration 2

Equal total quantities of products X and Y are produced. Product X is produced in one production run of 1,000 units while product Y is produced in ten separate production runs of 100 units. Each product has an equal direct material and direct labour content. The production overhead totals £3,300 which comprises production run set-up costs totalling £2,200 and quality inspection costs of £1,100. Set-up and inspection activities are identical for each production run irrespective of its product volume.

Total costs

	£
Direct material	4,000
Direct labour	1,000
Production overhead	3,300
	8,300

Product costs

| | Product X (1 large production run) | | Product Y (10 small production runs) | |
	Total cost	Unit cost	Total cost	Unit cost
	£	£	£	£
Conventional costing				
Direct material	2,000	2.00	2,000	2.00
Direct labour	500	0.50	500	0.50
Production overhead (330% of direct labour)	1,650	1.65	1,650	1.65
	4,150	4.15	4,150	4.15
'Real' costing				
Direct material	2,000	2.00	2,000	2.00
Direct labour	500	0.50	500	0.50
Production overhead:				
Quality inspection:				
1 inspection @ £100	100	0.10	–	–
10 inspections @ £100	–	–	1,000	1.00
Set-up: 1 set-up @ £200	200	0.20	–	–
10 set-ups @ £200	–	–	2000	2.00
	2,800	2.80	5,500	5.50

In summary, the fundamental problem with conventional product costing in many contemporary settings lies in the treatment of overhead costs. Traditional methods are perpetuated, perhaps for convenience, in changed circumstances where they are no longer appropriate. These methods of attaching overhead cost to products will frequently fail to adequately capture the causal relationship between individual products and overhead cost incurrence. To overcome this problem it is necessary to employ an overhead costing approach which more adequately reflects the cause–effect relationship between products and the consumption of the resources which have been acquired by the organization through overhead expenditure. ABC has been designed to ensure that overhead cost utilization is achieved in such a manner. A survey by Innes and Mitchell (1995) revealed that of *The Times* 1000 Companies (with a usable response rate of 25 per cent) approximately 20 per cent of respondents had adopted ABC.

Examining the mechanics of ABC

An ABC system for product costing involves a two-step process. First overheads are pooled in accordance with the activities which cause them. Second, a link, known as a cost driver, is found between each activity cost pool and product output. The computation of cost driver based rates (activity cost/period cost driver volume) then provides the means of actually attaching the overhead to the products. An overview of how such a system would work is provided in Illustration 3 (Figure 3.1). It should be noted that certain activities, normally those of production centres directly related to manufacturing operations, will contain predominantly volume-driven overheads. In these instances conventional cost drivers such as direct labour hours or machine hours will provide an acceptable means of unitizing overhead.

In simplified terms Illustration 3 represents the end result of an ABC system designed for product costing. In order to create an operational system of this type five major steps must first be achieved:

Step 1   Prepare an inventory of activities relating to overheads.
Step 2   Identify the resources and costs of each activity.
Step 3   Ascertain the cost drivers for each activity.
Step 4   Select the activity cost pools and cost drivers which will form the basis of the system.
Step 5   Apply the cost driver rates to the products.

Each of these steps is considered, in turn, below.

Step 1   Preparation of an inventory of activities

Fundamental to ABC is a knowledge of the activities which comprise the 'hidden factory' of indirect operations. This issue needs to be addressed in a systematic manner to ensure that a comprehensive capture of the relevant information is achieved. One approach is to begin with a map or plan of the production and office location and ascertain in broad terms what is done where. All of the available space should be accounted for as a location for operations or other functions. At this stage it will normally prove useful to take the organization's payroll name list and attach all staff to physical locations and broadly defined operational areas. This provides a check on the initial plan-based analysis. If all personnel have been taken into account the basis for the preparation of a detailed activity inventory should be complete.

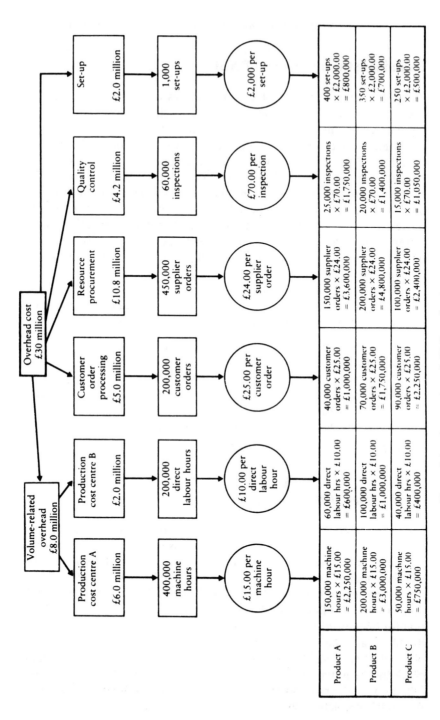

Figure 3.1 *An overview of ABC mechanics*

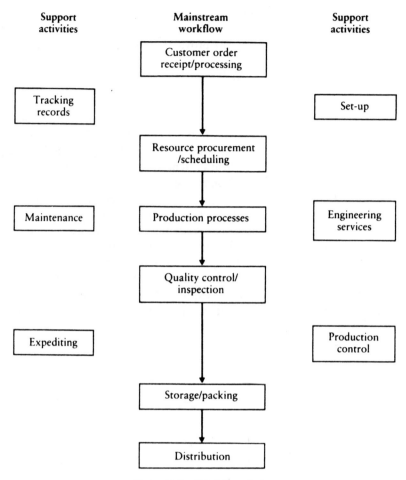

Figure 3.2   *Workflow chain*

The results of this preliminary activity analysis can be conveniently structured around a workflow chain. A simplified example of this is given in Illustration 4 (Figure 3.2).

This identification of the operations and processes of the organization provides the basis from which a more detailed listing of activities can be obtained in a structured manner. This is achieved by gathering information from those involved in the workflow chain about the activities which they carry out. Several alternative approaches have been adopted in order to obtain this information:

1   Managerial accountants interview senior staff in each area.
2   Consultants are brought in to interview senior staff in each area.
3   Senior staff are responsible for providing information of the activities undertaken in their area.
4   All staff fill in forms detailing the activities undertaken in, say, a normal working month.

The accuracy of data gathered at this stage is central to the validity of the final output from the ABC system. It may be worth considering more than one approach to permit cross-checking. It is also a highly sensitive area of investigation and at least one firm's attempts at ABC have floundered at this stage because staff viewed it simply as a first step towards cost cutting and job losses (Robinson, 1989). The improvement of product cost accuracy as the objective should be made clear to participants.

At the end of this step the specific activities relating to each item on the workflow analysis should be known. The information may have to be rationalized somewhat for example by grouping small tasks into significant activities in order to produce the basis of a workable system. The question of how much detail is required by the system must also be addressed. For example, rather than show customer order processing as one activity it may be decomposed into the constituent activities shown below in Illustration 5 (Figure 3.3).

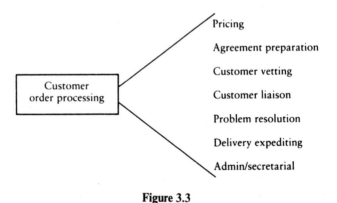

Figure 3.3

Step 2   Costing the specific activities

In terms of collecting the relevant data, much of this step may be combined with gathering the activity information in Step 1. A normal and convenient starting point is the ascertainment of the labour cost of each specific activity. Indeed, in some organizations seeking only an increased knowledge of the broad pattern of overhead spending rather than product cost information, the analysis has been restricted purely to this element of cost. At the time of ascertaining specific activities an analysis of time spent and grade of worker will permit the relevant labour costs to be determined. Information on the consumables and capital equipment employed in carrying out activities must also be obtained. Other overheads, for example occupancy costs such as heat, light, power, rent and rates may require to be allocated on a suitable basis (e.g. floor space or area) to each activity, but where possible costs should be directly charged in order to enhance accuracy. Continuing the example of customer order processing a schedule such as that contained in Illustration 6 would be produced.

Illustration 6   Customer order processing

Specific activities	Indirect labour	Occupancy costs	Depreciation	Consumables	Total
	£m	£m	£m	£m	£m
Pricing	0.25	0.18	0.02	0.08	0.53
Draw up agreements	0.42	0.23	0.03	0.10	0.78
Customer vetting	0.22	0.11	0.03	0.09	0.45
Customer liaison	0.95	0.69	0.14	0.11	1.89
Problem resolution	0.34	0.04	0.02	0.03	0.43
Expedite delivery	0.12	0.22	0.01	0.02	0.37
Admin./secretarial	0.10	0.33	0.05	0.07	0.55
	2.40	1.80	0.30	0.50	5.00

This type of analysis is of value in its own right. It gives a particular visibility, usually for the first time, to overhead cost incurrence. It details why and how overheads have been incurred, allows an assessment of relative magnitude and, as the system develops over time, will permit time period and inter-plant comparison at a detailed level. In addition supplementary analysis of activities into value added/non-value added categories or core/support activities can assist management in designing policies aimed at cost containment or reduction (see chapters on activity-based cost management for further details).

Step 3   Ascertain the cost drivers for each activity

A cost driver is a variable which determines the work volume or workload of a particular activity. It will provide a justification for the amount of resources consumed by an activity and hence its cost. Due to this close causal relationship it will be a significant measure of activity cost variation. To permit its practical application in an ABC system it must also, ideally, be conveniently measurable and readily attributed to individual products. In meeting these criteria most cost drivers will reflect the transactions which underlie the activity under consideration. Indeed in the USA the term transaction-based costing has been applied to ABC. Hence the number of purchase orders processed, number of customer orders processed, number of inspections undertaken or number of set-ups achieved all represent a volume of transactions related to an activity. However, there are also examples of characteristics of circumstances of the organization being used as cost drivers. They impact on the activity cost at an even more fundamental level as the characteristics chosen represent the factors which primarily determine the number of activities undertaken. For example the number of customers, number of suppliers or number of component parts have all been used as cost drivers. These are all situational factors which one would expect to influence the volume of transactions and hence the cost, respectively, of the customer order processing, procurement and scheduling activities. If this approach directs attention more directly to cost causality then the use of this more fundamental type of driver is preferable.

The ascertainment of cost drivers will normally involve repeat interviews with the personnel involved in the specific activities. These will centre on the topic of what causes a particular activity to consume resources and so incur cost. This is often facilitated by focusing not simply on a justification for the existing resources but also on the factors which would require a greater or lesser input of resources to the activity. Some typical questions aimed at teasing out cost drivers are provided in Illustration 7.

Illustration 7

- What staff work on this activity?
- Why are X number of staff needed?
- Have you sufficient staff? (If no, why?)
- What might cause you to need more/less staff?
- What determines the amount of time spent on this activity?
- Why is overtime worked?
- Why does idle time occur?

The end result of this step will typically be a set of potential cost drivers for each sub-activity. For the example chosen of customer order processing this might be as shown in Illustration 8.

Illustration 8   Customer order processing

Activities	Cost drivers
Pricing	Number of orders Number of customers Complexity of order
Setting agreements	Location of customer Number of orders Number of customers
Customer vetting	Number of customers Size of orders Location of customer
Customer liaison	Order book position Number of customers Number of orders Location of customer
Problem resolution	Delivery performance Product quality Number of orders Number of customers Location of customer
Expediting delivery	Location of customer Production hold-ups Number of orders
Admin./secretarial	Number of orders Number of problems Number of staff

Step 4   Final selection of activity cost pools and cost drivers

The completion of Steps 1 to 3 will result in a large volume of sub-activities and cost drivers. Some rationalization is then necessary to effect an operational system. This will involve the choice of a final set of activity cost pools and the selection of one cost driver for each pool.

The number and choice of cost pools differ considerably in practice. A very detailed system might simply employ a separate pool for every identified sub-activity. Indeed the existence of multiple cost drivers for any particular pool may give rise to some consideration to segment the pool further if fractions of its cost relate specifically to individual cost drivers. Several of the early US ABC systems were of a highly detailed nature with literally hundreds of cost pools and cost drivers. For purely product costing purposes several factors should be considered in determining the number of cost pools finally selected to form the basis of the ABC system:

1   The total cost of the particular pool. The activity cost must be material in size to justify separate treatment.
2   The homogeneity of the cost pool. The activity cost should be homogeneous in the sense that it can be accurately accommodated within the system through the use of one cost driver. Where this is not considered possible then a further division of the pool may be necessary. On the other hand where different activity cost pools utilize identical cost drivers there will be a case for aggregation.
3   Where there is a diversity of activity resource consumption by product lines then the aggregation of cost pools may result in inaccuracies. For example in Illustration 9 a marked distortion of cost would be caused by combining the two sub-activity pools within the parts ordering process because products X and Y make significantly different demands on the resources of these sub-activities.

The selection of one cost driver from a number of alternatives is also a judgemental matter. A statistical regression analysis of each competing alternative would provide the most objective means of coming to a decision, but it is unlikely that data will be available to permit this approach. In practice cost drivers have been selected by applying the criteria contained in Step 4 above, by having further discussions with the management of the sub-activity to ascertain their views on the possible alternatives, and considering the potential utility of the resultant ABC outputs. Monitoring the early use of a selected driver will also provide useful data to help decide whether change is required. Where more than one driver continues to appear pertinent it may be a sign that the activity pool can be further subdivided and both drivers used as appropriate for each new cost pool.

Illustration 10 progresses the customer order processing example to show three possible end results for the ABC system design. The first solution is based on the assumption of cost pool homogeneity. The single cost driver of number of orders has been chosen because of its relative preeminence through its appearance as a cost driver for six of the seven

Illustration 9   The effects of diversity in activity resource consumption

---

Data

Activity cost pool   *Cost driver rate*

I   Parts order preparation   £20 per order
II   Parts order verification   £50 per order
     (only for certain types of order)

Product costing

No diversity exists in activity resource consumption

	Product A		Product B	
	No. orders	Cost	No. orders	Cost
		£		£
Activity pool I	5	100.00	5	100.00
Activity pool II	3	150.00	3	150.00
	—		—	
	8	250.00	8	250.00
	=	======	=	======

Diversity exists in activity resource consumption

	Product X		Product Y	
	No. orders	Cost	No. orders	Cost
		£		£
Activity pool I	5	100.00	5	100.00
Activity pool II	2	100.00	4	200.00
	—		—	
	7	200.00	9	300.00
	=	======	=	======

---

sub-activities. It is the simplest and probably the cheapest approach but it does only provide feedback in total on the customer ordering process. It utilizes only two variables (cost and order volume) to reflect an area of activity which is clearly influenced by other factors.

The second solution lies at the other end of the spectrum. A cost driver which best represents each cost pool has been selected and a cost rate has been computed for each identified sub-activity. This will enhance the accuracy of the system and will provide more detailed feedback on cost variation within customer order processing, but it is also the most elaborate and costly alternative to operate. The third solution offers a half-way house with a limited amount of cost pool aggregation having been undertaken. Roughly half of the costs are concerned with administrative and

Illustration 10   Alternative cost driver rates for customer order processing

---

Solution 1

Full aggregation of sub-activities −1 cost driver

$$\frac{£5.00 \text{ million}}{200,000 \text{ orders}} = £25.00 \text{ per order}$$

Solution 2

No aggregation of sub-activities −1 cost driver per sub-activity

Activity	Cost (£ million)	Cost driver	Rate
Pricing	£0.53	Number of enquiries (300,000 enquiries)	£1.77 per enquiry
Agreements	£0.78	Number of orders (200,000 orders)	£3.90 per order
Vetting	£0.45	Number of customers (25,000 customers)	£18.00 per customer
Liaison	£1.89	Number of customers (25,000 customers)	£75.60 per customer
Problems	£0.43	Number of late deliveries (50,000 late deliveries)	£8.60 per late delivery
Expedite	£0.37	Number of orders (200,000 orders)	£1.85 per order
Administration	£0.55	Number of customers (25,000 customers)	£22.00 per customer

Solution 3

Partial aggregation

Activity	Cost (£ million)	Cost driver	Rate
Procedural activities (pricing agreements, vetting, admin.)	£2.31	Number of orders (200,000 orders)	£11.25 per order
Customer service activities (Liaison, problems, expedite)	£2.69	Number of late deliveries (50,000 late deliveries)	£53.80 per late delivery

procedural matters concerning order processing and are viewed as being influenced primarily by order volume. The remainder of the costs relate to the activities which facilitate the whole relationship with customers, particularly where problems occur, and these have been deemed to be driven by the volume of late order deliveries.

Step 5   Applying the cost driver rate to individual products

If a cost driver rate is to be practical the variable chosen must be measurable in a way which permits its identification with individual products. For example, the number of part orders associated with each product must be known if the products are to be individually costed. This requirement may represent one of the significant costs of ABC, especially where a new system has to be established to collect the cost driver information both in total and for each product (see Cobb *et al.*, 1993 for further details). The ability of a cost driver to meet this requirement should therefore also be considered during Step 3 when the cost driver is being chosen.

While the foregoing description outlines the basic characteristics of an ABC system, in practice ABC systems are not of uniform type. Many differences in design are apparent and the nature and rationale for several of these are explored in the following section.

Variation in ABC

One characteristic of ABC systems that is apparent from even the limited empirical evidence currently available is the extensive variation observable in existing operational systems. The nature of the adopting organization and the purpose for which the ABC system has been installed have both proved to be important contingencies influencing and resulting in differences in ABC system design. Seven of the major areas of variation are examined below.

(1)   The number of cost pools

ABC systems range from the very elaborate, involving hundreds of cost pools and cost drivers to the simple, involving only a small number of cost drivers. The former type of system is typically geared towards achieving the maximum accuracy in product line costing and, as described in the preceding section, it will also give a detailed visibility to overhead cost incurrence. The more simplistic systems, with a limited number of cost pools and drivers, have been designed not simply to enhance product cost accuracy but also to influence behaviour in the organization in a way which will improve cost consciousness and cost effectiveness. The prime examples of these less detailed systems evidence an orientation which is aimed at influencing product designers. A few cost drivers mean only a few highly significant cost driver rates and consequently the designers' attention becomes intensely focused on these factors if they are to ensure product cost targets are met at the design stage. Illustration 11 shows how one firm, Tektronix (Jonez, 1987), which had experienced growth in direct material-related overheads, designed its ABC system to ensure that designers would try to use existing standard parts in new products rather than proliferating the range of parts bought in. In essence the major cost driver of material-related overhead was the number of different parts involved in manufacturing operations and by having a system which imposed a cost penalty on the utilization of little used parts, a clear signal was given to designers to avoid them if at all possible.

Illustration 11   Motivational cost driver rates

Total direct material related overhead = £100 million
Total number of different part types utilized = 10,000
Cost per part type = £10,000 (£100 million ÷ 10,000)

Cost driver rates:
   High usage part (say 100,000 per annum) = £10,000 ÷ 100,000
                                                              = £0.10

   Low usage part (say 100 per annum) = £10,000 ÷ 100
                                                  = £100.00 per part

---

In summary the use of a limited number of cost drivers (say up to a dozen) may lack some of the accuracy and detail of a more elaborate system but it does concentrate attention on key areas. It can therefore be an important basis where a motivational impact is the objective. Indeed Japanese companies have largely stuck to a direct labour hours basis because they wish to reduce the costly labour input of their products (Hiromoto, 1988). In addition a small number of drivers provides a more easily managed basis for starting to develop ABC. It is easier to describe and communicate to management, its outputs are more easily analysed and it can be expanded gradually if expansion is considered necessary.

(2)   The nature of selected activity pools

The most common type of cost pooling (similar to that described in the preceding section) has been based on indirect activities. In other words the cost pools and costs have been limited purely to overheads. In a small number of cases, however, some firms have extended the ABC approach to include direct activities, i.e. those activities which comprise the actual production process. For example, this has occurred in the electronics sector where direct labour is typically very small (often as low as 2 per cent of costs) and production involves a sequential set of activities (Innes and Mitchell, 1990). In these situations direct labour and overheads have simply been aggregated and a full conversion cost added to the product as it passed through each operational activity. The cost drivers reflect the actual direct work being undertaken through that activity, e.g. number of holes drilled and number of wires inserted. In effect the organization of the system is akin to that of an operations costing system (Horngren and Foster, 1987) with the ABC idea of an activity-based cost driver built on.

While most ABC systems have been restricted to production and production support costs there have been suggestions that this approach is applicable to other types of overhead as well. R&D, distribution, selling, marketing and administration represent areas which may also be susceptible to ABC analysis. Indeed if the object of the exercise is to produce product cost information which will provide management with a view of the long-run total variable cost (Johnson and Kaplan, 1987) of their products then these costs should be included. In addition the enhanced cost visibility which ABC affords is equally applicable to non-production overheads.

(3)   Customizing cost driver rates

The straightforward computation of a cost driver rate involves

$$\frac{\text{Activity cost}}{\text{Cost driver volume}}$$

However it may be adjusted where appropriate to produce more meaningful rates. Illustration 11 earlier gave one example of how this might be done. In that instance it proved convenient for the rate to be computed in two stages to reflect the fact that overhead was driven by two factors – first simply the existence and maintenance of a part type and second the volume of usage of that part. Similarly it may be found that a transaction-based cost driver does not have a consistent (and linear) impact on cost and consequently a more complex mechanism has to be devised to maintain costing accuracy. For example, Illustration 12 shows how cost driver (number of orders) volume for customer order processing may have to be weighted if an accurate attribution of cost to products is to be achieved. An alternative approach would have involved splitting the cost pool of £5.0 million into three separate pools relating to the source order and, by applying appropriate order volumes to each, produce three separate cost driver rates. This approach would, however, involve a more detailed and costly analysis of the total cost. The use of unit weightings should achieve reasonable accuracy with less commitment of resources.

Illustration 12   Weighted driver rates

Customer location	Relative weight re. resource consumption	Number of orders	Weighted values
USA	30	80,000	2,400,000
Far East	60	20,000	1,200,000
Europe	10	100,000	1,000,000
			4,600,000

$$\text{Rate} \quad \frac{\text{£5.0 million}}{4,600,000 \text{ weighted order volume}}$$

$$= \text{£1.09 per weighted order}$$

Application
USA order   30 × £1.09 = £32.70
Far East order 60 × £1.09 = £65.40
Europe order   10 × £1.09 = £10.90

(4)   Activity cost structuring

The information generated by an ABC system is of particular value because it relates cost incurrence to causality (activities) through the range of cost drivers which are employed. It thus assists management to understand cost behaviour within the organization. However, to enhance this facility of ABC the cost information outputs of the system have, in some instances, been designed to classify activities costs with regard to the level at which their incurrence is driven. Essentially there will be six such levels:

1   The unit level where the activity and hence the level of cost is directly associated with the volume of production, e.g. drilling holes.
2   The batch level where the activity and hence the level of cost is directly associated with the number of batches produced, e.g. set-ups.
3   The process level where the activity and hence the level of cost is directly associated with the existence or otherwise of a particular process, e.g. maintenance.
4   The product level where the activity and hence the level of cost is directly associated with the existence or otherwise of a particular product line, e.g. part ordering.
5   The production facility where the activity and hence cost sustains the manufacturing plant, e.g. general management.
6   The customer where the activity and hence the level of cost is influenced by the particular customer being supplied, e.g. customization costs.

Structuring cost reports to reflect these levels can emphasize to management that although cost information may be reported in unit terms it is not simply by changing the number of units produced (or sold) that costs can be influenced. Illustration 13 exemplifies the type of report which might be produced to indicate underlying cost behaviour patterns or cost layering as it is usually called.

(5)   Cost of unused capacity

Just as cost layering in the previous section is one of the 1990s developments in ABC, so also is the development of the cost of unused capacity (see Kaplan, 1995). With its emphasis on activities an ABC system measures the cost of using resources rather that the cost of supplying resources. In other words if you incur expenditure in overhead areas but do not use part of the capacity of that overhead cost, you should report the cost of that unused capacity. It is very important that managers understand that reducing the use of a particular activity will not by itself necessarily save any expenditure.

Kaplan (1995, p. 253) summarizes the situation as follows:

$$\text{Cost of resources supplied} = \text{Cost of resources used} + \text{Cost of unused capacity}$$

'The difference between the resources supplied and the resources actually used during a period represents the unused capacity of the resource for the period.' In other words managers need to manage the unused capacity either by using it in some other way or by reducing or eliminating the unused capacity. As Kaplan (1995, p. 254) states 'what makes a resource cost "variable" in a downward direction is not inherent in the nature of the resource.'

Illustration 13   Costs: production period 1
(production 10,000 units in 10 batches)

	Total cost		Unit cost	
	£	£	£	£
Unit level				
Direct material 5,000lbs @ £10	50,000		5.00	
Conversion:				
Drilling – 50,000 holes @ £0.40	20,000		2.00	
Grinding – 10,000 bits @ £0.80	8,000		0.80	
		78,000		7.80
Batch level				
Quality control:				
10 inspections @ £250	2,500		0.25	
Set-up:				
10 set-ups @ £2,000	20,000		2.00	
		22,500		2.25
Process control				
Process supervision				
6 staff @ £1,000	6,000		0.60	
Process maintenance				
20 breakdowns @ £200	4,000		0.40	
		10,000		1.00
Product level				
Procurement:				
600 orders @ £30	18,000		1.80	
Expediting:				
30 expedites @ £100	3,000		0.30	
		21,000		2.10

	Total cost		Unit cost	
	£	£	£	£
Facility level				
Rent 14,000 sq.ft. @ £2.00 =	28,000		2.80	
Management:				
10 grade C managers @ £4,000 =	40,000		4.00	
		68,000		6.80
		199,500		19.95

(6)   A system or 'one-off' exercise?

Several of the early examples of ABC were conducted by small multi-disciplinary staff teams as 'one-off' exercises. A suitable recent past period was selected, data collected, and an ABC approach applied. Since then the development of more permanent systems routinely reporting ABC has become apparent. In some instances these systems have completely replaced conventional costing systems. The availability of software packages and specialist consultancy services has lent support to this trend. However, any firm contemplating ABC should address this issue. It is possible that many of the benefits of ABC can be achieved through periodic 'one-off' investigations especially in situations where the pace and extent of change is not great. Moreover, a 'one-off' analysis will provide a useful starting point in the assessment of ABC by providing a basis for comparing cost information differences and for obtaining the views and reactions of management. Potential benefits are then more apparent, and there is also the avoidance of routinely gathering information on staff time (necessitating the completion of time sheets?) and having resources committed to particular activities. On the other hand the speed of feedback and regularity of information will fall below that of a full system of ABC. In addition a systematic provision for ABC permits the use of predetermined or standard cost driver rates and can thus result in detailed analyses of overhead variances and capacity utilization. Clearly regular monitoring provides and enhances awareness of changes and facilitates a speedier managerial response. These benefits and costs will be situationally dependent and therefore require a company-by-company judgement.

(7) The extent of ABC

ABC can be designed to an extent which best suits the user. For example, some firms have emphasized the use of ABC for overhead control rather than product costing. They have found it necessary only to apply the ABC philosophy up to the stage of identifying activities and their respective costs. This analysis gives overhead cost incurrence the visibility and causality indications lacking in more conventional approaches. In other instances the second stage of linking activities to products is also pursued in order to produce the product cost information to support product-oriented strategic decisions. Another alternative cost object for the ABC system has been the customer. Activities (and hence cost) being associated with specific customers in order to measure the profitability of individual business relationships. If taken to a logical conclusion the construction of an activity/cost database would appear desirable with the facility to link costs as accurately as possible to a whole range of cost objects through the demands which they place on the activities.

Evaluating ABC

Any proper assessment of a management accounting system or technique should be made in relation to the purpose or objective which it is intended to fulfil. An objective will normally involve not simply the nature or type of information to be generated but the resultant use and impact of the information. The novelty of ABC has meant that, to date, little empirical evidence has been gathered even on its immediate or short-run effects within those organizations which have begun to implement it. The study of its medium-and long-term performance will have to wait several more years. Assessment is further complicated by the variation possible in the application of ABC ideas and by its relevance to more than one purpose. Advocates have suggested that its outputs can be used for strategic decision-making (product costs) and for cost analysis for operational control, cost control and management (Johnson, 1988; Kaplan, 1988). The assessment which follows is therefore largely reflective, being based on the authors' views of the limited amount of research and publication on ABC which exists to date.

ABC will generate product (or service) line costings which will differ from those produced by a traditional system primarily in respect of their indirect cost content. This is because costs will be attached to products in a way which reflects how these products have created a demand for, and effected the consumption of, the resources which comprise the organization's overheads. Where this element of cost is material and where traditional methods of overhead costing (e.g. labour hour/cost rates) do not adequately capture resource consumption then the use of ABC will improve the product cost information which is produced. Johnson and Kaplan (1987) suggest that it can be used to unitize all costs with the exception of excess capacity and research and development costs in order to provide a good indication of long-term average product costs. It therefore avoids the simplistic categorization of many costs as fixed period costs and provides a counterweight to conventional short-run marginal cost and contribution analysis. Over the long-term virtually all costs can be viewed as variable, not simply in respect of production volume but also in respect of the whole array of cost drivers which are associated in the application of ABC. When this is clarified by the costing system, managers can better appreciate the total demands which individual products place on the resources of the firm. Where the information is arranged and structured logically (see for example Illustration 13) then the ABC system will enhance an understanding of cost behaviour. ABC ensures that costs are associated with genuine causal factors; cost prediction is therefore facilitated and a basis for modelling costs is provided.

ABC will not however solve all of the complexities of product costing. Some arbitrariness will certainly remain. For example, some overheads are incurred at a level divorced from that of any individual product. Corporate name promotion in a multi-product firm, general management services and overall production facility costs are all 'joint' in respect of product lines. Any basis of attachment to individual products will be incorrigible and can be questioned. Furthermore cost drivers may also suffer from the problem of 'jointness'. If the 'number of orders' is being used as a driver for procurement overhead and the direct material for a number of products is made on each individual order then the association of the cost driver with the individual products becomes problematic. Indeed the identification of sets of cost drivers which explain 100 per cent of the relationship between products and activity costs is unlikely. ABC product costing has some technical difficulties.

The generation of product cost information implies that it has managerial utility. Advocates of ABC suggest that it is of use in the strategic assessment of the product range. The promotion, demotion, modification and elimination of individual products would all be a part of this process. As these decisions concern the future (and at a strategic level the medium- to long-run future) then it is future differential revenues and costs over that timescale which will represent the relevant information to decision-makers. The historic outputs of an ABC system will be relevant only as a basis for directing attention, in the first instance, to potential decision areas. While ABC information may give a good indication of how a product has consumed resources in the recent past, this may bear little relationship to future incremental cost (from expansion) or future avoidable cost (from dropping the product). Structured ABC information may however provide a sound basis for making such estimates.

The use of ABC will also generate information of relevance to cost control. Overheads are made more visible through pooling by activity and their underlying cause, to the extent it is reflected in their cost driver, is also indicated. The information is therefore in a useful form to support and direct managerial cost control action. Indeed the conventional controls of budgets and responsibility accounting can be conveniently incorporated within the ABC framework (Brimson and Fraser, 1990). There is some evidence to suggest that it is also in the area of cost control that most of the short-term benefits of ABC have been reported by those implementing it (Innes and Mitchell, 1990, 1991). Among its claimed advantages have been a greater understanding of cost behaviour, improved communication of cost information due to the logic of ABC, more cost-effective new product design as cost causality is understood more clearly by designers, new cost reduction initiatives by operational staff in response to ABC based feedback and the identification and elimination of some non-value added activities. Moreover the identification of activities and their capacities, as measured in cost driver terms, provides the basis for a profile of capacity usage. Where the system is operated on a standard costing basis, the level of detail in overhead variance analysis is considerably enhanced. Benefits such as these lend weight to the maxim that it is easier to manage activities than it is to manage costs.

However, because ABC is so directly related to how costs are incurred, particularly indirect labour costs, the gathering of information to run the system can be a matter of some sensitivity. Employees, frequently of a type not used to the exactitudes of the time-clock, may be reluctant to make accurate disclosure of exactly what activities they undertake. This may be especially so if they suspect that the information may be used to assess their performance, to tighten budgets or even to eliminate some labour resource. One of the few reported instances of ABC failure (Robinson, 1989) was because of just such a problem in obtaining the raw data upon which to base the system.

Finally ABC will result in a new set of information which can be used to measure aspects of operational performance within the organization, i.e. cost drivers and cost driver rates. These may provide useful and quick regular feedback to line management and may help to foster cost consciousness and efficiency (Johnson, 1988). Once again, however, care must be taken that the motivation engendered by these measures is as intended. This is especially so in respect of cost driver rates where an improvement can be achieved by increasing the volume of the denominator (the driver) providing there is a less than proportionate increase in the numerator (the activity cost). This will be so if there is an element of the activity cost fixed in relation to the driver. Thus, for example, if 'number of set-ups' is a cost driver there may be a motivation to increase these even where this is operationally unnecessary. The increase would boost total cost but also effect an improvement in the cost per set-up.

ABC possesses several compelling positive attributes. It has the potential to contribute to strategic decision-making, cost control and management and performance measurement. On balance, given the limitations inherent in any attempt to obtain full unit cost information in a complex business, it may well be that the cost control and management benefits of ABC will be the most enduring. It is also frequently competing with existing systems which have been discredited due to inherent inaccuracies such as those illustrated in the first part of this chapter. For these reasons the widespread and growing interest in ABC on both sides of the Atlantic can be soundly justified and is hardly surprising.

If this interest is followed up by a widespread adoption of ABC then some care must be exercised by both system designers and users in order to realize the benefits of ABC and minimize the costs. Implementation success will depend particularly on attention being given to the following three factors:

1 A recognition of the nature and variation in ABC and the creation of a system designed to meet the needs of the specific organization concerned.
2 A recognition that ABC is not a complete general purpose system which will meet all cost information needs.
3 A recognition that any ABC system will have some limitations and if not carefully designed and monitored will have the potential for dysfunctional consequences for the adopting organizations.

References

Brimson, J. and Fraser, R. (1991). The key features of ABC. *Management Accounting (UK)*, January, 42–3.

Cobb, I., Innes, J. and Mitchell, F. (1992). *Activity-Based Costing – Problems in Practice*. London: Chartered Institute of Management Accountants.

Cooper, R. (1988/9). The rise of activity based costing Parts 1–4. *Journal of Cost Management*, Summer, Fall, Winter, Spring.

Cooper, R. and Kaplan, R. (1988). Measure costs right: make the right decisions. *Harvard Business Review*, September/October.

Friedman, A. and Lyne, S. (1995). *Implementing Activity-Based Techniques – The Real Life Consequences*. London: Chartered Institute of Management Accountants.

Hiromoto, T. (1988) Another hidden edge – Japanese management accounting. *Harvard Business Review*, July/August.

Horngren, C. T. and Foster, G. (1987). *Cost Accounting: A Managerial Emphasis* (6th edition). New Jersey: Prentice-Hall.

Innes, J. and Mitchell, F. (1990). *Activity Based Costing: A Review with Case Studies*. London: Chartered Institute of Management Accountants.

Innes, J. and Mitchell, F. (1991). *Activity Based Cost Management*. London: Chartered Institute of Management Accountants.

Innes, J. and Mitchell, F. (1995). A survey of activity-based costing in the UK's largest companies, *Management Accounting Research*, June 137–53.

Johnson, H. T. (1988). Activity based information: a blueprint for world-class management accounting. *Management Accounting (USA)*.

Johnson, H. T. and Kaplan, R. (1987). The importance of long-term product costs. *The McKinsey Quarterly*, Autumn.

Jonez, J. W. (1987). Material burdening: management accounting can support competitive strategy. *Management Accounting (USA)*, August.

Kaplan, R. S. (1988). One cost system is not enough. *Harvard Business Review*, January/February.

Kaplan, R. S. (1994). Management accounting (1984–1994): development of new practice and theory, *Management Accounting Research*, September and December, 247–60.

Miller, J. G., Vollman, T. E. (1985). The hidden factory. *Harvard Business Review*, September/October.

Robinson, M. A., editor (1989). *Cases From Management Accounting Practice (Stanadyne Diesel Case)*. National Association of Accountants.

Staubus, G. (1971). *Activity Costing and Input-Output Accounting*. Richard D. Irwin Inc.

Acknowledgement

The authors would like to acknowledge both the Chartered Institute of Management Accountants and the Canon Foundation in Europe who have funded some of their research on activity-based costing.

4

The basics of activity-based management

James A. Brimson

This chapter explains the basic concepts of enterprise excellence and how activity-based management (ABM) can help a company achieve it. The chapter focuses on the way companies make decisions and how ABM changes company culture. It describes an ABM system and the three phases of implementation. It provides an overview of activity analysis, how to achieve short-term profit improvement, how a bill of activities improves activity product cost and how to implement an integrated activity accounting system that is compatible with enterprise excellence. Finally, a glossary of key ABM terms is provided.

The four cornerstones of enterprise excellence are total quality, continuous improvement, non-value added elimination, and cycle time reduction as illustrated in Figure 4.1. Activity-based management provides the tools and information needed to support managers in attaining enterprise excellence.

Enterprise excellence is achieved by identifying and eliminating waste, continually improving value added activities (reducing cost and time while improving quality) and streamlining management practices. Waste and inefficiency is a direct result of the management practices and management information systems that do not measure the factors critical to managerial excellence. As a consequence, every company in all industries has tremendous improvement potential. Consider what comprises the productivity improvement potential:

Waste   Most companies have between 20 and 40 per cent of total cost consumed in performing non-value added – wasteful – activities. Waste results from errors (correction, detection and disruption to operations),

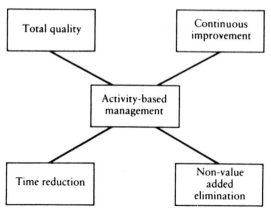

Figure 4.1 *Enterprise excellence*

useless paperwork, ineffective policies and procedures, mismanaged capacity and ineffectual physical/organizational structure.

Excessive bureaucracy Excessive layers of management and a burdensome administrative structure coupled with management doing inappropriate activities increases cost – often 5 to 10 per cent of total cost – and, more insidiously, decreases management time that might be spent on revenue-enhancing activities.

Inefficient value added activities No matter how well an activity is performed, there always exists a more efficient method of performing the activity by applying, for example, methods of improvement or state-of-the-art technology.

To illustrate these potentials, consider a company that recently applied activity analysis as the first step in implementing an activity-based management system. The company is a well known, profitable and highly respected global organization that is implementing cost management in a product line that is one of their cash cows. The analysis of their £10 million base of manufacturing cost revealed the following classification of cost:

Cost category	£ (mil)
Non-value added	3.3
Management	1.5
Value added	5.2

When these costs were analysed from a cost reduction perspective, the following potential was identified:

Cost category	Investment required £ (mil)	Potential annual savings £ (mil)
Non-value added	1.65	2.50
Management	—	0.50
Value added	1.00	0.50
Total	2.65	3.50

Looking closely at the activities in each category, the company concluded that approximately half of the non-value added cost could be eliminated in a period of eighteen months to two years without a significant capital investment. These reductions are a direct result of changes in policy, procedures and methods. The other half of the non-value added cost was related to structural problems, such as the plant layout and a proliferation of parts, that would require a much longer period of time and capital investment to remedy. In other words, by eliminating non-value added activities, streamlining management, continuously improving value-added activities and making strategic investments the company determined it was feasible to eliminate £3.50 million of annual cost on a base of £10 million for a one off investment of £2.65 million.

The savings in management costs were related to removing the need to manage non-value added activities that were eliminated, streamlining reports, removing layers of management, and instituting revised control procedures. The savings in value added activities relate to a continuous improvement programme where each manager is given a 10 per cent improvement goal.

It is also important to note that the cost reduction programme was only a part of a long-term plan of continued market dominance. Of equal or greater importance was to establish an ongoing measurement system that would highlight improvement opportunities on a continuous basis to *prevent* waste and inefficiencies from creeping back into the cost base.

However, it must be kept in mind that achieving enterprise excellence does not necessarily mean a company will gain a competitive advantage. Competitive advantage accrues to those companies that use manufacturing excellence as a proactive rather than reactive strategy. Long-term profitability is determined by the company's advantages or disadvantages relative to competitors. Companies that eliminate waste and strive for absolute quality in all aspects of management ahead of competitors can use the increased revenue to invest in R&D, reinvest in improving activity performance, lower cost, or build a strong cash liquidity position. The companies which achieve these results will be in a position to dictate the basis of competition in their industry.

To stay ahead of the competition companies must have information to provide the necessary understanding of the factors they can influence. Management must place unrelenting pressure on the entire organization for measurable profit improvement and productivity gains. Vigilance is critical because it is difficult to regain cost competitiveness once it is lost. Costs must not be allowed to get out of line in the first place.

Why did it happen?

Once a company has recognized the vast potential for improvement, as highlighted by the cost management system, the next logical question is how did such a large amount of waste and inefficiency occur in the first place? Was management that bad?

The reason that such a vast potential exists is that the business world has undergone dramatic changes in the recent past yet we cling to management practices and management information systems that hinder excellence. Consider how many of the following techniques you currently use to manage your firm and you begin to get an appreciation of why such vast improvement potential exists.

Managing the workforce – not workload Managers have traditionally managed costs through expanding or contracting the workforce. When asked to describe the magnitude of their responsibilities, a manager often specifies the number of employees. In the case of direct labour, traditional cost accounting systems can tell you to the fifth decimal point the direct labour content in a particular product.

The ultimate form of managing the workforce is downsizing – or restructuring as it is commonly referred to today. Managers know that costs are too high so they arbitrarily cut headcount by a certain percentage. Downsizing is ineffective because it does not correct the fundamental problem underlying the need to reduce resources. Costs cannot be permanently removed unless the workload is reduced. Workforce reductions will follow as a consequence.

Managing profits Directors of public companies believe the security of their jobs depends on reported profits and derivatives such as return on assets and earnings per share. As a consequence, middle management are given objectives, performance measures and rewards to support achievement of accounting profits. Unfavourable deviations in sales or cost are often compensated for by slashing the discretionary expenditures including long-term projects so as to stay on course for the committed profit figure.

The result is that when management decides to 'tighten the belt' with across-the-board cuts they generate a self-feeding cycle of competitive decay. They not only slash wasteful expenditures but also those activities critical to the future such as sales or marketing development, R&D, or forgo manufacturing improvements to make profits appear better. They do not address the demand for overhead resources – the activities that keep people busy and therefore incur costs.

A viciously deteriorating cycle works itself into worsening conditions. When short-term cutbacks are removed, spending returns at least to its previous level and often to a higher level since many important activities were delayed. Deterioration in the quality of service and pressures on an overburdened staff prompt renewed spending and overhead creeps up. Short-term crisis management inevitably leads to future crisis management.

While conflicts between short and long-term objectives have raged for ages, enterprise excellence requires management to differentiate between value added and wasteful activities. There must be an ongoing commitment to eliminating undesirable activities associated with waste and continuously improving value added and management activities. The short-term savings possible by this strategy should be used to fund future growth.

Managing variable costs – not the assets A company committed to enterprise excellence cannot afford to adopt a passive attitude toward managing fixed assets. A fixed asset represents a significant investment and management should be held accountable for *all* investments. Companies must recover fixed costs if they are to remain in business. Under traditional variable cost thinking if a worker is eliminated, a manager can visualize the savings. On the other hand, if the need for a machine is eliminated the manager does not see any cost savings because the machine has been bought. This attitude is reflected in traditional management accounting practice which advocates separating variable from fixed cost.

The consequence of this management philosophy was evident at the company referred to earlier in this article. Of the ten packing lines in the plant, certain ones were used three days a week while others were used two days a week based on product mix changes. No plant anywhere in the world would have their employees work two or three days a week and remain idle the other time. Yet because the cost for the packing lines was considered to be sunk it was not of paramount importance to keep them fully utilized. This is not to suggest that they should be kept busy building to stock but rather that the company should have acquired no more than six or seven lines rather than the current ten. The cost of a fixed asset is a cost of production and should be considered in all decisions impacting cost. Separating fixed cost led to complacency.

Successful companies are replacing the variable/fixed distinction with a used/unused asset management philosophy. An unused asset is waste since a cost is incurred without any corresponding revenue. A used asset should be continuously improved to shift capacity from used to unused. Unused assets should not be thought of as a sunk cost but rather as a prospective revenue.

To illustrate the used/unused concept, consider a company which streamlined their production facility and created unused factory floor space. According to contribution thinking they had not saved money because the cost of the floor space still had to be paid. Management believed, however, that working at greater efficiency must lead to greater competitiveness. Progressive management thinking prevailed and they lowered the facilities cost charged to production based on the actual floor space saved. This provided incentive to department managers to use facilities space as effectively as possible. The cost of the unused space was transferred to a management budget. The message conveyed by this approach was that facilities represented a revenue opportunity which was management's responsibility to achieve.

Organizing by functional specialization Functional specialization masks costs. The traditional approach is to disaggregate work into narrowly defined tasks, reaggregate the people performing those tasks into departments, install managers to administer them, and employ complex mechanisms to track progress. Management reporting emphasizes each organizational unit as if they were independent self-contained disciplines.

Conventional separation of organizational responsibility is dysfunctional since it encourages competition among departments and provides limited incentive to take action that hinders a department's performance, but is in the best overall interest of the company. People substitute the narrow goals of their particular department for the larger goals of the enterprise. When work is handed off from one department to another, delays and errors are inevitable. Accountability blurs, and critical issues fall between the cracks.

A classic example of this situation is found in the receiving department of the previously referred to company. An important activity of the receiving department is to unload and inspect incoming material. Because the shipments arrived randomly during the day, the staffing level had to be set to handle multiple trucks. Much of the time, as a consequence of random deliveries, the workers waited for trucks to arrive or were assigned to unnecessary work.

The obvious solution to the problem was to require the vendor to deliver according to a set delivery schedule. It was determined that £120,000 per year could be saved by this change. A natural question is: How did this significant level of non-value added costs arise? The management of the receiving department was aware of the problem but could not take any direct action because vendor delivery policy was the responsibility of the purchasing department which was located at corporate headquarters. On several occasions the receiving department manager had discussed the issue with the purchasing department. No action was initiated because the vendor responded that they wanted higher prices to deliver to a set schedule.

The cost management system was a major part of the problem. The purchasing manager had a negative incentive to incur an unfavourable purchase price variance to help the performance of the receiving department. Even if the purchasing department was willing to lower their performance, the enterprise did not have a simple way to determine whether the cost savings to the receiving department offset the higher purchase cost.

Setting relative improvement goals Most companies set performance goals relative to last year's performance. Thus management planning too often degenerates to taking last year's data and increasing expenditures by this year's planned level of growth. Standards are, consequently, relative rather than absolute. Setting relative standards does not motivate managers to the best possible level of performance especially when the relative standard is from a low base.

The composite performance of a company is a result of a mixture of good, average and poor performance. While an enterprise may operate within industry standards, it is a sure bet that its overall performance is a combination of outstanding performance for certain activities offset by poor performance elsewhere.

Imagine the insights to be gained if best practices could be identified across all units, and an action programme developed to bring all activities up to the highest standards. Imagine, furthermore, that a systematic analysis was undertaken to identify external best practices, and that the knowledge thus developed would also serve as a basis for the establishment of absolute performance standards.

Setting absolute performance standards is an important ingredient in achieving enterprise excellence. Such standards create discontinuity in organizations which have operated on a continuous (and under-performing) basis for years. For managers, the question ought to be: 'How good can we be?'

However, without the tools and techniques of ABM to provide data required to establish objective performance standards, managers revert to management of continuity rather than discontinuity. A new management planning technique known as activity-based budgeting enables a manager to plan and control workload and set an absolute baseline.

Accounting systems try to 'inspect in' cost   Conventional cost systems aggregate cost by cost element such as labour, travel and utilities at the end of the month. Monthly accounting is equivalent to trying to drive a car by only looking in the rear view mirror. The information is too late to impact decisions and does not encourage making the changes necessary to compete in the dynamic business world. Furthermore, cost element accounting does not show management what the organization does and, as a consequence, masks improvement potential. Cost can no more be inspected in through monthly reports than quality can be inspected in on the shop floor. Action to correct a problem from recurring can only be taken when the problem occurs – not at the end of the month when the actual results are compared with planned results and deviations are reviewed. The actual event that causes the deviation will already have occurred sometime during the month. The subsequent reporting of the variance is too late to solve the problem.

Managing symptoms – not causes   Management information systems detect problems when they occur. However, the cause of the problem has occurred in advance of when the problem is detected. If people do not understand the cause of the problem they cannot find the solution.

An important element of activity-based management is the identification of cost drivers. Cost drivers are those factors which cause cost to be incurred. For example, a company often incurs significant waste when an engineering change (ECNs) is issued. One impact of an ECN is that current production of a part will sit idle while notification is awaited of the disposition of the engineering change. While production supervisors have not caused the ECN, their activities are impacted and costs are incurred in their cost centre. A permanent improvement is not possible until the root cause (cost driver) has been addressed.

Management inertia   Perhaps the most damning of all the reasons for significant structural cost is management inertia. Management philosophies such as 'if it isn't broken, don't fix it' encourage an attitude of complacency. Management inertia becomes the rule. What management fails to realize is that current success is based on *past* decisions – not *current* decisions. Competitors, in the meantime, might be instituting change to capture additional market share. By the time their success is evident, a crisis has arisen for the complacent company. Thus management inertia directly leads to crises management. World class managers must be impatient.

The problem of management inertia is intensified by inappropriate information systems that lead to unfocused management. The external environment in which a company competes is constantly changing. Changes by competitors and state-of-the-art technology dramatically alter a company's competitive position. To stay ahead of the competition companies must have information to provide the necessary understanding of the factors they can influence. Management must place unrelenting pressure on the entire organization for measurable cost reduction and productivity gains. Vigilance is critical because it is difficult to regain cost competitiveness once it is lost.

Activity-based management

Activity-based management (ABM) reshapes how companies manage costs. By understanding its activities, a company can expose opportunities for performance improvement that conventional cost accounting systems seldom detect. Cost management is improved by identifying what the organization does and providing a benchmark to judge how much better a company's performance might be. Product cost accuracy is enhanced by more discrete tracing of activities to products.

The traditional view is that costs are best controlled by department managers who are responsible for minimizing the variance between budgeted and actual cost by cost element (salary and wages, travel, supplies, and similar costs). The emphasis is on *efficient* use of resources. The ABM view is that costs are best controlled by managing the workload, eliminating non-value added activities, managing the factors that drive cost, continuously improving value added activities, and streamlining management. The emphasis is on *effective* use of resources.

An understanding of activities is the heart of an ABM system. An activity is *how* an enterprise executes its business objective, i.e. the way the time is spent. To illustrate the concept of activities consider the major activities of a typical material control department. They would include:

- Handle incoming material
- Handle in-process material
- Handle outgoing material
- Store raw material
- Store WIP
- Store finished goods
- Management and administration
- Training
- Other

Each activity of the material control department represents a separate discrete process that recurs over time and produces a specific output – a material movement, stores requisition, etc. Incoming material handling is triggered by the receipt of materials and culminates in material being moved to the raw material store or the first manufacturing process. Raw material stores control, accounts, stocks and issues raw material.

Activities generate cost. How an activity is performed determines which factors of production, including people, machines, travel, supplies, and computer systems, are necessary. For example, the activity to schedule production requires a person to make a decision on scheduling production and a computer system to perform the necessary calculations and data manipulation. ABM would attach these costs to the schedule production activity of the scheduling department.

Attaching costs to activities allows a firm to understand not only how much cost is being incurred but also how effectively the factors of production are employed. For example, with the traditional approach of recording total salary and wages in the design engineering department, no insight is gained as to how the labour is used. The determination of the amount of time a design engineer spends on the various activities, such as new product design or engineering changes, provides a basis for understanding what causes cost. Excessive engineering change is often indicative of poor integration between the product design and the manufacturing engineering function which must determine how the product will be manufactured after it has been designed. Similarly, significant new product design suggests that design engineering may not be using standardized components, thereby resulting in an excessive number of new-part designs.

Finally, activities are 'natural' identifiers that are easily understood by such diverse groups as engineers, manufacturers, accountants and top management. They are readily understood because they correspond to familiar terms and events that occur in manufacturing. Today, much of the accounting information is presented in financial terms rather than in user terms. As an example, when costs are allocated between departments, users often do not understand what comprises the charge and consequently cannot relate it to the activities and tasks they perform. As a result, they often distrust the fairness of the charge and feel they have insufficient information to control the cost.

The importance of managing and associating cost to activities is not a new idea. Much of traditional management thinking has used activities as part of the strategic planning process, to improve operational performance, and as a basis for budgeting. Indeed much of industrial engineering and, more recently, total quality is founded on variations of activity analysis. However, many of the benefits of an activity approach have not been realized because of the absence of systematic process thinking. Few companies have rigorously analysed overhead or secondary activities. Even the notion of managerial activities involving defined outcomes (a central aspect of activity accounting) is somewhat foreign. How would such managerial processes as budgeting be improved if they were treated as processes – in other words, measured, brainstormed, and continually improved.

The components of an ABM system are summarized in Figure 4.2.

General ledger   The general ledger is the primary source of cost information for the ABM system. It is the recommended source of information because the costs reported under the activity accounting system would reconcile to the financial reporting system. This is important since it ensures consistency between financial accounting data and the management system. In the initial stages of implementation, the structure of the general ledger remains unchanged, with cost being accumulated by cost element within department. Eventually, the general ledger account structure will evolve to one where cost is accumulated by natural expense category for an activity within a department.

Manufacturing planning and control   The manufacturing planning and control system is the primary source of operational statistics. Bill of materials and product process plans provide an easy source of data such as the number of set-ups, the number of material moves, and the number of part numbers. The data is used to determine the volumes of output measures, activity lead times, and quality statistics.

Activity accounting   The activity accounting system collects the financial and operational performance information about the significant activities

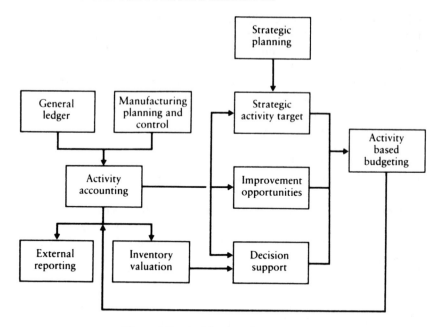

Figure 4.2   *Activity-based management*

of an enterprise. The activity accounting system is the repository of activity data used for management reports, external reports and inventory valuation. The system provides data for cost control on a real-time basis as the activity is performed. The monthly close simply verifies the daily cost results.

External reporting   The activity accounting system supports external reports such as financial statements, tax reports and government contract reports. This might require separate databases because the requirements of a tax authority and external agency might conflict with a management view of cost. As an example, the choice of depreciation methods varies significantly depending on the reporting objective. It is common practice to use accelerated depreciation for tax reporting because it results in the minimum tax liability within the taxing authority guidelines while straight line depreciation is often used by the same companies for external financial reports. Clearly the cost of the machine varies dramatically depending on the depreciation method chosen.

Inventory valuation   The activity accounting system supports inventory valuation. The activity-based product cost uses a bill of activities (BOA) to reflect the amount of resources required to build a unit of product. A BOA is developed for all significant products. Minor products will be costed using a product group bill of activities.

Strategic planning Activity strategic cost analysis uses activity cost and performance data to develop enterprise strategies, translate the strategy into its impact on activities, and provides feedback to determine whether the anticipated results of the strategy were obtained. Strategic cost analysis decomposes a company's mission and strategic objectives down to its impact on specific activities – from design to distribution – and determines where customer value can be enhanced or costs lowered. By clarifying the goals and how specific activities contribute, or not, to achieving the goals, a company can ensure as many priorities as possible are accomplished.

Strategic activity target As an output of the strategic planning process, a small number of specific activities will be designated as 'strategic' activities. These activities fall into two categories: (1) new activities required to support new production requirements, (2) existing activities where cost must be reduced from the current level to a new specified level in order to satisfy competitive requirements.

Improvement opportunities The ABM system must routinely identify improvement opportunities. It must establish a baseline for showing how much improvement is possible and to evaluate alternative courses of action based on their impact on cost and revenue. Key ABM tools for establishing a baseline include non-value added analysis, best practices, cost drivers, and performance targets.

Decision support Cost information is used to facilitate operational and strategic decisions including:

- Capital expenditure
- Make-or-buy
- Manufacturing methods selection
- Setting product prices
- Capacity expansion
- Product abandonment
- Product line expansion
- Production scheduling

These decision models must be updated to take advantage of the powerful data provided by ABM rather than being constrained by limitations of the conventional cost accounting system.

Activity-based budgeting   Activity-based budgeting is a quantitative expression of a plan or objective of the expected activities of an organization. The cost accounting information provides data for controlling the performance of organizational units and appraising managers. An activity-based budget reflects the anticipated workload at each department. By establishing the relationship between workload, as reflected in the output measure, and the activity, a preliminary understanding of the ratio of resources required to workload is established. Department managers can then focus their attention during the budgeting process on determining how they will improve their methods of performing the activity.

Implementing activity-based management

Activity-based management is typically implemented in several separate and distinct phases (see Figure 4.3). Phase 1a, activity analysis, collects the initial activity data. Phase 1b, eliminating wasteful activities, identifies specific short-term performance improvement projects to eliminate wasteful and inefficient activities where the savings should be achievable within a two-year period with minor capital investment. The majority of the savings result from elimination of non-value added activities. Phase 2, product and product group profitability, constructs a bill of activities by product group or for significant products. The resulting insight provided by the activity product cost supports strategic and operational decisions such as product abandonment/expansion, make/buy, and pricing. Phase 3, integrated activity accounting system, constructs an ongoing activity-based management system to support continuous improvement and prevent unwanted costs from accumulating.

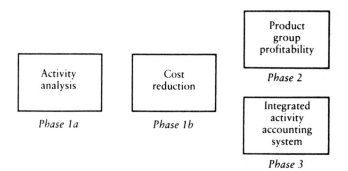

Figure 4.3   *Activity-based management implementation*

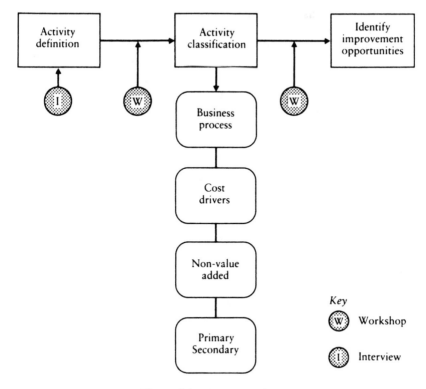

Figure 4.4   *Activity analysis*

Phase 1a – activity analysis

Activity analysis (see Figure 4.4) identifies the significant activities of an enterprise to establish a clear and concise basis for describing business operations and for determining their cost and performance. It fosters a common understanding of how an enterprise functions in order to improve enterprise performance, including profit, quality, and timeliness.

Activity analysis decomposes a large, complex organization into elemental processes (activities) and outputs of the activities that are understandable and manageable. Activity analysis is based on the observation that an entire system is too large to manage, but its individual components are not.

While activity analysis is a snapshot in time, the objective is to understand the process by which the activity is performed. Focusing on the process facilitates an understanding of the factors which influence the cost of the activity. Thus key factors such as changes to the activity volume can be analysed to determine their impact on cost and performance.

One objective of activity analysis is to improve enterprise profit and performance by emulating the best practices of an activity performed in several organizations – both internal and external. A comparison of cost and performance in several organizations that perform a common activity can identify useful similarities in the practices of those organizations. Such a determination of best practices is possible only if activities are consistently defined among the divisions and departments of a company.

Step 1   Activity definition
The objective of this step is to develop a comprehensive understanding of an enterprise's key processes (activities) and the resources assigned to each. Activity definition is done through the involvement of department managers in a series of structured interviews. The data gathered by the interview technique can be augmented by other means such as questionnaires or self-analysis. Activity analysis shows how staff are spending their time; the suppliers to, the customers of, the resources assigned to, the activity; the inputs of and outputs of the activity; and measures of the output.

An activity cost is calculated by tracing the total expense of all factors of production assigned to produce one output of an activity. It is derived for each enterprise activity by tracing the factors of production based on the 'usage' of the resources for each activity, and it is expressed in terms of an activity measure by which the cost of a given process varies most directly. Examples of activity measures include machine hours, number of inserts, and number of payroll cheques. Finally, activity costs are traced to cost objects such as products, customers, and channels of distribution based on the usage of the activity.

The procedures for tracing cost to an activity are described in Figure 4.5.

Initial cost data   The primary source of cost data is a general ledger. The level of detail in the existing general ledger system rarely limits the cost analysis but rather impacts the level of effort required to translate department cost into activity costs. For example, the accounts payable function may be performed by a separate department in a large organization. Translating this cost into an accounts payable activity is straightforward. On the other hand, if accounts payable was only one of several activities performed within a single finance department, a greater level of effort would be required to extract these costs in an activity analysis. Each general ledger account would have to be analysed to determine which finance department activity it supports. This would require significant effort, but eventually the accounts payable activity costs would be isolated.

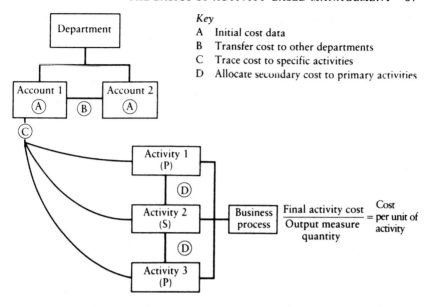

Figure 4.5   *ABM costing methodology flowchart*

The costed activity data is confirmed by managers at a workshop as being valid and as presenting an accurate picture of activities and processes.

Transfer cost to other departments   The prime purpose of certain departments is to support other departments. The primary activities of these departments are known as intercompany activities. Intercompany activities are coordinated by a central management group which delegates authority to specialized departments rather than each department having their own resources. Some important intercompany activities include management information system (MIS), administrative support, facilities maintenance. The cost of intercompany activities should be transferred to the using department in order to get a comprehensive view of total costs in a department.

Trace cost to specific activities   Costs are traced to activities where a causal relationship can be established between a factor of production and an activity. For example, employee costs are traced to activities on the basis of interviews with department managers to identify which people are involved in each activity by estimating the percentage of time they spend on an activity. Typical causal bases include:

Factor of production	Measure
People	Time
Technology	Machine/technology hours
Facilities	Square footage
Utilities	Kilowatt hours

Allocate secondary costs to primary activities   Not all department costs can be effectively traced to its activities. These non-traceable costs represent general department/cost centre support costs. Being related to a specific department, they should not be allocated on the basis of a company-wide cost pool. Therefore, it is recommended that a department's non-traceable costs be allocated to its primary activities on the basis of the department's primary factor of production.

Determine activity measure   An activity measure is an input, output, or physical attribute of an activity. The selection of an appropriate activity measure is critical to the success of an activity accounting system. There must be a direct correlation between the activity measure and the factors of production assigned to the activity. Activity measures are the best measures of workload. Finding a valid activity measure facilitates a simple, effective ongoing system.

In many cases, transactions can be associated with activities and are an excellent basis for defining an activity measure. An example of a transaction is a sales forecast prepared by marketing for manufacturing, or a material receipt.

A receipt transaction could be used to charge the receiving department cost to the specific material received. These costs could then be traced to products, used to evaluate the efficiency and effectiveness of the purchasing department, and as an input to purchase decisions such as quantity buys.

Step 2   Activity classification and focus
At workshops with relevant departmental managers, managers are asked to:

1 Classify activities as primary or secondary.
2 Classify activities as value added or non-value added.
3 Identify the root cause of cost (cost driver) – often a company procedure or policy. For example, demands for information from corporate headquarters.

4 Examine the key business processes that transcend departments, functions, or subsidiaries. For example, material procurement and security.

This analysis forms the basis for focusing on areas for improvement.

Step 3   Identify initial improvement opportunities
The final step in the analysis phase is to identify an initial list of performance improvement opportunities. At this point, the organization has
obtained a clear view of the opportunities for cost reduction. The opportunities are prioritized to balance the magnitude of gain with the cost and
effort of the change. This identification process should be achieved within
a short timescale, typically ten to twelve weeks.

   This intensive activity-based exercise yields a number of immediate
benefits. These include:

1 A high level of *visibility* of the potential for cost improvement
   particularly through highlighting levels of waste or non-value added.
2 The *quantification* of improvements through activity costing.
3 A *process* whereby managers have suggested and agreed to improvement opportunities.
4 A greater *understanding* of cost through the analysis of cost drivers.

Phase 1b – Cost reduction

The ensuing step after activity analysis is to make any necessary changes to
achieve an immediate performance improvement by eliminating wasteful
activities. *There is absolutely no excuse for waste or ineffective activities in
any organization at any time.* These problems divert valuable resources and
hinder competitiveness. Achieving short-term improvement typically
involves several actions: (1) the elimination of waste (non-value added),
(2) the simplification and methods improvement of value added activities,
(3) the redesign of business processes, and (4) the changing of company
policy and procedures.

   A common characteristic of enterprise excellence is continuous improvement. However, there is a significant difference between the traditional
approach to cost reduction and continuous improvement. The goal of cost
reduction is to eliminate cost. This leads to headcount cuts and reduction
in discretionary costs such as advertising, research and development,
training and special projects. These well-intentioned but misdirected
efforts do not consider the level of work and can lead to deterioration in
quality or customer service.

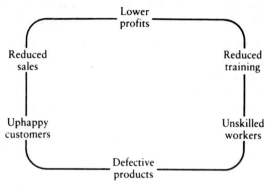

Figure 4.6

Continuous improvement is based on the premise that short-term cost reduction should only be focused on wasteful and inefficient activities. Managers are encouraged to brainstorm cost improvement actions by considering questions such as:

- Where activities are non-value added, can they be minimized or eliminated?
- Where the level of secondary activity is highest, can layers of management be taken out?
- What level of influence do we have over the cost drivers?
- Where activities are value added, can they be improved and made more efficient?
- How can we attack our cost drivers?

The goal of performance improvement is not only to eliminate non-productive resources but also to assign additional resources to activities whose performance must be improved to increase the overall effectiveness of the enterprise. To illustrate these differences consider the activity of training. It is often considered a discretionary cost and is often curtailed in recessionary times. However, this might have an undesired long-term effect as illustrated in Figure 4.6.

Performance improvement requires an escape from traditional mindsets where employees are motivated to treat the symptoms rather than trying to eliminate the cause. This usually involves dealing with organizational 'old chestnuts' (problems widely discussed in the past but no one wants to touch). Continuous improvement requires a culture not to fix the immediate problem you and your colleagues receive, or to improve the process of fixing problems but to find out the cause of the problem, and why the transferring group makes and sends these problems!

The activity cost reduction process is illustrated in Figure 4.7.

Evaluate improvement opportunities
This step requires the preparation of a detailed action plan for the elimination of non-value added activities and short-term improvements to value added activities. Here the feasibility of the initial opportunities is investigated in detail and confirmed, cost benefits of the proposals developed, prioritization of the potential projects made, projects selected and initiated.

Short-term cost reduction projects tend to fall into a number of categories:

Eliminate non-value added activities There is significant waste in most

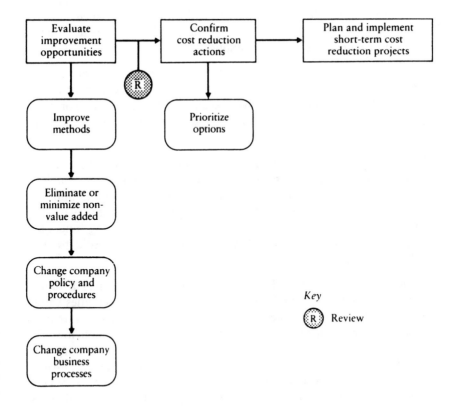

Figure 4.7 *Activity cost reduction*

organizations. Elimination of waste involves removing unnecessary or duplicate activities such as checking, correcting, or expediting.

Change company policies and procedures Company policies and procedures are a common cause of cost. Activities are controlled by company policies and procedures. They define the goals, strategies and regulations governing the activity. For example, the activity of scheduling production orders might be to accumulate several orders into a batch, when determining machining sequence, which would result from procedural rules embedded in scheduling techniques. This policy is contrary to process simplification and adds non-value added costs to manufacturing activities.

Changes to the organization Inappropriate organizational structures add unnecessary cost to an enterprise. Thus continuous improvement often leads to organizational change such as modifying spans of control and management chains where these are clearly inefficient. One common change is to create a new organization structure along process lines, in effect abandoning altogether other structural dimensions, such as function, product, or geography. Another approach would be to create a matrix of functional and process responsibilities.

Workload reduction One of the most effective methods of reducing cost is to eliminate or reduce the need to perform an activity. One must understand the factors which drive activity volume if one is to reduce workload. Output measures are important for cost reduction since they represent the volume of work of an activity.

Methods improvement Here changes are made to the way things are done by improving its effectiveness by eliminating obvious bottlenecks and inefficiencies, for example, through automation, simplification and improvement of paperwork, or redesign of processes. Workshop techniques allow for good ideas to flow through. For example, in a marketing function a simple manual was produced allowing some goods to be sold by mail order.

Business process redesign Business process redesign involves a fundamental change to the entire structure of the interrelated activities within the business process to yield more significant improvements than is possible by simply improving the methods of the individual activities. For example, a company may want to improve the sales order entry process. Rather than merely improving the individual activities, a superior approach is to re-evaluate the whole process – negotiating, receiving, and fulfilling orders. The redesign typically involves several changes: (1) simplification by eliminating unnecessary and duplicate activities,

(2) changing points of control so that they do not need to be separate activities but can be a by-product of the new structure.

Phase 2 – Product group profitability

Activity accounting provides a foundation for a more accurate and relevant product cost than a conventional system because it provides a discrete breakdown of cost which can be easily traced to products. Conventional cost accounting systems define product cost as the sum of direct labour, direct material and overhead. For example, consider material handling cost. Conventional cost accounting would allocate these costs on a global basis such as labour hours or machine hours neither of which reflects the need for moving material. Activity accounting would establish a causal relationship between the material movement activity and the product demand for the activity. One such relationship might be the number of material movements. Then the number of material movement transactions required to produce one unit of product could be used to trace material movement cost to a product. As a consequence, products requiring more moves would receive more material handling cost.

Costs are traced to a product through a bill of activities. A bill of activity (BOA) specifies the sequence of activities and the quantity of each activity consumed in manufacturing an individual product or a product family. The manufacturing process can be described in terms of production-related activities including those that do not physically touch the product. Material is purchased; labour and machines are assigned. Each discrete manufacturing operation in the transformation process whereby raw materials are converted to finished products is synonymous with an activity.

Labour costs are assigned to products as a component of the activity rate. For example, in an electronics company the cost of the manual insertion of components activity is charged to the product according to the number of insertions specified in the product bill of activities. The labour portion of the manual insertion activity that is assigned to the product is based on the pay scale and number of operators assigned to the manual insertion activity.

In addition to manufacturing activities, many support activities are required to manufacture a product. The product must be designed, the labour, machines, facilities and material must be procured, the manufacturing process scheduled and controlled, performance reported to internal and external parties, and a myriad of other activities. Each of these activities consume resources and are traceable to a product.

The bill of activities should include all activities over the entire lifecycle such as development-related activities, operational activities, and support-related activities. Those activities which support future production of a specific product should be amortized and included in the per unit cost.

Activity accounting represents a radical departure from conventional management practices. Traditionally manufacturers have emphasized the importance of products. As a consequence costs have been regarded as direct or indirect to product. Activity accounting challenges this assumption by emphasizing the manufacturing activities rather than the product. The new philosophy is *'excellent activities lead to excellent products'*. For example, an electronics manufacturer which inserts components, does surface mount, and assembles components better than any competitor can change the mix of products that use these core competencies and still remain a world class manufacturer.

Activity accounting is of critical importance to companies switching from a product to a process orientation. The underlying assumption of activity accounting is that resources are consumed in executing activities. Products consume activities. The BOA assumes new importance in this environment. The BOA provides management with the capability of understanding the quantity and cost of activities necessary to manufacture a product. This insight focuses attention on the individual processes so that improvement can be concentrated on these important controllable factors.

A bill of activities is created as follows:

Step 1   Identify traceable activities and business processes   The first step in constructing a bill of activities is to specify all activities or business processes necessary to manufacture a product. Key business processes that are consumed in a product are costed in total rather than listed individually.

An activity is traceable to a product when it is directly or indirectly triggered by a manufacturing order. Some of the important product traceable activities are shown in Table 4.1.

Step 2   For each traceable activity, determine the quantity consumed in manufacturing one unit of the product   The quantity of the output measure for each traceable activity consumed in manufacturing one unit of product must be specified. Defining the quantity of an activity at the unit level requires an understanding of its cost behaviour pattern. There are four primary categories of product-related cost behaviour patterns that include:

Cost behaviour	*Activity*
Lifecycle	Engineering
	Manufacturing engineering

Cost behaviour	Activity
	Research & development
	Industrial engineering
	Advertising
Customer order	Sales order
	Sales
Production batch	Scheduling
	Production control
Unit	Manufacturing
	Packaging
	Distribution

Activities related to the product lifecycle must be converted to a per unit basis over the planned production volume of the product. This is accomplished by dividing the total activity cost by the planned unit sales forecast. Similarly, customer order and production batch activities are traced based on the normal customer order or production batch size. Thus small lot size orders require a proportionally larger cost than large quantity orders.

Step 3   Extract activity rate from activity accounting system   The activity cost per output is computed within the activity accounting system separately from the product BOA. The activity cost is equivalent to a standard process cost based on the current methods and procedures.

Step 4   Determine total activity cost by multiplying the number of activity outputs by the activity rate   An activity cost is computed by multiplying the activity quantity (as specified in the BOA) by the activity unit cost previously computed by the activity accounting system.

Step 5   Determine the cost of raw materials and purchased components   Material costs are derived from the bills of material (BOM). Several activity product cost systems incorporate the detailed BOM into the product cost system, while others interface with the BOM and extract material cost in total.

The cost of purchased material consists of the purchase price and all traceable costs of bringing the material to the activity that consumes it. This would include the material acquisition, shipping, receiving, and incoming inspection.

Step 6   Allocate non-traceable infrastructure cost   The cost of non-traceable activities might, at the discretion of management, be allocated to the product in a conventional manner to determine a fully allocated cost.

Table 4.1

Activity	Lifecycle cost	Cost per unit
Research and development		
Applied research product	X	X
Applied research process	X	X
Engineering development		
Design product	X	X
Modify product	X	X
Manufacturing engineering		
Design manufacturing process	X	X
Modify manufacturing process	X	X
Quality planning	X	X
Tooling	X	X
Marketing and advertising		
Sell product		X
Product management		X
Material procurement		
Procure material		X
Laboratory acceptance testing		X
Production support		
Scheduling		X
Production control		X
Manufacturing		
Manufacturing process 1		X
Set-up		X
Move material		X
Store material		X
Manufacturing process n		X
Inspection and test		X
Logistics and support		
Shipping		X
Transport product		X
Store finished goods in warehouse		X
Supply spares		X
Evaluation at customers' sites		X
Logistics	X	X
Customer technical support	X	X
Field support	X	X
Warranty/service contract administration	X	X
Product liability	X	X

These non-traceable costs must be separately identified. It must be kept in mind by senior management that these non-traceable cost have no cause and effect relationship to the product. If included they should be viewed with full knowledge that they are equivalent to a 'franchise fee' for the product and cannot be influenced by product-related decisions.

Step 7   Determine the product cost by summing the individual activity costs and total material cost   A costed bill of activities for a product is computed by summing the individual activity costs and total material cost, and, if appropriate, the non-traceable infrastructure cost.

An example of a costed bill of activities follows:

Activity	Activity measure	Activity quantity	Activity cost £	Lifecycle cost (5,000) units	Current unit cost
Product engineering	Hours	1,000	50	50,000	10
Process planning	Hours	300	45	13,500	3
Material acquisition	Purchase orders	10	15		150
Manufacturing activity 1	Inserts	5	10		50
Manufacturing activity 2	Machine hours	5	60		300
Manufacturing activity 3	Burn-in hours	8	8		64
Manufacturing activity 4	Manhours	20	15		300
Packaging	Cubic feet	5	7		28
Shipping	Pounds	20	6		120
TOTAL					1025

Special considerations
Direct labour   In a pure activity accounting system labour costs are charged to the manufacturing process and not to the individual products. The approach is based on the observation that labourers perform activities and products consume activities. Labour cost is one component of activity cost.

An alternative activity accounting system structure is to continue to charge labour directly to products and use activity accounting for all other activities. This approach is only recommended where direct labour tracking is required by contract or the estimating system is so imprecise as to be useless.

There are several reasons for charging costs directly to activities rather than products. First, labour variances are more often the result of process variances than any aspect of the product. Demand changes (over or under), operator experience, and training variations result in operator efficiencies and inefficiencies. These factors cause variances to be related more to the activity than the product. Second, labour reporting is greatly simplified because there is no need to voucher labour to products.

Strategic decisions   An activity-based product cost system must be used very carefully for strategic decisions such as product line abandonment or expansion. There is a natural tendency to want to make changes in product mix when a new activity-based product cost reveals significant differences in cost from the traditional system. Such an immediate change is ill advised. The appropriate action an activity-based product cost should inspire is a careful study of the traceable activities to determine where performance improvement efforts should be directed based on competitive factors. In other words, the profit margin of a particular product may not be as favourable as other products offered by a company. Before a company abandons or decreases its effort in supporting the less profitable product it should first study the product to determine what its potential margin could be if wasteful activities were eliminated and value added activities improved. In other words, strategic decisions should only be made relative to the best feasible margin rather than the margin that currently exists.

Phase 3 – Integrated activity accounting system

A company striving for enterprise excellence must not only eliminate waste and streamline value added activities (phase 1b) but must place unrelenting pressure on preventing waste and inefficiency from occurring in the first place. The penalty associated with cost reduction rather than cost prevention is enormous. Adopting an objective of cost prevention requires: (1) undertaking strategic projects to address long-term improvements, (2) implementing an integrated activity accounting system to provide information essential to continuous improvement and cost prevention, and (3) changing decision support systems to be activity-based to improve the decision-making process. A secondary but important benefit of an integrated activity accounting system is the simplification that is possible by monitoring only the key factors that vary.

A prime factor in continuous improvement is to establish benchmarks to guide activity managers in determining how good their performance could be. The benchmark should provide an incentive to continuously improve performance. This requires a company to set absolute performance standards, where possible, and otherwise to set relative standards to the best possible level of performance.

Cost management techniques such as non-value added, best practices, and target cost can be used to establish benchmarks. For non-value added activities, the benchmark should be zero since they are waste and should be eliminated. Benchmarks based on best practices should be the lowest cost per output for any organization – internal or external – compared. Benchmarks based on target cost are set based on what the marketplace allows.

In addition to setting benchmarks, long-term improvement also requires a continuous programme to manage the cost drivers of an enterprise. Cost driver analysis identifies the cause of cost. For example, the factory layout is a key determinant of the cost of material movement and work-in-process. A plant organized by grouping similar machines results in significant movement of material (with a resulting large cost of work-in-process inventory) to each machine as the part is manufactured. A cellular manufacturing layout, on the other hand, locates all the machinery necessary to build a part in a single location to minimize material movement and work-in-process. Several other cost drivers, including transfer batch size and technology selection, contribute to material movement costs.

Unless cost drivers are managed, an activity manager can do nothing other than correct problems as they occur which means to merely await the next occurrence of the problem. Every occurrence of the problem results in additional cost to perform an activity even though the activity manager has no direct authority over the activity that caused the problem. An ongoing activity accounting system will support this process by identifying cost drivers and reporting their financial impact.

When a driver cannot be eliminated entirely its adverse impact should be minimized. For example, a company which competes in a market with low volumes of many products, should design products to share common processes to lower manufacturing cost. Costs are reduced by applying economies-of-scope principles to the common manufacturing processes (e.g., auto-insert, NC machining, assembly test, and others).

The process of implementing an integrated activity accounting system is illustrated in Figure 4.8.

Identification of long-term improvement opportunities
After activities have been streamlined in the waste elimination phase, the next step is to minimize the remaining structural cost through investment in strategic projects. These projects tend to involve a large capital investment and require a significant amount of time to implement. Rearranging the plant and standardizing components are examples.

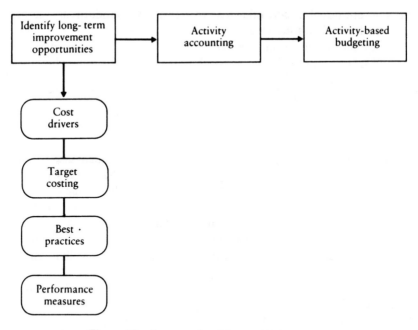

Figure 4.8 *Integrated activity accounting system*

These projects should be separated from the short-term waste elimination stage to ensure attention is not distracted from the immediate savings. However, progressive companies can often fund many of the strategic projects from the savings generated by the short-term cost reduction.

Cost drivers Cost and performance drivers should be investigated as near their cause as possible to identify the true causes of cost and performance variations (for instance design characteristics), generally very far from the analysed activity. Techniques such as cause and effect analysis and the 'five whys' (keep asking why until a root cause is determined) help lead to identification of the final cost driver.

Best practices A consistent definition of activities within all units of a company facilitates a ranking based on cost and performance. Activities that are lowest cost and highest performance are analysed to determine the source of excellence. The results of the analysis can then be shared with other groups within the company that perform the activity to determine the applicability in their operations.

Target cost Activities provide an excellent basis for identifying opportunities to achieve market generated target performance levels since the insight into non-value added activities and best practices provides a basis to apply value engineering techniques to improve these activities.

Activity performance measures   Activity performance must be judged on a basis other than only cost. The time it takes to perform an activity and the quality of the activity are keys to enterprise excellence. Specific improvement targets must be established at the activity level for time and quality improvements.

Development of an ongoing activity accounting system

An ongoing activity accounting system is an essential foundation for continuous improvement. Managers require information in a format that is compatible with the goals of enterprise excellence and at the right time to impact effective action. Activity information is ideally suited for this purpose because it focuses on the process of how the activity is performed, both at the department and inter-departmental level.

The primary requirements of an activity accounting system include the following:

- Capture actual costs to compare to costs planned at the activity level.
- Capture actual levels of activity workload.
- Identify non-value added costs.
- Identify best practices for understanding the gap with current performance.
- Identify total performance measures – cost per output, time, and quality – and their trends.

Actual activity costs are easily collected when resources are dedicated to a specific activity. Difficulties arise when resources are assigned to multiple activities. For example, a design engineer may work on new product design or change a product's design. In this case, a time recording system must be installed to assign time to the individual activities. Resource recording systems should only be used when the information is easily recorded as a by-product of an information system or the value of the information greatly exceeds the recording cost.

An alternative method of collecting actual cost for resources assigned to multiple activities is to use a surrogate. One possible surrogate is an earned activity cost which is computed by multiplying the actual workload by the standard cost per unit as output. The total of the earned cost is compared to total actual cost and a variance computed. A surrogate system can only work effectively when a complete activity definition has been performed and a total quality culture adopted.

Continued significant variations between actual and earned costs might indicate that the activity definition or product bills of activities must be reviewed. Those responsible for product profitability, such as the product/product line manager, should identify instances for above-normal activity usage. Those responsible for the process, such as the manufacturing manager, should identify instances of below-normal activity usage. Earned hours can be periodically validated by industrial engineering studies and random checks of actual time spent on activities as opposed to earned time.

The integrated activity system must be kept up-to-date since organizations are continually undergoing changes; changes in technology, management philosophy, new products, and others. Activity accounting must be structured to support change. As activities and factors of production change, the new activities and their associated cost and performance would be captured. Thus the existing reporting can be easily modified without altering the cost system itself. This permits a flexible cost management system that is structured to anticipate changes without restructuring the system.

Summary

Activity-based management reshapes the way companies manage costs. It attaches company costs to activities. Product cost is the sum of the cost of all traceable activities based on the usage of the activity. Cost control is focused on the source of the cost regardless of the organizational unit in which it is incurred.

Managers need activity information to help them achieve enterprise excellence. Activity accounting identifies what the organization does. In order to improve profitability and performance, it is critical to understand where the enterprise's precious time goes and, in detail, what the enterprise does and how it does it. Ultimately, an organization can only improve when management understands what is done, how well it is done, and whether it contributes to corporate objectives. Activity accounting facilitates improved traceability and, ultimately, improved accountability.

Activity-based management is a powerful tool for managing the complex operations of a business through a detailed assessment of its activities. Activity accounting attributes cost and performance data to activities. Activity cost and performance data provide management with information needed to determine an accurate product cost, improve business processes, eliminate waste (non-value added activities) identify cost drivers, plan operations, and set business strategies.

Activity-based management generates cost and production information in a manner that drives continuous improvement and total quality. Continuous improvement and total quality control are facilitated by treating each activity as a process and identifying the source of cost rather than focusing on the symptoms. In focusing attention on the source of problems, management must assign responsibility to those departmental activities that drive cost and monitor their execution to see if the planned results are achieved.

Activity information allows managers to identify and eliminate waste. It also confirms progress in removing waste from operating activities.

Eliminating waste and implementing a philosophy of continual improvement is not difficult if senior management has the will and if the cost management system is set up to assist. They can be impossible, however, if the accounting systems are designed around functional organizations rather than around activities.

Glossary

The items listed in this glossary represent the author's definition and may differ to some degree with definitions contained in the CIMA terminology publication.

Activity: A combination of people, technology, raw materials, methods, and environment that produces a given product or service. Activities describe what an enterprise does: the way time is spent and the outputs of the process. See Process.

Activity accounting: The collection of financial and operational performance information about significant activities of an enterprise.

Activity analysis: The breakdown of an enterprise into manageable segments for detailed analysis regarding cost and performance.

Activity-based cost (ABC): See Activity accounting.

Activity-based management (ABM): A management system that employs activities; in particular, with information on how activities consume resources to produce an output; whether they support the strategic objectives of the firm; the performance improvement potential by eliminating waste, minimizing cost drivers, and emulating best practices; and how they support operational and strategic decisions.

Activity measure: A quantitative measurement unit selected as a surrogate of the level of activity. Output measures may be based on an input (for example, a purchase requirement for the purchasing activity) or an output (for example, a purchase order for the purchasing activity) of the activity considered to drive the activity cost in a linear way.

Bill of Activities: A list of all activities required to build a unit of product.

Bill of material (BOM): A list of direct materials needed for the production of a given product.

BOM: See Bill of material.

Budget: A plan prepared and approved prior to a defined period of time, usually showing planned income to be generated and/or expenditure to be incurred during that period.

Business process: An orderly arrangement of activities operating under a set of procedures in order to accomplish specific objectives.

Cause: A source event or factor that impacts subsequent events or activities.

Cost: Resources sacrificed or forgone to achieve a specific objective.

Cost behaviour pattern: Estimation of how costs behave as volume changes over a relevant range of activity levels.

Cost driver: A factor whose occurrence creates cost; the factor represents a prime cause of the level of activity (for example, the number of active components for: production planning and control, inventory management, vendor contracting, and so on).

Cost elements: Types of costs (labour, material, service, supplies) associated with the manufacturing process.

Cost management: The management and control of activities to determine an accurate product cost, improve business processes, eliminate waste, identify cost drivers, plan operations, and set business strategies.

Direct labour: The cost of labour that can be identified with a specific product.

Direct materials: Acquisition costs of all materials that are identified as part of the finished goods and may be traced to the finished goods in an economically feasible manner.

Excellence: The cost-effective integration of activities within all units of an organization continually to improve the delivery of products and services to satisfy the customer.

Factors of production: All costs including labour, technology, utilities travel and so on.

Function: A group of activities having a common objective within a business.

Lifecycle: The progression of a product through growth stages and maturity. The five stages include: development, growth, shakeout, maturity and decline.

Natural expense category: The basic classifications of cost that are universal and independent of a company.

Non-value added cost: Any cost or activity, other than the minimum amount, which is not absolutely essential to the enterprise mission of manufacturing a product or performing a service.

Organization: A system delineating the structure and reporting relationships between management positions. Organization is the process of identifying and grouping work to be done, defining and delegating responsibility and authority and establishing relationships to accomplish objectives.

Output: The product of an activity. It is what users receive or what people produce.

Primary activity: Contributes directly to the central mission of a department or an organization unit. Typically the output is used outside the department.

Process: A combination of people, technology, raw materials, methods, and environment that produces a given product or service.

Product costs: Costs, including raw materials, direct labour, and technology, that are directly or indirectly involved in the production of goods and services for sale to customers. Indirect costs include such items as equipment maintenance, factory utilities, and wages for facilitating services in the plant. Indirect costs are customarily assigned to products or services by an appropriate allocation technique.

Resources: Factor of production such as labour, technology, and materials.

Secondary activity: An activity that supports an organization's primary activities. They tend to be of an administrative nature.

Strategic planning: A planning process that summarizes and articulates how the basic operational tasks are to be structured to implement the objectives, goals and strategies for the organization.

Target cost: A market-based cost that is calculated using a sales prices necessary to capture a predetermined market share.

Target cost = Sales price (for the target market share) minus desired profit

Tracing: The process of establishing a cause-and-effect relationship.

Transaction: Physical (including electronic) documents associated with activities that impact information.

Value added cost: The incremental cost of an activity to complete a required task at the lowest overall cost.

5

Activity-based cost management*
Robin Bellis-Jones

Introduction

The struggle to gain competitive advantage in markets that grow more fiercely contested day by day has radically altered the complexion of many businesses: the direct costs of products and services have been cut, technology and automation have been widely adopted and lifecycles of products and services shortened.

These changes have caused a major shift in the cost structure of many organizations. In the manufacturing sector, direct labour costs have given way to an increasing burden of overhead costs. Service industries, faced with diversification of customers and products, have seen their systems, support and control functions expand to meet the growing complexity and variety of ever more demanding markets.

Amid all this change, cost accounting has largely continued to employ the techniques of the 1950s and 1960s in providing management with the basic costing information on which key product and investment decisions are made. These techniques recover the cost of overheads using indices, such as direct labour or machine hours, which reflect production volume alone. They largely overlook the factors that increasingly drive costs, such as variety, complexity and change.

There is a growing recognition within professional bodies, the academic community and management itself that traditional cost accounting methods can distort crucial business costing information and that, as a result, both tactical and strategic decisions can be seriously flawed.

Activity-based cost management is an approach which addresses these issues. It is much wider in its scope than the original concept of ABC in that it addresses all aspects of management rather than just

*Based on material first published at Develin & Partners in 1990. All rights reserved.

product costing. It is also relevant to all fields of human endeavour, not just manufacturing.

Frequently, due to the shortcomings of conventional cost accounting, companies are unaware that a proportion of their products, services or customers contribute nothing to profits, and even erode them.

By focusing management attention on these items, activity-based cost management can improve profitability dramatically. Moreover, it enables the factors that drive operating costs, whether direct or overhead, to be identified so that costs can be reduced while ensuring that the important business and customer needs are met. In this chapter the author outlines the issues at stake.

What is cost management?

Our definition of cost management runs as follows:

> Cost management identifies the factors that drive costs. It also measures and analyses costs in a way that helps managers understand better what influences their business. It therefore helps them to exert effective control in achieving their objectives.

We contend that businesses incur costs which do not receive the management scrutiny their magnitude warrants, and that management accounts often do not attribute costs in a way which helps managers make decisions. The extent to which these problems exist varies from industry to industry, but all sectors, not just manufacturing, suffer from them.

Where are the problems?

The growth of overheads

Competitive forces are driving companies to become more responsive to customer needs; more rapid product supercessions, enhanced product features, wider range of choice, shorter order lead times, lower real prices. Meeting these needs has created a dramatic growth in the cost of 'support' functions, such as engineering, planning, marketing, product development, purchasing, materials handling, stock control, training and management services. As a result, while the direct labour content of products has reduced by a third in UK manufacturing over a period of just over 25 years, overheads have increased by almost 50 per cent in real terms (see Figure 5.1).

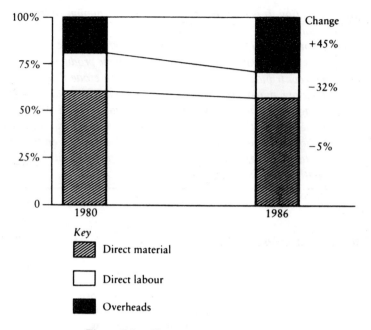

Figure 5.1 *Changing cost structures*

Not surprisingly, much attention has been focused on the dramatic change in the manufacturing sector. However, similar competitive pressures affect all other sectors of the economy. A recent study by Develin & Partners (The Effectiveness of the Corporate Overhead in British Business, 1988) showed that while *controllable* overhead costs typically account for 27 per cent of all costs in manufacturing industry, they account for significantly more in most other sectors of the economy (Figure 5.2).

Until the 1980s, competition in many service sectors was limited and profitability high. Structural changes such as market deregulation and the advent of the single European market are dramatically changing this picture, driving the need for better product, service and customer costing information and better cost management.

Timing

The link between the factors that drive costs and the costs themselves are frequently obscured by a combination of timing delays and the involvement of several different functions.

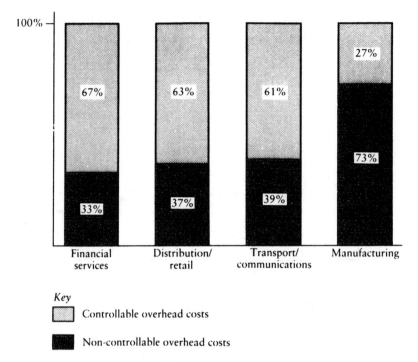

Figure 5.2 *Typical cost structures*

Take, as an example, a typical design and development cycle (Figure 5.3). (It could be the design of a product, the introduction of automatic telling machines or remote banking services, the building of a superstore or new school, or a civil engineering project, but the instance of a manufactured product is indicative of the issues at stake.) As a new product moves progressively from concept to production, the cumulative costs incurred are initially relatively low, but accelerate as the manufacturing facility gears up for production with component stock and equipment.

The finance department and other functional management focus their attention on the cash hungry production stage. However, the majority of future unit product costs are determined in the earlier stages.

In the case of automobile development, some 85 per cent of future unit product costs are determined by the end of the testing phase. This factor is the motivation behind simultaneous engineering in the automotive industry, in which the suppliers of the special production machines work with the car maker during vehicle design.

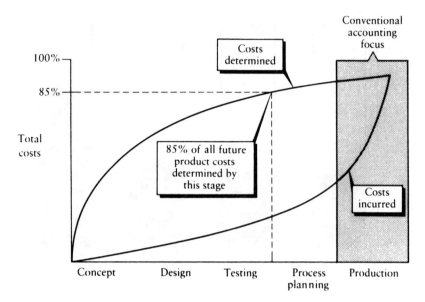

Figure 5.3   *Product development cycle*

Attention by management to the earlier stages of the design and development process has the greatest leverage on future product costs. A closer working relationship between suppliers, the purchasing and manufacturing functions, and the design and engineering teams will help ensure that the ramifications of early decisions are fully understood. Management accounting expertise in the design team provides a vital financial input to design decisions.

Control

In order to be able to manage costs, they have to be controllable. Although, in the long term, they can all be controlled, in the short term the fixed costs, by definition, cannot.

But even the variable costs are frequently not *controllable* in the short term. Much time and effort goes into measuring and tracking these costs, but there is little that managers can do to control them.

In the case of the automotive industry featured previously, only 15 per cent of direct product costs are controllable by management, through such actions as modifications to product specification, to design, and to method of manufacture. As a proportion of total costs, the direct costs (labour plus materials) typically represents 64 per cent of total costs. However, the *controllable* direct costs form only 10 per cent (that is, 15 per cent of 64 per cent) compared with controllable overhead costs, which constitute 27 per cent (Figure 5.4).

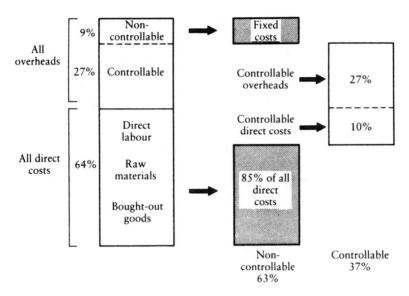

Figure 5.4   *Analysis of manufacturing costs*

That is to say, the leverage to control costs in the short to medium term is 2.7 times greater in the overhead areas than it is in the direct areas of material and labour in a manufacturing environment.

Does 2.7 times as much effort go into preparing management cost information in respect of the overhead areas as of the direct cost areas? The question is central to the theme of this chapter: cost accountants often gather information which is easy to measure and which at first sight is important to the business. But frequently its value is limited: it does not help managers to exercise control. Information which enables managers to exert real control over the direction of the business, but is difficult to measure, is simply not available. Take, as an example, waste. Is waste in your company measured? Almost certainly you will measure scrap resulting from production. But what about wasted time? The time wasted by overhead staff due to poor business processes averages 20 per cent. It will almost certainly be many times more costly than material scrap. But the cost of material scrap is relatively easy to measure, and will appear as an item in the management accounts. Time wasted is not easy to measure and is therefore ignored.

Product costing

As has been highlighted in a recent survey (Activity Based Cost Management: The Overheads Revolution. A CBI/Develin & Partners Survey, 1991) the majority of companies recover their manufacturing overheads on volume-driven indices (see Figure 5.5). When overhead cost content was low and direct labour high, this approach was an acceptable approximation. It had the additional virtue of being easy for all to understand and easy to compute and apply. However, because overheads have grown so greatly at the expense of direct labour, overhead recovery rates now often exceed 500 per cent and can easily reach as high as 1,000 per cent. In such circumstances product costs can become hopelessly inaccurate, seriously affecting margin management and the associated allocation of resources.

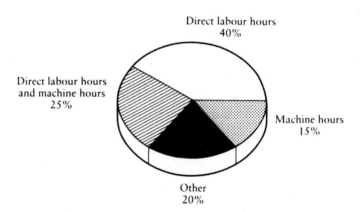

Figure 5.5   *Basis for overhead recovery: current practice*

In sectors where prices are market-led, product profitability can be dramatically over or under-stated. The result is that valuable operational resources, such as sales effort and major plant investments, are directed towards the support of unprofitable products or customers at the expense of those which are, in reality, much more attractive. In contrast, incorrect cost estimates in a sector where prices are determined on a cost-plus basis will cause profitable business to be lost through overpricing and much unprofitable business to be won through underpricing.

Cost management

Organizations are structured hierarchically and in the main on a functional basis (Figure 5.6). It is apparent in their organization and grading structure, their cost and profit centre structures and their charts of accounts. Costs are reported, and control exercised, to reflect this functionality, under commonly recognized general ledger headings. Within this system, departments are 'controlled' against budget and past performance. It is a well tried and well understood approach, but it fails on three counts:

1   Senior management devote much effort to the development of corporate strategies, but often fail to communicate them to the middle and lower levels of their organization for fear of breaches in confidentiality. The budgeting process often acts as a surrogate for this communication process, fragmenting the elements of the strategy on a functional 'need-to-know' basis to each individual department. This diminishes the initiative of management at departmental level and thereby stultifies corporate responsiveness to opportunities.
2   Businesses try to meet their corporate objectives and to meet the needs of their customers. Each department will have its role to play and be given a cost budget in which to do so. All too often, departments allow

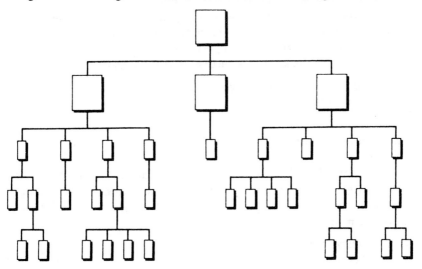

Figure 5.6   *Company organization structure*

budgetary targets to dominate, so that their contribution to meeting business and customer needs is neglected.

For example, the purchasing function of a large engineering firm had regularly met budget and was therefore regarded as a well-managed department. However, its ability to convert requisitions into orders, and then to ensure that suppliers met their *agreed* delivery dates was highly unpredictable (Figure 5.7). In other words the service it provided to the engineers and the production schedulers who required the bought-out goods was wholly unsatisfactory. It caused much wasted effort and prejudiced the company's ability to deliver to its customers on time.

Conventional cost accounting tells management only about the costs of a department, not about the quality or importance of the service it provides. If a department's costs are over budget the accounts alert management to the unfavourable variance, but give no help in identifying what should be done: merely cutting a resource to bring costs back to budget may seriously harm an important service.

3   Conventional cost management fails to recognize that corporate success depends on the effectiveness of key business processes. Such processes (see Figure 5.8) frequently cross several functional boundaries. Inadequacies in any department which contributes to a business process can adversely affect the entire process – a cross-functional business process is only as strong as its weakest link.

Traditional management accounting and financial control systems reflect the needs of the hierarchical, functional organization structure. They rarely recognize or support the effectiveness of the business process which are key to the success of an organization.

Existing financial and management control systems are not redundant, but they are insufficient.

Customer profitability

The commercial needs of different customers can vary radically. In their efforts to retain existing customers and attract new ones, companies can be drawn into providing widely different levels of service in respect of many service elements, such as:

- frequency of delivery
- number of order lines
- quantity per order line
- customer location

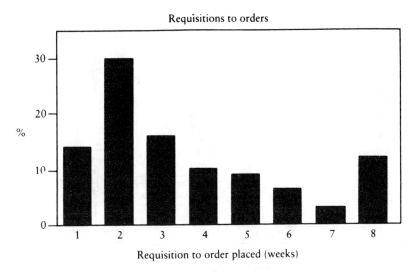

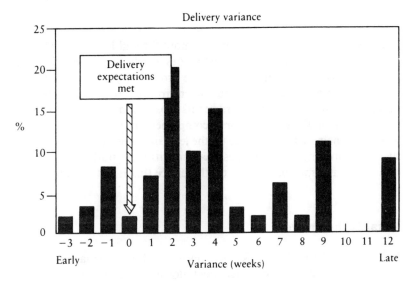

Figure 5.7 *Service outputs: purchasing function*

- discounts given
- salesmen's visits
- special orders

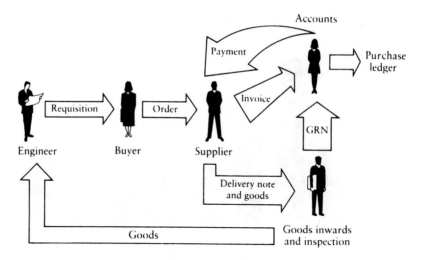

Figure 5.8 *The purchasing process*

These elements have one thing in common: they all have associated costs. Conventional cost accounting techniques rarely recognize them. As a result, companies do not know the true profitability of trading with individual customers, or even with customer groups. Certain customers, often those whom the company regards as its most important, may provide no contribution at all. What is worse, companies can be unaware of the true value that their customers place on the level of service they provide. Under such circumstances, companies may unwittingly trade at a loss with customers, and may be giving a costly service that is not actually required.

What is the answer?

In view of all the drawbacks of conventional cost management, a new approach is needed. It must meet the following conditions:

- It must be able to generate product costs that more accurately reflect all the factors which drive them, such as variety, complexity, scope and change, and not just volume.
- It must be able to attribute the costs of delivering different elements of service to individual customers in order to establish true customer profitability.
- It must be able to measure the cost of failure throughout the organiza-

tion, particularly in the overhead functions, so as to focus management attention on the major opportunities for improvement.

- It must be capable of identifying the factors that drive costs so that managers can be guided as to where and when they can best direct their efforts in order to control costs.
- It must recognize and reflect the crucial importance of key business processes.

Activity-based cost management

Data collection

The cornerstone of activity-based cost management (ABCM) is data collection. By collecting the *right* information it is possible to build an activity database from which various analyses can be undertaken. Depending on the part of the organization being measured, data is collected in different ways: in some areas staff complete their own forms, in others activity sampling is undertaken. In yet other, existing records, such as sales invoices, are analysed.

The data collected differs from conventional management accounting information in one fundamental respect: it is not precise. It is an accurate estimate of what takes place in the business. This enables the data to be collected quickly and with minimum disruption. Because it is used to help managers make decisions, it only needs to be accurate enough to ensure they make the *right* decisions. This is superior to having a precise quantification of a meaningless measure, which we contend is the case with much conventional accounting information.

Data collection is the cornerstone of activity-based cost management. But it is valueless without analysis and interpretation, which requires an understanding of the needs of the business and its customers. This understanding is often assumed to exist and is equally often found to be lacking. It can be gained, or confirmed, through two exercises: a *customer needs survey* and a statement of *critical success factors*.

Customer needs survey

A business must consistently meet, and at times exceed, the needs of its customers if it is to prosper. Barely meeting the needs of customers is no longer sufficient. At times, customers must be delighted by a company's performance if they are to maintain their allegiance.

In ABCM, an external customer needs survey (Figure 5.9) is carried out to determine what factors are regarded as important by customers in

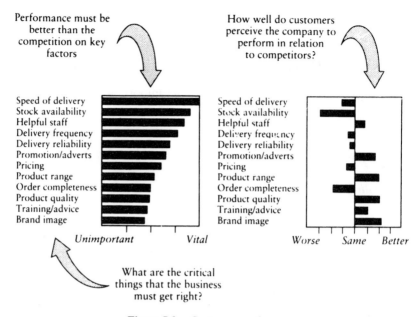

Figure 5.9 *Customer needs survey*

providing the level of service that they require. These factors are prioritized and a quantified assessment of how well the business performs them is obtained from customers. Similar assessments are obtained from management within the business.

ABCM highlights the difference between management's perceptions and those of the customer. It indicates the areas where improved service levels are required and where opportunities to reduce service levels exist.

Critical success factors

A central objective of ABCM is to ensure that adequate resources are in place to satisfy the important current and future demands facing the business. In order to do so, it is necessary to know the strategic direction of the company and the key requirements of its external customers.

Strategic direction should be identified through a series of interviews with the Board, senior management and the business planning group. The key requirements of external customers are identified through the external customer needs survey. These inputs are translated into a series of critical success factors (CSFs): the key issues that the company must accomplish well if it is to be successful (Figure 5.10). The critical success factors are

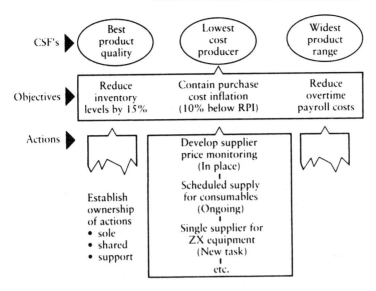

Figure 5.10   *Structuring of CSFs*

used as a guide for proposing and agreeing change. For example, tasks that enable the critical success factors to be achieved are identified, so that special attention can be given to improving the level of service provided.

There are three main types of exercise that can be undertaken once activity data collection has been completed, customer needs surveyed and critical success factors established. Each addresses a different view of the business and overcomes a shortfall of conventional cost management. They are *business process improvement, customer profitability* and *product costing*.

Business process improvement

People at work engage in a range of activities. The activity database that is constructed in ABCM documents all these activities in a quantified form. However, the activities people perform are not isolated: they occur in logical sequences which together combine into a business process. It is the performance of the business processes as a whole that is important. Individual activities might be undertaken well, but if they are not well coordinated into the overall process, or if one of the key activities in the process is done badly, the process will not be effective.

The coordination of a number of management groups, each controlling a different part of a process, is difficult because of the communication barriers that organizational boundaries cause (see Figure 5.11). Frequently, the problem is made worse by contradictory, functional objectives.

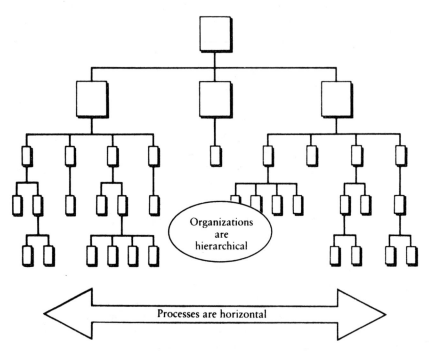

Figure 5.11 *Organizations and processes*

In ABCM, activities are grouped into processes so that all the activities forming a process, usually involving several groups, are reviewed together. Recognizing that not all the activities in a process add equal value is crucial to improving business performance. Therefore ABCM puts each activity into one of three categories: *core, support* and *diversionary*.

Core activities are those for which the groups exist. They involve a specific expertise, add value to the business, and therefore provide a service to internal or external customers.

Support activities make it possible for the core activities to take place. For example, a salesman's time spent negotiating an order with a customer is core activity. Travelling to the customer is a support activity.

Diversionary activities are caused by inadequacies somewhere within the organization. Such activities include correcting errors and chasing other people. Diversionary activities have many causes, for example:

- inadequate training, tools or procedures
- poor documentation
- poor suppliers (internal or external)
- inadequate understanding of customer needs
- inter-functional barriers

Past ABCM studies have found the distribution of time across the whole of a business to be, typically, as shown in Figure 5.12.

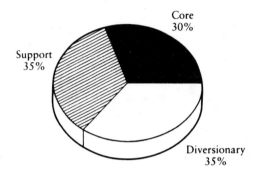

Figure 5.12   *Typical distribution of activity before ABCM*

The activity analysis provides a focus for the business to concentrate on getting the most cost-effective balance of activity.

Diversionary activity cannot be eliminated entirely, but must be minimized. This is done by identifying the *root causes* of problems and eradicating them. Because processes move through the organization, failures frequently progress through a number of departments, causing widespread diversionary activity as they go. The cost of eradicating the root cause of failure is always a great deal less than the cost of the diversionary activity that the failures caused elsewhere.

Support activity must be undertaken as efficiently as possible, by using, for example, the most appropriate systems.

Core activities can be reduced or enhanced. By analysing business processes in the context of the company's critical success factors, and in the context of its customers' needs, management can make *rational* decisions on improving the service provided by core activities in the *key* business processes. Conversely it can examine the possibilities for reducing the service levels provided by the core activities of less important business processes. The scope for change depends on the importance attached to a service by customers and their perceptions of how well their needs are presently met. Emphasis is placed on *quantifying* the risks of reducing service levels and the benefits of enhancing them.

A key outcome of ABCM is to *change the mix* of core, support and diversionary activity within the business. There will be far more emphasis on core activity to enhance service quality, to displace diversionary activity elsewhere and to improve services to external customers where necessary (see Figure 5.13).

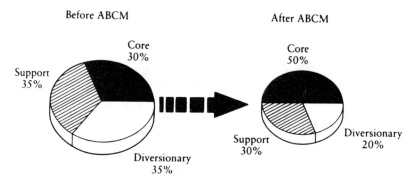

Figure 5.13   *Changing the mix of activity*

ABCM thereby provides a radically new way of looking at business costs: instead of merely providing costs by department or cost centre, it supplies the cost of processes within the business and identifies the factors that drive them. It enables management to pinpoint and measure opportunities for process improvement in the context of meeting business and customer needs. In other words, ABCM delivers the means by which management can make decisions that will improve business performance.

Because diversionary activities have been eradicated, support activities made more efficient and some activities reduced, ABCM always provides a cost saving – usually around 20 per cent.

Investment appraisal

ABCM helps management to identify and evaluate the most important and attractive investment opportunities, be they in information systems, in plant and equipment or in staff.

Management can focus its attention on the key core activities and the worst cases of diversionary activity. Furthermore, it can *quantify* the improvements that investment can make; the enhanced service provided by core activities; the increased efficiency of support activities; the elimination of diversionary activities. By doing so, it allows management to make more informed investment decisions.

Case study: business process improvement

The company is a market leader in office equipment and supplies, mainly selling direct to major retailers.

The exploded part of the activity pie chart (Figure 5.14) relates to the mobile sales force. They spent more time dealing with complaints from customers than they did selling to them! Why were complaints so time-consuming?

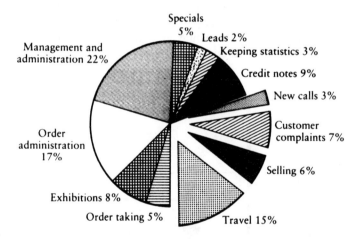

Figure 5.14   *Sales and sales administration*

The remaining segments of the pie chart represent the sales administration department. The main activities *they* performed also raised questions:

- Why was so much time spent on credit notes and order administration?
- Why did they need to keep statistics?
- Why did they need to raise special invoices?
- Why was there so much management and administration?

The fundamental answer to all these questions was that salesmen were having to call on customers to placate them because of late and incomplete deliveries. Sales administration was in turn having to raise a very high number of credit notes and special invoices, as well as keeping detailed statistics on the problems.

If the salesmen had got the order right the first time, if manufacturing had organized the production schedule to provide adequate inventory cover, and if distribution had organized warehousing and vehicle routeing to meet the customers' required delivery dates, the salesmen's placatory visits would not have been necessary.

Under these circumstances the time spent by salesmen dealing with problems could be radically reduced, and the time saved redeployed into selling and new business development. The time saved in sales administration could partly be used to improve dealer support and partly taken as a cost saving – and the company would have much happier customers!

But to achieve this position, each function involved in the chain of servicing the company's external customers had to recognize the impact of its failure on other functions and, ultimately, on the external customer. It required the forging of effective partnerships between functions by establishing levels of service that would minimize diversionary activity and meet internal and external customers' needs consistently. In order to do

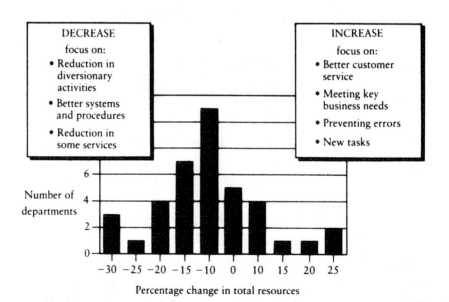

Figure 5.15 *ABCM: typical rebalancing of resources*

this, extra core resource was needed selectively to break out of the vicious circle of failure. By rebalancing resources (Figure 5.15), it was possible to prevent problems at source and thereby save diversionary activity elsewhere. An overall saving of 18 per cent of controllable overhead costs was achieved. *None of the opportunities for improvement was apparent from the conventional management accounts available prior to ABCM.*

Customer profitability

Cost driving factors

Activities in a business do not occur spontaneously; they are triggered by other events. These events are important because they drive the activities and the costs associated with them.

By identifying the cost driving factors and understanding the chain of events they trigger (Figure 5.16), managers are able to measure the cost of processes that take place in the business. For example, when a sales order is raised, certain activities will occur in response, such as an internal production order, a warehouse picking list, a delivery note, an invoice, as well as the direct activities associated with manufacture and delivery.

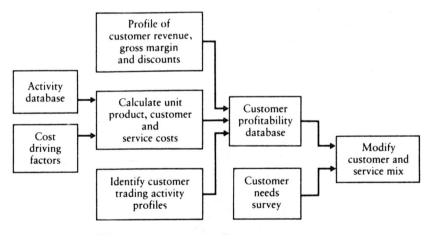

Figure 5.16 *Customer profitability: main steps*

Cost driving factors are particularly important in calculating product/service costs and customer costs. Typical of the many customer driven overhead costs are product customization, special delivery requirements, special orders, discount terms and payment arrangements.

To establish the profitability of individual customers or customer groups three factors are considered:

- the profile of customer revenue, gross margin and discounts, obtained by analysing sales by product and customer;
- the unit product, customer and service costs, calculated from the activity database and cost driving factors;
- the trading activity profile for each individual customer.

Having established these factors, the profit margin provided by each customer can be determined, thereby giving a true measure of its value to the organization. This enables management to consider tactical ways to improve the contribution of its least profitable customers. For example:

- Do the results of the customer needs survey suggest any elements of service that could be reduced so as to lower operating costs?
- Can discount terms be varied in a way which selectively penalizes the least profitable customers and rewards the most profitable?
- If all else fails, can unprofitable customers be shed so that they become a burden to one of the competitors?

Case study: customer profitability

A wholesaler/distributor of a mature product range to the retail sector had grown, through extensive acquisition and organic growth, from a struggling medium-sized regional player into the market leader. It provided a nationwide delivery service to 18,000 customers through more than sixty warehouses.

Management recognized that, given the maturity of the market, further profit growth could only come through better cost management.

The company operated a complex volume-related discount and incentive structure and believed it to be effective in ensuring that all customers, whether large or small, were sources of profitable business. However, this view was intuitive. No evidence of customer profitability was available other than at gross margin level.

The warehouse and distribution network was a major element of operating costs and was substantially fixed in the short to medium term. The company therefore planned to rationalize and redesign the network to gain economics of scale and to take advantage of the major improvements in the trunk road network.

It undertook a customer service needs survey. The most important finding was that a delivery service that was predictable and reliable was significantly more important to customers than one which was fast. This led to a major policy shift in the delivery pattern and allowed distribution and sales managers to plan for a much more cost-effective use of sales and delivery resources.

Once the activity costs of servicing customers had been set against the gross margin generated at the level of individual customer outlets, it was possible to draw a cumulative contribution chart (Figure 5.17). This revealed two surprises:

- the cumulative contribution of the least profitable 60 per cent of customers was zero;
- the cost of serving each of the least profitable 28 per cent of customers was significantly greater than the gross margin they generated

An even more astonishing revelation was that the largest customer, a major company representing some 20 per cent of total turnover, was generating a large negative contribution. Management sought to improve this situation through detailed negotiations with the customer to reduce the cost of incompatible documentation and to modify the discount structure. Had the negotiations failed the company would have declined the business, and would have removed all associated operating costs, so overall profitability would have improved whatever the outcome. However, the negotiations succeeded and served the mutual long-term benefit of both parties.

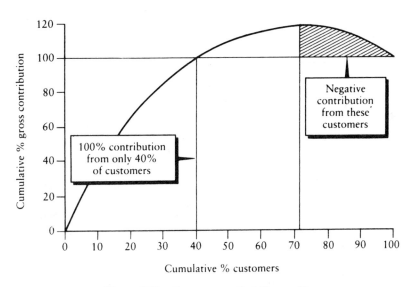

Figure 5.17 *Customer profitability profile*

The review of logistics indicated that eighteen warehouses, located correctly, could replace the existing network of sixty, and led to a saving of £13m per year in operating costs. One of the new sites coincided with that of an existing location. However, even when converted from single to three shift operation, it could not cope with the required throughput of orders. Examination of the profitability of the different customer types in the areas to be served by the new warehouse revealed a particular group who generated a great deal of work in proportion to gross margin. By actively encouraging these customers to switch their business to competitors, it was possible to close eight warehouses and service the remaining, profitable volume through the upgraded existing location. Thus for minimal capital expenditure, profitability was dramatically improved and capital released through the sale of redundant sites.

Product costing

From a knowledge of the cost driving factors that are product-related, it is possible to identify the overhead activities which contribute to product costs. These activity costs are attributed to individual products and are added to the costs of direct labour and material. The remaining pool of overhead costs, which are not directly product-attributable, is now significantly smaller than with a conventional approach, rendering their subsequent treatment much less likely to distort product cost information (see Figure 5.18).

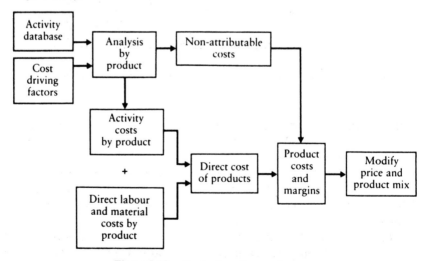

Figure 5.18   *Product costing: main steps*

For the purpose of product portfolio and make-or-buy decisions this amounts to a marginal approach to product costing on an activity basis and takes account of only the elements of cost that management are *prepared* to vary in the short to medium term. Focusing on such *avoidable* costs makes this a much more powerful decision support tool as a consequence. By contrast, for product pricing and competitor comparison purposes it may be necessary to adopt a full absorbtion approach to product costing. As such, this use of an activity-based approach is merely a refinement of conventional management accounting thinking.

The key difference between conventional product-costing and the ABCM approach is that ABCM attributes activity costs to the specific products that drive them. These costs are conventionally hidden as part of 'the overhead' and their impact on the true cost of the product is therefore lost.

The inaccuracy that conventional product costing can introduce is shown by the example (Figures 5.19 and 5.20) in which two products, A

	Product A	Product B
Direct labour	50	200
Direct material	200	100
Manufacturing overheads	150	600
Total	400	900

$$\text{Overhead recovery rate} = \frac{\text{Total overheads}}{\text{Total direct labour}} = \frac{750}{250}$$
$$= 300\%$$

Figure 5.19   *Product cost calculation: using allocation based on direct labour cost*

and B, are costed using two different methods. The first method apportions overheads based on direct labour; the second uses activity as a basis for attributing overhead costs.

In the first method, the manufacturing overheads allocated to product B are four times as great as those allocated to product A, because B uses four times as much direct labour. Consequently, product B costs 900 units whereas product A costs only 400 units.

In activity-based costing, the manufacturing overhead is broken down into its constituent parts, each of which is attributed to product A and product B according to the overhead activity actually devoted to it. In

		Product A		Product B
Direct labour		50		200
Direct material		200		100
Manufacturing overheads	Purchasing	120	30	
	Product development	50	80	
	Materials handling	100	50	
	Inspection	180	40	
	Maintenance	80	20	
		530		220
Total		780		520
	Product cost difference =	+95%		−42%

Figure 5.20 *Product cost calculation: allocation based on activities*

this instance, it transpired that product B consumed only 220 units of overhead, not 600 as the allocation based on direct labour had indicated. Conversely, product A consumed 530 units, not 150.

Product B happened to be a line that used simple production plant requiring a heavy direct labour involvement. It was a well-established customer favourite, with a steady demand. Over time, the wrinkles had been ironed out of the overhead processes associated with it, and attributable overhead costs were low.

As a result of inaccuracies in the conventional method of calculation, the cost of product A had been underestimated by a factor of 95 per cent. That of product B had been overestimated by 42 per cent.

Case study: product costing

A British engineering company with a long history of manufacturing high quality, heavy duty equipment was importing a complementary range from the Far East which they sold from stock with little modification. Its profit record fluctuated with the fortunes of the economy but showed a long-term decline.

Overhead costs were recovered conventionally on the basis of the direct labour hour content of each product sold, as recorded by the direct labour booking system.

The range of imported products were bought off-the-shelf, had no direct labour content and therefore carried no overhead burden.

The activity-based costing exercise revealed that the imported equipment *did* drive some of the overhead costs such as purchasing, sales, invoicing, advertising, materials handling and distribution. However, due to the existing basis of recovering overheads, these were *incorrectly* recovered on the made-to-order range. As a result, tenders for made-to-order products were often over-priced, causing a poor bid success rate. This in turn reduced the need for direct labour and caused the overhead recovery rate to increase, exacerbating the pricing problem.

Conversely, the range of imported products was under-priced and sales volumes grew.

Following the product costing exercise, the prices of the imported equipment were raised slightly to reflect the market price more closely. Nevertheless, they remained competitive, so that volume loss was slight. Because of the higher margin, the profit generated actually rose.

In recognition of the lower costs of the made-to-order equipment, prices were reduced, causing the success rate of tenders to increase significantly, while maintaining acceptable profit margins. These changes enabled the company to reverse its downward profits trend.

Prior to the ABCM study, management had initiated a review of overhead effectiveness in order to return to profitability. They had taken this action because their management accounts had led them to believe overhead ineffectiveness was the problem. Activity-based cost management revealed the problem's true nature and enabled management to regain effective control of their profits.

Concluding note

Traditional management accounts which do not reflect the decision-making needs of management have the potential to do business a grave disservice. They measure, with great preciseness and in great volume, those costs which it is convenient to measure rather than those which help managers to make effective management decisions. Consequently, such management accounts are either ignored, or used only as a crude instrument of budgetary control. This is a terrible waste. Management accounts should and could be a key source of management information. The answer must not be to ignore the accounts, but to ensure that the cost information they provide *helps managers manage*.

ABCM is an approach that does just this: it provides a base of cost data and a range of analysis tools that enable management to control the business. It does so by presenting information which directly relates to the decisions that managers are able to make about the resources they control.

Ironically, the amount of extra work required to produce useful cost information is not necessarily a great deal more than traditional techniques demand. The primary need is for the will and commitment to change.

Summary

Activity-based cost management is founded on the identification of the needs of the business and its customers, on an objective quantification of the activities undertaken in all areas of the company, and on the development of a clear understanding of the factors which drive costs.

It is an approach which touches all aspects of cost management in every sector of the economy. It brings specific competitive advantage through:

- greatly increased awareness of how and when costs are incurred throughout the organization and of what drives them;
- measuring the effectiveness of the key business processes, and identifying how they may be improved;
- recognizing the factors that are critical to the business and the needs that are important to its customers, and applying them to management's decision-making process;
- establishing customer terms and product/service pricing that reflect the real costs of serving customers.

By exploring opportunities to improve the effectiveness of business processes, by analysing customer profitability and by determining true product costs, it gives to management the quantified information it needs to control the business.

In other words, it fulfils the true purpose of cost management in a way that conventional techniques do not.

6

Accounting for just-in-time
Ian Cobb

The success of Japanese firms in international markets has generated interest among many Western companies as to how this success was achieved. It is claimed that the implementation of just-in-time (JIT) production methods has been one of the factors contributing to this success. In this chapter Ian Cobb describes the major features of the JIT philosophy and discusses the management accounting implications of moving from a traditional manufacturing environment to a JIT production environment. In the final section some examples of observed changes in management accounting systems arising from a field study are described.

Introduction

Just-in-time (JIT) is a management 'philosophy' in the sense of being a general way of thinking about the management of an organization. According to Blackburn (1988, p. 5), it '. . . profoundly affect[s] the entire manufacturing organisation . . .' It was developed initially by Toyota of Japan as the Toyota Production System described by Monden (1983, p. 1) as a '. . . revolutionary production management system . . .' following the earlier revolutions of Taylorism (scientific management) and Fordism (mass assembly).

JIT was initially viewed in the West as an inventory reduction technique (Blackburn, 1988, p. 5) but has gradually come to be seen as a much wider phenomenon. Perhaps that initial impression arose, as Harrison (1992, p. 14) suggests, because of inadequate understanding of the Japanese language and reticence on the part of Japanese companies.

The aim of JIT is the '. . . total elimination of waste . . .' (Japan Management Association, 1989, p. 16) from all parts of the manufacturing process, from design to delivery, by a process of continuous improvement which Turney and Anderson (1989, p. 38) define as 'the relentless pursuit of improvement in the delivery of value to the customer'. Value in this context is as perceived by the customer, not the provider.

Although the initial development and adoption of JIT was within manufacturing companies, it can be applied more widely as in education (Tatikonda, 1993) and other service organizations (Schniederjans, 1993, Chapter 7; Blackburn, 1992; Lee, 1990; Collins, 1992).

The first section of this chapter provides an overview of JIT to enable changes in the management accounting system (MAS) to be viewed in the wider context of organizational change. Next the accounting implications of JIT adoption are considered and finally some examples of MAS change from a field study are presented.

The JIT philosophy

This section provides an overview of the JIT philosophy. For more detailed information about the adoption and operation of JIT, readers are referred to Schniederjans (1993), Harrison (1992), Lamming (1993), Vollmann *et al.* (1992) and Voss and Clutterbuck (1989).

JIT is often explained in terms of the many techniques which are part of its implementation. This approach is adopted here, but it should be borne in mind that these techniques do not comprise JIT, they are the means of its realization. In a similar manner, the sculptor's tools are not the sculpture, they are the means of its realization.

Following Hay (1988), JIT can be considered in seven broad aspects as illustrated in Figure 6.1.

Employee involvement This is arguably the most important aspect, as JIT implies major cultural change in the organization, in particular in the relationship between management and workforce. Indeed such terminology may be inappropriate for a JIT company. Thus Harrison (1992, p. 46) quotes Konosuke Matsushita, founder of Matsushita Electric, '. . . management is the entire workforce's intellectual commitment at the service of the company – without self-imposed functional or class barriers'. Increased participation, flexibility and responsibility on the part of the 'workforce' – employee empowerment – has as a corollary, a changed role for managers from that of controller to that of facilitator. Managers and employees with traditional views of their roles may have difficulty adapting to JIT.

Increased participation, flexibility and responsibility also have implica-

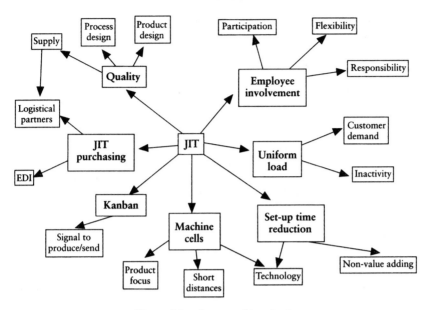

Figure 6.1 *Aspects of just-in-time*

tions for payment systems. Piecework or individual bonus schemes may require review in the light of JIT. Group schemes which recognize and share the benefits of innovation and improvement may be more appropriate.

Quality With the JIT focus on the elimination of waste, quality can be viewed as doing the right things, to meet customer needs, correctly the first time. This involves three interrelated aspects:

a designing the product to provide the functions required by the customer with the least input of resources and also for ease of manufacture;
b designing the process – layout, plant and machinery, procedures, skill-training – to ensure that the designed quality is achieved;
c ensuring that in-coming goods and services are of the quality required.

Uniform factory load The intention of this aspect is to have all parts of the production process operate at a speed which matches customer demand for the final product. Thus some parts of the process may remain idle if they have capacity above that required by customer demand.

Set-up time reduction Under JIT, setting-up is considered a non-value adding activity rather than an inherent feature of production processes. A JIT company will endeavour to eliminate the down-time traditionally associated with set-ups and product change-overs. Many of the technology aspects of JIT, such as modifications to equipment, are associated with this area. A detailed account of this aspect is given in Shingo (1985).

Machine cells   A machine (or work) cell brings together the diverse processes and skills required to produce a complete component, major sub-assembly or final product. The work carried out in a cell would traditionally have involved a component travelling around a factory to the various specialist processes. The establishment of machine cells will involve the rearrangement of the factory and possibly the purchase of new equipment.

Pull production control (Kanban)   Monden (1983) describes the Kanban as 'an information system'. It uses a card, an empty workspace, an empty container or a computer record to provide a signal from one production stage to an earlier stage that more components or materials are required. Without the signal, the earlier stage produces no output; there is no production in anticipation of demand.

Inventory within the manufacturing process is controlled by limiting the number of Kanbans (cards, containers, etc.) in circulation. A method of calculating the optimal number of Kanbans is given in Vollmann *et al.* (1992, pp. 507–12).

JIT purchasing   Long-term relationships are developed with a limited range of suppliers (Lamming, 1993). Such suppliers effectively become part of an 'extended factory' with partial integration into the company's systems, often through the use of electronic data interchange (EDI).

From this brief overview it is perhaps apparent that JIT is about management processes, not technology.

Accounting implications

As has been explained above, the JIT philosophy affects the way in which a company operates and is managed. Given that the management accounting system (MAS) of an organization attempts to model these processes, the adoption of JIT will have implications for the design and operation of the MAS. Some of the issues involved are illustrated in Figure 6.2 and discussed below.

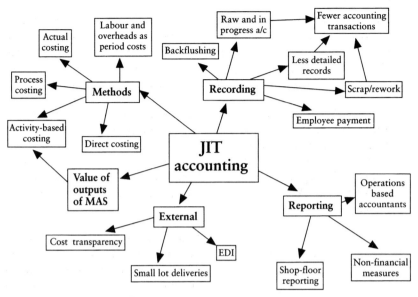

Figure 6.2 *JIT accounting issues*

Methods

A number of writers (for example McNair *et al.* (1988), Swenson and Cassidy (1993)) have noted a trend away from job/works order costing to process costing to reflect the simplification of the flow of work in companies they studied. With JIT's emphasis on the elimination of waste and continuous improvement, the use of standard costing, which institutionalizes waste through the inclusion of allowances for expected downtime, scrap and defectives, would be inconsistent. A move to the use of actual costing was reported by McNair *et al.* (1988).

Under a JIT philosophy there will be much less work in progress (WIP) and individual materials will spend much less time in progress. With this reduced significance of WIP, it is suggested that detailed tracking of direct labour in WIP is inappropriate. Instead, direct labour may be treated as a part of overhead (Dugdale and Shrimpton, 1990) or indeed the combined amount may be treated as a period cost with appropriate adjustments for external reporting purposes.

Increased traceability of costs as a feature of JIT systems is suggested by Bromwich and Bhimani (1994, pp. 47/8). Thus many costs previously considered as indirect, such as material handling and energy, could be classified as direct, reducing the need for cost allocations.

Since the aim of waste elimination is central to JIT, a company's costing system should generate product costs that reflect as accurately as possible the resources consumed in the manufacture of the specific products. Kaplan and Cooper (1988) have proposed 'activity-based costing' (ABC) as a method of getting to a 'truer' cost of resource consumption than traditional methods. Many of the cases recorded of US companies adopting JIT note that they have also adopted ABC.

Recording

The changes noted above imply a different approach to the recording of cost transactions. Thus the WIP and raw material accounts may be combined into a single Raw and In Progress account (RIP), leading to a reduction in detailed record keeping and a potential reduction in the number of accounting transactions. Thus Patell (1987) found a 'much less finely detailed' cost recording system in his study of Hewlett-Packard whilst Bailes and Kleinsorge (1992) noted that 'transaction processing was reduced drastically' in their study.

It should be remembered that whilst there may be a single RIP account, with aggregated periodic entries, in the general ledger, this will normally be supported by a subsidiary ledger, a file containing the movements and status of every material and component used by the company.

A very abbreviated form of inventory accounting is proposed by Schonberger (1986) with a 'four-wall' approach; material receipts are debited to, and the material content of sales is credited from, a single inventory account. He does caution however that the inventory file and the bill of material (BOM) file must be 'highly accurate' (p. 182). He also recognizes that companies are generally not able to adopt the 'four-wall' approach because of supplier failures.

Other writers (CMA (1993), Swenson and Cassidy (1993), Foster and Horngren (1988), Neumann and Jaouen (1986), Bhimani and Bromwich (1991)) have made similar comments about JIT leading to a simpler accounting system with fewer transactions.

Backflushing

A type of accounting process often associated with JIT is 'backflushing' with a 'greatly reduced' level of detail (Bromwich and Bhimani, 1994, p. 48). Using this process, raw materials and components are held in the RIP account until the product is completed. At that point, the individual materials and components in the product's BOM are credited to the RIP account and the product's standard material cost is debited to the finished goods account.

Consider the following simplified example of a product, whose BOM contains 200 different components, which the company traditionally produced in batches of 100. The transactions referred to here are those in the subsidiary ledgers, not the periodic, aggregated entries in the general ledger.

Traditional approach

- Issue batches of components (100 of each) from raw material (RM) to WIP – 200 credit transactions to RM and 200 debit transactions to WIP (the WIP transactions may be aggregated into a single debit in some systems).
- Process the components – 200 debit transactions to WIP and 200 credit transactions to direct labour recovery plus 200 debit transactions to WIP and 200 credit transactions to overhead recovery. The assumption here is that there will be a single labour and overhead input for each component.
- Transfer to finished goods – one credit to WIP and one debit to Finished Goods account.
- Total number of transactions to process 100 units = 1202.

JIT approach

- Issue components using a Kanban system – no transactions.
- Process the components – no transactions
- Transfer to finished goods – for each individual product, 200 credit transactions to RIP and one debit transaction to Finished Goods, i.e. 20,100 transactions for 100 products. If production is still controlled in batches of 100 then a total of 200 credit transactions to RIP will be required plus one debit transaction to Finished Goods. Batches of less than 100 may also be used resulting in between 201 and 20,100 transactions.
- Total number of transactions to process 100 units = 201 to 20,100.

Thus a JIT approach may produce an increase or a reduction in the number of transactions in the subsidiary ledgers. The impact will vary from company to company depending on product complexity and variety, and the batch size, remembering that an ultimate aim of JIT is a batch size of one. In the general ledger there will be a reduction since the there will be no transactions to a WIP account.

The BOM file is a key element in the backflushing process. Consider the following illustration of the effect of inaccuracies in the BOM file.

Suppose the BOM for product A erroneously includes a component X which does not form part of the product. When the product is completed and the BOM is backflushed, the RIP stock for component X will be reduced, that is the 'book stock' of X will be less than the physical stock. If this discrepancy is not noticed, the reorder process for X may be triggered, leading to over-stocking.

Alternatively, suppose that the BOM for product B erroneously excludes a component Y which does form part of the product. When the BOM for product B is backflushed, the stock of component Y will not be affected, that is the 'book stock' of Y will exceed the physical stock. If undetected, this discrepancy can lead to a stock-out and disruption of production.

Thus BOM accuracy is crucial to the operation of a backflushing system.

External interactions

The adoption of JIT means that the boundary of the MAS is extended beyond that of the legal entity. Thus there is a growth in the use of electronic data interchange (EDI) systems (Sadhwani and Sarhan, 1987) which lead to a partial integration of the accounting systems of the company and its customers and suppliers. Also, the close relationship with suppliers and customers may lead to 'cost transparency' – the two-way sharing of cost information proposed by Lamming (1993).

A further feature of JIT purchasing is the use of many small-lot deliveries in place of less frequent bulk deliveries with implications for the material accounting and accounts payable systems. In a USA case study, Forbes *et al.* (1989) describe 'partnership accounting' in which the supplier delivers components directly to the production line in weekly lots. A monthly invoice is submitted, and provided this is within 2 per cent of the company's assessment of component usage based on final product output, the invoice is paid.

Reporting

Under JIT a company will aim for a low inventory, closely coupled manufacturing system. A consequence of this is that management reporting will tend to become shop-floor based and non-financial in orientation. In their study, Bailes and Kleinsorge (1992) reported the introduction of a chart-based reporting system, containing no financial data, directed at operations management who termed this approach 'management by eye'. This echoed the earlier article by Foster and Horngren (1988) in which they noted as a general trend in JIT factories, a '. . . declining role for financial measures, and an increasing role for personal observation and non-financial measures in cost control activities' (p. 11).

If management accountants are to play a central role in this new reporting scenario they will need to detach themselves from their central departments and become involved in the basic processes of the organization by working alongside operations managers.

Value of outputs

Consideration of the value to its 'customers' of the outputs of the MAS may also lead to changes in those outputs and in the MAS itself. Thus, Bromwich and Bhimani (1989, p. 12) suggest that the role of management accounting should be reassessed due to the 'novel demands' of modern production systems, and in particular that the use of activity-based costing should be considered.

Simpler accounting?

A major theme of the literature discussed above is that the adoption of JIT will result in simpler cost accounting procedures and in particular, a reduction in the number of accounting entries. This can be illustrated by comparing the flow of transactions through a conventional manufacturing company with that of a JIT manufacturing company.

First, consider a conventional manufacturing accounting system as shown in Figure 6.3.

The significant features of such a system are,

a   a purchase price variance is extracted on receipt of raw materials and components and charged to a variance account;
b   raw materials and components are posted to the stock account at standard cost;
c   raw materials and components are issued to production against a scheduled works order requirement;
d   completed components and sub-assemblies, produced in 'economic batch quantities', are returned to stock for later reissue;
e   materials and components issued to replace scrap or defectives are charged to a variance account;

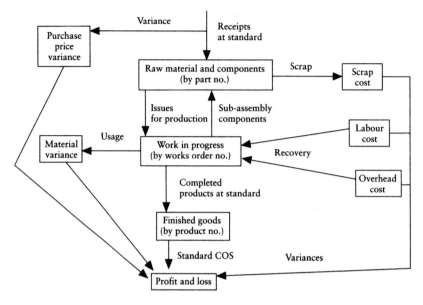

Figure 6.3 *Conventional manufacturing accounting*

f any usage variance detected on completion of the works order is charged to a material usage variance account;

g labour and overheads are recovered at standard rates as work progresses through work in progress (WIP);

h completed products are transferred to finished goods stock at standard material, labour and overhead cost;

i the profit and loss account will include the standard cost of sales plus the variances recorded for the period.

Compare this with the JIT manufacturing accounting system shown in Figure 6.4.

The main differences are,

a works orders are no longer used; the physical movement of raw materials and components from stores, through WIP to finished goods is controlled by a Kanban system;

b raw materials and components are held in a Raw and In Progress (RIP) account until the product is completed;

c on product completion, the individual materials and components listed in the product's BOM are backflushed (as described earlier) from the RIP account into the finished goods account;

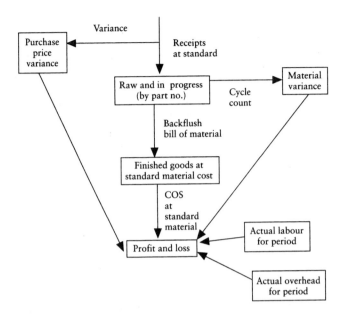

Figure 6.4 *JIT manufacturing accounting*

d   periodic cycle counting of items in stores and WIP areas is necessary to detect material usage variances;

e   the profit and loss account includes the standard material cost of sales plus the material variances and the actual labour and overhead costs for the period;

f   for periodic external reporting purposes, an adjustment will be required to reflect the labour and overhead content of WIP and finished goods inventory.

Thus the expectation would be that a company adopting JIT would change to a simpler accounting system with a reduced number of accounting transactions.

The field study

This section is based on a field study carried out at companies which had adopted JIT between two and ten years prior to the visits. Multiple data sources were used in the study. A semi-structured interview, using an interview schedule with space for note taking, was conducted with a senior management accountant at each of the sites. To enable the collection of as much data as possible, the interviews were taped; none of the interviewees expressed any reservations about the use of the recorder. A shop-floor visit at each site gave the opportunity to observe the factory layout, the various production processes and data collection systems as well as shop-floor displays of performance indicators. Management reports and other documents were also examined and in some cases copies of these were obtained.

Full details of the companies and findings are given in Cobb (1993). In this chapter the manufacturing accounting systems of four of the companies will be used to illustrate that accounting in a JIT company is not necessarily simple accounting. Brief profiles of these companies are given to provide a context for the explanations of their accounting systems.

Company Q

The company assembles a wide range of high-volume computer products which are subject to frequent specification changes and sold through associated sales companies throughout Europe. Annual turnover exceeds £500m and the company has about 500 employees. The company views customer satisfaction, that is, a combination of quality, value for money and support services, as the main success factor. Product technology is also important in this market. The company adopted JIT in 1988. The European cost manager was interviewed.

The company's manufacturing accounting system is illustrated in Figure 6.5. When JIT was adopted, the system was extended to include a 'Kanban' account and works orders were retained as a method of batching products through production. The company passes all receipts through a Quality Control (QC) account into a Stockroom account after inspection. Non-inspected parts from approved suppliers are also passed through the QC account because of constraints within the existing software.

Small, low-value parts such as fasteners are issued to the shop-floor in bulk and are charged to a Material Expense account. Items such as packaging, which are delivered directly by suppliers to the work in progress (WIP) area are also charged to this account.

A Kanban system is used to physically withdraw materials from the stockroom with each Kanban being individually transacted into the Kanban account. On shipment of a batch of products, entries are trig-

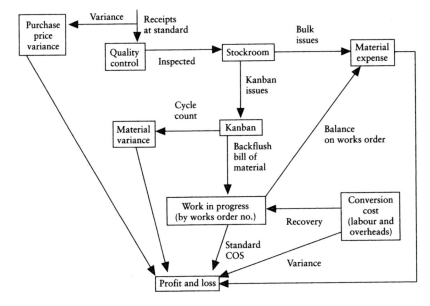

Figure 6.5 *Company Q*

gered in an individual works order record within the WIP account as
follows:

a   the current BOM, excluding bulk issue and packaging, is backflushed
from the Kanban account into the WIP record;
b   the standard conversion cost (labour and overheads), taken from the
standard cost listing, is added to the record;
c   the full standard cost (material, labour and overhead), from the standard cost listing, of the products is credited to the record and charged as
cost of sales to the profit and loss account.

A balance will remain on the works order record for two reasons. The cost
of the bulk issue parts and packaging are included in the standard product
cost but not in the backflushed BOM. This factor will result in a credit
balance in the WIP record. Also, the current BOM may differ from that
included in the standard product cost due to specification changes. This
factor may have a credit or debit effect on the WIP record. The record balance is transferred to the Material Expense account to offset the earlier
debits for bulk issues and packaging. Any large balances are investigated
as they may result from errors in the BOM. The detection of such errors is
crucial as they can lead to out-of-stock conditions since the company

attempts to keep stocks at a very low level. Thus, from a narrow accounting viewpoint, the WIP account is used simply to close off the works order and would not normally show any net balance. However, it also provides a vital material control function.

A cycle count of WIP stock on the shop-floor is necessary to detect discrepancies in the Kanban account due to undeclared scrap and BOM errors. The cost of such discrepancies is transferred to a Material Variance account.

The profit and loss account includes the standard cost of sales, the under/over recovery of conversion costs, the net material expense, the material variance and purchase price variance.

The company has experienced an increase in the number of transactions as a result of more frequent deliveries from suppliers, the issue of smaller lots to the shop-floor and the backflushing of smaller production quantities. Bar coding is used as a means of coping with the increase.

Company R

This company manufactures business equipment and has a turnover of about £200m and approximately 1,400 employees. The company's processes include assembly, printed circuit board (PCB) assembly and component manufacture. Although the product range is limited there are many potential variations as the company customizes the products to meet particular customer requirements. Thus individual product volumes are low. The company sells worldwide through group sales companies and views quality and technical features followed by price as the main success factors in the market. The company has developed the JIT concept over the past five years. Interviews were conducted with the company accountant and the costing and inventory manager.

The company's manufacturing accounting system is shown in Figure 6.6. As in company Q, this company also retained works orders and introduced an additional Kanban account with the adoption of JIT. The works orders are issued weekly for each individual product type, usually for very small numbers or even a single unit.

On receipt, materials are debited to a 'Loading Bank' account at standard, with any purchase price variance being debited/credited to the variance account. Materials are physically issued using Kanbans which are transacted from the Loading Bank account through the Stores account into the Kanban account. The simultaneous debit and credit to the Stores account is necessary because of existing software constraints. The Kanban account is the equivalent of a conventional WIP material account.

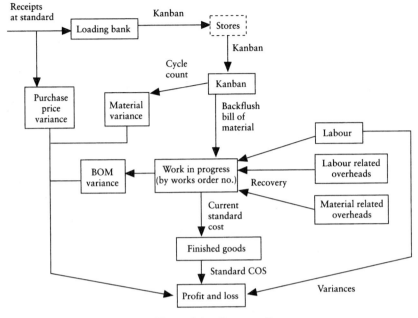

Figure 6.6   *Company R*

When the product(s) on a works order are completed the following entries are made:

a   the BOM current at the time of issue of the works order is backflushed from the Kanban account into the WIP record;

b   standard labour and overhead recoveries (the company uses both labour related and material related overhead recovery rates) are added to the WIP record; and

c   the current BOM value including labour and overhead is credited to the WIP record and debited to finished goods.

Any balance remaining on the WIP record will represent the difference between the current BOM and the BOM at the time of issue of the works order and is transferred to a BOM variance account. Thus, as in company Q, the WIP account is used to close off the works orders and would not normally show any net balance.

This company also carries out a cycle count of the Kanban stock on the shop-floor to detect discrepancies caused by BOM errors, undeclared scrap, 'shrinkage', and the unrecorded use of production materials by development engineers.

Although only one set of summary entries is posted to the general ledger each month, the number of transactions in the material recording system is 'enormous'.

Company S

A manufacturer of electronic instrumentation and test equipment, the company has a turnover in the £50–100m range and about 1,200 employees. The company has a printed circuit board (PCB) manufacturing facility as well as PCB assembly, sub- and final assembly departments. The wide product range is sold throughout the world through group sales companies. Technical features and value for money are the main success factors for the company. JIT was adopted in the early 1980s following a total quality management (TQM) initiative in 1979. The divisional controller was interviewed.

The company S manufacturing accounting system is shown below in Figure 6.7. This company comes closer to the JIT system shown in figure 6.4 than the other companies discussed here, although a separate WIP is still maintained. A Kanban system is used physically to issue components

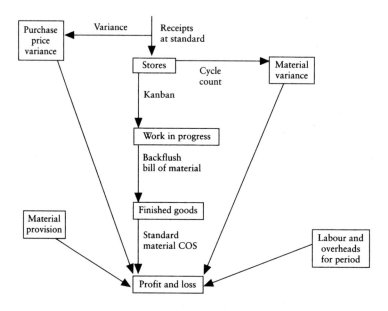

Figure 6.7 *Company S*

and materials from stores and transfer their cost to work in progress. In some instances, aggregated pick-lists for a number of components are used for issuing and accounting purposes. Completion of a batch of products backflushes the BOM from the WIP account into Finished Goods account which is at standard material cost.

A cycle count of stores stock is used to detect discrepancies but the company does not attempt to track material variances or BOM differences occurring in WIP. The company sets up a provision for such variances by charging a standard percentage of material cost in the profit and loss account each month. Provided the difference revealed at the annual physical stock-take does not exceed the accumulated provision, no further investigation ensues.

The company treats labour and overheads as period costs. An appropriate adjustment for the labour and overhead content of WIP and finished goods is made for external reporting purposes.

A single journal entry is posted each month to the general ledger to account for material movements with no attempt being made accurately to track WIP. The company's management accountant is relatively indifferent to possible discrepancies in WIP given the company's provision procedure. Also, the company has total stocks of about twelve weeks and is thus protected (at a cost) from the dangerous combination of inaccurate inventory data and low inventory levels.

Company T

This company manufactures consumer durables and has a turnover in the £100/500m range with about 1,600 employees. The company has basic component manufacturing operations as well as sub- and final assembly. Although there are many product types and variations, unit volumes are high. The company operates in highly competitive European markets where the key success factor is quality combined with price. The company started its major JIT initiatives in the late 1980s, but certain aspects such as quality, employee involvement and machine cells have been in place since the 1970s. The financial planning manager was interviewed.

Figure 6.8 shows a simplified version of the company's manufacturing accounting system. Only two of the many WIP stages are included in the diagram for clarity. This company's system is also complicated by its use of four separate overhead recovery bases applied at different stages of the production process. These multiple bases are part of the company's development of an activity-based costing system.

On receipt, the standard cost of materials, to which is added the

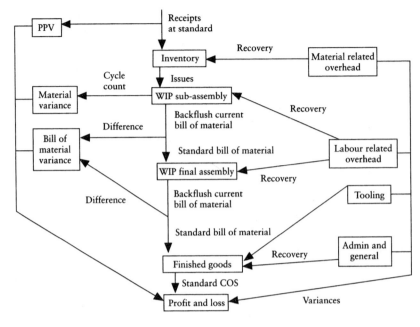

Figure 6.8 *Company T*

material related overhead recovery rate, is debited to the Inventory account, with any purchase price variance being posted to the variance account. The company does not use a Kanban system; materials are issued in batches and charged to the sub-assembly WIP account.

The company maintains two BOMs for each product or sub-assembly; a standard BOM derived from the standard setting process for the financial year and a current BOM reflecting specification changes during the year.

On completion of a batch of sub-assemblies, the following entries are made:

a   the standard labour and labour related overhead is debited to sub-assembly WIP; and
b   the current BOM (including labour and overhead) is backflushed out of sub-assembly WIP;
c   the standard BOM is debited to the final assembly WIP;
d   the difference between the standard and current BOMs is debited/ credited to the BOM variance account.

A similar procedure applies when a batch of products is completed, though here the debit of the standard BOM to finished goods attracts a recovery of tooling and administration and general overheads.

Frequent cycle counting of WIP detects about 90 per cent of discrepancies which arise, the balance being revealed at the half-yearly WIP stocktake. Shop-floor material controllers have on-line access to stock records to assist in this process.

The company has experienced a 'massive' increase in the number of goods-inward transactions since the mid-1980s with local suppliers now delivering once per shift instead of every second day. Some bulky components are delivered three times per shift. In addition, the backflushing of smaller production batches has also increased the number of transactions in the manufacturing accounting system. However the company's computer system had sufficient capacity to cope with the increase without staff increases.

Discussion

Earlier in the chapter reference was made to many articles and books which suggested that the adoption of JIT should lead to a simplified MAS and in particular to a reduction in the number of accounting transactions. The cases described above clearly show that the accounting system will not necessarily be simplified. Also the number of transactions will not always reduce and may in fact increase under a JIT system. It may be that the writers considered the accounting system and its transactions to be limited to the general ledger. The general ledger by its very nature is a summary of aggregated transactions which cannot reflect the detailed changes in state within a complex manufacturing organization. Thus, the companies described above, probably in common with many manufacturing companies, make one set of month-end aggregate entries to their general ledgers to summarize the many hundreds of thousands or even millions of individual transactions in the manufacturing accounting systems.

The companies all have complex BOMs for a large number of products subject to frequent change as a result of customer feedback, shop-floor feedback, cost reduction programmes, product improvement, material supply problems, etc. If a company is to maintain its production flow with very low inventory levels it is essential that its BOM and inventory records are accurate. A minor discrepancy in a BOM could lead to a production stoppage and non-delivery to a customer.

Thus companies Q, R, and T continue to use complex material tracking and accounting systems to ensure the integrity of their BOM and inventory files. Company S does not attempt to identify such discrepancies.

However, the company has about twelve weeks of inventory and is thus relatively immune to inaccuracies in its inventory records. Also, its stock loss provision procedure protects it from any financial shocks resulting from inventory losses.

A further factor which limits the scope for MAS simplification is the software already in use by the company. This represents a major investment of resources, which, although a sunk cost, is indicative of the resources required to design and implement a new system. The interviewee in one of the companies regarded the possible replacement of the cost accounting system as a 'horrendous prospect'.

Conclusion

Management accounting extends far beyond the general ledger. To view changes in management accounting practice it is necessary to examine its finer detail in context. This chapter has attempted to do this, looking at some of the consequences of adopting a new management philosophy. As Hopwood (1990) warns us, the 'impact of new technologies is not singular'. Their impact on accounting 'is likely to be mediated and influenced by the organizational and cultural terrains into which the technologies are introduced'.

The MASs of the companies featured in this chapter have responded in different ways to the challenge presented by the adoption of JIT. They have generally become more complex, not simpler, as a consequence.

Any management accountant faced with the challenge of a company adopting JIT should consider the current technological, organizational and cultural environments of the company in developing a response to that challenge. There is no single solution which will meet the needs of all companies – but isn't that what makes management accounting interesting?

Acknowledgements

The author wishes to thank the Research Foundation of the Chartered Institute of Management Accountants for funding the field research on which this chapter is based and the accountants and managers who participated in the study.

References

Bailes, J. C. and Kleinsorge, I. K. (1992). Cutting waste with JIT, *Management Accounting (USA)*, May, 28–32.

Bhimani, A. and Bromwich, M. (1991). Accounting for just-in-time manufacturing systems, *CMA Magazine*, February, **65**(1), 31–34.

Blackburn, J. D. (1988). The new manufacturing environment, *Journal of Cost Management*, Summer, 4–10.

Blackburn, J. D. (1992). Time-based competition: white-collar activities, *Business Horizons*, July–August, 96–101.

Bromwich, M. and Bhimani, A. (1989). *Management Accounting: Evolution not Revolution*. London: CIMA.

Bromwich, M. and Bhimani, A. (1994). *Management Accounting Pathways to Progress*, London: CIMA.

CMA (1993). *Implementing Just-in-Time Production Systems*, Management Accounting Guidelines no. 19, The Society of Management Accountants of Canada, Hamilton.

Cobb, I. (1993). *JIT and the Management Accountant: A Study of Current UK Practice*, London: CIMA.

Collins, P. (1992). Admin JIT, *Management Services*, April, 24–26.

Dugdale, D. and Shrimpton, S. (1990). Product costing in a JIT environment, *Management Accounting*, March, 40–2.

Forbes, R. S., Jones, D. F. and Marty, S. T. (1989). Managerial accounting and vendor relations for JIT: a case study, *Production and Inventory Management Journal*, First Quarter, 76–81.

Foster, G. and Horngren, C. T. (1988). Cost accounting and cost management in a JIT Environment, *Journal of Cost Management*, Winter, 4–14.

Harrison, A. (1992). *Just-in-Time Manufacturing in Perspective*. Hemel Hempstead: Prentice Hall.

Hay, E. J. (1988). *The Just-in-Time Breakthrough*. John Wiley.

Hopwood, A. G. (1990). Accounting and organisation change, *Accounting, Auditing and Accountability Journal*, **3**(1), 7–17.

Japan Management Association, translated by D. J. Lu (1989). *Kanban: Just-in-Time at Toyota*. Cambridge, USA: Productivity Press.

Kaplan, R. S. and Cooper, R. (1988). How cost accounting distorts product costs. *Management Accounting (USA)*, April, 20–7.

Lamming, R. (1993). *Beyond Partnership: Strategies for Innovation and Lean Supply*. Hemel Hempstead: Prentice Hall.

Lee, J. Y. (1990). JIT works for services too. *CMA Magazine*, 20–23.

McNair, C. J., Mosconi, W. and Norris, T. (1988). *Meeting the Technology Challenge: Cost Accounting in a JIT Environment*, Montvale, New Jersey: NAA.

Monden, Y. (1983). *Toyota Production System*. Norcross: Industrial Engineering and Management Press.

Neumann, B. R. and Jaouen, P. R. (1986). Kanban, ZIPS and cost accounting: a case study. *Journal of Accountancy*, August, 132–141.

Patell, J. M. (1987). Adapting a cost accounting system to just-in-time manufacturing: the Hewlett-Packard personal office computer division. In *Accounting and Management Field Study Perspectives*, (eds) W. J. Bruns Jnr and R. S. Kaplan), Harvard Business School Press, 229–67.

Sadhwani, A. T. and Sarhan, M. H. (1987). Electronic systems enhance JIT operations. *Management Accounting (USA)*, December, 25–30.

Schniederjans, M. J. (1993). *Topics in Just-in-Time Management*. Needham Heights: Allyn & Bacon.

Schonberger, R. J. (1986). *World Class Manufacturing: The Lessons of Simplicity Applied*, The Free Press.

Shingo, S. (1985). *A Revolution in Manufacturing: the SMED system*. Cambridge, USA: Productivity Press.

Swenson, D. W. and Cassidy, J. (1993). The Effect of JIT on Management Accounting. *Journal of Cost Management*, Spring, 7, No. 1, 39–47.

Tatikonda, L. U. (1993). JIT can save accounting education. *Management Accounting (USA)*, December, 53–55.

Turney, P. B. B. and Anderson, B. (1989). Accounting for continuous improvement. *Sloan Management Review*, Winter, 37–47.

Vollmann, T. E., Berry, W. L. and Whybark, D. C. (1992). *Manufacturing Planning and Control Systems*, 3rd edn, Irwin.

Voss, C. and Clutterbuck, D. (1989). *Just-in-Time: A Global Status Report*, IFS.

7

Throughput accounting: theory, techniques and practice
David Dugdale and T. Colwyn Jones

During the past decade an enormous amount of publicity has been generated by the publications of Goldratt and Cox (1984, 1986, 1993) relating to the theory of constraints and the maximization of throughput to enhance profitability. In this chapter David Dugdale and Colwyn Jones describe the theory, techniques and practice of accounting for throughput. The first section deals with the origins of throughput thinking in the theory of constraints. The second section introduces throughput accounting. The third section describes the experience of one company in introducing the theory of constraints in production and the idea of throughput in its accounting. The chapter concludes with a discussion of competing theories and lessons which can be drawn from the experiences of the case study company.

The 1980s can be seen as a period when established manufacturing and accounting practices came under attack. The success of Japanese manufacturers using 'just-in-time' (JIT) and 'total quality management' (TQM) caused a re-evaluation of traditional approaches, and by the mid-1980s there was widespread acceptance of the efficacy of these new practices. Many Western companies adopted new manufacturing 'philosophies' and these changes led to a re-evaluation of accounting, especially management accounting.

Johnson and Kaplan (1987) claimed that management accounting had lost its relevance. Their main thesis was that relevant **cost management** techniques, developed during the nineteenth century, have given way, during the twentieth century, to **cost accounting**, subservient to the demands of financial reporting and generating irrelevant and misleading management information. They identified two major deficiencies in traditional cost accounting systems. First, traditional systems concentrated on production costs – to the detriment of marketing, distribution and development costs – expensed in the profit and loss account and often not subject to detailed analysis. Second, the attribution of production overhead itself was undertaken very simplistically – often based on a single or very few overhead 'pools' and inappropriate (but convenient) recovery bases (such as direct labour).

This general historical critique of accounting was reinforced by more immediate concerns in 'the new manufacturing environment' of the 1980s. Brimson (1988) claimed that conventional accounting provided old-style information which misled managers whilst simultaneously disregarding important new-style information. A wide range of measures were seen as inducing managers and supervisors to follow actions which improved their 'scores' but which resulted in the production of excess inventory and missed opportunities for cost reduction (see Table 7.1).

Management accounting, reeling from the charges that its controls were antipathetic to JIT and TQM, and that traditional cost accounting could generate misleading product costs, was challenged from yet another quarter. Eli Goldratt developed the 'Theory of Constraints' in which the maximization of 'throughput' was identified as the most salient factor in increasing profitability. Here cost accounting was seen as 'enemy number one of productivity' (Goldratt and Cox, 1993, introduction) since its local performance measures obscure the goal of the organization and hinder the realization of potential throughput.

This chapter covers the theory, techniques, and practice of accounting for throughput. The first section deals with the theory of constraints and the concept of throughput. The second section introduces throughput accounting. The third section shows how one company fared in introducing the theory of constraints in production and the idea of throughput in its accounting. The chapter concludes with discussion of the competing theories and the lessons which can be drawn from the experiences of the case study company.

The theory of constraints

TOC and production

The theory of constraints (TOC) has its roots in the development of the production scheduling software *optimized production technology* (OPT) in the mid 1970s. Although trained as a physicist, Goldratt became

Table 7.1 Some traditional measures that encourage waste

Measurement	Action	Result
Purchase price	Purchasing increases order quantity to get lower price. Ignores quality and delivery.	Excess inventory. Increased carrying cost. Supplier with best quality and delivery is overlooked.
Machine utilization	Supervisor runs machine in excess of daily unit requirement to maximize machine utilization.	Excess inventory. Wrong inventory.
Scrap factor built into a standard cost	Supervisor takes no action if no variance.	Inflated standard. Scrap threshold built in.
Standard cost overhead absorption WIP	Supervisor overproduces to get overhead absorption in excess of his expenses.	Excess inventory.
Indirect/direct head count ratio	Management controls the ratio not total cost. Total cost not in control.	Indirect labour standards wrongly established.
Scrap (£)	Scrap £ drives corrective action priority.	Defect level impact on flow hidden in £.
Cost centre reporting	Management focus is on cost centre instead of activities.	Missed cost reduction opportunities because common activities among cost centres are overlooked.
Labour reporting	Management focus is on direct labour, which is fixed and relatively small. Overhead which is large, is overlooked.	Missed cost reduction opportunities. Major overhead activities not exposed.
Earned labour (£)	Supervisor maximizes earned labour. Keeps workers busy.	Excess inventory. Scheduled attainment given lower priority. Output is emphasized.
Overhead rate	Management controls the rate not total cost.	Overhead levels improperly established. High cost activities hidden.

Source: Brimson (1988)

interested in scheduling problems when he realized that existing materials requirements planning (MRP) systems, typically, assumed that production capacity was either available or could be readily made available. This was a massive over-simplification because, in practice, production bottlenecks often limited production output. Goldratt noted that existing MRP systems could easily lead to excessive production on non-bottleneck facilities and this would lead, not to sales, but to excess work-in-progress. These reflections led him to consider the problems inherent in finite production scheduling (where the finite capacities of production facilities are taken into account) and OPT was developed as computer software which addressed these problems and marketed through the company Creative Output.

The ideas underlying OPT might have languished in the obscure world of production scheduling if they had not been given massive publicity with publication, in 1984, of *The Goal* (Goldratt and Cox), a novel with a serious message which has since become a best seller, and was republished in extended form in 1993. The thoughts and activities of plant manager, Alex Rogo, are traced as he strives to save his plant from closure by improving its performance.

Prompted by his old college professor, Jonah, Alex realizes that the goal of his company is to 'make money' and the way to achieve this is to increase plant throughput. As throughput is limited by output from the plant's bottleneck facilities Alex concentrates attention on managing them. Stock 'buffers' are located in front of the bottlenecks (so they are never starved of work), parts are inspected before bottleneck processing (so that bottleneck capacity is not wasted processing defective parts) and alternative production routings are investigated (so as to release bottleneck capacity).

Whilst bottleneck production must be maximized Alex realizes that non-bottleneck facilities must be managed differently. Since they have excess capacity they must *not* run constantly because this would merely build inventory. Instead production on non-bottleneck facilities is restricted so that they produce only to serve the bottlenecks. As Alex puts these ideas into practice inventory is maintained or increased in the buffers but declines in the rest of the plant. The changes lead to improved plant performance and further improvements follow as batch sizes are reduced. The plant is saved and Alex is promoted.

In improving the performance of his plant Alex is handicapped by conventional accounting. Non-bottleneck facilities, no longer producing for stock, run under capacity and the efficiency and utilization measures reported to division deteriorate. The bad news is apparently confirmed in the profit and loss account which suffers as falling work-in-progress reduces overhead recovery. Only improved cash flow consequent upon improved customer focus and stock liquidation allows Alex to stave off criticism long enough for the underlying improvement to become evident.

Having introduced OPT ideas to a wide audience in *The Goal*, Goldratt then turned to the codification of these ideas in *The Race* (Goldratt and Fox, 1986). The importance of production bottlenecks is emphasized and the whole plant is to be paced by the speed of the bottleneck facilities. The idea is graphically illustrated by an imaginary drummer who paces the whole plant by beating a *drum*. Non-bottleneck facilities must produce to the beat of the drum, feeding the bottlenecks and not building stock by over producing. The bottlenecks are protected by stock *buffers* held in front of them so that, if problems arise in providing parts to the bottlenecks, production is not lost because the bottlenecks continue to work by reducing the stock buffers. Stock buffers are rebuilt as soon as production difficulties are resolved. Lastly, the idea of a *rope* which connects facilities together is introduced. The imaginary rope pulls production from the non-bottleneck facilities in order to feed the bottlenecks. (In fact, production is pulled before it is strictly needed so as to maintain the bottleneck stock buffers at their planned levels.)

By the late 1980s Goldratt had developed the thinking which underpinned bottleneck management to the more general 'theory of constraints'. In *The Haystack Syndrome* (Goldratt, 1990a), and in *The Theory of Constraints* (Goldratt, 1990b), TOC is set out as five focusing steps (see Figure 7.1).

1. Identify the system's constraints.

2. Decide how to exploit the system's constraints.

3. Subordinate everything else to the above decision.

4. Elevate the system's constraints.

5. If in the previous steps a constraint has been broken, go back to step 1, but do not allow inertia to cause a system constraint.

Figure 7.1   *The five steps*

Goldratt's ideas have had a significant impact on production scheduling theory, the original OPT software has been developed over the past fifteen years and an increasing number of companies are interested in finite production scheduling. Goldratt himself has become interested in increasingly general problems and has developed 'the thinking process', a generic approach which is intended to help managers resolve problems in a logical manner. This most recent development in Goldratt's thinking is set out in *It's Not Luck* (Goldratt, 1994) and reviewed in *The Theory of Constraints and its Implications for Management Accounting* (Noreen *et al.*, 1995).

TOC and accounting

Goldratt has caused some consternation by arguing on a number of occasions that cost accounting is 'enemy number one of productivity'. His reasons relate to the problems which Alex Rogo faced in *The Goal*: the sub-optimal behaviour which can be encouraged by local efficiency and utilization measures and the standard accounting practice of recovering overhead into stock as goods are produced (not sold). These difficulties caused Goldratt to reconsider basic accounting principles and to conclude that managers need to know the answer to:

> Three simple questions: 'How much money is generated by our company? How much money is captured by our company? And how much money do we have to spend to operate it?'
>
> (Goldratt, 1990a, p. 19)

To answer these questions Goldratt identified three key measures: throughput, inventory and operational expense. They are defined in both editions of *The Goal*:

> Throughput ... is the rate at which the system generates money through *sales* ... Inventory is all the money that the system invests in purchasing things which it intends to sell ... Operational expense is all the money the system spends in order to turn inventory into throughput.
>
> (Goldratt and Cox, 1993, pp. 59–60)

The definition of throughput is important: sales revenue less materials (accountants would see this as closely related to traditional contribution: sales revenue less variable costs). Rather awkwardly Goldratt defines inventory as including plant and buildings (and accountants would normally define Goldratt's 'inventory' as total assets or capital employed). Finally, operational expense covers all the costs of conversion including *all* employee costs, whether direct or indirect.

In Goldratt's analysis virtually all company costs are fixed (hence the definition of throughput which treats only material costs as variable). Goldratt is very suspicious of 'efficiency gains' (which ought to lead to reduction in those costs traditionally identified as 'variable') because his experience suggests that such claims are often spurious. In *The Goal* Alex claims that efficiency is improving following the introduction of robots. Jonah's analysis, however, reveals that there has been no reduction in operating expense (no workers have lost their jobs); no reduction in inventory (which remains high) and no increase in throughput for the plant as a whole – so where is the efficiency gain?

Because of the manner in which Goldratt has defined 'throughput' and 'operational expense' it follows that profit can be derived by subtracting one from the other:

$$\text{Net profit} = \text{Throughput} - \text{Operational expense}$$

Also, because inventory has been defined in a way which would usually relate to 'assets' or 'capital employed', it follows that 'return on investment' can also be calculated:

$$\text{Return on investment} = \frac{\text{Throughput} - \text{Operational expense}}{\text{Inventory}}$$

Accountants might be inclined to dismiss Goldratt's analysis at this point because there seems to be little new here. Throughput and operational expense seem to be variations on the traditional analysis of profit into contribution and fixed cost and the definition of 'inventory' is more familiar as a definition of 'investment', 'assets' or 'capital employed'. Nevertheless we believe that this would seriously underestimate Goldratt's message. Goldratt is not trying to introduce new accounting techniques (although he does devote several pages in *The Haystack Syndrome* to a 'throughput per bottleneck minute' example), he is trying to induce a **paradigm shift** in management thinking.

Goldratt (1990) evaluates the RoI ratio in the context of the new production 'philosophies' of the 1970s and 1980s: TQM, JIT and TOC. He concludes that these philosophies 'work' because of the emphasis they give (either by accident or design) to increasing throughput. TOC, derived from the ideas of bottleneck management, concentrates attention on the maximization of throughput. TQM aids throughput by its customer focus with emphasis on quality, reliability and customer satisfaction. Goldratt argues that the major impact of JIT is not the reduction of stock levels but the improvement of throughput. According to Goldratt, JIT leads to reduced customer lead-time and an operation which is increasingly responsive to customer needs – and, hence, encourages increased throughput.

Thus the three 'new' philosophies make the maximization of throughput the first priority for management. Goldratt contrasts this with the traditional emphasis of the 'cost world', obsessed with controlling and reducing operational expense – a process which is inherently limited because operational expense can only approach zero. Similarly, reductions in stock, whilst desirable because of their indirect impact on throughput, are inherently limited. Figure 7.2 summarizes Goldratt's analysis.

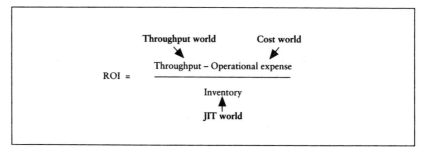

Figure 7.2　*A paradigm shift in management*

This analysis leads Goldratt to his recommendation for a crucial change in managerial priorities. Traditionally the emphasis has been, first, on cost reduction, second, on increasing throughput and third, on inventory reduction. Instead Goldratt urges throughput first, inventory second and cost third. A vital change in mind-set for many managers.

Throughput accounting

In the UK 'throughput accounting' (TA) is most widely connected with the work of two consultants, David Galloway and David Waldron, who coined the term in 1988 and publicized it in a series of articles in the professional journal of the Chartered Institute of Management Accountants, *Management Accounting*. In the US the term 'throughput accounting' refers to the work of Goldratt and is developed from his theory of constraints. In the UK confusion can arise because, while Galloway and Waldron share many of Goldratt's ideas (Waldron having worked for a Goldratt company in the mid 1980s), there are many points of difference and some antipathy between the two camps. We have, therefore, tried to separate the work of Goldratt from that of Galloway and Waldron as clearly as possible.

Galloway and Waldron's TA

Galloway and Waldron claim that a new language for manufacturing is needed to replace traditional concepts such as direct/indirect costs, economic batch sizes and the idea of adding value to stock. Waldron (1988) contrasted traditional concepts with the new throughput ideas (see Table 7.2).

Table 7.2 Throughput accounting

Fundamental concepts of conventional cost accounting	*New principles of throughput accounting*
There are direct and indirect costs: direct costs are variable and indirect costs are fixed	Distinguishing between indirect and direct costs is no longer useful
Summing component costs to derive a product cost and subtracting the result from the sales price is a good way to determine relative product profitability	It is the rate at which the factory earns money that determines profitability, not the contribution of each product
Inventory is an asset and working on material increases its value	Inventory is not an asset. It is the product of unsynchronized manufacturing and stands between you and profit
Reducing component costs directly increases profit	Profit is a function of material cost, total factory cost and throughput

Adapted from: Waldron, 1988

Galloway and Waldron claim that, with the introduction of JIT, TQM and computer integrated manufacturing, a new approach is needed to link manufacturing response time, inventory and profit. Manufacturing should be seen as an integrated whole with costs which are largely pre-determined:

> It is most useful and infinitely simpler to consider the entire cost, excluding material, as fixed and to call this cost the 'Total Factory Cost'
> (Galloway and Waldron 1988a, p. 34)

In their second article Galloway and Waldron (1988b) introduce the 'TA ratio'. They suggest that the TA ratio be used to rank individual products:

$$\text{If:} \quad \text{Return per factory hour} = \frac{\text{Sales} - \text{Material cost}}{\text{Time on key resource}}$$

And: Cost per factory hour $=\dfrac{\text{Total factory cost}}{\text{Total time on the key resource}}$

Then: TA ratio $=\dfrac{\text{Return per factory hour}}{\text{Cost per factory hour}}$

Galloway and Waldron furnish an example (based on a knitwear factory) in order to make the use of the TA ratio clear (see Table 7.3).

Table 7.3 An example of the TA ratio in use

Product Line	Sales price less materials (£)	Bottleneck time (minutes)	Return per hour (£)	TA ratio
Centaur	117	91	77	1.10
Oxford	137	43	191	2.73
Jesmeda	76	38	120	1.72
Iris	129	180	43	0.61
Westminster	90	44	123	1.75

Note: Cost per factory hour = £70
Adapted from: Galloway and Waldron, 1988b, p. 35

Galloway and Waldron would argue that the 'best' product is Oxford followed by Westminster. We should note that the same ranking of products is derived whether it is based on the TA ratio or on the penultimate column 'Return per hour'. This latter measure is, of course, better known to accountants as 'contribution per unit of limiting factor' (the limiting factor here being time on the bottleneck). The TA ratio can indicate whether, if a single product were manufactured, a profit would result. However, as a means of ranking products it seems to be unnecessarily complicated. (In order to derive the TA ratio for each product the return per hour for each product is divided by 'Cost per factory hour' – but this is the same for every product and so, for ranking purposes, provides no additional information.)

The TA ratio embodies the same idea as contribution per unit of limiting factor. Indeed, if materials *were* the only variable cost, contribution and throughput would be identical and there would be no difference between traditional contribution analysis and 'throughput' analysis.

In their third article Galloway and Waldron (1989a) introduce the 'primary ratio'. Instead of defining profit as 'Throughput less factory cost' (analogous to Goldratt's 'Throughput less operational expense') Galloway and Waldron prefer a ratio:

$$\text{Primary ratio} = \frac{\text{Throughput}}{\text{Total Factory Cost}} \qquad \text{or T/TFC}$$

For a profitable operation the 'primary ratio' will be greater than one.

Galloway and Waldron go on to construct departmental performance measures and, to do this, they need a measure of 'departmental throughput'. Remembering that throughput has been defined as 'Sales revenue less materials' the reader might expect to see a departmental measure based on departmental 'sales'. However this would imply transfer pricing between departments, and, perhaps in order to avoid this potential quagmire, Galloway and Waldron preferred a time-based measure:

$$\begin{array}{lll} \text{Departmental} & \text{Standard} & \text{Budgeted} \\ \text{throughput} & = \text{minutes} & \times \text{departmental} \\ & \text{of throughput} & \text{cost per minute} \end{array}$$

Throughput is based on the standard minute content of components made to schedule, and valuation of departmental output is then based on budgeted departmental cost per minute which is itself calculated by dividing the department's operating cost by total budgeted time. Galloway and Waldron do not provide an example so it is unclear whether the evaluation of departmental throughput is to relate only to output from the departmental 'bottleneck' or 'focal point'. However, to be consistent with their approach to product costing (Galloway and Waldron, 1989b), the evaluation would be based on output from the bottleneck only. For example, if budgeted departmental costs were £250,000 and budgeted focal point capacity 2,000 hours then:

$$\text{Cost per minute} = \frac{£250,000}{2,000 \text{ hours}} = £125 \text{ per hour}$$

If 100 units were produced, each worth six standard hours of focal point time, then:

Departmental thoughput =
100 units × 6 hours × £125 per hour = £75,000

The reader should note that, in constructing this new departmental measure, Galloway and Waldron have been driven into using concepts from the outmoded 'cost world': standard minutes and budgeted costs. Nevertheless, if only output from the focal point is to count as throughput, then the new measure might encourage output from the key resource and discourage unneeded output from other resources.

An interview with Waldron (1994) revealed a continuing commitment to departmental measures and he had now evolved a different measure:

$$\text{Departmental ratio} = \frac{\text{Throughput}}{\text{Total facility cost}} \quad \text{or } \mathbf{t/tfc}$$

Although, superficially, this ratio appears to be consistent with the 'primary ratio' for the factory as a whole (**T/TFC**), attempts to define departmental throughput still pose problems. Departmental throughput is to be evaluated only in terms of product produced to schedule (neither early nor late) and, in order to place a value on this output, Waldron proposed:

> Material value or some form of product cost value. It doesn't matter as long as it is consistent.
>
> (Waldron, 1994)

But, **t** is not related to revenue, and so is inconsistent with **T**.

Determining **tfc** also posed problems. In theory we might expect all the individual facility costs to sum to the 'Total Factory Cost' but this would, of course, lead into traditional problems of cost allocation and apportionment. Waldron side-stepped these problems:

> One of the big steps was to say that the sum of all the 'little tfc' didn't have to equal 'big TFC' – in other words I didn't have to allocate things that are difficult to allocate.
>
> (Waldron, 1994)

Thus, neither the numerator nor the denominator in **t/tfc** is consistent with **T/TFC**. Given the emphasis in throughput accounting on aligning local measures with the global goal of 'making money' these deficiencies seem to be a significant theoretical defect in TA.

Whether such theoretical niceties matter in practice depends upon whether the proposed measures have the desired effect. According to Waldron the use of **t/tfc** will encourage supervisors to strive to meet schedule (increasing **t**) whilst simultaneously using less materials, people and power (reducing **tfc**).

> This has totally changed the supervisor's job. I've made him responsible – financially – for his section.
>
> (Waldron, 1994)

Whilst the use of the departmental ratio may have the consequences desired by Waldron we should note the almost total divergence from Goldratt's thinking. If the supervisor succeeds in meeting schedules the only avenue for improvement then becomes reduction in facility costs – indeed the supervisor, now financially responsible for his section, may concentrate on cost reduction. But this is hardly in line with Goldratt's emphasis on throughput as management's number one priority. It smacks more of a reversion to 'cost world' thinking and even seems to be somewhat inconsistent with Galloway and Waldron's earlier insistence that Total Factory Cost be considered fixed.

In their fourth article Galloway and Waldron (1989b) note that, in a complex manufacturing environment, there may be several manufacturing facilities and, within each facility, the 'focal point' needs to be identified. Then:

$$\text{Cost per focal point minute} = \frac{\text{Total facility cost}}{\text{Focal point capacity (minutes)}}$$

Galloway and Waldron conclude by showing how product costs can be compiled on TA principles:

$$\text{Product cost} = \begin{array}{c}\text{Time required} \\ \text{on focal point}\end{array} \times \begin{array}{c}\text{Cost per focal} \\ \text{point minute}\end{array} + \begin{array}{c}\text{Material} \\ \text{cost}\end{array}$$

Galloway and Waldron clarify their ideas with an example of a facility for pressing chassis components involving six separate operations, where operation number 4 is on the presses themselves – the focal point of the facility (see Box 7.6).

Throughput based product costs would penalize products which make heavy use of the focal points while products which do not pass through these points would be costed as materials only. We were rather sceptical about the practical application of throughput product costs and, when we put this to Waldron, he agreed that he no longer regarded TA as a product costing system. He now saw activity-based costing (ABC) as more appropriate for product costing:

> Some sectors of the accounting world would want to set TA against ABC . . . that's a whole lot of junk because you need the added information and they're both adding something . . . [ABC] doesn't tell you anything about how the business can make money . . . It doesn't tell you how many [products] I can make, or how fast . . . [but] TA will never tell you the right price to go to the market with for a product. So you need both . . . TA is not a product costing system.
>
> (Waldron, 1994)

Box 7.1 An example of product costing

1 Processing time for three products

Product	Production operations (minutes)						Total
	1	2	3	4	5	6	
A	0.34	–	0.41	0.12	0.22	–	1.09
B	–	0.13	0.41	0.14	–	0.18	0.86
C	0.27	0.44	–	0.09	–	0.23	1.03

The cost of the facility is £9,503 per week (based only on those costs which can be readily attributed to the facility) and focal point capacity is 7,920 minutes per week. Therefore:

tfc per minute = 9,503/7,920 = £1.20 per minute

The cost of each component can then be calculated.

2 TA product costing for the three products

Product	Focal point time (minutes)	Total facility cost per minute (£)	Product cost (£)
A	0.12	1.20	0.144
B	0.14	1.20	0.168
C	0.09	1.20	0.108

For complex products, component costs would be calculated and then summed.

Adapted from: Galloway and Waldron, 1989b, p. 41

Goldratt versus Galloway and Waldron

Although there are similarities in the work of Goldratt and that of Galloway and Waldron there are also major differences. The main similarities are in the definitions of throughput and operating expense (Galloway and Waldron's factory cost). And both Goldratt and Galloway and Waldron place some emphasis on the use of 'throughput per bottleneck minute' in making product mix decisions.

However, Galloway and Waldron diverge from Goldratt in their attempt to derive local performance measures consistent with overall measures of throughput. They have encountered a number of technical problems in this endeavour (relating to the measurement of 'throughput' at departmental level and the allocation/apportionment of costs) and Goldratt would be suspicious of *any* attempt to create local measures of 'efficiency' because of the dangers of local sub-optimization. The difficulties encountered by Galloway and Waldron will be familiar to many accountants!

Galloway and Waldron also diverge from Goldratt in their attempt to create throughput-based product costs. Although the use of TA as a product costing system is no longer advocated, Waldron sees a key role in modern management accounting for ABC. Goldratt, on the other hand, sees activity-based costing as symptomatic of accountants continuing emphasis on 'the cost world':

> The financial community is totally immersed in an attempt to save the obsolete situation . . . 'cost drivers' and 'activity-based costing' are the names of these fruitless efforts . . . We fell in love with a technique. We forgot the purpose – to be able to judge the impact of any local decision on the bottom line.
>
> (Goldratt, 1990, pp. 40–41)

Finally, compare Galloway and Waldron's views on stock holding and stock reduction with those of Goldratt. Galloway and Waldron are unequivocal:

> Above all else, we must remember the one truth – any decision which increases inventory is a bad decision.
>
> (1989a, p33)

Again, Galloway and Waldron diverge from Goldratt because this would apply to the stock buffers which, in the theory of constraints, protect production bottlenecks. When we put this to Waldron (1994) he argued that TOC's buffers incline managers to be relaxed about production constraints instead of striving to break them. Waldron preferred JIT principles, setting a target of zero stock, rather than TOC.

Accounting for throughput in practice

This section presents a detailed case study of one company where accountants were influenced by throughput thinking. It is constructed from interviews we carried out between 1993 and 1995 with accounting, production, production control and marketing staff. We have disguised the name of the company and made some minor changes to the data to preserve anonymity.

Automek(UK) is a component supplier to the automotive industry. Founded in 1970 it manufactures 'meks' which, traditionally, have been supplied to the commercial diesel engine market (for trucks, tractors, etc.) but, in the 1980s, a new market emerged for meks in both the diesel and petrol engine passenger car market. The company experienced expanding markets even when the UK and world economies have suffered recessions. In fact, demand always outstripped supply so, in essence, the levels of sales achieved by the company was determined by its ability to increase its manufacturing output.

Such a position may appear enviable, but it brought attendant problems for managers. Customers, many of whom represented the giant automobile corporations, were constantly complaining about missed due dates. Supervisors spent much of their time frantically expediting to get orders out of the factory. Managers regarded their workers as ill-disciplined (and their trade union as too powerful) because they had not experienced the economic insecurity of other workforces. When the company became part of PolyCo (a US multinational) it was also affected by a corporate strategy in the late 1980s which directed passenger mek production to another European division and left Automek(UK) with the less profitable commercial business. The lower-volume, shorter-run lines of commercial meks created more production difficulties. These were exacerbated when an attempted tougher approach to industrial relations culminated in a strike in the summer of 1989. With the supply of meks cut off, major automotive companies put pressure on the PolyCo head office in the USA, Automek(UK) management was instructed to settle with the union, and the dispute left a legacy of bitterness on both sides. In 1990 the company made an operating loss, and the pressure from PolyCo for improvements in performance increased.

Changes in production

Production in the mid-1980s was a mixture of the long-established commercial meks (low volumes and a competitive market) and the new passenger meks (where volumes were increasing in a rapidly expanding market). Production was typically conducted in large batches, the whole batch would be milled, then held as work-in-progress, drilled and tapped, again held as work-in-progress, then deburred and washed. Lead-times were long, stock high (over £6 million) and the assembly section could still be stopped for lack of parts.

1980s' accounting practices were typical of many companies in the period. A traditional standard costing system was in place for financial reporting and management accounting. Production variances for labour, material and overhead were calculated and monthly reports distributed to managers. There was a commonly held view that variances were used to 'beat up' production management and both production managers and accountants were aware of the dangers of over-zealous use of these measures. Efficiency and utilization measures could be manipulated, unproductive witch-hunts could be started and managers could build parts for stock knowing this would impact favourably on efficiency and recovery measures.

Probably the most important change came in 1988 with the introduction of OPT. This was championed by the production control manager and considerable effort was expended in training managers and workers in the new system. In programming OPT, managers first identified the production of one of the five mek sub-assemblies as the overall constraint on the plant, since it was here that the greatest variation was experienced incurring many time-consuming set-up changes. Then key machines were identified in every section of production and production managers' attention was focused on maximizing their utilization whilst being instructed to run non-bottleneck machines under capacity so as not to produce unnecessary stock. There was a considerable change in emphasis in production thinking. Now throughput was seen as more important than individual machine utilizations and the production control schedule adherence reports took on greater importance. The introduction of OPT led to a steady reduction in work-in-progress – which fell to about £2.5 million over two years – and this, together with smaller batch sizes, led to reduced production lead-times.

The late 1980s also saw rationalization of production accomplished by consolidation of the operation on a single site. This was accompanied by re-organization of production into six 'cells' based on the five mek sub-assemblies and an assembly cell. A plant management/supervision structure was replaced by one based on six cell managers and the intent was to integrate production support services such as manufacturing engineering into the cell management structure. The re-organization and rationalization included an attempt to enforce redundancies which led to the 1989 strike.

There were difficulties in implementing OPT. Several production managers commented on the problems inherent in setting up for excessively small batches and the OPT schedules did not always seem sensible from a production management standpoint. Nevertheless, the key ideas embodied in OPT *were* implemented. There was considerable commitment to the ideas and the work of Eli Goldratt, especially his novel *The Goal*, was well known. Production managers and workers were familiar with the book:

Reading *The Goal* was important. It was readily available [in the company].

It was promoted at the same time as OPT.

> It's all basic stuff, but that book – *The Goal* –put it into perspective, into an actual situation . . . It's well written, it's so logical.

The Goal and later works by Goldratt introduced TOC to the plant with its language of 'throughput', 'drum-buffer-rope' and 'constraints' and, to some extent, this replaced the older vocabulary of 'efficiency', 'utilization' and 'control'. The impact of the ideas on production managers varied considerably. Some (perhaps because of previous experience or training) saw the ideas as just common sense. Some found the change to be quite revolutionary:

> You used to go round a factory and see all the work-in-progress stacked about the shop and say, 'Blimey, you're doing well'. Today I see the same thing and think, 'Blimey, you're in a mess'.

The introduction of new scheduling ideas, organization structure and production rationalization was accompanied by efforts to streamline production. Where possible, production flow-lines and U-lines were set up and some managers worked to improve the flexibility of labour within their cells. This was in line with the corporate 'philosophy' of the time which emphasized team-work, cycle-time reduction and continuous improvement.

Impact of throughput thinking on accounting

In many companies the introduction of OPT software has little, if any, impact on accounting. Typically, production management install and implement the software without impacting accounting tasks and reports. Our case study company was different.

With the company losing money in 1990, the financial controller felt that existing financial measures were unhelpful and was receptive to new ideas. Even so, his first reading of *The Goal* had not impressed him and neither had a visit to the plant by Galloway and Waldron. Given the publicity which activity-based costing was receiving at the time, the technique was considered and a major consulting group prepared a proposal to introduce a major system. The financial controller remembered that they were 'On the verge of saying "Yes"', but attendance at an ABC conference did not enthuse him. By chance, whilst attending this conference, invitations to a Goldratt event were received, and the financial controller left the unfinished conference to hear Goldratt speak to a large forum. This experience changed the direction of accounting within Automek(UK).

The introduction of OPT at Automek(UK) had not been expected to affect the finance function at all. However, the tight schedules generated by this software had the effect of limiting production in some areas. This did not affect deliveries because production through manufacturing bottlenecks was still maximized. It did, however, begin to reduce the substantial investment in inventory and under-recovery of overhead (consequent on limited production schedules) had an adverse effect on reported profits. Automek(UK) management were pleased with the changes taking place, as production became slicker and the liquidation of stock generated a healthy cash inflow. However, the financial controller identified two problems. First, there was pressure from PolyCo head office who wanted cost cutting measures and headcount reductions: 'their knee-jerk reaction to a loss-making plant'. Second, the accounting measures used internally, 'especially the efficiency report' were not congruent with the impact of OPT. Hearing Goldratt crystallized these issues and led to rapid change in management accounting and production management philosophy.

A number of traditional measures were now seen as unhelpful. Measures of efficiency and overhead recovery were no longer considered useful: 'We realized that we were pushing for overhead recovery [and there was] no point'. The danger of traditional measures causing sub-optimal behaviour was now recognized and the key measure became 'schedule adherence'. Production managers should ensure that OPT schedules were met precisely – no more and no less. The switch to schedule adherence was made during 1991 and traditional efficiency reporting was abruptly withdrawn. Whether such an abrupt change was desirable is unclear; certainly it provoked adverse reaction:

> We withdrew variances, efficiencies and recoveries and replaced them with monitoring schedule adherence overnight. Reaction was terrible.

Although production management had previously been 'battered' for low efficiency and recovery they were not pleased by the new measures:

> They wanted to know their efficiencies again [so as to] transfer hours [from direct labour to overhead categories], build for stock, etc.

> Cell managers knew how to manipulate efficiency. They didn't know what schedule adherence was.

The management accountant thought that more preparation and education would have been desirable while the financial controller was less concerned. He noted that schedule adherence as a 'naive measure' worked well while cell managers were also naive!

The use of schedule adherence was later accompanied by the introduction of a 'throughput profit and loss account' which replaced the 'standard cost profit and loss account' inside the company (whilst reports to division were still based on the standard cost P&L). The throughput P&L was extremely simple (see Figure 7.3).

	£
Sales revenue	xxx
Materials	(xx)
Materials price and exchange variances	x
Throughput	xx
Expense	(xx)
Net profit	x

Figure 7.3   *Automek (UK) throughput P&L*

The format is obviously heavily influenced by Goldratt's ideas, and can be seen as an extreme form of direct or variable costing. Only materials are treated as direct costs whilst the remainder, including so-called 'direct' labour, are treated as fixed and written off as period expenses. Whilst it is clearly unsuitable for financial reporting it is simple and easily understood by operating managers. The throughput P&L was: 'Wonderfully received, they liked it because it was a lot simpler'. The financial controller also preferred the throughput P&L as an indicator of business performance because it was not distorted by spurious 'under recovery' of production overhead whilst stock was falling as was the traditional 'standard cost' P&L. Gradually other measures were added to cell managers' monthly accounting packages – days inventory on-hand, manufacturing cycle time, cost of quality, customer due-date performance. To facilitate the flow of information accountants were allocated, on a fractional time basis, to work closely with production staff.

Accountants considered providing a throughput P&L at cell level, but were very aware of the potential problems:

> Do you give it a transfer price of, say, you've recovered so many hours, therefore its the standard cost sent to another cell ... It's always been a problem hasn't it, reducing global perspectives down to [something] like a manufacturing cell.

Given their new antipathy to standard costing, this approach was rejected and no cell level P&L was produced.

Like Galloway and Waldron, these accountants were interested in developing local measures consistent with overall throughput ideas. An attempt was made to compare the value of throughput with the cost of a production cell, but:

> We did try to work out how much each cell was costing and [compare with] . . . throughput for the month [but it was]. . . getting very complicated trying to value throughput on these particular units.

Again only standard costs seemed to provide a basis for deriving transfer prices and the attempt was not pursued further.

The financial controller ensured the commitment of the accounting department to 'throughput thinking' by his recruitment and training policies. He took the ideas to local universities and presented them to economics and accounting undergraduates. This initiative led to the appointment of three graduates in the department. All three confirmed the commitment to throughput ideas when they arrived. The financial controller's infectious enthusiasm was transmitted to his staff who were given *The Goal* to read. They also played the 'P&Q' simulation model (developed by Goldratt to illustrate the importance of basing decisions on throughput/constraint analysis) well into the evenings.

The two recruits who had concentrated on management accounting still clearly favoured throughput approaches:

> People took to [the throughput P&L] quite readily because it's a lot easier to look at than to start talking about overhead rates and under/over recovery.

> We're not busy allocating [cost] . . . we're not going to run a machine just to get an efficiency out of it.

There was strong antipathy to activity-based costing:

> Polyco (France) use activity-based costing . . . The time they've taken. I just couldn't believe it.

> [The Financial Controller] wouldn't allow ABC books in the office.

However, the third graduate who worked on traditional reports for the division was less emphatic. The traditional standard costing system has been maintained to facilitate preparation of the requisite divisional reports and this accountant saw dangers in the production of two P&Ls:

> I think that's very dangerous because the local people will see one set of profits, the Corporation will see another . . . perhaps we're showing more throughput profits . . . [This could encourage] a pay claim . . . but to America we've done averagely.

Although standard costing remained in place for financial reporting purposes, it was considered inappropriate for management decisions at cell level and efforts were made to keep the information off the shop-floor. Standard cost information was kept in a separate computer directory with a special password which was not available to those outside the finance department except for senior management:

> Here's some more information we don't allow anyone to see – efficiency rates used to grade managers good, bad or efficient, inefficient. [They were] dropped just before I came [because they] caused people to produce things they didn't need to produce.

> We never used to let standard costs out of the department, we didn't really consider them reliable enough to be able to make decisions on.

The financial controller was emphatic that the negative influence of traditional cost accounting should not confuse or hinder the positive potential of the new throughput accounting he had created.

Accounting for throughput in production

Cell managers remembered the abrupt introduction of the schedule adherence measure in place of traditional efficiency measures. In principle, most thought that schedule adherence was a good measure but its credibility depended on the creation of realistic schedules. Managers had always treated the schedules somewhat flexibly by combining some batches and there was always some schedule slippage. Slavish application of the schedule adherence measure could be counterproductive because, once a schedule was missed, the manager had no incentive to produce the requisite product – no credit would be received for late manufacture.

When the other measures of WIP, cycle-times, cost of quality, and customer performance were introduced with the package, cell managers had a clearer picture of their overall performance, but this was not of immediate significance in their management of cells. Later, figures were supplied at cell level and were converted into colourful graphics and prominently displayed on shop-floor noticeboards. However, some cell managers still felt that a single overall indication of cell performance was needed. Production managers liked the throughput P&L and some expressed interest in a throughput P&L at cell level and did not appear to appreciate the transfer pricing complications of this. They did, however, recognize a 'boundary problem' since more flexible working practices meant that labour was often shifted from cell to cell during the day. Cell managers wanted this to be effectively recorded before any 'profit' or 'loss' was ascribed to their cell.

Following the abandonment of standard hours and variances, work study was discontinued in 1991. This left cell managers with only schedule adherence as the key measure, but they were convinced that they were producing more efficiently by ignoring the detailed OPT instructions. Whether the solution would be the return of the traditional efficiency measures was influenced by their evaluation of previous practices. Some thought standard hours had been used in an unfair battering of the workforce and were out of step with modern manufacturing thinking with its emphasis on improving performance through teamwork. Others saw them as vital for planning and control purposes, and were appalled when they were removed. Some cell managers identified the new situation as a kind of 'measurement vacuum' and produced their own 'efficiency' figures. Eventually their views were accepted by higher management, and work study was re-introduced in 1994.

One change proposed by the finance department seemed to have almost universal support in principle but was difficult to achieve in practice. All the cell managers welcomed the idea of a specific accountant from the finance department being assigned as their own cell accountant, even on a part-time basis. However, some of the cell accountants were not often seen on the shop-floor, and the initiative seems to have faded. Perhaps this was due to time pressure, or lack of commitment from the top. Though accountants were notionally allocated to cells, this did not appear to imply a significant commitment, nor to lead to significant change in the relationship between production and finance.

Accounting for throughput in marketing

Whilst there was some disagreement about the use of throughput measures in production there were no such reservations in marketing. As a form of marginal costing (only material costs treated as variable) throughput accounting supported the marketing manager's drive for new business:

> How much can you *really* make the product for? . . . Business where, up to that point in time, we said 'Well this isn't worth having', if you looked at it on a throughput basis it *was* worth having.

Business was sought aggressively, quoting very competitive prices if necessary. The marketing manager was prepared to set prices below 'full absorption' break-even in order to compete with European and US competition and 'to keep the Japanese out'. The use of marginal cost based pricing when necessary was a conscious decision and the marketing manager was able to discuss the merits of other costing approaches (such as traditional absorption and activity-based) in some depth. An activity-based cost might indicate that small production quantities were not viable but:

> As soon as we start making decisions like that the business goes on to the slippery slope . . . I'm still a great believer in if there is business out there we need to have every part of it, every part we can get.

For marketing, the move towards marginal cost pricing and away from absorbed costs and gross margin targets was an unmitigated success. The insistence that a full-cost plus mark-up had to be achieved was castigated because, 'That's how you go about losing business'. The subjective and unscientific assumptions in absorbed costs were cited as problems in using them.

Throughput and company performance

The fortunes of Automek(UK) improved significantly in the 1990s. From being a loss making company in the late 1980s, by early 1994 it was showing healthy profits – in both conventional and throughput accounts (see Table 7.4). Production levels were very significantly higher, due-date delivery performance much improved, and work-in-progress slashed to less than a third of its 1990 level. A change in corporate strategy allowed Automek(UK) to bid for the more profitable passenger car business, and two new products were launched in 1993. As the financial controller put it, 'These were very sophisticated meks – and they had a very sophisticated price!' A dramatic increase in demand for meks during 1994 caused considerable production difficulties, but also led to profits 'going through the roof' later in the year. The financial controller ascribed this success to 'throughput thinking' which he had supported through the development of TA. He had got rid of the negative effects of traditional measures by purging them from the shop-floor, and had begun to encourage positive effects with the throughput P&L and new measures based around schedule adherence. Perhaps as recognition of his personal contribution to improvements he was promoted to another company within Automek (Europe).

Throughput accounting and change

This case study provides some insight into the consequences of introducing throughput ideas into accounting, production and marketing.

In accounting the most important change was in a re-evaluation of traditional performance measures and the introduction of the throughput

Table 7.4 Automek(UK) financial performance (conventional accounting)

Year	Sales (£000s)	Operating profit/(loss) (£000s)
1989	44,000	(200)
1990	44,800	50
1991	45,600	200
1992	46,000	600
1993	50,000	3000
1994	70,000	6000

Note: These numbers have been rounded.

P&L. There are now many references in the accounting literature to the unfortunate consequences of traditional efficiency and utilization measures, especially for companies which aspire to be 'world class manufacturers' employing JIT and TQM approaches. The accountants in this company now felt that efficiency and absorption measures were counterproductive and should be kept away from the shop-floor. Interestingly, they still felt that *some* measures were needed and set about the development of a new management information package based on schedule adherence, days' inventory, cost of quality, etc. Although they were not influenced by Galloway and Waldron, they have, to some extent, followed the same path. Whilst Goldratt may be correct in drawing attention to the dangers of local sub-optimization, it seems that the derivation of local measures is an important issue. This could be expected from consultants – who need new techniques and measures for their commercial credibility. However, we also think that both accountants and production managers see local measures as important. If existing measures are removed there seems to be an irresistible urge to fill the 'measurement vacuum' so that managers can have an answer to the question 'How am I doing?'.

Accountants might not see the introduction of the 'throughput P&L' as a major innovation (direct or variable costing systems being standard textbook theory). However, this was operated alongside the existing financial reporting system and the consequences of operating two systems should not be underestimated. Initially we expected accountants to see the necessary reconciliations of the two systems as a major task. However, this was not the case. The relationship between the 'throughput' and the 'standard cost' P&L was well understood and reconciliation of the two was not seen as a problem. Accountants were, however, very conscious of the dangers of supplying managers with two sets of possibly conflicting information.

In theory, throughput information was used only for internal purposes and standard cost information only for financial reporting to the division. In practice, production managers knew that efficiency calculations were still made and, occasionally, these 'came out of the closet':

> I had it thrown at me the other week . . . the pressure comes on and suddenly 'How come you're only 53 per cent efficient?'

Attempts were made to separate the two systems – for example by password protecting all standard cost information (which accountants now perceived to be dangerous in the hands of operations management). Still, there was scope for the misuse of information and one accountant expressed concern that profit information which was reported to the division differed from that used internally.

Production management in the 1990s was significantly different from that of the 1980s. Rationalization of production, the introduction of the scheduling software, OPT, and re-organization of management based on production 'cells' had all had a significant impact. Production managers broadly approved of the new accounting information and 'schedule adherence' as a measure seemed consistent with the introduction of OPT. Perhaps surprisingly, since efficiencies had historically been used to 'batter production management', a number of managers wanted standards and efficiency information to be routinely available. Whilst this might simply be seen as conservatism, the desire to retain tried and trusted measures which were well understood and 'manipulable', we think that the issue runs deeper than this. Both for planning production and for controlling what was (arguably) a recalcitrant workforce, some managers argued that standards and variances were needed. The argument in favour of work study seemed to have been won in 1994 when it was re-introduced. The arguments around efficiency calculations either as an indicator of 'whether we are getting better' or as an aid in 'getting a fair day's work for a fair day's pay' rumble on.

In marketing the introduction of 'throughput thinking' will be interpreted by many accountants as a willingness to consider marginal rather than, or as well as, full cost information in making sensitive pricing decisions. This is hardly a novel issue; the use of marginal prices based on the idea of 'contribution generation' is standard textbook theory. It seems likely that the financial controller in the case study company was rather untypical in being prepared to consider less than full-cost pricing. This can, of course, be seen as a reflection of his commitment to throughput ideas – which, for both Goldratt and Galloway and Waldron, see the majority of 'operational expense' or 'factory cost' as fixed in relation to volume. (The opposite of ABC which sees much of this expense as variable.) We suspect that the views of the company's new financial controller are more typical of finance managers in general:

> I was aware that there were some 'interesting' pricing decisions being made on the back of throughput accounting and I would regard marginal costing, which I would describe that as in its broadest sense, as a 'slippery slope to ruin'.

As the new financial controller has also introduced 'the largest ABC system in Europe' in a previous company, Automek(UK) may face some more interesting accounting changes in the future!

Whether throughput or marginal cost pricing is desirable seems, to us, to be an open question. No doubt the intransigent insistence on 'full-cost' plus target margin as a pricing policy can lead to unfortunate commercial decisions and 'throughput pricing' may provide some relief from such a rigid policy. However, many finance managers would sympathize with the views of the new financial controller, especially in a company which has consistently struggled to meet customer demand.

Conclusion

We suspect that many accountants will conclude that there is little new in throughput accounting. Certainly specific prescriptions such as the maximization of throughput (contribution) per bottleneck (constraint) minute, and the use of a variable cost P&L statement are not new. These approaches have been textbook recommendations for many years. Academic support for marginal costing has also been around for a long time. The point is that, despite this, few companies have made the kind of changes we describe in our case study company. Perhaps, as Johnson and Kaplan (1987) argued, this is because accounting information has been dominated by financial reporting. What throughput thinking offers is a new challenge to the hegemony of financial reporting systems.

The form which 'throughput accounting' takes depends upon whether practising accountants subscribe to the ideas of Goldratt, or Galloway and Waldron, or generate new ideas of their own. We have seen similarities in the work of Goldratt and Galloway and Waldron, particularly in relation to the definition of throughput and operational expense and the use of limiting factor analysis to maximize throughput. These ideas were adopted and operationalized in our case study company. Both 'throughput' and 'operational expense' appear in the 'throughput P&L', now used to disseminate information to management within the company. And the financial controller calculated 'throughput' by product line as an informational aid when making product mix decisions.

Many accountants would not see the introduction of a 'throughput P&L' or the use of 'product throughput' as particularly novel. The theory of marginal or variable cost accounting has been in the textbooks for many years. It has also been pointed out to us that the throughput P&L is no more than a 'value added' statement – an idea which had a short vogue in the 1970s. We do think, however, that this view understates the developments in our case study company. Whilst the idea of a variable cost P&L is well understood there is little evidence that companies actually use them. One of the authors visited 20 companies in the late 1980s without finding one. Our case study company was an exception and provides an example of information being developed for **management information** alongside traditional systems, still needed for **financial reporting**.

If there is common ground in the definition and use of basic throughput ideas there is less agreement on the manner in which the basic ideas might be developed and extended. Galloway and Waldron devote considerable effort to the development of local (departmental) performance measures. They encountered considerable difficulties in this and Goldratt would see the whole effort as mistaken. However, accountants in our case study company also devoted considerable effort to the development of local performance measures. Like Galloway and Waldron they concentrated on schedule adherence as a key departmental measure but, unlike Galloway and Waldron, they did not place a financial valuation on this.

In their original work Galloway and Waldron went to some lengths to derive throughput based product costs. However, Waldron now sees activity-based costs as more useful and no longer regards TA as a product costing system. Goldratt would see the development of *any* 'absorbed' product cost as mistaken. In our case study company accountants were suspicious of traditional 'standard' costs and their potential for mis-use. Their use of material costs as a form of marginal product cost in advising marketing management is very much in line with Goldratt's thinking.

Whilst Goldratt and Galloway and Waldron share some common definitions and basic ideas (not surprisingly since Waldron was heavily influenced by Goldratt in the mid 1980s) there are major differences in their work. Galloway and Waldron concentrate on the development of detailed performance measures including an emphasis on local (facility) cost control. Goldratt abhors local measures in general and calls for a **paradigm shift** away from the **cost world** and in favour of the **throughput world**. Our case study company has been most heavily influenced by Goldratt's thinking, both through the implementation of OPT which incorporates much of Goldratt's early thinking and through Goldratt's writing and the work of the Goldratt Institute which has organized training courses for company personnel.

The changes in our case study company do not go as far as those advocated by Goldratt. They do include the removal of traditional control measures from the shop-floor and the introduction of an internal P&L for 'management information' alongside traditional financial reporting (now used only for reporting to the division). However, there is continuing commitment in the case study company both to cost control (partly a consequence of very tight controls imposed by PolyCo) and to the development of local performance measures.

It may be that neither Goldratt's broad vision of a throughput paradigm nor the particular detailed measures derived by Galloway and Waldron can be easily implemented. However, we conclude that TOC and TA *have* changed the way information is presented in one company and, through the introduction of OPT, use of the schedule adherence measure, and greater flexibility in the use of marginal costing have affected both production and marketing management. The company's journey from operating loss in 1990 to significant operating profit in 1994 clearly involved many factors not directly related to accounting – improvements in manufacturing techniques and re-entry to the passenger vehicle market being especially important. However, to the extent that throughput thinking led to removal of some of the negative features of conventional accounting, and TA provided positive encouragement to managers who were persuaded by the TOC approach, we conclude that the new accounting facilitated change in the company.

References

Brimson, J. A. (1988). CAM-I cost management systems project, in (eds R. Cappettini and D. K. Clancy) *Cost Accounting, Robotics and the New Manufacturing Environment*, New York: American Accounting Association.

Galloway, D. and Waldron, D. (1988a). Throughput Accounting – 1: The need for a new language for manufacturing, *Management Accounting*, November, 34–5.

Galloway, D. and Waldron, D. (1988b). Throughput Accounting – 2: Ranking products profitably, *Management Accounting*, December, 34–5.

Galloway, D. and Waldron, D. (1989a). Throughput Accounting – 3: A better way to control labour costs, *Management Accounting*, January, 32–3.

Galloway, D. and Waldron, D. (1989b). Throughput Accounting – 4: Moving on to complex products, *Management Accounting*, February, 40–41.

Goldratt, E. M. (1994). *It's Not Luck*, London: Gower.

Goldratt, E. M. (1990a). *The Haystack Syndrome*, New York: North River Press.

Goldratt, E. M. (1990b). *Theory of Constraints*, New York: North River Press.

Goldratt, E. M. and Cox, J. (1984). *The Goal*, London: Gower.

Goldratt, E. M. and Cox, J. (1993). *The Goal* (2nd edition), London: Gower.

Goldratt, E. M. and Fox, R. (1986). *The Race*, New York: North River Press.

Johnson, H. T. and Kaplan, R. S. (1987). *Relevance Lost: The Rise and Fall of Management Accounting*, Cambridge, Mass.: Harvard Business School Press.

Noreen, E., Smith, D. and Mackey, J. T. (1995). *The Theory of Constraints and its Implications for Management Accounting*, New York: North River Press.

Waldron, D. (1988). Accounting for CIM: the new yardsticks, *EMAP Business and Computing Supplement*, February, 1–2.

Waldron, D. (1994). *Research Interview*, February.

8

Measuring for today and tomorrow: the role of non-financial performance assessment

Mohamed Zairi

Financial measures have traditionally been the cornerstone of the performance measured system. To counterbalance the over-emphasis on financial measures increasing attention is now being given to non-financial measures that provide feedback on the key variables that are required to compete successfully in today's competitive environment. In recent years there has been a shift from treating financial figures as the foundation for performance measurement and control to treating them as one among a broader set of measures. In this chapter Professor Mohammed Zairi describes how non-financial measures are being applied in a modern business context.

The evolution of financial measurement systems

Traditional performance measurement systems go back a long way in their origin and applications. It is thought, for instance, that double-entry book-keeping was first used in Venice around the fourteenth century. The following evolutionary steps then took place:

- The period of the nineteenth century and the coming of the industrial revolution led to the creation of more comprehensive financial measurement systems, to meet the requirements of entrepreneurs.
- Systems developed included conversion costs, costs per tonne/per unit, material and labour costs, allocation of overheads.
- Cost and profit centres and financial companies were developed by the mid-nineteenth century. Indicators used were all efficiency based.
- Frederick Taylor's scientific management was introduced around 1911

where it was argued that division and specialization of labour would lead to greater productivity. Workers were considered as a standard extension to machines doing routine and tightly controlled jobs. Standard production methods were used and standard costing techniques applied.

- The principles of capital investment appraisal, budgeting, performance measurement, variance accounting and return on investment (ROI) were introduced in the 1920s.
- By the 1930s fully integrated cost and management accounting systems were developed, regulated, subjected to independent auditing and linked to external financial operating systems (Taylor, 1992).
- However, since the 1930s there was no real change to the existing systems apart from occasional cosmetic changes. The cost management accounting systems therefore became unable to meet modern business requirements and incompatible with the fast pace of change and technological advancement that had been witnessed particularly in the 1980s and 1990s.

The concern about the limitations of existing performance measurement systems has been in both academic circles and by most industrialists. Most arguments presented seem to be about the fact that existing cost management systems are unable to help organizations implement modern management concepts such as just-in-time (JIT) and total quality management (TQM) amongst others (Maskell, 1989; Dixon et al., 1990; Goldratt and Cox, 1986; Kaplan, 1984; Edwards, 1985; Drury, 1990).

Management accounting systems were particularly criticized for:

- their incompatibility and lack of relevance to the demands of the modern business environment;
- big distortions and inaccuracies since they focused on product costs and not the process;
- their inability to incorporate change and their remoteness from the process; and
- making the vision of best-in-class difficult to achieve since they only focused on short-term results.

Johnson and Kaplan (1987) for instance voiced their concern as follows:

> Today's management accounting information, driven by the procedures and cycle of the organisation's financial reporting system, is too late, too aggregated, and too distorted to be relevant for managers' planning and control decisions.

These criticisms were also echoed elsewhere by McNair et al. (1990). They insist that:

Managers need clear, timely and relevant signals from their internal information systems to understand root causes or problems, to initiate corrective action, and to support decisions at all levels of the organisation.

Further explanations and discussions on the shortcomings of financial performance measurement systems are provided in the following sections.

The traditional approach to performance measurement

The traditional approach to performance measurement (PM) is based on cost accounting techniques that have been found to have a large number of limitations associated with them.

- Most performance measures are derived from cost accounting information (most of which is over fifty years old).
- Cost accounting data is often based on out-dated and irrelevant principles. Most of the time it produces irrelevant or misleading information.
- Performance is often tracked in isolated areas (single dimensions).
- Management decisions are based on cost accounting information. Since performance is measured in specific areas only, managers tend to find themselves unable to assess whether they have implemented their strategies effectively.
- Cost accounting information is unable to map process performance. PM is designed by people who are often too remote from the process and with very little understanding of how it works.
- One of the biggest shortcomings of traditional PM is the failure to take into account the customer perspective, whether internal or external. This encouraged the development of an attitude based on 'Let's carve the market for ourselves!'
- Cost accounting techniques were more relevant in a business environment based on low technology and high labour content. This, however, is no longer the case in the context of modern businesses.
- Performance measures that produced bottom-line financial results are too late for carrying out corrective action.

Economic models of performance measurement

Amongst the various economic models of PM the most widely used is perhaps return on investment, a measure developed by DuPont in 1919. Figure 8.1 illustrates the breakdown of the ROI formula.

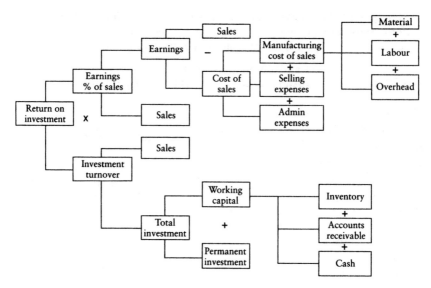

Figure 8.1   *An example of an economic measure: return on investment (ROI)*

ROI, although still very widely used, has many shortcomings.

- ROI has originally been designed as a long-term measure. However, it is being used as a short-term measure.
- ROI is inaccurate and irrelevant for detailed and complex projects. It has proved to be ineffective in justifying investment in innovations such as advanced manufacturing technology.
- Many managers, particularly in the West, are interested only in short-term measures. This is because executive bonuses are based on short-term performance.
- Many managers have a very poor understanding of processes and products, hence their interest in financial indicators.
- Financial indicators have remained static whilst the business environment has changed dramatically.
- ROI is a single-period measurement – it ignores events beyond the current period. As such, ROI tells us what happened, not what is happening or what will happen.
- ROI can only be worked out after profits are calculated for a period of time.
- The use of ROI as a long-term measure is often abused. For example, the evaluation of strategic requirements (long-term) and PM (short-term) can lead to a discriminatory allocation of resources, often to

ensure that short-term goals are achieved to the detriment of long-term objectives.

Traditional and improvement measures: a comparison

The basic difference between PM based on standard, for example, and TQM-based PM is that the former places more emphasis on the method and the latter on people.

Table 8.1 illustrates the difference between the two approaches. TQM-based performance is based on people productivity, their empowerment and involvement and giving them total ownership in the design, control and measurement of their processes.

Table 8.1 Performance management: people versus method approach

The people approach	*The method approach*
High performance can be achieved through people.	High performance can be best secured by first analysing the work which needs to be done, and then designing the most efficient sequence or method of work activities.
Competent, motivated people will evolve their own best methods of working.	People follow method.

Table 8.2 on the other hand compares some management techniques based on the method approach and others that are geared towards optimizing human creativity. Some of the techniques still used, such as management by objectives and job evaluation, are detrimental to people's creativity since they instigate fear, resentment, isolation and do not encourage participation and employee involvement at all. Other methods are more about producing quotas and statistics which managers will use to make decisions without consultation, involvement or listening to the voice of the performers – those who own and manage various organizational processes on an everyday basis.

Table 8.2 illustrates a complete shift in emphasis. In the traditional approach, PM tended to be based on methods. Managers were, therefore, trained to use a wide variety of methods that would enable them to plan, control and measure activities with a selective approach of fitting people in according to the task and based on the requirements set by the method. In

Table 8.2 Performance management techniques based on method versus people approach

The people approach	The method approach
Selection test techniques	Work study
Training need analysis	Critical path analysis
Training techniques	Operational research
Joint consultation	O&M
Industrial democracy	PPBR
Merit rating	Cost/benefit analysis
Quality circles	Job evaluation
Human resource planning	Statistical manpower planning
Performance related pay	Management by objectives

a TQM-based environment, however, the whole emphasis on running business operations is based on people: from their recruitment to their developing and setting the climate which would enable them to be most creative.

Why do we need new measures?

The following arguments are presented to help provide explanations about the need for new performance measures.

1 The management approach has moved from manager-centred to customer-centred. The emphasis in a modern business context is delivering quality rather than producing quantity.
2 Direct physical measures are an effective means to decision making; unlike traditional measures, the new measures such as cost, quality and time can lead to action on the spot and decisions taken at the right time to make necessary adjustments and bring about any corrections. Hence, what is delivered to the customer can remain of high quality.
3 Measuring through the voice of the process: measuring the capability of the process (i.e. control measures such as SPC) and the consistency of the process (i.e. feedback measures such as time, quality and cost) determines the overall capability of the organization and as such enables senior managers to define parameters of competitiveness.
4 New measures can support strategic direction and make goal setting a more achievable task. The lack of performance measurement with strategy is recognized by most authors. Vollmann (1991) for instance argued that one of the fundamental attributes of an effective performance measurement system is that it should 'encourage actions congruent with the company's business strategy'.

As will be argued later, the effectiveness of the implementation of TQ-based performance measurement systems is heavily dependent on strategy formulation and implementation. There is total inter-dependence and effective strategic planning has to rely on continuous feedback resulting from continuous measurement. As Sink (1991) argues:

> Improving strategic planning is critical to developing measurement systems for world-class competition.

Examples of best practice measures

Table 8.3 EQA Award winners

Quality	Defects improvement (% better than previous year); quality certification (% part, processes, operators certified as meeting quality standards)
Delivery	% production delivery (commitments met)
Cycle time reduction	Manufacturing inventory including work in progress (days of supply)
Time to market	Time from decision to market a product through the design and development, prototypes to the start of production
Manufacturing	Supplier lead time improvements (% who achieved better than 8 week's lead time, % within a day's transport time of factory)
Logistics	Order to install time improvement (order, allocate, deliver, install)
Customer service response times	Product repair cycle times (% better than target); customer queries outstanding over 5 days

Examples of non-financial performance measurement systems

The balanced scoreboard model

- Proposed by Kaplan and Norton (1993) and based on a 12 month research project involving twelve leading companies.
- The model covers areas which are all core to business competitiveness. It addresses four critical sets of issues:
  - Having a customer perspective: All businesses exist to satisfy customer requirements. In order to compete successfully, there is a

Table 8.4 MBNQA Award winners

Measure	Indicator(s)
Service measures to customers (Wallace)	On-time delivery performance; complete and accurate shipments; error-free transactions
Service quality indicators (SQI) (Federal Express)	Right day late service failures; wrong day late service failures; traces (no proof of performance request where some information cannot be located); complaints reopened by customers; missing proof of delivery (MOD); invoice adjustments requested; missed pickups, damaged packages; lost packages; abandoned calls
Productivity measures (IBM Rochester)	% increase in world-wide production installations against previous year; % customers who would recommend IBM products to other users (compared with previous years); revenue increase per employee; total cycle time reduction; % decrease in write-offs; engineering change costs as % of output; employee absence; employee turnover

need to start with the customer first. In addition, measurement has to be externally focused using external data such as service, quality, responsiveness and cost.

- Process capability: Building capability internally is essential to becoming competitive.
- Focus on innovation: Modern competitiveness is based on fulfilling customer requirements through creativity and innovation. The consideration of people as the main asset is crucial and measurement of employee satisfaction and employee attitudes is crucial. The challenge is to compete on a set of competencies that are capable of delivering future strategies.
- The financial perspective focusing on the shareholder: Shareholders are another set of customers and value added to shareholders has to be continuously monitored and measured (see Figures 8.2 and 8.3).

Royal Mail systematic approach to measurement

- This model is based on a series of steps that, if and when applied properly, will lead to 'good added value' measurement.
- There are 10 steps in this model which, most of the time, apply to both in-process situations and results oriented situations:
    1 Step 1: Identify Measurement classification – process or results – and overall purpose.

2 Step 2: Identify precise aim and the type of measurement.
3 Step 3: Determine who will use it.
4 Step 4: Position the measurement (if attached to the process).
5 Step 5: Identify specifically what to measure.
6 Step 6: Select an appropriate measurement technique.
7 Step 7: Define the measurement feedback characteristics.
8 Step 8: Ensure a healthy mix of measurement is established.
9 Step 9: Apply the measurement 'added value' test questions.
10 Step 10: Develop and implement measurements.

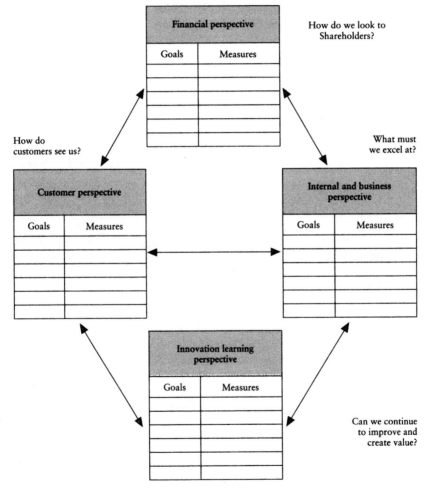

Figure 8.2 *The balanced scorecard model: an integrated performance measurement system*

The internal/external integrated measurement model

- This model is complete since it addresses internal measurement aspects (effectiveness and efficiency) and external measurement aspects (competitiveness) (General Accounting Office, 1991).

Financial perspective	
Goals	Measures
Survive	Cash flow
Succeed	Quarterly sales growth and operating income by division
Prosper	Increased market share and ROE

Customer perspective	
Goals	Measures
New products	Per cent of sales from new products Per cent of sales from proprietary products
Responsive supply	On-time delivery (defined by customer)
Preferred supplier	Share of key accounts purchases Ranking by key accounts
Customer partnership	Number of cooperative engineering efforts

Internal and business perspective	
Goals	Measures
Technology capability	Manufacturing geometry versus competition
Manufacturing excellence	Cycle time Unit cost Yield
Design Productivity	Silicon efficiency Engineering efficiency
New product introduction	Actual introduction schedule versus plan

Innovation and learning perspective	
Goals	Measures
Technology leadership	Time to develop next generation
Manufacturing learning	Process time to maturity
Product focus	Per cent of products that equal 80% of sales
Time to market	New product introduction versus competition

Figure 8.3   *An applied example of the balanced scoreboard model in electronics*

Table 8.5 Deming Prize winners

Measure/Indicator	Management measures
Earning rate	Profit; net profit; profit before tax (amount, rate); profit after turnover tax; ordinary profit (amount, rate); per capital ordinary profit; profit ratio of total liabilities and net worth; break even point ratio
Productivity	Value-added productivity; per capital value-added productivity; per capital sales; break even point operating rate
Growth rate	Sales; growth rate of sales; exports
Safety	Net worth rate; debt ratio; ratio of financial expense to sales
	Departmental activities
Product develop-ment capability	New product sales (amount, rate), period for new product development; number of design alterations; enrichment of model assortment; improvement in new product mass production start-up; number of patent applications
Marketing capability	Sales target attainment rate; scheduled contract securing rate
	Human resources aspect
Manpower resources	Number of improvement proposals; number of completed QCC themes; number of newly acquired qualifications; number of training courses participants; attendance rate; industrial accident occurrence rate
	Functional aspects
Cost	
Cost reduction	Cost reduction; failure rate; target cost attainment condition; new product mass production start up cost; customer C/D amount
Rationalization	Rationalization amount; inventory turnover; delivery price reduction
Production/delivery time	
Production quality	Production quality
Inventory	Inventory reduction; inventory turnover; number of days held
Delivery time	Delivery time
Quality	
Manufacturing failure	Process per cent defective; failure cost; processed material per cent defective per unit; yield

Functional aspects

Finished goods inspection	QA department inspection rejection rate; delivery inspection rejection rate
User disadvantages	Customer acceptance inspection rejection rate; claims (amount, rate, number of cases); compensation work cost
User disadvantages	Market quality evaluation data; comparison with international standards; changes in quality problems; extension of warranty period
Marketability	Market share

Applications of non-financial performance measurement: some examples

Table 8.6 BOC UK Gases

Critical success factors	*Key performance indicators*
Customer satisfaction	• Customer surveys (Maurice Vernon) performance – biannual • Business retained/lost report – quarterly • Customer service management statistics – quarterly • Segmentation analysis – quarterly
Continuous improvement	• Profit growth in excess of sales growth compared to last year – quarterly • Employee involvement in quaity projects – biannual • LWCR – quarterly • Motor vehicle accident rate – quarterly • ISRS involvement – biannual
Growth	• Real growth in turnover – quarterly • Sureflow turnover growth compared to plan – quarterly • Special gases turnover compared to plan – quarterly
Market position/leadership (including technology)	• Bulk business gained/lost report – quarterly • Compressed market share trend – quarterly • Non-cryogenic plant placements – quarterly • Applications signing – quarterly • Technology plan implementation – biannual
Profitability/cost effectiveness	• Profit/turnover – monthly • ROCE – quarterly • Profit/employee – quarterly
Organization effectiveness	• Overheads/turnover – quarterly • Turnover/employee – quarterly • Direct overheads/total overheads – quarterly

SmithKline Beecham world-wide operations

Table 8.7 Performance improvement methodology

Principles:
- Identify achievable, early successes
- Implement some short-term, incremental improvements
- Focus on quantifiable benefits
- Progress a balance of short-term and longer-term opportunities
- Develop low-tech soutions
- Prepare for continuous improvment after step changes
- Focus on simplification and standardization
- Build on best practice and knowledge within the organization and the other PIPs
- Take a proactive approach and break down 'sacred cows'
- Underpin the project with formal, frequent communications

Critical success factors:
- Senior management commitment
- Business ownership
- Fresh, original perspective
- A core of full-time team members
- Adequate time from nominated people on programme
- Real cross-functional teamwork
- Identification and use of 'change leaders/change champions'
- Clearly defined objectives (both personal and project)
- Realistic (but stretching) workload
- Detailed workplan, clearly defined and adhered to

Objective
To improve the operational performance of the existing business by undertaking a programme of performance improvement across the entire pipeline

- It focuses on continuous improvement and addresses measurement issues from a short-term, feedback perspective.
- Leadership for continuous improvement is recognized as the key driver for successful measurement.
- Having quality systems and involving people closely, helps create the right discipline for doing the right things, right first time and consistently, by focusing on the needs of internal and external customers.
- Internal measurement aspects are those which relate to aspects of the process and the output (product/service).
- External measurement aspects relate to customer satisfaction and performance in the marketplace.
- This model highlights measurements that are geared towards lowering levels (i.e. those dealing with negative quality aspects) and

Table 8.8 Performance improvement scope at SmithKline Beecham Consumer Brands

People	• Organization and structure
	• Manning levels
	• Skill levels
	• Communication/motivation
	• Training
	• Pay/incentives
	• Absenteeism
Sales and marketing	• Forecast accuracy
	• Forecast timing
	• Promotions
	• Sales demand
	• Order processing
	• Order invoicing
Planning	• Inventory levels
	• Inventory accuracy
	• Integrated planning
	• Adherence to schedule
	• Timeliness of planning
Purchasing	• Vendor profile
	• Material cost
	• Call-off
	• Vendor management
	• Specification
Production	• Material flow
	• WIP level
	• Line efficiency
	• Layout
	• Changeovers
	• Scrap/wastage/rework

measurements that seek to optimize added value (i.e. dealing with positive quality aspects).
- This model is based on a continuous improvement approach and constant feedback is injected into the various areas for action, corrections and drive the improvement effort forward.
- A similar model was developed by a sister company to Hewlett Packard, which shows that quality works in two different ways, both complementary to each other
  - Internally, drives productivity up and costs down so that there is an impact on profit improvement
  - Externally, drives customer satisfaction up and prices down, so that there is an impact on market share and profit improvement.

Conclusions

- Performance measurement takes place through a methodological approach which is the key determinant of its effectiveness.
- Good measurement is one that provides quality information that will lead to action and things to be changed.
- Good measurement therefore has to have the following characteristics:
  - Timeliness
  - Clarity of purpose
  - Correct and precise
  - Provides information for right people
  - Reflect process visibility
  - Reflects progress visibility
  - Focuses on core value added activity
  - Helps corporate targets
  - Reflects a culture of continuous improvement
- Measurement therefore is the key driver for continuous improvement and the discipline required to eliminate complacency.
- Measurement has to encapsulate all aspects of business operations so that the right decisions can be made.

Table 8.9

Process-based measures	*Results-based measures*
• Relate to a particular process	• Relate to broader business, or unit targets
• Used by people working in the process	• Used more as management information
• Maintained by people working in the • process	• Data collected in workplace but analysed and presented elsewhere
• Provide very quick feedback on performance	• Usually gives retrospective results, often weekly or monthly
• Visually displayed in the workplace	• Often too detailed to be fully communicated but 'vital few' are displayed in workplace

Source: Royal Mail (1990–91)

- Measures for improvement can be classified as two sorts:
  - In-process measures (attached to process)
    Effectiveness
    Efficiency
    Process consistency/variability
    Quality output level
  - Output measures (results-based measures) (outside the process)
    Customer satisfaction
    Employee satisfaction
    Product performance
    Other key business targets
- The difference between process-based measures and results-based measures is illustrated in Table 8.9:
- A recommended Performance Measurement System has six key elements to it. These include:

  1. Strategy development and deployment
  2. Measurement system design
  3. Measurement planning
  4. Measurement implementation
  5. Review and action
  6. Performance audit through self-assessment

- Measurement is meaningful at all levels within the organization. Primary, secondary and tertiary measures have all got sponsors, and action is taken according to process importance and line of authority and responsibility.
- Critical elements for successful performance measurement systems include:
  - Leadership and commitment to measurement and continuous improvement
  - Full employee involvement and participation in the design, implementation, review and audit of aspects of measurement linked to their processes
  - Good planning, monitoring and review mechanisms
  - Good measurement reflects good progress – the two are inseparable
  - Measurement is relative and has to lead to stretch objectives as a result of benchmarking activity
  - Good measurement is only concerned with value adding activity – focusing on the customer

- Measurement has to focus on 'negative quality' aspects but also has to be used proactively for developing a competitive advantage, in the market place
- Measurement in a TQ context is geared for continuous improvement, the **control** of processes and activities, **not** the people
- Effectiveness of measurement can be greatly enhanced by **reward** and **recognition** systems.

References

Dixon, J. R. *et al.* (1990). *The New Performance Challenge: Measuring Operations for World Class Competition*, Homewood, Illinois: Business One Irwin.

Drury, C. (1990). Cost control and performance measurement in an AMT environment, *Management Accounting (UK)*, **46**, November, 40–42.

Edwards, J. B. (1985). Are management accountants marching towards inevitable decline because of outmoded techniques? *Management Accounting (US)*, September, 45–50.

General Accounting Office (1991). The internal/external integrated measurement model.

Goldratt, E. M. and Cox, J. (1986). *The Goal: A Process of Ongoing Improvement* (revised ed.), New York: North River Press.

Johnson, H. T. and Kaplan, R. S. (1987). *Relevance Lost: the Rise and Fall of Management Accounting*, Boston, Mass.: Harvard Business School.

Kaplan, R. S. (1984). Yesterday's accounting undermines production, *Harvard Business Review*, **96**, July–August.

Kaplan, R. S. and Norton, D. P. (1993). The balanced scoreboard – measures that drive performance. *Quality and Productivity Management* **10**(3), 47–54.

Maskell, B. (1989). Performance measurement for World Class Manufacturing, Part 1, *Management Accounting*, **67**(5), 32–3.

McNair, C. J. *et al.* (1990) Do financial and non-financial performance measures have to agree? *Management Accounting (US)*, November, 28–36.

Øvretveit, J. (1993). *Measuring service quality: practical guidelines*, Letchworth: Technical Communications (Publishing) Ltd.

Royal Mail (1990–91). The framework for measurement – A systematic approach for creating added value measurement activity.

Sink, D. S. (1991). The role of measurement in achieving world class quality and productivity management, *Industrial Engineering*, **23**(6), 23–8, 70.

Taylor, M. C. (1992). Total quality based performance measurement, MBA dissertation, Bradford University Management Centre, UK.

Vollman, T. E. (1991). Cutting the Gordian knot of misguided performance measurement, *Industrial Management & Data Systems* (UK), **91**, 24–6.

Recommended reading

Zairi, M. (1994). *Measuring Performance for Business Results*, London: Chapman and Hall.

9

Strategic management accounting
Michael Bromwich

Empirical evidence suggests that Western management accounting practice focuses almost exclusively on internal activities within the firm. With regard to information external to the firm, most management accounting systems do not go beyond reporting sales revenues. In this chapter Professor Bromwich emphasizes the need for management accounting to adopt a more strategic perspective by reporting information relating to the firm's markets and its competitors.

He begins by outlining two major aims of strategic management accounting. First, strategic excellence requires that the product characteristics offered by the firm are determined and then costed. By adopting this approach management accounting helps to focus managerial efforts more on markets where customers have to be won and retained and competitors repulsed. The second aim of strategic management accounting is to ascertain the enterprises's cost positioning relative to its rivals. This positioning is crucial in determining the sustainability of the firm's product characteristics and price/output strategies against competitors. For such sustainability to be achieved the enterprise needs to have cost advantages over its rivals.

Professor Bromwich then proceeds to outline the essential characteristics of strategic management accounting and some of its limitations. He also provides a brief review of the literature. The following section illustrates why this approach is needed by showing that conventional management accounting may fail to deal with strategic issues, and how these problems may be overcome using strategic management accounting.

The next two sections of the chapter first describe the role of product characteristics in strategy and their impact on the firm's cost structure, and then introduce a method of strategic cost analysis which allows the value of product attributes provided to consumers by the firm to be

> *costed, usually over the product life-cycle, in a far more systematic way*
> *than is available with conventional management accounting.*
>   *The final substantive section of the chapter considers in less detail*
> *that aspect of strategic management accounting which seeks to ascer-*
> *tain, understand and analyse the cost structures of competitors.*

Introduction

That firms must be able to compete globally over a wide range of strategic variables not just price to survive and grow has become a commonplace recently (Haas, 1987; Porter, 1980 and 1985). Competition now focuses on strategic product and service characteristics, such as operating performance, product finish, low cost to consumers, high reliability and quality, good after-sales services, and a sensitive and rapid supply response to customer demands. It is these product and service attributes which appeal to consumers and for which they are willing to pay. Demands for goods are really requirements for consumer value. Their match with consumer tastes relative to competitive offerings are important in determining enterprise market share and in sustaining enterprise products in the market.

This is the way in which some Japanese companies, for example, determine their product strategies (Hasegawa, 1986, pp. 59–60; Hiromoto, 1988). These companies choose a bundle of characteristics which is larger and richer than those offered by competitors and determine a price based on a target price aimed to yield a desired market share. Cost savings are then engineered to obtain this target price and to allow the product and service characteristics offered to be further improved over time and for prices to decline similarly in a planned way, thereby increasing future market share. Management accounting as a control or evaluation device is utilized in Japan to encourage the associated continual search for cost reductions and thereby serves to reinforce long-term manufacturing strategies at all levels of the organization. Thus Hiromoto (1988) can write that accounting in Japan reflects and reinforces an overriding commitment to market-driven management.

Porter (1985, Chapter 1) says that satisfying consumer needs is necessary, but not sufficient, for sustained competitive success. The firm also needs to have a competitive advantage over actual and potential competitors. This advantage may be manifested in terms of either a superior way of meeting consumer needs relative to competitive products by offering a clearly differentiated product or set of services related to the product, or in terms of marketing a relatively low cost product. Competitive strategies may span the whole product range of an industry or may be focused on only a target segment. Accounting has a clear role in helping to formulate strategies of this type. Differentiation is only worthwhile if the revenues obtained exceed the costs of satisfying consumer needs. Accounting obviously plays a major role in achieving a cost leadership strategy and in maintaining this strategy by continuing cost engineering.

Given the importance accorded to accounting systems in Western decision-making, the costs of offering strategically excellent products need to be fully integrated into enterprise cost systems and reported on by these systems. This is one of the objectives of what has come to be called 'strategic management accounting'. This new approach to management accounting helps to focus managerial efforts more on their markets where customers have to be won and retained and competitors repulsed and on the costs of these market activities. The second aim of strategic management accounting is to ascertain the enterprise's cost positioning relative to its rivals (see Bromwich, 1990, pp. 37–46; Shank, 1989). This positioning is crucial in determining the sustainability of the firm's product characteristics and price/output strategies against competitors. For such sustainability to be achieved the enterprise needs to have cost advantages over its rivals.

The next section will briefly introduce strategic management accounting and outline its essential characteristics and some of its advantages. This section also provides a brief review of the literature. The following section illustrates why this approach is needed by showing that conventional management accounting may fail to deal with strategic issues, and how these problems may be overcome using strategic management accounting.

The next two sections of the chapter first describe the role of product characteristics in strategy and their impact on the firm's cost structure and then introduce a method of strategic cost analysis which allows the value of product attributes provided to consumers by the firm to be costed, usually over the product life-cycle, in a far more systematic way than is available with conventional management accounting.

The final substantive section of the chapter considers, in less detail, that aspect of strategic management accounting which seeks to ascertain, understand and analyse the cost structures of competitors. The chapter is completed by a brief set of conclusions.

What is strategic management accounting?

Strategic orientated accounting complements the traditional concerns of Western accounting by additionally focusing on the costs incurred to maintain the competitive advantages of the enterprise's actual and potential product portfolio and on the cost structures of actual and possible rivals. This innovatory focus on the cost implications of the enterprise's product and market strategies can be seen as essential for success in meeting today's global challenges in an ever increasing number of markets.

More generally, such a reorientation permits management accounting additionally to concentrate upon the consumer value generated relative to competitors. It also aids in monitoring the firm's performance in the marketplace using a whole range of strategic variables over a decision horizon sufficiently long for strategic plans to come to fruition. These concepts form the core of the new concept of strategic management accounting. A working definition of strategic management accounting is:

> The provision and analysis of financial information on the firm's product markets and competitors' costs and cost structures and the monitoring of the enterprise's strategies and those of its competitors in these markets over a number of periods.

Providing a strategic perspective on management accounting requires the role of accounting to be extended in two directions. Full strategic excellence first requires that the product characteristics offered by the firm are determined and then costed. It secondly requires that similar operations are undertaken for the enterprise's actual and potential competitors and that their cost structures are determined and monitored.

The uses and advantages of strategic management accounting

The term strategic management accounting is new, though many firms have practised elements of this approach for a long time. Many firms, when faced with competitive challenges, hastily undertake competitive investigations of product benefits offered by themselves and their competitors. Often, however, the costs of providing such benefits are not considered in this process. These costs are subject to the same swingeing overall cuts introduced to beat off the competitive threat as all other costs even though these costs may need to be increased to meet this challenge. Such information is also often gathered in connection with takeover bids and is sometimes crucial to either a successful takeover or the successful defence of such a bid. Similarly, in automotive firms for example, product planners when developing a new model are often provided with figures based on product characteristics. Many consultants offer services in this area. Indeed, this sector of the consultancy industry in the USA has been estimated to amount to a billion dollar industry. Similarly, for example, variants of this approach have recently been successfully introduced in large European firms in the computer, pharmaceutical and steel industries by the consultants Coopers & Lybrand Deloittes.

Strategic management accounting gives additional support and a stronger role to the surprisingly substantial number of the Fortune 500 controllers that do participate in strategic planning activities but presently only by giving informal advice or providing data or analyses. Only some 25 to 33 per cent claim to get involved in choosing options or to be involved in all the phases of the two crucial steps in strategic planning of developing the mission and establishing objectives (Fern and Tipgos, 1988). Strategic planning can only gain from having a strategically aware finance function on its side. This should ensure that the informal systems for determining the costs of product benefits that are burgeoning all over the enterprise use sensible cost determination methods for their purposes.

Harnessing the finance department to corporate strategy may give additional impetus to the need to match the strong strategic thrust of many global competitors. There is ample evidence that Western firms lag behind in this area. A recent study of product development in Japan, Korea and Denmark indicated that Danish firms tended to allow the problems experienced by existing customers to drive product development whereas the Japanese relied much more on innovative product research and competitor analysis and employed a substantial number of market scanning devices. Similarly, a recent study by the Harris Research Centre (1990) of information for strategic management in large UK companies found that the use of external information is generally rare. Only about half the companies used competitor information and market research results a lot. Annual financial reports seemed to be the major item of public information used.

Strategic management accounting is still in its infancy and its successful application yields results which are highly commercially sensitive. This makes it difficult to give many examples of how actual enterprises use the approaches advocated here. Some relevant examples will be introduced but concentrating on how firms use elements of the approach advocated here in strategic planning as do many Japanese and advanced Western organizations. Allen (1986) gives an example of strategic financial management in a UK company which puts the emphasis on determining the present value of future plans and on appraising suggested plans in these terms.

Goldstar Electronics, a major Korean electronics firm adopts a very similar procedure when planning for those projects fundamental to the company's success but about which the company lacks detailed information. Their first step in appraising such projects is to determine what are called environmental factors in the company's planning process. This involves answering detailed questions including the following:

- Uses of product by consumers
- Characteristics of users
- Technology required
- Current/future competition and their products
- Who is the market leader
- How did competitors start
- What markets are they in and what are their plans (see Kang and Soong, 1986).

Similarly, many firms have attempted to isolate their key strategic success factors which they must sustain if the firm is to survive and succeed, and to determine the strategic dimensions of the goods and services they provide. It is well known, for example, that the McDonald's Corporation uses as major items of strategic importance detailed measures of quality, cleanliness and value. Similarly, a large supplier to the aircraft industry has identified a number of customer-orientated strategic objectives including reduced delivery times resulting from shortening lead times, reliability and high quality, incorporating the need to obtain zero defects and to provide flexible responses to customer demands whilst matching industry innovation levels at a low buyer cost.

Without the adoption of strategic management accounting, the control and monitoring of strategic objectives may have to take place outside the financial management system using disaggregated measures thereby losing the ability to easily consider the overall impact of the enterprise's achievements in these areas.

The public excitement generated over strategic management accounting does not yet match that which now surrounds activity costing. There may be a number of reasons for this. In many ways the revisions required to current management accounting are much more radical than those needed to implement activity costing and are not as well-founded on existing management accounting expertise as activity costing. Strategic management accounting requires that accountants extend their interests beyond their usual areas and cooperate much more with general management, corporate strategists and marketing and product development, who may not have a good image of accountants. William Whipple, manager of financial analysis at du Pont exemplified this problem in an 'imaginary' conversation between a strategic planner and business director when considering whether to invite finance to a major meeting to review the five year business plan. The strategic planner doubts whether the 'number crunchers would add much at this stage. Of course they'll generate a forecast later, after we've decided which way the business is headed'. The approach suggested here may help to convert the business director so that he or she can say of accountants, as Mr Whipple clearly hopes, that 'I've noticed that they're getting more savvy about the planning process' (Whipple, 1988).

Strategic management accounting provides a system that helps answer the major concerns that management have about the inability of conventional management accounting to deal well with strategic matters. It also raises many problems which at first glance seem insoluble to those inexperienced in this area. For example, the usual reaction to being told to consider competitors cost structures is that it can not be done even in the face of evidence that many global competitors devote considerable resources to this endeavour. A firm involved with its competitor in a joint venture did learn about its competitor's costs but did not use them in competitive analysis because the competitor used a different system of overhead allocation. It is difficult to see how a business can be managed without a broad understanding of the enterprise's competitive cost structure.

These ideas have had less public support from consultants than activity costing because although, as indicated above, many of the ideas of strategic management accounting are extensively used by consultants, they have not yet been able to offer a comprehensive package in this area. Intensified global competition and a better understanding of business strategy have produced a new interest in this area and a new literature has begun to emerge.

The existing literature

So far, however, there exists only a very small body of literature describing the approach, explaining models which can be used in applying a strategic approach to management accounting and providing a theoretical foundation for the approach.

The credit for coining the term and first advocating the approach goes to Kenneth Simmonds, a CIMA member in a paper presented to an Institute technical symposium in 1981 (see Simmonds, 1981a). At this lime, he also set much of the later agenda for strategic management accounting especially in the area of determining competitive cost position. His wish was to incorporate the findings of the relatively new subject of business strategy into management accounting. He argued that accounting should be much more outward looking and should help the firm evaluate its competitive position. He first outlined the importance of the learning curve and the strategic importance of the long-term behaviour of costs yielded by this approach in terms of providing competitive advantages. He emphasized the importance of costing competitors in order to determine their competitive position and their likely responses to changes in the enterprise's business strategies and investments. Simmonds also joined a number of other commentators who were urging the use of market-related data in management accounts and arguing that variance analysis only made sense if it was interpretated in the light of market changes (Simmonds, 1981a and 1981b).

The leading set of proponents in the USA are Shank and Govindarajan who call their approach strategic cost analysis. A good indication of their work is given in their recent book (1989). Their approach relies heavily on the work of Porter and other competitive strategists. They commence their studies of a firm by defining the firm's or the strategic business unit's value chain which isolates each activity which creates consumer value and spans all the functions of the organization from supply to the customer after-sales service and the honouring of warranties. The next step is to assign costs and assets to each value activity comprising the chain and to identify the cost drivers for each activity to ascertain the total costs of the value chain and the resources it uses. In this chapter, it is sought to extend this approach and assign costs to product attributes. The final step is to build sustainable competitive advantage either by operating on the cost drivers or by rearranging the value chain focusing on those activities in which the firm has competitive advantage. Here, the cost drivers in mind are much more general than those now familiar from activity costing. They are really the cost characteristics of the value activities and of their linkages which may give competitive advantage. They thus include economies of scale, learning curve effects and economies of scope (which allow two or more products to be produced together cheaper than if they were produced in separate free-standing facilities).

Mainly using the case study method, Shank and Govindarajan seek to change accounting systems so that they better fit with the organization's strategy and can contribute to the formulation of strategy, the communication of strategies throughout the organization, and the development of methods to implement, monitor and change strategies. Their work suggests that existing accounting methods which were designed for different purposes cannot be expected to aid greatly in the strategic area. This is, perhaps, most startlingly illustrated in their Kinstead Equipment Company case where they look at profit variance analysis from a strategic focus (Shank and Govindarajan, 1989, Chapter 6). For a similar UK criticism see Goold, 1986.

Because of the scarcity of other authors in the UK, much of the remainder of this chapter focuses on research which looks not at products but rather their attributes and seek to cost the provision of these attributes. It also concentrates more on the strategic importance of patterns of cost behaviour than other writers. The next section looks at some of the problems that conventional management accounting has in coping with strategic issues.

Conventional management accounting: strategic problems

Existing management accounting procedures assign costs only to products and to responsibility centres and not to the benefits provided to consumers. These conventional accounting methods therefore cannot match the Japanese target price method, described above, which automatically considers product benefits and their costs simultaneously by requiring these costs to be reduced so that the target price can be achieved.

The focus of conventional management accounting reports is on a detailed understanding of the enterprise's internal costs, each categorized according to the input to which they relate and attributed to a product or products and to a responsibility centre or centres. Generally far more detail is given concerning direct or variable costs than overheads, even though the latter expenses often relate more to the accomplishment of enterprise strategy. Comparisons with budgets and standards yield a rich set of information for management concerning the firm's internal activities. The focus is almost exclusively on activities within the enterprise rather than the market results of such endeavours. Even the inclusion of market share detail may be rare, see, for example, Horngren and Foster, 1987 and Howell *et al.*, 1987.

Cost drivers with the conventional accounting approach are thus activities performed within the organization whereas, from a strategic perspective the benefits provided by products to consumers, are the ultimate cost drivers. This lack of strategic relevance lies at the heart of many of the problems presently being experienced with accounting.

Key success factors and management accounting

As was said above, many firms have attempted to isolate those key strategic success factors which they must sustain if the firm is to survive and succeed, and to determine the strategic dimensions of the goods and services they provide. Conventional accounting systems are unable to say much about the cost aspects of these, and similar, items, because of their lack of focus on determining the costs of providing product characteristics and ultimately value to the consumer. One of the objectives of conventional accounting is to ascertain the costs of individual responsibility centres rather than the costs of the enterprise's strategic activities, which generally involve many departments working together in a way not fully reflected in the enterprise's formal accountability structure.

The costs of most strategic activities just cannot be deduced from existing accounting reports. Often these costs are treated as part of enterprise-wide overheads (for example, much of the development expenditure relevant to these activities and much of product planning may be treated in this way) and may not be allocated to products at all.

Thus, items which are recognized as crucial to enterprise success are not costed in any systematic way. When these costs are allocated to products, this operation is likely to distort costs so that they do not reflect their true incidence as driven by the requirements of each individual product or class of product.

Most of these costs tend to be treated as overheads with current accounting systems. The move towards activity costing by many firms may help to provide information relevant to strategy (Cooper and Kaplan, 1987; Berliner and Brimson, 1988), providing that the cost drivers employed are linked to the customer benefits which they ultimately yield and are not selected simply on the basis of the amount of enterprise costs they explain which is sometimes seen as an initial surrogate for value added.

Strategic management accounting directly faces up to these problems by seeking to measure the costs of those enterprise strategic objectives concerned to give benefit to consumers.

Recognizing the difficulty of monitoring the attainment of key success factors and strategic objectives by traditional accounting means, many firms have been forced to measure these items outside the traditional accounting system using disaggregated measures, thereby losing the ability to see easily the overall impact of achievements in these areas.

Goldstar Electronics, referred to earlier, provides an example of these difficulties. It sets its strategic objectives in terms of ability to provide what customers may want, good after-sales service, product development and innovative production management but does not appraise the achievement of these goals directly using its management accounting system. Rather, the company relies on a number of key performance indicators of the familiar type, such as indices of sales growth and of new market development, per capita sales ratios and product mix ratios. These measures which are not all fully reflective of the chosen goals, may give conflicting signals, do not fully reflect cost factors and cannot be aggregated in a meaningful way and therefore cannot be used easily to seek trade-offs between product benefits to consumers and their costs.

The use of these and of other non-financial measures related directly to key success factors is increasing and seems to be contributing to success in industry and commerce, especially at the level of the strategic business unit. Seeking to change the accounting system so that it also captures strategic factors supplements this movement by sharing its concentration on key success factors but reporting on these in a way that is more meaningful and somewhat more familiar at the higher levels of decision-making. Strategic management accounting allows each material customer benefit provided by a product to be related to its cost yielding what may be called financial key performance indicators and integrating these with the more usual indicators of this type.

Thus, Goldstar's strategy for after-sales service could be monitored by comparing revenue generated by after-sales service with the cost of providing that service.

Problems in investment appraisal

That the traditional management accounting system cannot properly deal with strategic and customer-orientated items is also clear from the recent problems firms have found in appraising investments in new technologies, such as flexible manufacturing systems, including robotics and CAD/CAM. One of the major problems here is that many of the benefits claimed for these technologies, such as higher reliability and quality, flexible response to changing customer demand, better fit with existing products and new skills which enhance the firm's image with customers, are difficult to quantify using conventional accounting tools, and their appraisal requires the cooperation of many departments in the firm. Many controllers trained in traditional accounting have been unable to abandon their concern to use only 'hard' figures in investment appraisal, thereby helping to ensure that less 'high-tech' investments are undertaken than in competing countries where the strategic benefits of investments are more heavily weighted, by a variety of means. Other firms have just given up the attempt to appraise such investments in any formal way (Woods et al., 1984). The approach to costing the provision of product value to consumers suggested here should help to ensure that more of the consequences of such investments are considered and that customer benefits may become to be seen as reasonably hard numbers crucial to the appraisal of 'high-tech' investments (see Bromwich and Bhimani, 1991).

The search for non-value added activities

The current drive to eliminate non-value added activities by activity costers and other reformers of management accounting can be aided by the approach suggested here. This search also illustrates that strategic variables and costs are intertwined and must be considered together. Cost reduction exercises of this type ideally require that studies be mounted to investigate whether each activity does yield customer benefits and to identify such benefits. Strategic cost analysis has been found to answer this need. In default of such a linking between costs and customer benefits, those seeking to demonstrate the existence of non-value added activities have had to be content to argue that such activities can be stopped without affecting the total product being offered to the consumer. However, the customer's views of the product may not be easily established without a detailed analysis seeking to link costs and consumer benefits. Seemingly unnecessary costs may provide clear benefits to the consumer, for example, by suggesting that the firm is determined to 'over' engineer its products to enhance reliability. Similarly, the existence of resources which do not seem directly to give rise to value added (such as excess production capacity) may be seen as indicating that the firm has resources which can be used to be flexible in the face of changing consumer demands. Excess capacity is deliberately planned for this purpose in Japan. Providing customer benefits such as these may be crucial in sustaining product prices in the market but this may not be visible without a detailed costing of product benefits.

This problem of not linking costs and customer benefits and basing strategic decisions on conventional accounting figures is illustrated by a process industry which saw the price quoted for one of its more complex products halved by one of the firms in industry. All the remaining firms quickly ceased production after a brief inspection of their conventionally defined costs. On later investigation, and after foreign competitors had entered the market, it was found that the new technology which was being employed could not meet all the consumers' needs associated with the product nor could it satisfy anything other than a small proportion of the demand for the product. A different decision might have been made if customer benefits and the costs of providing these benefits had been considered in more detail. The next section looks at how the costs of product attributes can be incorporated into strategic management accounting.

Costing product characteristics or attributes

The revenues generated by the product characteristics and ultimately the consumer benefits provided by a product and the costs of these benefits are intertwined and need to be evaluated together. Similarly, strategic decision-making requires that the usual trade-offs between benefits and costs need to be explored.

In many firms, including some in Japan, strategic decisions are initially made in the marketing, product planning and engineering areas. A study of 407 top European managers in 109 organizations confirmed the overwhelming influence of these functions on product–market decisions (Hegarty and Hoffman, 1987). Similar findings have been obtained in the USA. Strategic decisions thus tend to concentrate on strategic product characteristics without fully considering their costs and any interrelationships between costs and benefits.

This approach captures only part of the strategy problem. Firms that also pay attention to the absolute and relative costs of providing value to the customer might expect to be in a better position than those firms that focus only on part of the strategic aspects of products.

Product characteristics as cost drivers

The benefits provided by products which generate enterprise revenues are the ultimate cost drivers. From a strategic perspective, this category of cost drivers dominate those cost drivers used in traditional accounting and in activity costing if this approach is used in a routine way to attribute costs to products and not to the benefits which the activities represented by these costs provide to the consumer.

With the customer value perspective, each cost incurred by the enterprise is seen as being linked to providing to the customer benefits which meet their needs (except for some costs which are incurred to meet regulations imposed by authorities external to the firm). It is these benefits for which customers are willing to pay. Strategic cost analysis allows these costs to be integrated with operational plans because it seeks to make the links between costs and customer benefits visible to management at the operational level. With this approach, the utility of training costs, for example, becomes much more transparent. Training should be carried out only if it provides specific benefits to customers for which they are willing to pay more than the consequent costs of these benefits. Thus all enterprise costs should be linked to the benefits they provide. This test can be applied to training decisions at all levels in the organization thereby integrating the strategic benefits of training into operational plans. More importantly, this approach provides a way of driving strategy right down the organization. It has always been impossible to provide this integration within conventional management accounting where strategic planning has generally had to be decoupled from current operations because accounting systems report only the costs of enterprise current operations.

Customer benefits

Customer benefits need to be sufficient to either retain existing customers or to win new ones in a market where rivals compete in terms of lower product cost, higher quality delivery times and, as corporate strategists recognize, across a wide range of strategic product variables, not simply price. Indeed, the price of the given package of benefits contained in a product may not be a decision variable for many firms in strongly competitive markets. Concern with consumer benefits suggests that a wide range of techniques are required to produce a detailed analysis of the firm's products and the offerings of its competitors.

The key perspective that allows strategic management accounting to be introduced at this level is to see each product not as a whole or as a unity but to perceive it as comprised of a number of separate characteristics offered to the consumer. With this view, products are seen as being comprised of a package of attributes or characteristics which they offer to consumers (Lancaster, 1979). It is these attributes that actually constitute commodities and which appeal to consumers and for which they are willing to pay. Demands for goods are derived demands stemming from the demands for their underlying characteristics. These attributes might include a variety of quality elements, such as operating performance variables, reliability and warranty arrangements; physical items, including the degree of finish and trim; and service factors, like the assurance of supply and of after-sales service. It is these elements which differentiate products and appeal to consumers. A firm's market share depends on the match between the attributes provided by its products and consumers' tastes and on the supply of these attributes by competitors.

Only efficient products, each of which yields the *maximum* amount of a *specific* bundle of characteristics for the amount of money the consumer wishes to spend, will survive in the market. Whether a product represents an efficient way for the consumer to buy the bundle of characteristics offered by the product depends on product prices as well as the quantities of characteristics offered by products. If the relative price of a product decreases, for example, the quantity of the characteristics per monetary unit it offers increases and more would be spent on it to the detriment of other products. Changes in the prices of products and in the amount of characteristics obtainable for a given price would alter views as to which products were regarded as efficient in obtaining the bundle of characteristics they offer.

With this perspective, product characteristics and product cost (and therefore price) are deeply intertwined. Neither of these matters can be considered in isolation.

The market share accruing to each product will depend on consumer tastes and on product prices. Each product will attract that clientele of consumers who like the bundle of characteristics it offers, conditional on its relative price. The firm's strategic decision is therefore to determine the amount of characteristics which will be offered and the product price. A change in market share can be won by offering a different bundle of characteristics, that is by differentiating products, by offering a greater bundle of characteristics at the same price by, for example, introducing cost-saving technology and by supplying an existing set of characteristics at a lower price. Introducing a cheaper way of obtaining characteristics should attract demand from the other products depending on competitors' technology and cost structures (and, more generally, on their strategic behaviour in the face of a challenge). The amount of any increase in market share will also depend on consumers' preferences. The introduction of a cheaper way of obtaining characteristics may mean that existing competiting products are no longer worthwhile.

New technologies that allow additional combinations of characteristics will yield new products. Products which mimic the characteristics of existing products have to sell for no more than the price of these existing products. Similarly, new products which offer combinations of characteristics which combine or span the characteristics offered by existing products must be priced so that each of the characteristics they offer are no more expensive than with the existing products which they span.

In real world markets, firms supplying outputs which otherwise would be inefficient in terms of the mixture of characteristics they provide may well survive in the market. Such products may be sustainable in market settings where products are not divisible and cannot easily be used together, as with some consumer durables, provided that they yield a combination of characteristics desired by some consumers. However, such firms are unlikely to be able to resist entry because they are charging a higher price for units of characteristics offered by other firms which are either charging less using the same technology or using a lower cost technology.

The above approach can easily include a large number of products and a large number of characteristics. Expanding the number of characteristics allows other strategic problems to be treated. For example, the choice between producing either a high quality and high price product or a low quality and low price product requires a comparison between a product offering a large number of characteristics with a product which yields but a few characteristics.

Decision-driven costs

Focusing on product value provided to customers also allows a better understanding and treatment of those costs which are incurred because they contribute to the provision of a planned level of product characteristics but do not change either with output or with production activity. Rather they are incurred following policy choices by the enterprise and they will continue to be incurred until such decisions are altered or their objectives are accomplished. Thus, they can be called *decision-driven* costs.

Such costs cover a very wide range of costs reflecting policy decisions, including at least some of those concerning research, engineering, design and development, capacity availability, product quality and advertising and promotion activities. Many of the resources represented by these costs provide those benefits which appeal especially to the consumer although these benefits are not directly reflected in physical products. For example, the strength of IBM in the personal computer market is argued to stem less from its physical products than from software, service and advertising advantages and the perceived long-term sustainability of the firm in the market.

Strategic cost analysis

With this background, it is possible to see how product attributes can be incorporated into strategic management accounting reports. There are problems with such reports but they are variants of the problems that plague conventional management accounting. The aim of strategic cost analysis is to determine as well as possible the costs of providing product characteristics to the consumer, given the existing state of the art in cost determination. A detailed application of this approach is given in Bromwich (1991).

Such an analysis does not need to be undertaken for all products. Similar products can be linked together and indeed must be for common activities. Nor is the detailed accuracy of costs of crucial importance. Even the benefits of fairly inexact statements are likely to yield substantial information which can be used to generate competitive advantage.

Comprehensive strategic cost analysis of the type suggested here will be used by enterprises which compete in terms of the product characteristics they offer and their costs. Here, strategic cost analysis will be carried out regularly. Not all costs can necessarily be attributed to consumer benefits and for some costs and benefits, such an attribution may not be worth the cost of undertaking such an exercise.

The timespan encompassed in any strategic cost analysis and the frequency of reports in this area, will depend on the type of businesses in which the enterprise is involved, the importance of providing customer benefits in these businesses and the stability of the economic and competitive environment. For many businesses, the costs reported should be those for the entire product life-cycle, as many costs, especially decision-driven costs, will be dependent on stages in the product life-cycle. With this approach, the costs included in the strategic cost analysis will be both actual and planned costs. The frequency of the reporting strategic cost analyses will again depend on the type of business and especially the turbulence of the economic and competitive environments faced by the business. The reporting cycle will be shortest for those enterprises facing highly uncertain markets.

Many of the cost figures needed can be obtained from a re-analysis of existing databases and more detailed analyses of existing figures. Indeed, an important virtue of the system is that it does not require the existing method of reporting the cost structure of the enterprise to be abandoned.

Consumer benefits in strategic cost analysis

The first step in a strategic cost analysis of this type is to list separately the product benefits or groups of benefits offered to consumers. These benefits will differ fundamentally depending on whether the consumer in mind is in the final goods market or is an intermediatory firm in the chain leading to the final customer. With the latter type of customer, strategic cost analysis facilitates analysis by customer rather than product; an exercise that many firms are finding difficult in the confines of conventional management accounting.

The number of consumer benefits or packages of consumer benefits to which it is sought to assign a cost will depend on the strategy adopted by the enterprise. Thus a firm which concentrates on giving high benefits for only a few characteristics will report only the costs associated with these characteristics. In practice, the firm might bundle together a number of items depending on its competitive strategy.

Consumer benefits can be categorized in a number of ways. Generally, those items directly related to a unit of product would be shown separately from those relating to sales outlets and those relating to the organization as a whole. Often in practice a number of these benefits will be added together.

Costs in strategic cost analysis

The second step in strategic cost analysis is to decide on a set of cost categories. Often a variant of the firm's usual cost classification will be best because this will encompass the matters seen as of concern to that firm and thus reflect its economic environment. A generally useful classification would be variable product costs, activity-related costs, capacity-related costs and decision-related costs. These costs categories can be further subdivided into other categories.

Variable product cost shows the normal direct cost of production which give rise to specific consumer benefits. The second category of costs is that of the activity or transaction-related costs attributable to the product. The inclusion of such activity-related costs indicates that the approach is sufficiently flexible to incorporate the results of a variety of ways of collecting costs.

Some benefits may not cause costs in all categories and although offered at the product or outlet level may cause no or few costs at this level. How far the provision of consumer benefits change variable costs will depend on the nature of the business. More consumer benefits may have variable costs associated with them in manufacturing industry than in financial services but even here their incidence may be small.

Surprisingly, the technical but important problem of common costs may arise in strategic cost analysis with respect to costs which are variable with output or with activity, whereas this problem is generally encountered with respect to overheads in conventional management accounting. These common cost problems arise in strategic cost analysis because with costs such as materials, labour and variable overheads, each cost component may contribute simultaneously to a number of product characteristics and it may be impossible to attribute these costs to each of the product attributes to which they contribute. For example, in a confectionery business, an operation which blends two or more raw materials together may contribute to a number of consumer attributes, such as appearance, taste and texture. Any assignment of the costs of the operation to these attributes would be arbitrary.

The obvious solution to this problem is to bundle these benefits together for the relevant sub-category of direct cost where this problem arises. For example, a fast food supplier, which is a low cost provider of its products using minimally sized and equipped outlets, might well only cost the relative value of its products and the costs of providing a good geographical coverage in convenient locations. A more up-market supplier would report on more product and outlet benefits. The incremental costs for these additional consumer benefits would be reported separately for each benefit. More generally, some of the costs of providing benefits in a cost category may be bundled together and others reported separately.

Many of the activity costs necessary to sustain benefits reflect quality control and quality monitoring activities.

The other major costs of sustaining quality benefits are planning and specification costs which comprise decision-related costs (see below).

The next major category of costs is capacity-related costs which include machinery and equipment costs, such as depreciation and land and building occupancy costs. These two sub-cost categories illustrate both advantages and disadvantages of the approach. The approach associates these costs directly with products or groups of products, whereas normally they are aggregated into overheads and allocated on some arbitrary basis. With depreciation and occupancy costs, at least in some instances, it will be possible to determine what assets and capacity are attributable to the product or class of product.

Strategic cost analysis at least seeks to report sensibly on the costs of resources that may be very important in attracting customers. However, if these costs are just taken from the financial accounting reports, any numbers entered here may have little economic meaning. For many businesses, substituting leasing charges for depreciation charges may be feasible, as may be charging a market-based rental for space, especially if these approaches are used in the company's conventional management accounts as they are, for example, by many well-known store and hotel chains.

This class of costs may also raise the problem of the common use of resources by more than one product. The general problem of common costs plagues conventional management accounting and it is not intended to attempt to solve these more general problems here. However, as was suggested above, this problem with regard to this cost category may be less important with the perspective employed here because these costs in strategic cost analysis will refer to resources specifically identified with a product or group of products.

The final category of costs, decision-related costs, are those the level of which depends not on operational activity but on managerial decisions concerning the level of resources to be provided for certain functions. The costs associated with these decisions will generally not be affected by the actual level of activity in the enterprise at any given time. They are, however, the costs which are often especially geared to providing consumer value. Seeking to attribute them to the consumer benefits they generate represents a major step forward in providing strategically orientated management accounting information. These costs are not rendered visible with conventional management accounting where, as was said earlier, they are generally subsumed into fixed costs. The approach suggested here focuses directly on these costs which are often of great strategic importance to the enterprise.

Generally, an analysis of the type suggested here will be undertaken separately for each group of similar products. There will also be a need to provide additional statements at the level of the strategic business unit or the enterprise to encompass any customer benefits flowing from diversification of the enterprise product portfolio and other benefits generated at this level in the firm, such as non-product related advertising and providing a 'high-tech' image for all the firm's products.

This part of the chapter has considered how the product characteristics offered by the firm can be costed. Strategic management accounting also requires that similar operations are undertaken for the enterprise's actual and potential competitors and that their cost structures are determined and monitored. This task is taken up briefly in the last substantive part of this chapter. A more detailed analysis can be found in Bromwich, 1990; pp. 37–46.

Cost behaviour in competitive markets

A firm needs to be able to assess a number of cost factors if it is to expect that its cost structure will not militate against the sustainability in the market of the bundle of product attributes it offers and of its price and output strategy. It must first determine whether it has greater economies of scale in multi-production than its rivals for all outputs and also whether it has any products which are better produced on their own. If it does not possess either of these advantages, it needs to consider whether these disadvantages can be offset by any economies of scope it may possess in multi-product production over all volumes. Cost disadvantages can also be overcome where a unique product or products is offered which is protected by some type of barriers restricting the ability of other enterprises to offer competitive products.

Sustainability may not be guaranteed even where these rigorous cost conditions are met. This is because demand conditions are also important. For example, demand must be sufficient for sustainable volumes to be achieved at the point where the firm's costs are lower than those of their rivals. This suggests that a strategic management accounting information system needs to encompass demand information and collect all the internal and external cost data discussed above if fully informed decisions are to be achieved. Elements of the cost theory from which these ideas are taken (the theory of contestable markets, see Baumol *et al.*, 1988) would seem to yield considerable theoretical support for the ideas of strategic management accounting, especially its requirement to look beyond the firm.

Any manager or industrial accountant reading this section may well feel that the information required for decision-making when adopting this perspective on costs is far too burdensome. For the firm seeking to utilize this approach only for cost analysis, some relaxation of these information requirements is possible where the assumptions of the theory do not fully apply. If an incumbent firm does have the protection of barriers to entry, then the cost conditions for sustainability become less important for the maintenance of its market strategies. Incumbents possessing barriers to entry may not be so concerned with minor entry into their markets because such entry will not necessarily cause them to become unprofitable as it would with fully competitive markets. Even the prospect of larger-scale entry may not be a cause of great concern because incumbent firms may practice or threaten to resort to entry preventing strategies. Such relaxations of the assumptions necessary for sustainability allow incumbent firms interested in sustainability in such conditions to avoid the need to scan the entire spans of the cost structures of either actual or potential rivals. They can rather restrict themselves to the relevant range of outputs where entry would cause the profits of the incumbent firm to be reduced. However, additional information concerning entry conditions and entry prevention strategies in the industry will need to be collected by such firms if they are to maintain the sustainability of their strategies.

The above analysis suggests that information about barriers to entry may be important to the firm's strategy. Thus, the information concerning barriers to entry should comprise part of strategic management accounting. Although many barriers to entry are cost-based (Bain, 1956), the discipline of management accounting seems to ignore them entirely. Little, if any, mention of them can be found in accounting research or in management accounting textbooks. This may be due to the tendency, alluded to earlier, of management accounting to focus only on costs incurred by the enterprise. In contrast, the analysis of cost-based barriers by management accountants also requires the adoption of a more external focus because these barriers to entry relate to favourable cost advantages possessed by the incumbent firm or firms relative to potential entrants. Any lack of concern with barriers to entry in management accounting may be also explained either by the perceived stability of these barriers from one period to another or by the view that they are strategic matters to be considered by top management. With this latter view, the provision of information concerning them would seem to fall within the area of strategic management accounting.

Barriers to entry to a market have long been considered crucial determinants of industrial structure. Baumol *et al.* (1988) emphasize the importance of costs in determining barriers to exit. The existence of barriers of either type may allow some relaxation of the rigorous conditions concerning costs which were argued above to be necessary for the sustainability of enterprise strategies.

Accountants could have a role in providing information to enterprise management about these barriers, if only in measuring their costs. The current view is that barriers to entry arise only where a potential entrant cannot match, by purchases on the market, the advantages of existing firms. With this view, economies of scale or scope do not constitute barriers where new entrants have access to the same technology as existing firms at the same prices. Here, any restriction on entry is regarded as resulting from the size of the market being too small to support additional firms when incumbent firms are producing at their minimum average cost. Knowledge of how the spreading of fixed costs yield economies of scale is important in the determination of the cost sustainability of enterprise strategies but not in terms of barriers to entry. With this view, the only barriers flowing from enterprise cost structures are those resulting from absolute cost advantages. Accountants may help in evaluating the strength of such barriers by providing the relevant cost information for incumbent firms and that concerning potential competitors highlighting the source of such barriers.

An important source of absolute cost advantages are what are called sunk costs. These are costs, the price of which cannot be recouped or can only be partially recouped from the market by selling the relevant resources on the market. They yield a cost advantage to incumbent firms based on the need for new entrants to recoup these costs fully in product prices if entry is to be worthwhile. Thus, accountants should seek to provide information on sunk costs because of the strategic advantages they may bring to the enterprises which possess them. This really requires a continual study of fixed costs because any given fixed cost may be expected to have a sunk component, at least, over some short time period. Thus the role of sunk costs in terms of generating barriers to entry increases the general importance accorded to information concerning fixed costs because of their importance in maintaining the sustainability of enterprise product market strategies.

Conclusions

It has been suggested that there may be a role for accountants in helping to provide information for strategic decision-making and for the monitoring of strategies. This chapter has reviewed the arguments for applying strategic management accounting and reviewed the existing literature in this area. This chapter emphasized the role of the characteristics or attributes possessed by products in strategic planning and suggested that information about a number of demand and cost factors appertaining to the attributes possessed by a firm's products and those of its actual and potential rivals is needed for optimal decision-making. Accountants play an important role here in costing the characteristics provided by goods and in monitoring and reporting on these costs regularly. Similarly, they need to be involved in determining the cost of any package of attributes which is being considered for introduction to the market. However, where a strategic perspective is adopted by accountants, costs have to be considered in the context of demand factors because of the likely interplay between costs and demand in determining successful strategic conduct when considering product attributes.

Further reasons why accountants should be involved in strategy formation and should adopt the perspective provided by strategic management accounting were also considered here but rather more briefly. For example, the important role accountants can play in modelling the cost structures of competitors was discussed as was their part in ascertaining the importance of any barriers to entry the firm may possess.

Note

Some of the material in this chapter is based upon Bromwich (1990) and (1991) and is reproduced with permission.

I am grateful to the Chartered Institute of Management Accountants for financing the research utilized in this chapter as part of a study considering the treatment of fixed overheads with special reference to high-technology industries.

References

Allen, D. (1986). Strategic financial management. In *Research & Current Issues in Management Accounting* (eds M. Bromwich and A. G. Hopwood), London: Pitman, pp. 47–51.

Bain, J. S. (1965). *Barriers to New Competition*. Boston: Harvard University Press.

Baumol, W. J., Panzer, J. D. and Willig, R. D. (1988). *Contestable Markets and the Theory of Industry Structure*. San Diego: Harcourt Brace and Jovanovich.

Berliner, C. and Brimson, J. (eds) (1988). *Cost Management in Today's Advanced Manufacturing Environments; The CAM-I Conceptual Design*. Boston: Harvard Business School Press.

Bromwich, M. (1990). The case for strategic management accounting: the role of accounting information for strategy in competitive markets. *Accounting, Organisations and Society*, January, 27–46.

Bromwich, M. (1991). *Accounting for Strategic Excellence*, (forthcoming, 1991).

Bromwich, M. and Bhimani, A. (1991). Strategic investment appraisal. *Management Accounting (USA)*, March, 45–48.

Cooper, R. and Kaplan, R. S. (1987). How cost accounting systematically distorts product costs. In *Accounting and Management: Field Study Perspectives* (eds W. J. Bruns and R. S. Kaplan), Boston: Harvard Business School Press.

Dahlgaard, J. J., Kanji, G. K., Kristensen, K. and Norreklit, L. (1989). *A Comparative Study of Quality Control Methods and Principles in Japan, Korea and Denmark*. Arhus, Denmark: Institut for informationsbehandling.

Fern, R. H. and Tipgos, M. (1988). Controllers as business strategists: a progress report. *Management Accounting (USA)*, March, 25–29.

Goold, M. C. (1986). Accounting and strategy. In *Research & Current Issues in Management Accounting* (eds M. Bromwich and A. G. Hopwood), London: Pitman, pp. 181–91.

Haas, E. A. (1987). Breakthrough manufacturing. *Harvard Business Review*, March–April, 75–81.

Harris Research Centre (1990). *Information for Strategic Management: A Survey of Leading Companies*, 1990. KPMG Peat Marwick Management Consultants.

Hasegawa, K. (1986). *Japanese Style Management – An Insider's Analysis*. Tokyo: Kodasha International.

Hegarty, W. H., Hoffman R. C. (1987). Who influences strategic decisions? *Long Range Planning*, April, 76–85.

Hiromoto, T. (1988). Another hidden edge – Japanese management accounting. *Harvard Business Review*, July–August, 22–6.

Horngren, C. and Foster, G. (1987). *Cost Accounting: A Managerial Emphasis*. Englewood Cliffs, New Jersey: Prentice Hall.

Howell, R. A., Brown, J. D., Soucy, S. R., Seed, A. H. III (1987). *Management Accounting in the New Manufacturing Environment*. National Association of Accountants.

Kang, K. W. and Soong, H. Park (1986). Goldstar Electronics. In *Managerial Accounting and Analysis in Multinational Enterprises* (eds Holzer, H. P. and H. M. Schoenfeld), Berlin: Walter de Gruyter.

Lancaster, K. J. (1979). *Variety, Equity and Efficiency: Product Variety in an Industrial Society*. New York: Columbia University Press, pp. 16–36.

Porter, M. E. (1980). *Competitive Strategy: Techniques for Analysing Industries and Competitors*. New York: The Free Press.

Porter, M. E. (1985). *Competitive Advantage: Creating and Sustaining Superior Performance*. New York: The Free Press.

Shank, J. K. (1989). Strategic cost management: new wine or just new bottles. *Journal of Management Accounting Research*, Fall, 47–65.

Shank, J. K. and Govindarajan, V. (1989). *Strategic Cost Analysis: The Evolution from Managerial to Strategic Accounting*. Homewood II.: Irwin.

Simmonds, K. (1981a). Strategic management accounting. *Management Accounting*, April, 26–29.

Simmonds, K. (1981b). *The Fundamentals of Strategic Management Accounting, ICMA Occasional Papers Series*. London: ICMA.

Whipple, W., III (1988). How finance can contribute to strategic planning. *Journal of Accountancy*, January, 116–21.

Woods, M., Polorny, M., Lintner, V. and Blinkhorn, M. (1984). Investment appraisal in mechanical engineering. *Management Accounting*, October.

10

Accounting for marketing strategies

Keith Ward

Historically management accounting has been heavily biased towards the internal comparisons of costs and revenues and relatively little attention has been given to the external environment in which the business operates. In this chapter Keith Ward argues for a more strategic thrust to management accounting which focuses on both the external environment and the internal workings of the organization.

Ward begins by stressing that a successful business strategy requires the development and maintenance of some form of sustainable relative competitive advantage. Profits are likely to follow from achieving such a competitive advantage. Thus strategic management accounting should highlight the relative competitive positioning of the organization. In the long-term commercial success can only be achieved by implementing a succession of appropriately changing business strategies, which build on or maintain the relative competitive advantage of the business. An important role of strategic management accounting is therefore to highlight the need for a change in competitive strategy.

Having argued the case that management accounting should focus on external relative comparisons with competitors, Ward outlines some of the problems associated with this approach. In particular, he discusses problems relating to segmental profitability analysis and the financial evaluation of competitive marketing strategies.

The author then concentrates on the decision support information required to develop and implement specific competitive strategies. A competitive strategy at this level relates to a specific product in a specific market against identified competitors. Ward therefore advocates that management accounting should provide information on competitive strategies relating to product, markets (i.e. customers) and competition. The author then proceeds to describe in detail competitor

> *accounting, customer account profitability analysis and product profit-ability analysis within a strategic management accounting context.*

Introduction

In the past, the management accounting function within most businesses concentrated on the internal relationships among various costs and revenues. Most of the financial comparisons of current achievements were made against historic levels of actual performance or expected levels for this current period, as incorporated in the budgets or financial plans of the business. Unfortunately such an inwardly focused process ignores the potentially significant changes which occur, all too frequently and rapidly, in the external environment in which any business operates. Consequently, if management accounting is to contribute most effectively in its role as a decision support system, it must take account of the impact of the external environment as well as the relevant internal financial interrelationships.

This overall area of management accounting has become known as strategic management accounting, because 'strategic management' has a clearly identified interest in both the external environment and the internal workings of the organization. In January 1981 Professor Kenneth Simmonds in 'Strategic Management Accounting', a paper presented to CIMA: technical symposium, defined strategic management accounting as 'the provision and analysis of management accounting data about a business and its competitors for use in developing and maintaining the business strategy, particularly relative levels and trends in real costs and prices, volume, market share, cash flow and the proportion demanded of a firm's total resources'.

Given this definition, it is disappointing that in many businesses the financial performance measures in use are still predominantly indicators of short-term performance and often are heavily biased towards internal comparisons, rather than having the external, longer term relative emphasis which is so obviously important to business strategy. A successful business strategy requires the development and maintenance of some form of sustainable relative competitive advantage. It can be very strongly argued that profits follow from achieving such a competitive advantage, so that strategic management accounting should highlight the relative competitive positioning of the organization. However, given the dynamic nature of the external environment and the complexity of modern large, diversified organizations, these relative competitive advantages may change both over time and across the different parts of the business at any particular time. In the long term, therefore, commercial success can only be achieved by implementing a succession of appropriately changing business strategies, which build on or maintain the relative competitive advantage of the business.

This can be achieved in a multitude of ways depending on the selected strategic thrust for each particular part of the firm, and it is important that the management accounting system is appropriately tailored to support each particular business strategy.

Corporate and competitive strategies

Strategic management decisions are clearly required at several levels in any large organization. At the highest level, they drive the overall corporate strategy, and strategic management accounting systems must be developed to provide appropriately tailored financial information to support the strategic decisions taken at this level. Thus the complications created by various organizational structures must be allowed for. However, strategic management is also involved at the more detailed level of developing and implementing specific competitive strategies. The ultimate level of a competitive strategy relates to a specific product (product refers to both goods and services) in a specific market against identified competitors. Hence management accounting at this level must provide decision support information on products, markets (i.e. customers) and competition. In most cases, this requires that the organization is broken down into appropriate segments, so that specific information can be generated which focuses on the particular strategic decision under consideration. The ideal subdivision for this purpose is, not surprisingly, the strategic business unit (SBU) which is usually defined as a part of the overall organization having distinct external customers and readily identifiable competitors, as well as producing and selling a specified range of products. This part of strategic management accounting is considered in detail in this chapter and each element of accounting for these competitive marketing strategies (i.e. accounting for competitors, customers and products) is considered in detail, following a brief overview of the problems associated with such an approach.

Overview

Success is a relative measure and, even more clearly, a competitive advantage is a relative concept; having a good quality, cheap product is not a competitive advantage if the competition have better quality, cheaper products. Despite this, most management accounting information is still produced without any external form of comparison and, in many cases, even the internal comparisons which are used are not very helpful. Successful strategic management is also a long-term relative concept and therefore accounting measures which place undue emphasis on the short-term performance of the business are also not conducive to supporting good strategic decision-making. This is particularly true when applied to the important issue of improving the relative competitive positioning of the firm's products or its place in the market. In many cases, such an improvement requires expenditure which is treated as an accounting expense and therefore, in the short term, the profitability of the business may be reduced, even though over the longer term its financial performance has been enhanced.

There is a consequent need for a dramatic change in the way much internal management accounting information is presented to managers if the key objectives of strategic management accounting are to be achieved. Both the relative financial impact of strategic decisions and their longer term implications must be accurately and clearly reflected in the management reports generated by an appropriately designed accounting system. An important role for this detailed level of strategic management accounting is to highlight the need for a change in competitive strategy and, preferably, to indicate a few key indicators which will give advance warning that such a change will be necessary in the future. For many marketing-orientated companies, such an indicator would be any unexpected movement in the relative market share of major products. Yet very few businesses regularly incorporate such information into their internal management accounting reports, even though the information may be readily available and is probably already separately reported through the sales and marketing information system. Using such externally based comparisons to explain the relative current changes in sales revenues, profits and cash flows and their future implications can add considerable value to the accounting system in its function of supporting financially based strategic decisions.

There are also two aspects of all good management accounting systems which have particularly important implications in accounting for competitive strategies. First, managers, who are responsible for implementing specific elements of the competitive strategy, must be set objectives which are in line with the overall corporate objectives of the organization, so as to achieve goal congruence for individuals, SBUs and the group. This can easily be illustrated by reference to the potential timing conflict which is implicit in the way sales targets are set in many organizations. If sales managers are targeted to achieve particular sales revenue levels in the current accounting period and this forms their sole form of performance measurement, they cannot be expected to be overly concerned with either the profitability of those sales or, more importantly, the long-term development of customer relationships.

Second, there should be a clear distinction between assessing the economic performance of the business unit and the managerial performance of the responsible individuals. It is a fundamental issue of good financial control systems that managers should only be held accountable for those areas which are under their control. Inevitably in many SBUs of a large group, there will be certain internal areas of central costs which are not directly under the control of the divisional managers. However, when assessing the relative success of any competitive strategy, there will also be certain external influences which cannot be regarded as being under managerial control. This does not mean that these external non-controllable elements are unimportant and should be excluded from the strategic management accounting process. All the relevant elements must be included in the financial analysis if the correct strategic decision is to be taken. The important separation is that the economically justified decision does not necessarily reflect the relative managerial performance within the particular business. If an industry is depressed and loss-making, it may be sensible in economic terms to leave the industry or, if that is not practical, to minimize any new investment in that particular business. This may be valid no matter how good the managers are; in a hostile environment, the best managers simply lose less money than the rest. Equally in a booming economy, the worst managers in the world may find it relatively easy to make a reasonably good financial return, but they will always make a lower return than the best management team. Consequently the assessment of managerial performance should be made against a relative standard, which shows how well competitors are doing. Economic performance should be assessed against a more overall objective measure of the financial return being achieved as compared to the alternative investment returns which could be earned at a similar level of risk.

Segment profitability analysis problems

The most important aspect of a strategic management accounting system is that it helps in the strategic decision process; in other words, it should be a decision-based system and hence it must produce economically valid financial analysis of the available alternative opportunities. This creates several problems because most management accounting systems are based on the actual historic costs incurred by the business which are duly apportioned to the various subdivisions, such as products and customers. Unfortunately the relevant costs for strategic decisions are not the historic costs already incurred, but should be the incremental costs or the avoidable costs depending on the particular nature of the decision. Also, after many years of practice, management accountants have become very sophisticated in the ways in which shared costs can be apportioned across the relevant areas, and this normally means that the total cost is exactly absorbed by the various business segments. This obsession with excessive accounting neatness does not normally help the decision-based analysis at all, as the appropriate proportions which should be charged to individual segments depend upon how the total costs will change, as levels of activity alter. This is illustrated in Figure 10.1.

Segmented analysis within a business can be one, two or three dimen-

		Individual customers XYZ						Product's total profit
£000s								
I n d i v i d u a l	ABC	6	6					
			4	10	5	15	20	60
			5					
			4					
			16					
p r o d u c t			15					
			9					
			11					
'X' Customer's total profit			70					Business total profit

Note: All costs are spread to a specific product and a specific customer, so that every customer's total profit (Row X) is split across each of the individual products. Similarly each product's total profit (Column Y) is spread to individual customers. This means that the sum of all the customers' individual profits will equal the sum of all the products' individual profits and both will equal the business' total profits.

Comment: Very neat and completely useless!

Figure 10.1   *The 'ultimate neat' segment profitability analysis*

sional as it may focus on a particular product, customer, or competitor or a combination of two or three. The accounting problems are increased if an initially one-dimensionally based analysis (say, a product profitability analysis) is subsequently used as part of a customer account profitability evaluation. In arriving at the product profitability analysis, the business would have first deducted from the sales revenue for the product all the directly attributable costs for that product (e.g. direct raw materials, direct labour and product-based marketing costs). However, there would also have been a large number of relevant but indirect shared costs which need to be taken into account in such an exercise. These costs, such as distribution and customer-based marketing, would be apportioned on the most appropriate basis, so as to arrive at a net contribution for each product. As mentioned this apportionment process can be, and unfortunately often is, applied to all shared costs, including those committed fixed costs which cannot change as a result of any subsequent business decision. The appropriate decision-based level of analysis clearly depends on the particular decision which is being faced and this demands that the accounting system is sufficiently flexible and can react fast enough to supply the required financial information in time to support the strategic decisions.

Some of these decisions will not focus on specific products but may concentrate on particular customers or the appropriate response to an unexpected initiative from a competitor. This previously established product profitability analysis does not provide a sound starting point for such a differently focused segmented analysis, as some costs which were direct and others which are indirect to a particular product may be the other way round for a specific customer. Thus customer marketing costs, and possibly distribution expenses, can be directly allocated to each customer, while the product marketing costs will have to be apportioned depending on the mix of products bought by each customer. Consequently each different type of segmented profitability analysis has to be compiled from scratch, which has severe resourcing implications if the accounting system is not carefully specified. The ideal solution is to use a relational database which enables the coded basic financial data to be rapidly analysed in the most appropriate manner for particular segmented decisions. This type of accounting system also copes very easily with the added complexity for hierarchical segmented financial analysis. As well as requiring profitability analyses for individual products and customers, managers need information on the relative performance of groups of products and customers (e.g. particular channels of distribution) and combinations thereof (such as the profitability of sales of the specific product offerings which face off against a particular competitor and were sold to customers also served by this competitor). Unless a flexible, computerized coding system has been developed, the clerical workload involved in responding to these irregular but normally urgent demands from senior management can make providing timely yet accurate financial information impossible.

Understanding of cost relationships

The decision support emphasis of this type of marketing accounting system has implications for the ways in which costs should be classified. Strategic decisions tend to be long term and externally focused, which means that the traditional accounting classification between fixed and variable costs may be irrelevant. The concepts of committed and avoidable/incremental costs are usually more helpful because, by definition, the time-scale of the particular decision dictates whether the costs really are committed (i.e. will have to be spent whatever decision is taken) or can be avoided (these avoidable costs are also known as severable costs) by the business as a result of a change in competitive strategy now. Incremental costs are clearly the opposite side of avoidable costs and represent the additional costs which will be incurred as a result of the decision.

It is very well understood that the relevant costs for financially evaluating all decisions are the future costs which will be affected by the particular decision; hence truly committed costs can be ignored while the avoidable or incremental costs must be taken into account. However, the problem with all these relevant decision costs is that, by definition, they are in the future and can change, i.e. they are uncertain. Consequently an important aspect of all management accounting systems is that they must assist in the forecasting of these future costs. The potential forecasting accuracy for most costs depends upon the kind of predictive relationship which can be established from an historical analysis of past movements.

In some areas of the business, a very good input–output relationship can be established, which enables very accurate predictions for the future to be made. Most of these 'engineering' type relationships are restricted to the physical interactions involved, e.g. how many tonnes of silver are needed to produce 100,000 rolls of photographic film, rather than the total cost which will depend on the future cost per unit, i.e. the cost of each tonne of silver. Engineering costs are not restricted to the production area and can be used wherever there is this clearly established predictable relationship between units of input used and the level of output produced. Thus repetitive clerical functions are an area where these relationships can be established. The certainty of forecasting the physical relationship enables the accounting resources to concentrate on forecasting the relevant future cost per unit of input, and this can make the overall financial evaluation much more accurate.

Many businesses not only do not apply this concept of 'standard costing' to service and other non-production areas of the business, such as marketing, but even in the traditional areas, its use has become stereotyped and of almost no relevance to strategic decisions. It is very common for companies to prepare detailed variance analyses which are little more than accounting reconciliation statements, because they do not indicate decisions which should be taken, such as specific changes in current competitive strategies. Competitive strategies should be based on relative financial information which must include an up-to-date assessment of the external environment, rather than an historic reconciliation of actual results with an outdated prediction of what the results might be. Management accountants within the business have normally built up a very good understanding of the dynamic relationships among the various important cost elements, but this knowledge is often not effectively utilized in the evaluation of alternative possible competitive strategies. One clear area where this could be used very beneficially is by applying this knowledge to developing an understanding of competitors' relative cost structures, thus enabling models to be built of potential competitive responses to strategic initiatives. Before considering this area in detail, there is another major accounting problem which is highlighted by segmented financial analysis which needs to be considered.

Marketing investment analysis

Most companies in competitive markets now agree that their overall long-term success is closely linked to the success of their marketing strategy. Consequently, levels of marketing expenditure are often significant and yet these are often subjected to far less rigorous financial evaluations than smaller financial commitments on more tangible assets. Few sophisticated companies even apply their normal discounted cash flow procedures to major expenditures on marketing activities, and still fewer have challenged the traditional method of accounting for such expenditures. Accounting procedures have developed very complex ways of distinguishing between capital and revenue expenditure on all sorts of tangible fixed assets, even where the future benefits of having such long term assets are highly dependent upon the company continuing to have successful products and loyal customers willing to buy these products.

The potential strategic implications of the current expensing of all marketing expenditures in the accounting period in which they are incurred are significant; and this issue is not concerned with the current debate regarding the capitalization of marketing assets on externally published balance sheets. Much more important is the impact of the management accounting treatment of these intangible assets on the strategic decision-making process of the business. In the case of an investment in a tangible asset, the financial evaluation is automatically carried out over the full economic life of the asset and the accounting 'matching' principle avoids any dramatically adverse short-term financial consequences of such an investment. The 'prudent' method of immediately expensing all marketing expenditures highlights the short-term financial pressure on such activities and this is often exacerbated by the absence of the use of any appropriate long-term evaluation procedure.

For many marketing-led businesses, their most valuable assets are their brands and their customers and yet, if they are under pressure to improve financial performance in the short-term, the easiest way to improve profitability is to reduce expenditure on marketing or on research and development into new products. As with most assets, if they are not properly maintained, marketing assets will decline in value, and so the long-term consequences of this short-term expediency may be horrendous. Even worse this reduction in marketing activity may have been done at a time when the marketing strategy called for an increase in relative market share; the result may have been the opposite with market share falling sharply.

What is required is a close linkage between the specific objectives of the marketing and competitive strategy for the business unit and the management accounting controls used by the business. Thus marketing expenditures should be split between development and maintenance activities. Development marketing is designed to increase the value of the marketing assets, in the same way as capital improvements would be regarded for a more normal, tangible asset. Maintenance activity is obviously carried out to keep the existing attributes of the asset at their current levels, so as to maintain the overall value. If inadequate maintenance expenditure takes place, the value of the marketing asset will decline. This type of financial evaluation can only be carried out if the existing attributes of a marketing asset (e.g. a brand) can be defined, and the objectives of a development marketing strategy can be quantified and evaluated.

Many companies do indeed carry out this type of quantified, specific marketing planning so that desired levels of brand awareness, effective distribution and customer preference are established, with detailed plans for achieving these objectives. What is missing in most of these businesses is the involvement of their management accountants in any meaningful form of financial evaluation and monitoring of the resulting marketing budget. Thus the marketing objectives may specify an increase in customer awareness of three per cent over the next year and the marketing plan includes £2 million for a television advertising campaign to achieve this. It is quite possible to construct a simple financial model to link the proposed change in customer awareness to the possible increase in future sales of the product and thus to evaluate the potential financial return from the proposed advertising expenditure. Indeed a more comprehensive model could attempt to optimize the planned advertising expenditure. Clearly the initial attempts at such models are going to be highly inaccurate but the learning curve is normally very steep, and the financial evaluation process itself forces line managers to question the assumed relationships inherent in their plans (e.g. what is the relationship between customer awareness and sales levels?).

Some companies are attempting to tackle this area, but even in most of these leading companies, the sophistication of the marketing evaluation techniques is far ahead of the corresponding financial analysis. This whole area of marketing accounting represents one of the most important development opportunities for financial managers who wish to make a major strategic contribution to their companies.

Competitor accounting

Strategic management has already been stated as being interested in creating a sustainable competitive advantage and this can clearly only be created by direct comparison to competitors. This comparison should be as precise and clearly identified as is practical. Therefore the business must conduct detailed relative financial evaluations of its major competitors. In any such competitor accounting analysis relative costs and prices are much more important than the absolute levels. This is of considerable assistance as it should be much easier to build up a picture of the relative cost structure of these competitors by using the knowledge of all the appropriate managers within the business and the wide range of potential external sources. Thus competitor accounting should not be seen as the exclusive preserve of the accounting department, but neither should it focus exclusively on relative cost comparisons. The competitor's marketing strategy must be understood and factored into the analysis; for example, if its product positioning is one of very high quality and this enables it to command a substantial price premium in the market, due to the high value perceived by customers, the relative cost comparison is likely to indicate an apparent but irrelevant cost disadvantage.

The process for undertaking a competitor accounting analysis is fairly straightforward. The existing and current competition should be identified by reference to the strategic objectives of the business unit, but it is important to include other companies which satisfy similar customer needs, even if in very different ways. In other words, this stage should be done from the perspective of the targeted customers by considering which other businesses they would consider as alternative suppliers.

The most important element in the competitor analysis is now to consider what alternative competitive strategies could be implemented by each of these identified competitors. This strategic analysis clearly requires an assessment of their relative cost positions and customer value propositions, but it must also include their commitment to this particular business segment and its importance to their overall business. This should indicate their likely response both to changes in the external environment and to any possible new strategic competitive initiatives.

Clearly for many companies it is very difficult even to measure the historic level of competitors' costs, particularly when these competitors are part of very large diversified businesses, which only publish overall financial results for the group. However, by using a combination of externally published figures and deductive reasoning from both direct observation and a whole series of indirect sources, such as are indicated in Figure 10.2,

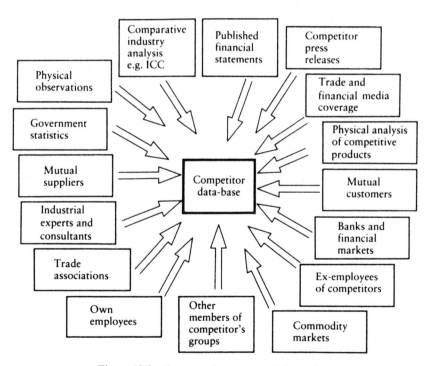

Figure 10.2 *Sources of competitor information*

it is normally possible to build up a reasonable picture of the major differences in cost between the competitor and the originating business. It is important to remember that none of these analytical forecasting methods can ever produce a precisely accurate result, and an absolute snapshot of the competitor's cost level is not the objective. Consistent application of the technique on a regular basis will start to show up the trend in relative cost levels, and this can of be great value in selecting the most appropriate competitive strategy in the future.

It is also not necessary even to develop a complete cost picture in some cases, as the key relative items can be defined by the stage of development of the products and markets in which the businesses compete. If the product is very new in the market and the market development is not yet guaranteed, a key competitive issue may be the relative strengths of the research and development teams. The relative levels of expenditure on R&D can be assessed by building up an estimate of competitive spending; if by no other means than using the size of their physical facilities and applying a normal level of space allocation per person, etc.

Where there is a high growth market, the critical competitive factor will often be growth in market share and this can be monitored over time. Forecasts can be generated by reference to estimates of relative levels of marketing expenditure, and these relationships can be tested over time and the models updated. As always, it is important to take account of possible differences in strategic thrusts for particular competitors. It is normally prudent to carry out a particularly careful review for any competitor which appears to be implementing a competitive strategy which is directly contrary to everyone else in the market; perhaps they have got it right! When the market matures and the rate of growth declines rapidly, it is quite common for price competition to become much more important. Consequently in this environment relative cost comparisons become particularly important and quite small, but sustainable, differences can make significant differences to the financial success of the mature business.

However, once again allowance must be made for competitors who successfully maintain their premium pricing strategy during this maturity phase. If their market share is retained, their customers must place an even higher premium value on their enhanced product attributes. It is important to try to assess if any cost penalty being incurred by this competitor more than offsets the pricing premium obtained in the market.

This information can be of value in assessing possible future opportunities for, and threats to, the competitive strategy of the business. It must be remembered that this is the main objective of competitor financial analysis. This should focus the analytical effort on areas which can add value to future competitive strategy decisions, rather than merely improve the detailed accuracy of the relative cost assessment for a particular competitor if the existing level of accuracy is satisfactory.

Customer account profitability

Customer account profitability (CAP) analysis can be defined as 'the total sales revenue generated from a customer or customer group less all the costs that are incurred in servicing that customer or customer group'. The fundamental strategic importance of CAP can be illustrated by the philosophy of one major marketing-led company which argues that it does not have profitable products, only profitable customers. Indeed an immediate impact of introducing any level of segmented financial analysis into an organization is to destroy totally any illusion that the same level of profit is derived from all customers. Groups of customers or different channels of distribution can often be distinguished in terms of the effective selling prices achieved and variations in the mix of products purchased. However, in many cases, these factors may be much less important than the varying levels of customer service that are supplied to each category of customer or market segment. It may well be that the lower selling prices charged to one such segment are more than justified by the cost savings which are generated by the way in which these customers are serviced. Hence these customers may, in reality, be more profitable than those in areas where the higher selling prices achieved are more than offset by the increased costs incurred in achieving the sales. If the business is to allocate its limited resources most effectively in the future, so as to achieve its corporate objectives, it must have reliable information on which of its potential customer groupings are its most profitable and whether there are any existing areas in which the business actually makes a loss.

This is the major benefit to a business of carrying out CAP analysis and indicates that, once again, relative comparative performance is much more important than the absolute profitability levels of individual segments. Thus the financial analysis can concentrate on quantifying the impact of the differences in the way in which the various customers groups are dealt with by the business. It is, as previously discussed, important that these resource allocation decisions are based on relevant costs. Neither gross contribution margins, before taking account of different servicing costs, nor net profit levels, after arbitrarily apportioning committed shared costs across the different customer groups, are therefore appropriate levels of financial analysis for this purpose.

CAP has become a major area of interest for many companies, particularly due to the increasing focus on customers as 'the most important assets which the company has'. The increasing demands from major customers for individual, tailored treatment in terms of pricing, distribution, sales support, specialized packaging, etc. have accelerated the need for more accurate financial evaluations of the impact of these potential changes in competitive strategies.

For many companies, the main strategic thrust is attempting to expand the range of products sold to existing loyal customers, as is shown in Figure 10.3. This indicates the importance of 'customer assets' to the business. It is also important that the financial analysis ensures that increasing sales to *these* existing customers will enhance the long-term profitability of the business. The logic of such a marketing strategy is that it is more cost-effective to build on the established loyalty of these existing customers, rather than to try to develop new markets in which to sell the existing product range. Clearly the comparative competitor analysis of relative strengths should have indicated which strategy was most appropriate for the particular business.

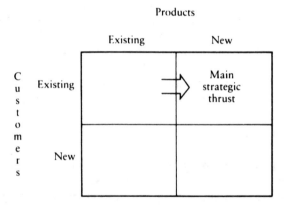

Figure 10.3 *Utilizing 'customer assets'*

However, this customer asset-based strategy must not be seen as risk free, even though the effective intangible asset turnover ratio is being improved as well as potentially enhancing the profit margin level through better absorption of existing fixed costs. If the new products are not well accepted by these vitally important existing customers, there is an obvious danger of a rebound effect on the sales levels of existing products. This risk needs to be taken into account when financially evaluating the benefits of such an integrated marketing strategy; it also helps to explain why some leading marketing-orientated companies insist that all their products are separately and independently branded, despite the loss of economies of scale and synergy benefits in their advertising.

When implementing a system of CAP, the business must highlight the differences in costs between two categories of customer, but the relevant size of the difference may change depending on the strategic decision under consideration. An example using sales-force costs may make this clearer. One category of customer may be considering doing away with the services of the field sales-force of its suppliers and is seeking to negotiate an appropriate discount to reflect the prospective savings to be made by the suppliers. From the supplier's perspective, the potential discount should reflect the avoidable cost of the sales-force which will be saved if the change is made. However, this avoidable cost will not normally be the same as the historic actual cost which may have been apportioned to this particular customer, as this will include some shared costs (such as sales managers) which will not change if only this customer stops using these support services. Clearly the CAP analysis must reflect increasing levels of attributable cost as the customer groupings are made more general; thus if a change is made for the whole of the distribution channel, the savings might be much greater. Also the potential cost saving may not be equal to the potential incremental cost which would be incurred if a single customer or group of customers wanted to start using the services of the field sales-force.

Unfortunately if segment profitability analysis is to be of maximum value as a decision support tool, it must be tailored to the needs of each category of decision.

Product profitability analysis

Product costing has been a mainstay of management accounting for many years and many companies have developed very complex cost apportionment systems in this area. However, even for many of these apparently financially sophisticated businesses, the concept of applying an externally focused, strategic decision-based analysis to relative product profitabilities is still new and, in some sectors of industry, is as yet not widely in use. Most existing product costing systems are oriented around production technology or some other product attributes, rather than being designed from the perspective of the external marketplace and the competitive strategy of the business. Thus accounting systems often emphasize the impact of sales volumes, by assuming a linear relationship between volume and product profitability. This clearly is an invalid assumption in the long-term, when all costs must be regarded as variable, but it is also unrealistic to assume that, in the short-term, sales volumes can be increased without altering the effective contribution per unit achieved on product sales. The classical profit/volume straight line graph becomes a complex set of curves when trying to assess the financial impact of alternative product-based marketing strategies.

This financial analysis of relative product profitabilities is obviously of critical importance to those businesses which have as their main strategic thrust the development of new markets in which to sell their existing products, as shown in Figure 10.4. Instead of their major strengths being based on loyal customers, these businesses have a relative competitive advantage in their existing products, and this should form the basis for their future competitive strategy. In many cases, this strength is embodied in the well-established branding of the particular product attributes and the proposed marketing strategy is to exploit this brand in other markets and with other new customers. Once again, the basis of this competitive strategy should be financially analysed to ensure both that the relative product profitability of the core brand is sufficiently strong to justify its further development and that the proposed developments into new markets will improve, rather than dissipate, this existing level of profitability.

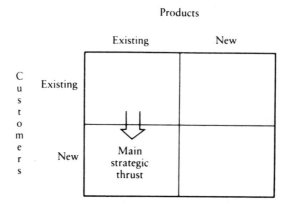

Figure 10.4 *Maximizing value of existing products*

Not surprisingly therefore, the early developments in systems for decision-based product profitability analysis were driven by such strongly product-orientated and highly branded companies. These companies, of which Procter and Gamble (P&G) was the leader, wanted to use the analysis as a major strategic marketing tool in order to expand both their customer base and their share of the existing customer base. This strategy was based on preparing the product profitability analysis, not from the traditionally inwardly focused perspective, but from the point of view of their customers. P&G's products are principally sold through retailers (i.e. an intermediary channel of distribution), who are mainly concerned with the relative financial performance of the alternative products which they are asked to stock in their stores. The selling space in the stores is clearly limited and thus constitutes a critical limiting factor on which to base the relative product contribution analysis. The strategic objective of the companies introducing this innovative use of product profitability analyses was to show that their products made a relatively high rate of profit contribution when expressed in terms of the customers' limiting factor (the retail selling space in the current example). This would be particularly helpful for products which, on a more superficial financial comparison, appeared less attractive than rivals for the limited shelf space; high unit volume products with relatively low unit selling prices, such as toilet rolls and washing powders, would fit into this category. By including the higher rate of sale of these products, it was possible to show that they made a perfectly acceptable overall contribution for the space which they occupied.

The financial analysis was made more sophisticated by including other differences in relative costs across the various product categories. Thus specific financial allowances were made for ease or difficulty of ordering, delivery, handling, storage, display in-store, and the period of credit granted to the retailer, as well as the more obvious marketing promotional offers made by the suppliers. Clearly such a financial analysis focuses on relative contribution levels per unit of limiting factor and this makes the process considerably more practical.

When it was introduced this type of direct product profitability (DPP), as it has become known, had a significant impact and it was quickly picked up and applied by the retailers themselves, using their in-depth internal knowledge of the operational cost differences among the products. It has also been applied as a positive marketing tool in many other areas of business (it has particular application where an intermediary channel of distribution is involved) and is now available in a range of tailored computer software application packages.

Indeed many companies are now linking DPP analysis and CAP analysis in order to devise financially justified, specifically tailored marketing strategies for individual customer groups purchasing a range of products. These applications indicate the potential added value which can be generated by a sound strategic application of segmented financial analysis in the area of accounting for marketing strategies.

Linking performance measures and competitive strategies in service businesses: three case studies

T. J. Brignall, L. Fitzgerald, R. Johnston and R. Silvestro

Most of the management accounting literature has tended to focus on the application of management accounting techniques within the manufacturing sector. The service sector has been virtually ignored even though it constitutes a larger proportion of economic output than manufacturing activities in both the UK and the USA. This chapter focuses on performance measurement and control systems in service organizations and the extent to which they support corporate objectives and competitive strategies.

The chapter begins with a brief review of the relevant literature. Drawing off recent research, the authors outline six performance dimensions against which divisional or strategic business unit performance can be monitored and controlled, and indicate the types of performance measures which can be used for each dimension. The authors stress, however, that the managers of every service organization will need to develop their own set of performance measures to help them gain and retain competitive advantage. This set will be affected by the interaction of three contingent variables: the competitive environment they face, their chosen strategy and the type of service business they are running.

This chapter also contains case studies relating to different service organizations: a major UK high street bank, a hotel chain and a home electronics rental service organization. The strategies and performance measurement systems of these organizations are examined in order to ascertain the extent to which these service companies' strategies are supported with appropriate performance measurement systems. The authors briefly discuss the matches or mismatches observed between the strategies and measurement systems for each case.

In the concluding section the authors discuss the need for companies to develop systems for the monitoring and control of those aspects of performance which are critical to the successful realization of their strategy.

Choice of appropriate [performance] measures is an art that must be practised in conjunction with the strategic goals of the firm and in close communication with the rapid changes occurring in firms' . . . processes (Kaplan 1984a).

Introduction

In this chapter we argue that performance measurement and control systems in for-profit service organizations should support corporate objectives and competitive strategies. Organizational control is the process of ensuring that an organization is pursuing actions and strategies which will enable it to achieve its goals. The measurement and evaluation of performance is central to control, and means posing three questions: what has happened? why has it happened? what are we going to do about it? A number of authors across several management disciplines have claimed that performance measurement often focuses narrowly on the easily quantifiable aspects of performance such as productivity and cost, to the neglect of other performance criteria such as quality or flexibility, which are equally critical to competitive business success. Recognizing this, many successful companies now use non-financial performance indicators, whether quantitative (hard) or qualitative (soft), to supplement traditional performance indicators such as financial or operating ratios. These performance measures are usually part of a feedforward-feedback control model in which progress against plans, budgets, standards and targets is monitored by the analysis of significant variances and the use of a balanced set of performance measures across various dimensions (see Figure 11.1).

This chapter briefly reviews the relevant literature and, drawing on recent research, identifies six performance dimensions against which divisional or strategic business unit (SBU) performance in service industries can be monitored and controlled, and indicates the types of performance measure which can be used against each criterion. This chapter also contains three case studies.

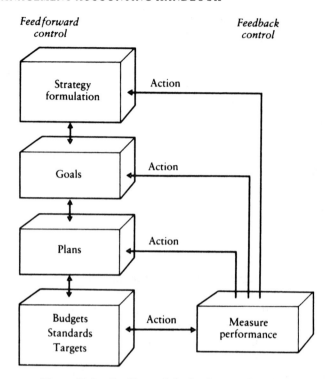

Figure 11.1 *Feedforward:feedback control model*

A division/SBU is a natural grouping of part of an organization, which may contain one or more SBUs/divisions. SBUs/divisions will also serve as a link between corporate, SBU, functional and product managers. The SBU/divisional type of organizational structure therefore helps overcome some of the problems of size and diversity by breaking strategic planning into three levels: corporate, SBU/division and function. We concentrate on performance measurement at this second level.

Service industries now make up 64 per cent of GDP and 70 per cent of UK employment and are the fastest growing sector of the economy, yet they are almost completely neglected in traditional management accounting textbooks, which concentrate on the problems of manufacturing industry (see, for example, Drury, 1988). The following typology of performance criteria may be used as a tool to analyse the match between service strategy and the range of measures used to control performance against strategy. The aim is to develop a management tool for identifying mismatches between strategy and control.

Performance criteria

In 1953 the management guru Peter Drucker identified seven generic performance criteria and argued that the objectives set by organizations for each performance area should be supported by appropriate measures which could be used continually to monitor and control performance against objectives. Drucker (1953) goes some way towards providing a classification of the multiple facets of business performance, and has received some support in the field of management education (see, for example, Rowe *et al.*, 1986). More recently Sink (1985) developed Drucker's framework with the enrichment of observations drawn from Peters and Waterman's *In Search of Excellence* and redefined his own set of performance criteria: profitability, effectiveness, productivity, efficiency, quality, quality of working life and innovation.

Kaplan (1983) also identified a range of performance areas which organizations have to control and measure. His work referred specifically to manufacturing but the following dimensions are also applicable to services: profitability, cost control, competitiveness, product leadership, productivity, quality, delivery performance, innovation and flexibility.

These performance criteria, drawn from the production/operations management and management accounting literatures, can be synthesized into the following six generic categories: financial performance, competitive performance, resource utilization, quality of service, innovation and flexibility (Fitzgerald *et al.*, 1991). Sink (1985) also includes quality of working life in his list of performance criteria. It is arguable that it is even more crucial to generate job satisfaction and employee loyalty in a service organization because of the frequently high degree of customer contact: as J. Willard Marriott of the Marriott Corporation argued, happy employees make happy customers (Hostage, 1975). Nevertheless, it is our contention that whilst providing quality of working life may be a necessary prerequisite for successful business performance, it is not itself a dimension of performance. To summarize, we suggest that there are six dimensions against which measurement of business performance can take place (see Table 11.1).

We believe that the managers of every service organization will need to develop their own set of performance measures to help them gain and retain a competitive advantage. This set will be affected by the interaction of three contingent variables: the competitive environment they face, their chosen strategy and the type of service business they are running. These three variables primarily determine, respectively, the why, the what and the how of performance measurement. The design of a performance

Table 11.1 Business performance criteria

Financial performance	Profitability
	Liquidity
	Capital structure
	Market ratios
Competitiveness	Relative market share and position
	Sales growth
	Measures of the customer base
Resource utilization	Productivity (input : output)
	Efficiency (resources planned : consumed)
	Utilization (resources available : consumed)
Quality of service	Overall service indicators
	Measures of the twelve determinants of service quality; reliability, responsiveness, aesthetics, cleanliness, comfort, friendliness, communication, courtesy, competence, access, availability, security
Innovation	Proportion of new to old products and services
	New product and service sales levels
Flexibility	Product/service introduction flexibility
	Product/service mix flexibility
	Volume flexibility
	Delivery flexibility

measurement system is therefore best done in three steps linked to these variables.

To a large extent it is the presence of some degree of competition which causes a need for management information and affects the nature of the information system. Thus the first step in developing a balanced set of performance measures across all six dimensions is to decide what kind of competitive environment the business faces: relatively turbulent and competitive, or not. This will in turn determine whether its managers need to build an interactive information system focusing on strategic threats and uncertainties and facilitating regular dialogue between top management and operating management to speed organizational learning, or can rely on delegated control of day-to-day operations to ensure sustained competitive success (Simons, 1987, 1990 and 1991). This need to tailor the type of information system (interactive or by exception) to the nature of the competitive environment reminds us of the vital link between performance measurement and appropriate action at the right organizational level. The need for action in response to environmental changes is the why of performance measurement. Obviously, in a dynamic environment those items which are monitored interactively will tend to change over time, but in many businesses most items will be treated on an exception basis.

What one should measure in any organization depends on strategic intentions. If a company decides, for example, to differentiate itself in the market on the basis of service quality, then it should have measures in place to monitor and control service quality. If technological leadership and innovation is the key source of a company's competitive advantage, then it should be measuring its performance in this area relative to its competitors. Cost leaders will therefore tend to focus on measuring their resource utilization and controlling costs along the value chain; differentiators will give greater emphasis to measuring service quality, flexibility and innovation.

The third step in developing a set of performance measures across six dimensions is to decide what kind of service business you are dealing with: professional service, service shop or mass service (see classification scheme later). Some measures may be infeasible or inappropriate in certain types of service, but not in others. Given one's strategy, it may be quite easy to see what should be measured, but this does not always mean that you can see how to measure it! This is where firms in the same class may learn from each other – most notably, perhaps, from their competitors.

There is a further important point to be made about the six performance dimensions, which is that they fall into two conceptually different classes. The first two, financial performance and competitiveness, are measures of the results of the company's strategy: the other four are measures of factors that determine competitive success. Whereas all companies will wish to measure the results of their strategy, the mix of factors that determine their competitive success will vary. In consequence, while one would not expect much difference between companies' management accounting systems and use of competitiveness measures, one would anticipate systematic differences in their overall performance measurement systems, which will include measures of determinants. Finally, measurement against this range of criteria may make visible the trade-offs which can exist between them: for example, trade-offs between short-term financial return and long-term competitive position, or between resource utilization and service quality.

The task of how to control service organizations may be usefully approached by viewing them in the terms of a simple input: process: output model, in which human and other resources flow through the process of designing, producing and delivering a product or service – what Porter

(1980) has called the 'value chain' (see Figure 11.2). Organizational performance on the six dimensions may be measured at any or all of these three stages. However, this simple model does not reflect the wide differences in processes, mixes of inputs and types of output that may be found in a sample of real service organizations. These differences may have profound implications for how to measure performance. A useful way of coping with such complexity is to use a classification scheme such as that developed by Fitzgerald *et al.* (1991). Fitzgerald *et al.* proposed the three service archetypes mentioned earlier: professional services, service shops and mass services (see Figure 11.3). In their classification scheme the number of customers processed by a typical business unit per day determines the level of demand placed on the business, and six other dimensions measure aspects of the response to that demand. Professional services deal with comparatively low numbers of customers per day, whereas mass services have many customers with service shops falling between the two.

Figure 11.2 *Input-process-output model*

However, while services may vary among themselves, they tend to have five characteristics in common which distinguish them from other businesses and which will also have implications for how to measure performance. First, with most services the customer is present during the process of delivering the service, which is a source of both threats and opportunities to service managers. Second, there are often intangible aspects of service which are difficult to measure. Third, customers' service expectations may not be homogeneous; nor may staff performance. Fourth, in many services the production and consumption of the service may be simultaneous. This, together with the fifth characteristic, perishability, means that inventory cannot be used as a buffer between peaks and troughs in demand.

With this background in mind we proceed to examine three case studies

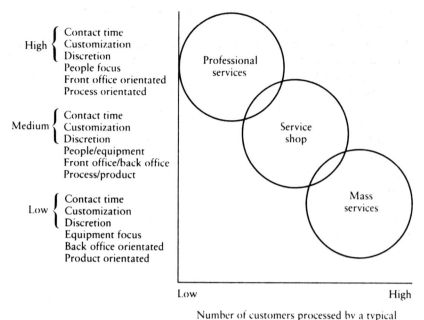

High {
Contact time
Customization
Discretion
}
People focus
Front office orientated
Process orientated

Medium {
Contact time
Customization
Discretion
}
People/equipment
Front office/back office
Process/product

Low {
Contact time
Customization
Discretion
}
Equipment focus
Back office orientated
Product orientated

Professional
services

Service
shop

Mass
services

Low   High

Number of customers processed by a typical
unit per day

Figure 11.3   *Service classification scheme*

in service performance measurement. To simplify comparisons, all three
are service shops.

Links between strategy and performance measurement in three service organizations

As we have said before, most management accounting textbooks still focus
on the problems of manufacturing industry. To do something to redress
the balance, in this section the above categorization of performance criteria is used as a tool to examine the performance measures used by three
service shop organizations, investigated in the light of their strategic intentions. The strategies and measurement systems of a major UK high street
bank, a hotel chain and a home electronics rental service were researched
(Fitzgerald *et al.*, 1991) with a view to identifying the extent to which these
service companies' strategies are supported with appropriate performance

measurement systems. The research methodology included interviews and the analysis of documentation. A profile of each company will include an outline of corporate strategy and of the financial and operational performance measures implemented, followed by a brief discussion of the matches or mismatches observed between the strategies and measurement systems in each case.

High street bank

The interviews were based in one region of this major high street bank, offering both corporate and retail banking services, and included the regional director, his executive team and supporting branch management and staff. The regional director had been instated some eighteen months previously with the brief of improving regional profit performance. The region's comparatively low profitability was partly explained by the declining local economy, nevertheless, the director felt that there was considerable scope for improvement.

Whilst the region had enjoyed a tradition of customer loyalty, with the entry of new competitors (such as building societies, foreign banks and credit card companies), competition was becoming increasingly fierce and it was recognized that the bank could no longer rely so heavily on its historical reputation in order to gain and retain custom. Indeed, the bank had lost its regional position as market leader over the past two years; it was, therefore, one of the regional director's prime aims to restore its previous position in terms of market share. He planned to achieve this by means of a differentiation strategy based on service quality, but recognized that this would necessitate a change in the bank's culture towards a market orientation and greater profit consciousness.

Table 11.2 itemizes the performance measures which were used to monitor and control branch performance (both retail and corporate sectors), together with the methods and frequency of reporting.

This list of performance measures is dominated by financial, volume and productivity measures. No measures of competitiveness were reported which reflected branch performance relative to local markets, although branch managers were required to produce annual business plans outlining their competitive position and plans for improving it. Branch targets were not set for market share but only for financial performance – despite the clear concern expressed by senior managers about the recent erosion of market share.

When asked how service quality was measured, managers referred to letters of complaint as the prime indicator used by regional office to gauge

Table 11.2 Performance measures used by Regional Office (RO) to monitor Branch performance

---

Financial performance

Profit and loss account	Quarterly report to RO
Average gross margins as percentage average interest rate	Reported half yearly by branches to RO
Ratio of total commissions and expenses	Calculated annually by RO and circulated to branches
Return on notional capital	Calculated annually by RO and circulated to branches in the form of a league table
Level of bad debts	Branches supply list of all high-risk accounts/out of order accounts to RO every two months

Competitive performance

Number of accounts by product category	Quarterly report to RO
Number of corporate accounts lost and gained, with reasons for transfer	Quarterly report to RO

Resource utilization

Ratio of total workload and total available man hours	Monthly reporting to RO
Average debit and credit balance per head of staff	Calculated annually by RO for each branch and circulated as a league table

Service quality

Number of customer complaints received	Continuously monitored by RO
Number of corporate accounts lost and gained, with reasons for transfer	Quarterly report to RO
Audit of the quality of branch lending decisions	Carried out every three years by RO

Innovation and flexibility

None identified

---

branch performance in delivering quality and generating customer satisfaction. It was, nevertheless, recognized that such letters facilitated only reaction rather than proaction, and that they could not be interpreted as accurate measures of satisfaction since many customers either remained silent or moved their accounts elsewhere when dissatisfied.

Customer reasons for transferring their accounts to or from the bank were also recorded, although this practice was restricted to large corporate accounts. There were no other routines for reporting customer perceptions of service at branch or at regional level, in either the corporate or retail sectors, despite considerable variation in customer profiles between geographical locations.

Branch audits were carried out by regional office to check the quality of lending decisions, but these were only carried out once every three years and the quality control system was internally rather than customer-orientated.

The fact that so few service quality measures were reported to regional office does not, of course, necessarily imply poor service quality control at branch level. However, if the improvement of service quality and customer care is a strategic objective, then some means of monitoring performance in this respect is necessary for senior management to ensure that the organization is in control and moving in the right strategic direction. Given the time lag which can occur between a noticeable drop in service standards and a decrease in the customer base, managers (who usually remained in position for no longer than three years in any one branch) may well be tempted to improve their bottom line performance by cutting costs, despite the strategy of service differentiation. There may also be pressure to improve branch productivity targets without due consideration for the negative effect this may have on service levels. The development of performance measures with which to monitor the less easily quantifiable dimensions of competitiveness and service quality might provide some degree of safeguard against the dangers outlined earlier of focusing on short-term profit and productivity measures. In particular, one would advocate regular customer satisfaction surveys and monitoring of the bank's relative share of end-user segments in order to support its strategy of differentiation by quality of service.

Hotel chain

This company was a large international hotel chain with a well-known brand name. Its hotels provided three or four star accommodation with a range of leisure and conference facilities. Interviews were conducted with the management team: directors and managers at head office as well as a number of hotel general managers.

The company targeted the growing business market, although cheaper weekend rates were used to attract holiday travellers and improve facility utilization during periods of low demand. The company competed primarily against a core of about six hotel chains, although there was some local variation. The customer base contained a substantial proportion of international travellers, so exchange rates and other economic factors had a significant impact upon the business.

The company differentiated itself by service quality and its provision of business and leisure facilities. The high profile of the brand name in the UK was also a competitive advantage, together with the chain's reputation for consistent quality standards.

The management team consisted of a board of directors and the hotel general managers, who met once a month to discuss and review hotel performance. The reports which were prepared for discussion contained the performance measures given in Table 11.3.

The monthly management meetings focused on relative competitive performance as well as financial performance against budget. The reporting of the competitive performance of each hotel included share of the local market, the number of rooms available and occupied for each of the top six local competitors, together with the average room rates charged by each competing hotel. (This data was shared by agreement between the local competitors.) This information meant that any trade-offs which might exist between financial and competitive performance were made explicit, so that a general manager who adopted a strategy of focusing on one rather than another would have to be prepared to account for this on an ongoing basis. In the case of the bank, by contrast, competitive performance of a branch was reviewed on a quarterly basis and the business plan discussed in detail only once a year, so that a time lag was more likely to occur between managerial action and the effects of competitive performance visible to regional office.

Service quality indicators were also discussed during the management review meetings. These were measures of customer satisfaction with overall service levels and with a range of the components of the service package, both tangible and intangible. The data was drawn from questionnaires which were left in the bedrooms and which guests were invited to complete at the end of their visit. The response rate was small (an average of one in two hundred guests responded), and those guests who did reply were recognized to be unrepresentative in as much as they tended to be polarized in their opinions: they were typically either extremely pleased or highly dissatisfied with the service. Nevertheless, if service levels dropped

Table 11.3 Performance measures used to monitor hotel performance

---

Financial performance

Profit and loss (P/L) account	Monthly report to management team; costs and revenues broken down by department
Budget variance analysis	Each month general managers have to submit with their P/L account explanations for the three largest variances
Breakdown of payroll costs, days absence, overtime etc.	Reported by each hotel every two weeks to head office

Competitive performance

Market share (number of rooms occupied out of total number of rooms available in the local market	Monthly report to management team
Number and percentage of rooms occupied for each of the top six local competitors	Monthly report to management team
Average room rates charged by the top six local competitors	Monthly report to management team
Number of rooms sold by customer type	Monthly report to management team
Customer loyalty: number of repeat bookings	Data available from automated booking system

Resource utilization measures

Percentage of rooms occupied out of total number available	Monthly report to management team

Service quality measures

Customer satisfaction with: overall service levels; staff friendliness, helpfulness, attentiveness, efficiency and discretion; cleanliness, appearance and comfort of rooms; functionality of facilities; quality of food; handling of check-in; value for money.	Guest questionnaires: data compiled into a monthly report to management team with statistics on all the items listed opposite
Likelihood of repeat custom	Guest questionnaires
Staff turnover by avoidable/unavoidable reasons for transfer	Monthly report to management committee

Innovation and flexibility

None identified

---

significantly this was likely to be reflected in the customer data so that head office had some means, albeit crude, of monitoring hotel standards. Moreover, it did make managers aware that their performance was being monitored not in solely short-term financial and volume terms. Performance-related pay was used as an incentive for hotel managers to maintain service standards, although the majority of the bonus was based on performance against budget.

The customer questionnaire also invited guests to comment on ways in which the service could be improved. This meant that customer feedback could be used as an input into service design at a local level. In the bank, however, customer surveys were carried out by head office and not at regional level, despite the recognized differences between customer bases of different geographical areas. This meant that branches and regional offices only received *ad hoc* feedback from customers rather than system-atic and regular data on customer perceptions of service levels. The data was thus gathered at only one level; at the corporate rather than the SBU level as well.

In summary, the hotel chain seemed to have addressed the need to use a range of performance measures to monitor and control hotel perform-ance. The regular reporting of financial, competitive, resource utilization and quality measures meant that any potential trade-offs were made explicit and enabled head office to develop an up-to-date understanding and proactive approach towards the overall performance of its hotels.

Equipment rental service

This company offered both rental and retail of home electronic equip-ment, although the former was the core service, representing over 90 per cent of the business. In recent years the rental market has been in decline mainly because of the increasing attractiveness to the consumer of equipment retail; thus rental organizations are in direct competition with equipment retailers as well as with each other. Retail has increased in popularity at the expense of rental for the following reasons:

1 Reduced product prices of the equipment, making purchase of equip-ment within the reach of more customers.
2 Improved product reliability, meaning that the benefits of equipment rental in terms of field service repairs is a less important criterion in choosing between purchase and rental.
3 In previous years the advent of new facilities and features such as colour and video meant that rental enabled customers to update

equipment as the new products were introduced. Indeed, this is still believed to be the main attraction of rental for the customer over and above retail. More recently, however, product innovations have been largely cosmetic and there has been a reduction in the number of major technological changes.

Nevertheless, a recent merger between this rental organization and a sister company had resulted in a 50 per cent growth at the time of interview, and the company had adopted a corporate strategy of growth based on the acquisition of independent operators. A change in the culture of the organization was also taking place. Whilst the traditional focus of the business had been the increase in the number of rental units, the company was now emphasizing rental margins and profit. The company directors considered that the key towards improved profitability was the increase of income per household, the ability to retain existing customers and the minimization of rental contract terminations.

The company was therefore implementing a differentiation strategy based upon service quality and technological innovation. Shops were being refitted to convey an up-market image and considerable investment was being made in the most up-to-date and comprehensive range of products – the company took pride in the fact that 80 per cent of rental equipment was less than two years old.

A considerable number of performance measures were used by the rental organization, ranging across several performance dimensions. They are summarized in Table 11.4.

The range of performance measures used by this organization contrasts sharply with those used by the bank. The company focused as much on measures of branch competitiveness as on financial and productivity measures. It also had performance measures to support its differentiation strategy of service quality and technological lead. The latter was measured by age of stock. The company also monitored its technological lead relative to competitors. Area managers made routine checks of the products offered by competitors in the locality of each of its shops on a monthly basis. Reports were submitted as a result to head office in order to support central purchasing decisions.

The number of service calls per product was used as a hard measure of product reliability. A range of soft quality measures was also used and there were two principal mechanisms for gathering the more qualitative data:

1 Area managers made monthly visits to each shop and scored each one against a detailed checklist. S/he checked stock levels, the appearance

Table 11.4 Performance measures used to monitor shop performance

Financial measures	
Profit and loss account	Monthly report by shops and service centres
Ratio of profit to sales	Monthly report by shops
Ratio of gross profit to sales	Monthly report by shops
Ratio of arrears to rental income	Monthly report by shops
A range of ratios comparing income, costs and profit	Monthly report by shops
Cash flow analysis	Monthly report at senior management level
Total value of stock by product category	Monthly report by shops
Measures of competitiveness	
Market share	Monthly reporting at senior management level
Number of customers	Monthly reporting by shops
Net gain/loss in number of customers	Monthly reporting by shops
Number of units rented/sold by product and per customer	Monthly reporting by shops
Value of units rented/sold	Monthly reporting by shops
Rental/retail income per household	Monthly reporting by shops
Number of rental terminations	Monthly reporting by shops
Resource utilization measures	
Number of service calls per man day of service staff	Monthly reporting by service centres
Number of customer accounts per clerical employee	Monthly reporting at senior management levels
Average human resource costs per full-time employee	Monthly reporting at senior management levels
Service quality measures	
First time fix	Monthly reporting by service centres
Average time taken to respond to a customer's service request	Monthly reporting by service centres
Number of service calls per product	Monthly reporting by service centres
Perceptual data drawn from customer	Continuous monitoring by means of after service telephone call
Stock levels by product	Monthly reporting by shops

Number of training days per employee	Monthly reporting at senior management level
Number of staff leaving voluntarily/non-voluntarily	Monthly reporting at senior management level
Staff turnover	Monthly reporting at senior management level
Number of shop refits per month	Monthly reporting at senior management level
Complaints per 10,000 customers	Monthly reporting at senior management level
Perceptual measures: shop appearance and cleanliness; stock levels and condition; staff competence, courtesy, appearance and attitude; adherence to specification of shop layout, product displays and promotions; accuracy and clarity of labelling and pricing.	See below for details of reporting methods

Innovation measures

Average age of stock	Continuous monitoring at senior management level
Scan of product offerings of competitors in every shop locality	Carried out monthly by area managers

Flexibility measures

Average time taken to respond to a customer's service request	Monthly reporting by service centres

---

of the service facilities and staff, adherence to centrally specified shop layouts and promotion plans, clarity of pricing and labelling. The product knowledge, communication skills and attitude of staff were also scored.

2 Mystery shoppers, external to the organization, were employed to make spot visits to each shop, sampling the service from a customer perspective. Again, shoppers completed a questionnaire after each visit, commenting on the quality of service received with respect to both tangible and intangible aspects of service. They were also instructed to 'award' each shop with fun stickers ('raspberry' and 'jackpot' stickers) indicating their overall assessment of shop performance. This was intended to add an element of fun to the process and reduce the threatening feeling of being 'policed' that branch staff might feel upon initial introduction of the scheme.

The quality of service delivered by field engineers was also measured on a routine basis. 'First time fix' (i.e. the percentage of service repairs completed during the first visit) was used to monitor the competence of service engineers, together with average service response times. Perceptual data were also collected. Customers were telephoned after the first equipment installation and were asked questions to establish that the engineer had performed certain key tasks and to make sure that they were satisfied with the product and service received.

The fact that this rental organization had implemented systems for measuring a range of performance dimensions, including the areas which were critical to its competitive success, does not necessarily entail successful realization of strategy. Nor does the fact that formal measures of service quality, for instance, were more prevalent here than in the bank, mean that service standards must have been higher in the rental company. Our contention is, however, that the implementation of these measurement systems put the rental organization in a stronger position to monitor and respond to changes in performance levels, thus facilitating a more proactive approach to the control of the business. The use of a range of performance measures meant the trade-offs which may exist between the different performance criteria were made explicit in the control system. This appears to be one way of guarding against opportunistic management behaviour, the dangers of which have been repeatedly expounded in the management accounting literature (for example Kaplan, 1984b).

Summary of the three case studies

These three organizations would be classed as 'service shops', with the corporate arm of the bank having certain features similar to a professional service. All three claimed to be following a differentiation strategy, primarily on service quality. In such businesses it is seldom apparent how the attributes that are important to the customer influenced by activities in the value chain. One would therefore expect their performance measures at the SBU level to be 'customer-focused', and to include customer satisfaction surveys and estimates of customer loyalty, together with measures of their relative share of end-user segments. An examination of the performance measures in use shows the rental company coming closest to this prescribed 'ideal', with the bank faring worst. This may reflect the relatively recent increase in competition in high street banking, which was notably uncompetitive until cartelized oligopoly was ended by the freeing of restrictions on the range of activities permissible to building societies and the TSB. This change in the industry's structure and its impact on customers' perceptions of value appear to have outstripped the bank's ability to adapt its organizational culture in the short-term, although it is now making some progress in this area.

Conclusion

In response to the widespread appeal in the management literature for the use of a range of measures to control business performance, this chapter has categorized a range of six performance dimensions against which measurement can take place for each of two generic strategies in services. The list of dimensions was then used as a tool to analyse the performance measures used by three service organizations in order to identify mismatches between their corporate strategies and performance measurement systems. This tool should help managers to analyse and re-evaluate their performance measurement systems in the light of their chosen strategy. Whilst it is the nature of the competitive environment which will determine how the performance measurement system is used, it is the type of business that will determine how performance should be measured. The why, the what and the how of performance measurement are therefore contingent on the interaction of environment, strategy and business type.

Our conclusion is that the measurement of service business performance involves measurement against a range of performance criteria across six dimensions. What should be measured and the relative importance of each criterion in any given organization will depend upon its existing competitive strategy. Companies should therefore set out to develop systems for the monitoring and control of those aspects of performance which are critical to the successful realization of their strategy. Equally, they need to assess continually their distinctive competences, look for sources of positional advantage and identify key success factors in the process of assessing, adjusting and re-formulating their existing strategy.

Measurement against a range of performance criteria may also make visible (and thus enhance management understanding of) the trade-offs which can exist between different performance criteria: for example, trade-offs between financial return and competitive position, or between resource utilization and service quality. Unfortunately the things which need to be measured are not necessarily the easiest to quantify. Nevertheless, our empirical evidence suggests that some service managers are addressing the challenge of developing a range of measures to monitor the performance of their business units.

Acknowledgements

This chapter is one output from a two and a half year research project funded by CIMA, to whom we are grateful for their financial support. The views expressed are those of the authors.

References

Drucker, P. (1953). *The Practice of Management*. New York: Harper and Brothers.

Drury, C. (1988). *Management and Cost Accounting*. 2nd edition. Van Nostrand Reinhold.

Fitzgerald, L., Johnston, R., Brignall, T. J., Silvestro, R. and Voss, C. (1991). Performance Measurement in Service Businesses, CIMA, forthcoming.

Hostage, G. M. (1975). Quality control in a service business. *Harvard Business Review*, July–August.

Kaplan, R. S. (1983). Measuring manufacturing performance: a new challenge for accounting research. *The Accounting Review*, **LVIII**, (4).

Kaplan, R. S. (1984a). Accounting lag: the obsolescence of cost accounting systems. Harvard Business School, 75th Anniversary Colloquium on Productivity and Technology.

Kaplan, R. S. (1984b). The evolution of management accounting. *The Accounting Review*, **LIX** (3).

Peters, T. J. and Waterman, R. H. (1982). *In Search of Excellence*. New York: Harper and Row Publishers.

Porter, M. (1980). *Competitive Strategy*. Free Press.

Rowe, Mason and Dickel (1986) *Strategic Management: A Methodological Approach*. Addison-Wesley.

Simons, R. (1987). Accounting control systems and business strategy: an empirical analysis. *Accounting, Organizations and Society*, **12** (4).

Simons, R. (1990). The role of management control systems in creating competitive advantage: new perspectives. *Accounting, Organizations and Society*, **15** (1/2).

Simons, R. (1991). Strategic orientation and top management attention to control systems. *Strategic Management Journal*, **12**.

Sink, D. S. (1985). *Productivity Management: Planning, Measurement and Evaluation, Control and Improvement*. John Wiley.

12

Management accounting in retail organizations

Nigel Coulthurst

Management accounting in retailing organizations has been virtually ignored in the accounting literature. In this chapter Nigel Coulthurst describes various aspects of management accounting within the Boots Company Plc, with particular reference to Boots the Chemists.

The author describes the unique features of retail organizations, the difficulties that arise in satisfying management's accounting information requirements in such organizations, and especially, how developments in information technology provide an opportunity for these difficulties to be overcome.

After completing this chapter, the reader should have an appreciation of how investment in electronic point of sale technology, and utilization/development of sophisticated cost allocation models, are providing the means for retail managers to enhance the profitability of their organizations.

The content of the chapter draws upon the author's experience of management accounting within the Boots Company Plc, and should not be assumed to reflect the state of the art in retail organizations generally.

Retailing

Retailing is an example of a service industry with its own unique features and accounting aspects. However, as with any other commercial organization, goods must be sold profitably and cash must be managed effectively, in order to ensure that the organization survives and thrives.

Since the space available in retail stores is limited, the goods which provide the 'best' profit levels should be stocked if profitability is to be maximized. It is necessary, however, that inventories fall within the scope of business strategy, with the correct balance of goods to provide adequate customer choice and retain retail authority.

Profitability of an item (or group of similar items) will depend not only upon the profit per unit of the item(s) but also upon the volume of sales achieved. Profit per unit will be affected by the retail value of the item and the percentage buying margin. However, consideration must also be given to the costs of converting bought-in product into sales. Costs include: the marketing costs involved in launching and continuing to merchandise a line; the costs of storage and of distributing goods to stores; in-store costs such as the cost of space occupied by goods on display, the cost of store labour and the interest cost of stockholding. Ultimately, if store space is the limiting factor, profitability should be measured in relation to space occupied.

Unique features and difficulties

Retailing has traditionally had three special accounting problems which are not to be found in other organizations.

Sales analysis

First, there has been a problem of identifying sales, and thus profitability, of different products/product groups. Whilst supplies to retail outlets (stores) could be recorded accurately by product, no direct measure has traditionally been available of individual product sales due to lack of information at the cash taking point.

In the long-run, even if opening and closing stocks in stores, as well as supplies to stores and other stock adjustments (e.g. returns), were known in detail, units sold could not be determined by product/product group because stock losses through breakage and pilfering may have occurred.

Determining the value of sales from stock movements has been further complicated where price changes took place during the period. Stocks are, in any case, difficult (and costly via stocktakes) to determine accurately at a particular point in time if there are many products and several outlets.

In the short-term, e.g. from week to week or month to month, it has traditionally been even more difficult to establish a breakdown of sales by product/product group, which is critical to the effective use of space, and for justification of promotional offers.

Inventory size

A second accounting problem for many retailers results from the very large number of different products which are frequently stocked, and thus sold, and the fact that the inventory may be constantly changing. It increases considerably the difficulties of both providing and interpreting product information. The greater the number of products the greater the difficulty in establishing an analysis of sales. Complexity is increased for retailers with a large number of outlets, of differing size, in different locations.

To take Boots the Chemists as an example of a large and complex retail chain, it has over 1,000 retail stores in the UK varying from approximately 'front-room' sized up to over 4,000 square metres, each stocking up to 40,000 different items. The smallest band of shop size will typically stock a quarter to one-third of the inventory available to the largest. In some years up to one-third of items can change, although in most cases they will be replaced with different versions of the same thing.

Stock losses

A third problem for many retailers has been the vulnerability of store stock to pilferage, coupled with the absence of related control information.

Cost apportionment

A further accounting problem which retailers have in common with other organizations is the proportion of costs which are difficult to apportion to products/product groups. This problem is exacerbated the greater the number of products, and if the retailer also has its own warehousing and distribution facilities.

Again using Boots the Chemists as an example, the company has a highly centralized distribution system, which has evolved over many years, consisting of six main central warehouses delivering to twenty redistribution centres which then deliver to stores on a daily basis. Fastest selling lines are delivered to stores from common stock rooms which are co-located with the redistribution centres. Some lines are delivered direct from suppliers to common stock rooms; others via warehouses.

The six main central warehouses are all different – different ages, types of building and operating methods which vary with the nature of the merchandise and technology employed. Although they nominally house particular ranges of merchandise the need for flexibility often means that items can be despatched from more than one warehouse.

The variation in store size and inventory stocked has repercussions back up the supply chain. It would be impossible to operate if all goods were sent to stores in unbroken outers. Stores would be more than full and stock investment would be excessive. Whilst complete outers are enforced wherever practical, for many lines stores have to be allowed to order in singles.

Goods have to be protected in transit and are despatched from warehouses using three basic travel units:

- Travel outers where the outer is enforced and strong enough to need no further protection.
- Roll containers (wire cages on wheels) into which singles or outers can be packed. Not all stores can accept these because of access problems.
- Black plastic boxes called town trays. A town tray can hold approximately a tenth of a roll container's worth of stock.

An item can go to different sizes of store in a combination of these three units.

There are up to thirty-six different possible splits of a single item's output from one warehouse, all of which will have different characteristics for costing purposes. The thirty-six arise from three factors:

- Category of store (six sizes)
- Travel unit (three types)
- Allocation or normal stock order (two types)

All of the factors just mentioned are highly relevant to any analysis of costs, and illustrate the complexity of the task.

Accounting and technological developments

Because of the above accounting problems, the measure of product/product group profitability that has traditionally been established in retail organizations has been *gross profit* (i.e. retail value less product bought-in cost) on *supplies* to stores. Control over store stock losses, to the extent that control has been possible, has been effected by maintenance of the store stock account at retail value. Stock losses are identified as the balancing item upon reconciliation of the store stock account following periodic (often annual) stocktake, having adjusted the stock account for all other value movements, including retail price changes. This has only been possible for a store in total due to absence of sales and stock adjustment information by product grouping.

Two very significant developments, resulting from advances in computer technology, have had a dramatic effect on the above mentioned processes and measures within Boots the Chemists.

Direct product profitability

First, the advent of computer hardware and software capable of handling the detailed analysis of products moving through the distribution chain to point-of-sale has enabled a closer quantification of the different elements, and the establishment of product costs other than the cost of the goods themselves. This analysis is called direct product profitability (DPP). DPP fills in some of the gaps between gross profit and net profit by identifying, on an item by item basis, the cost profiles and profit contribution of each product sold. This gives an indication of the absolute performance of an item and also allows comparison between items or ranges of items. It is important to note that this is not net profit but the contribution to unallocated costs and net profit.

Electronic point-of-sale

The second significant development has been the introduction of electronic point-of-sale (EPOS) equipment at store check-out points to record every sales transaction that takes place. Advancements made in information systems, with the growth of laser and microchip technology, have enabled EPOS hardware and software to be developed. Whilst investment in EPOS technology is expensive, the potential benefits are considerable, and such investment is increasingly seen by major retailers as an essential competitive tool. Boots the Chemists, for example, have made a very significant investment in developing and implementing, working closely with IBM, the largest EPOS network in Europe.

In addition to providing detailed analysis of sales and gross profit, EPOS enables the development of improved accounting reports. In particular, it makes it possible to move the basis of all management accounting information to sales, rather than a mixture of supplies and sales. EPOS implementation also enables cost savings to be made in-store.

Together DPP and EPOS have enabled the establishment of product sales as well as supplies, with profit on sales determined after the inclusion of costs other than simply the cost of the goods. Both DPP and EPOS will now be considered in more detail as utilized by Boots the Chemists (BTC).

Direct product profitability

Direct product costs and profit

The concept of direct product profitability (DPP) is not new. It basically follows absorption costing principles in seeking to establish product profitability for a retailer. It does not, however, use traditional absorption bases. A very large number of activity measures are established and utilized.

Product profit is measured as sales minus 'direct' product cost. However, product costs are not 'direct' as applied typically in manufacturing organizations and thus the term can be confusing. In the retail operation the only 'direct' product cost (using the term as in a manufacturing situation) is the cost of the goods for resale, which is already deducted from sales in the traditional measure of gross profit. DPP adds a share of indirect costs to the cost of the goods, working from an individual item level and building information up into relevant inventory groups.

Indirect costs included in the BTC DPP system, which is a tailor-made mainframe system, are those where cost drivers and associated product characteristics can be determined, and as a result costs identified with individual products, with reasonable accuracy (hence the term 'direct'). For example, cubic volume has been shown to be a prime determinant of certain distribution costs, and as data on item cubic volume and throughput is available, the information is used for cost apportionment. A number of costs are not included because of the difficulty in identifying cost drivers and/or relating them to products. Examples are store management, store general administration, central administration, and information technology costs.

Indirect costs in DPP include store labour (filling-up and selling), store space and certain other store operating costs, inventory carrying costs, promotion, and warehousing and distribution costs.

Analysis

The availability of computer technology has facilitated such analysis and thus enabled DPP to be carried out within Boots the Chemists. Data regarding item characteristics and throughput during a twelve month period is combined with the costs of activities that those products gave rise to during the same time period. A complex set of rules within the system calculates the amount of workload associated with an item's throughput from which the cost is then derived. This reflects the complexity of warehousing and distribution operations, the variation in size of products/stores, breadth of inventory carried, differences in display and so on.

The scale and sophistication of the BTC system, and the difficulties of product costing for retailers, can be appreciated from the fact that a print-out of all the data held on an individual item (one of the 60,000 items held on the system at any one time), either extracted from other systems or calculated within DPP, can end up with over fifty pages of report. The system has over 2,000 activities analysed.

This complexity means that the cost of an activity per single item handled will be different in different circumstances. Take order picking in the warehouse as an example. For a store large enough to take a full outer of something, the time per order will clearly be different from an order where, for example, only two singles are required for a much smaller store.

Thus, the product profitability system uses a large amount of item information. At each stage of a product's passage through the network of warehousing, distribution and selling, item characteristics (e.g. unit cubic volume; warehouse, semi-direct or direct supply; level of throughput; size of store order; normal or allocation supply; type of transit container and finished package) are taken into account to produce a fair and reasonable charge for the workload associated with the item.

The costs involved in getting an item to the store, and the costs of handling it in store, will not be directly related to the value of the item. The physical and logistical characteristics of the item – its size, weight, level of throughput and the way it is handled – determine the amount of workload associated with the item and thence the charge it attracts.

Although in principle similar to absorption costing, DPP has become a more refined and sophisticated method of establishing product costs because of its development in conjunction with advances in computer technology, and because of the rationale that has been adopted. Traditional absorption costing systems have much to learn from DPP.

The sheer volume of data in the BTC DPP system, and the complexity of the task, restricts the frequency of analysis to a few times a year. However, known changes can be allowed for manually if required, although the characteristics of products and their handling do not change frequently.

Reports

The BTC DPP system is flexible, enabling a variety of reports to be produced (on screen or paper), ranging from an individual item to large inventory grouping. Report formats include profit reports, cost profiles, and space productivity. Appendix 12.1 provides an example of the format of a report that is made available. The rows are presented to show the revenue, gross profit, costs, and final profit contribution values in a logical sequence.

The user is able to further analyse the make-up of the costs to establish in more detail where costs have been incurred within any of the cost groups. For example, the warehouse and distribution cost group may be viewed to reveal details of the individual receiving, space, assembly, despatch, and local delivery costs that go to make it up.

Two types of report are available to users:

1 *On-line reports* – these present selected information to users, about particular items or merchandise groups, on screen for immediate reading. A paper copy of the screen details can be produced.
2 *Batch reports* – these would cover a larger range of inventory which would be too time-consuming and too detailed to produce and present on-line. They are produced as paper reports, which are printed overnight in response to a request entered at the terminal, and are complementary to the on-line system.

The system has been made as 'user friendly' as possible. Throughout the on-line part of the system, every screen that a user sees has a back-up help screen telling them how to make their selections, what data they are looking at, or giving suggestions on interpretation of the data. A user guide booklet introduces users to the system and takes them through it step-by-step.

Modelling

The BTC DPP system also has a modelling facility.

The requirement for a modelling system comes from the fact that a user is presented with an historical database derived from a huge volume of variables which a general user could not hope to amend for himself in a modelling situation. The statistical derivation of simplified equations provided in the modelling system enables the profit contribution for a new product line, or the effect of changes to an existing line, to be estimated from the input of a small number of parameters.

Estimated product costs require careful interpretation. Modelling does not supplement the need for judgement in decision-making and cannot provide all the answers to all possible queries. However, inventory managers can quickly (the facility is available on screen) distinguish between likely winners and more doubtful additions (or changes) to the inventory.

Utility of DPP

Critics of absorption costing would also question the validity of the DPP approach. However, five factors should be recognized.

First, it should be seen particularly as a guide to the long-run allocation of resources and thus an aid in strategic planning rather than for short-term tactical decisions. Second, a major use of DPP is in comparing performance of one product (or group of products) with another rather than looking at absolute numbers in isolation. Third, space is a limiting factor and thus ultimately profit in relation to space will be the crucial measure. As a result the apportionment of space costs, which will be largely fixed, will have no effect on comparisons of profitability from one product to another. The fourth factor to recognize is that certain costs, which tend to remain fixed and are remote from the product (for example, general administration, general store labour), are excluded from DPP. Finally, marginal costing may also be usefully applied to product profit analysis. A shorter-term view can be taken of cost variability in order to assist tactical decision-making in the retailing environment.

DPP and EPOS should be used together to select the most profitable item mix for a given product group within the constraints of strategic direction. If properly used, DPP provides an invaluable decision support system. Its more specific uses include:

1   Helping to determine whether to add/drop product ranges. In the long-run, products must make a sufficient contribution to the space that they occupy in store (and in the warehouse also). Identifying the contribution using DPP provides a guide to the longer-term situation and enables a clearer view to be formed as to the relative contributions of different types of merchandise. A more clearly defined strategy and a more sharply focused product offering should result.

  One of the most revealing aspects of DPP has been the highlighting of the high costs of stockholding and related storage and rehandling costs. DPP also provides a good indication of the economics of bulky, low-value products. Despite an initial high gross profit margin, products may well have a negative DPP contribution. It is important to appreciate the variability of the different costs included and over what time horizon.

2   Helping to determine mix within ranges of products. The cost of

having variety is not reflected by gross profit. DPP measures draw greater attention to the question of product mix and its space allocation. EPOS provides the means to test the effect of making changes, particularly to reduce variety.

It is important to stress, in all product mix decisions, that DPP costs (e.g. space) may not be saved through inventory reduction, especially in the short-term. Focus, through DPP, should be on increasing the absolute profit generated by the mix of products in store.

3 Providing a better understanding of the business and of the incidence of cost, especially to buyers within BTC. As a result buyers, in consultation with suppliers, may discuss the possibility of changing product characteristics in order to reduce cost. Outer packaging size may be increased for high volume lines or reduced for slow movers. Product configuration may even be changed in order to provide easier handling, distribution and display. Customer appeal has to be weighed against bad pallet fit, damage, delay and cost in the distribution chain, and ultimately poor presentation at the point of sale.

Appreciation of the incidence of cost may also lead to changes in supply routes/methods, or to changes in display types, display space or selling method.

Changing product characteristics in order to reduce cost is relevant to manufacturers as well as to retailers and goes far beyond the more traditional value engineering which simply looked for cheaper materials whilst maintaining functional capability and aesthetic appeal.

It is important for manufacturers to consider the implications for wholesalers and retailers of aspects of the product's shape and packaging, and thus to consider costs right through to the point of sale. Changes made can result in reduced packaging and packing costs for the manufacturer and savings in the retailer operation in the areas of labour, space and inventory as the product passes through the warehouse, transport and store environments. Manufacturers may also find DPP useful in providing an indication of the true cost of variety, and may even point to improvements in their own absorption costing. It certainly helps to direct attention to other than simply the costing of the manufacturing operation.

4 Use in margin negotiations with suppliers. Clear demonstration of the DPP implications of different products (according to gross profit margin, configuration and size) may enable retailer margins to be increased. Relative performance of suppliers against competitors can be highlighted.

5 Determining the true profitability of promotions. DPP has helped to measure the true cost of 'added value' promotions, where the added

value was an additional item stuck to the side of the original pack. The costs of handling, the frequently reduced margin and the loss of sales of alternative packs with easier handling and higher margins, may well offset the increased volume that may be generated by the promotion. Rapid feedback from EPOS equipment has also helped in such decisions.

6 The detailed structure of the DPP process (i.e. sophisticated absorption costing) provides management (e.g. buying teams) with an increased appreciation of the practical side of the way other functions perform their duties.

7 Establishing sales targets for particular merchandise to break even taking into account the cost of resources utilized.

8 Helping to maximize return on space. Store space is one of the biggest costs and is the overriding limiting factor. DPP information can be used to reallocate display space between product groups, ranges or brands, and to manipulate the quality of space. The final measure of DPP performance will be profit in relation to space.

However, it is difficult to determine the optimum use of space. For example, poor performance may be because insufficient space has been allocated to a product/product range for it to establish the necessary authority. An increase in space may result in an increase in DPP per unit of space. In other situations the reverse may be the case. It is also difficult to measure, and reflect in DPP analysis, the quality of space. For example, certain parts of the store have more passing traffic, generating greater customer awareness, and impulse purchase. Investment in EPOS equipment enables experimentation to be carried out which may provide useful information to assist in space allocation.

Thus DPP has provided considerable benefits for Boots the Chemists. It is not, however, a panacea, as for example the above discussion about space allocation shows, and it is not without its difficulties. The quality of information is dependent upon the ability to identify input/output relationships. Ultimately cost apportionment assumptions have to be made. Because of its complexity and the cost of operating the DPP system it provides an infrequent, and only broad, indication of profit incidence on ranges of products and cannot be expected to provide rapid response to changed tactics on individual products. It also tends to provide a bias against variety, because of its emphasis on cost. An adequate range of products is necessary in order to provide authority and sufficient choice for the consumer.

DPP has, however, much to offer those who appreciate what it can reasonably be used for. It is especially important to provide indications of significant differences between products at an acceptable level of accuracy, and this DPP does. The kinds of decisions are not new; DPP has provided much better quantification and has had a significant effect on management thinking. Positive profit enhancement can be achieved with such information at hand.

Epos

Data collection and control

EPOS sales information can be collected by store and item for all bar-coded items on a daily basis. The information is then summarized on central databases at various levels, e.g. store/item/week, store/product group/week, sales area/item/week. It is then normally held at each of these levels for up to two years enabling required comparisons of current year performance with previous year. Maintenance of a vast EPOS network, to ensure reliability and timeliness of data, is a major exercise.

Controls are required within EPOS computer systems to ensure that price details entered on head office mainframe systems are successfully transmitted to store computers and implemented correctly. It is also necessary to ensure that shelf edge pricing tickets are consistent with EPOS system prices applied to bar-code readings. Regular checks are required to ensure maintenance of required trading standards.

Information provided

EPOS information made available to management takes two main forms. Firstly, standard reports are available on a regular basis (e.g. weekly/four-weekly) which compare sales and gross profit performance of standard inventory groupings (or individual stores/standard groupings of stores) with budget and/or with a previous period (e.g. same period last year). Appendix 12.2 provides an example of a possible routine report format where sales for various product groupings are identified by week for the most recent four-week period and year-on-year percentage changes are shown for the last week and the last four weeks.

Secondly, the EPOS database can be accessed (at item level, by store, if required) in order to carry out *ad hoc* analysis of sales. Such information would be used to provide analysis of resource, selling price or inventory changes. These changes may involve capital investment, where *ad hoc* EPOS data will be required for justification and post-audit purposes.

Benefits from EPOS

1   The strength of EPOS is that it records every sales transaction that takes place in a retail store. It is thus capable of distinguishing, clearly and immediately, between the sale of different products, both units and value. It is especially useful in identifying not only the absolute sales of product/product groups on a regular basis but also the response of sales to changes in the marketing mix, e.g. pricing trials, changes in space allocation, sales promotions. Provision of such detailed sales information is a vital source of information to support product mix, pricing and resource allocation decisions, and a major justification for EPOS investment.

2   In addition to the management information benefits that result from EPOS implementation, significant cost savings can also be made in-store. With an EPOS system, there is no requirement for individual items to be priced using price tickets and ticket guns. The EPOS technology reads bar-codes imprinted on item packaging, which provides the necessary point of sale information on selling price. Shelf edge ticketing on display units within the store is sufficient to convey pricing information to customers. Cash points have a greater throughput due to the speed of bar-code reading. The need for periodic stock counting is eliminated since the in-store EPOS controller has details of all item stock movements. This can also be used to drive store stock replenishment systems with a resultant reduction in stockholding. Stock counts are still necessary because of wastage and pilferage, but this can be done on a perpetual inventory basis and targetted towards vulnerable items, producing more accurate information and thus helping to overcome one of the traditional problem areas for retailers.

3   Routine management accounts for inventory groups within retail organizations have traditionally been supplies based, as a breakdown of retail sales has not been available. Supplies to stores at retail value have been reconciled with store takings via estimated store stocks and the estimated profit margin in store stocks used to convert profit on supplies to profit on sales. With the advent of EPOS, sales-based management accounts have become a reality with sales analysis by inventory group, and gross profit on sales calculated directly by having cost prices as well as retail prices on the EPOS system. Details of supplies to stores and store stocks are no longer required in order to establish profit.

Reporting cycle

For those retail companies who have traditionally produced monthly management accounts an important issue which arises in the process of making the change to sales-based management accounts concerns the length of the reporting cycle or accounting period. The dilemma revolves around the fact that retail sales information is naturally weekly. The sales information benefits of moving to a reporting cycle based on weeks must be balanced against the cost of changing systems from a monthly cycle and any resultant information loss.

Full weeks enable more meaningful comparisons of sales from period to period, and a better basis for budgeting, by eliminating calendar effects. Against this, however, balance sheet comparisons and cash flow monitoring is rendered more difficult and less useful if accounting period ends occur at different times of the month. Other systems (e.g. expense accounting, general ledger, purchases accounting), would have to change. If monthly reporting was retained, costs would be incurred to calculate monthly sales from EPOS data.

Store performance

A further important aspect of retail accounting is the measurement of store performance. This is more straightforward. Total sales and cost of sales can be relatively easily identified and many more costs are directly allocatable at store level. From this information contribution and attributable profit can be determined. In addition, it may be decided to approximate each store's net profit performance through the apportionment of central costs of administration, marketing, warehousing and distribution. This is more problematic and arbitrary, but some costs, for example warehousing and distribution, may be accumulated via the DPP system.

The performance of a store can be judged on its own merits in relation to budget/target. It may also be judged in relation to the performance of other stores.

Summary

The chapter has sought in particular to provide an insight into how information technology developments (cost allocation models and electronic point of sale equipment) are advancing the state of the art of retailing (with particular reference to Boots the Chemists) through improved sales, cost and profit information. Although management information provided through DPP and EPOS cannot give a complete picture of profitability, nevertheless such information enables managers to undertake effective profit enhancement through well informed decision-making.

Direct product profitability has enabled the establishment of certain product costs in addition to the cost of the goods themselves, enabling item profit contributions and cost profiles to be established and compared. The main benefit of EPOS investment is that it provides detailed analysis of sales on the basis of which more effective resource allocation decisions (based upon relevant DPP costs) can be made.

Appendix 12.1 Product profitability

	Total (£000s)	Percentage of sales (exc. VAT)	Average per unit (pence) Item	Product group
Sales (inc. VAT)	x	x	x	x
Sales (exc. VAT)	x	x	x	x
Gross profit	x	x	x ·	x
*Warehouse & distribution	x	x	x	x
*Marketing	x	x	x	x
*Stock investment	x	x	x	x
*Store labour	x	x	x	x
*Store space	x	x	x	x
*Gross profit adj.	x	x	x	x
Sum of costs	x	x	x	x
Profit contribution	x	x	x	x

Notes

(a)   Further details would be available of the cost items within the cost groups (denoted by *).

(b)   The report would be available for:
    (i)   an individual item;
    (ii)   a merchandise group.

Appendix 12.2 Standard EPOS report
EPOS sales report (by product group)

£000

	Last week	Last week −1	Last week −2	Last week −3	Last week last year	Last week year-on-year % change	Last 4 weeks this year	Last 4 weeks last year	Last 4 weeks year-on-year % change
Product group									
A	x	x	x	x	x	x	x	x	x
B	x	x	x	x	x	x	x	x	x
C	x	x	x	x	x	x	x	x	x
D	x	x	x	x	x	x	x	x	x
	—	—	—	—	—	—	—	—	—
Inventory group A	x	x	x	x	x	x	x	x	x
	—	—	—	—	—	—	—	—	—
Product group									
E	x	x	x	x	x	x	x	x	x
F etc.	x	x	x	x	x	x	x	x	x
	—	—	—	—	—	—	—	—	—
Inventory group B	x	x	x	x	x	x	x	x	x
	—	—	—	—	—	—	—	—	—

Notes

(a) The report would be available for:
   (i) sales;
   (ii) gross profit.

(b) The report would be available for:
   (i) total stores;

13

Management accounting in local government

Maurice Pendlebury

Local government is responsible for the provision of a wide range of services of major importance which constitute a significant share of gross domestic product. Over the past decade radical changes in local government have resulted in important changes in the management and control of various activities. In this chapter Professor Pendlebury outlines some of the changes which have taken place and describes the nature and role of local government management accounting practices.

The author begins by focusing on budget preparation and budgetary control. He then proceeds to outline some of the recent developments in local government 'commercial' activities and discuss the role of management accounting in direct labour and direct service organizations. In the final sections the charging for central services and the move towards devolved financial management are considered.

Introduction

For several years now virtually the whole of the public sector has frequently had to respond to significant and often radical changes. Local government has been no exception. Changes in functions, changes in structure, changes in financing, changes in methods of service delivery and changes in market force pressures have all left their mark on the management and control practices and on the role and nature of management accounting in local government.

The characteristic features of many of the services provided by local government are that the precise objectives are difficult to define in a quantifiable way and that the actual accomplishments are even more difficult to measure. The techniques of management accounting that can be found in the mainstream (i.e. private sector dominated) management accounting literature tend to assume that output can be measured in terms of either sales value or units of production/service that will eventually be sold. For local government services such as education or police or social services there is no equivalent market related output measure. It is true that measures of usage or activity are obtainable, such as number of school children being educated or elderly people cared for, but these convey only limited information about the quality or effectiveness of the service and say nothing about the satisfaction felt by users of the service. It is a reality that for services where market priced outputs are not available, or not appropriate, then the adequacy of the outputs is a matter for political or subjective judgement. Traditionally the role of management accounting in local government has been closely involved with the inputs (i.e. the costs of the services) but much less so with the outputs.

Management and control of inputs is achieved through the annual budget and budgetary control cycle. Budgets use detailed expenditure headings to provide specific spending authorizations and actual spending is then monitored against budget throughout the fiscal year. The annual budget is therefore at the very heart of local government management, and Marshall (1974, p. 73) states that:

> Local government would be unworkable without the annual budget, the centrepiece of the financial year. All departments and most officers participate in its making: and must abide by its contents. It is the most pervasive financial activity . . . Legally its purpose is to fix the rate: managerially it is both a decision making and a control document.

Given that for several local services management accounting consists of the annual budget/budgetary control process and little else, it is this that forms the emphasis of the remaining sections of this chapter. However, a more recent development in local government has been for the more 'commercial' activities, such as housing maintenance, highways maintenance and construction, refuse collection, repair and maintenance of vehicles, school meals and so on, to be required to be accounted for separately from other local authority activities. There is then a further requirement to earn a specified rate of return on capital employed. For these activities the role of management accounting will clearly extend beyond budgeting and this will also be discussed.

The budget cycle

Local authorities prepare two types of budget: annual revenue budgets; and capital budgets. The basic distinction between the two is that annual revenue budgets are concerned with items of a short-term recurrent nature, such as wages, heating, lighting, etc., whereas the expenditure that is contained in capital budgets will be on such things as buildings, roads, equipment, etc., which provide benefits for several years ahead.

Although in a typical local authority, work on the annual revenue budget might begin in June or July for the financial year that will commence on the following 1 April, the final decision on the level of local spending can not be made until January or February. This is because of the high proportion of local spending that is financed by central government, which means that until central government's spending levels are finalized the level of grants to local government will not finally be known. An early indication of the likely level of government grant for the coming financial year is provided in the autumn budget statement, which, since 1993, has been presented in late November or early December. More detailed information on the government's spending plans for the coming financial year are provided in the annual departmental reports, which are published in February.

Budget preparation

A frequent criticism of the prominent role played by the annual revenue budget in the financial planning of a local authority is that a one-year time horizon is too short a period for effective planning. For many services, particularly those that are affected by factors such as demographic changes, this is undoubtedly true. Even in times of relative stability and certainty the use of medium-term revenue budgeting has never been very widespread in local government. The uncertainty that has surrounded local government finance in recent years has meant that financial planning beyond the next budget year is now virtually non-existent.

A further criticism of the annual revenue budget is that, in its conventional form, it doesn't attempt to show the purposes or objectives of the expenditure but the nature of the spending. For example, the budget for the police service of a local authority might be analysed so as to reveal the expenditure on wages, salaries, supplies, services, etc. This approach, which is often referred to as 'line-item' budgeting, shows the *nature* of the spending but not the *purpose*. Although it might be difficult to obtain precise agreement on the overall objective or objectives of a police service, there are several sub-objectives or programmes that might find general acceptance. Examples of these might include: deterring and preventing crime; apprehending criminals; control of traffic; and control of crowds. Analysing the total budget request for the police service in this programme structure manner would give a clearer picture of what the money is to be used for and would, it is argued, help in the making of rational allocations of scarce resources.

One of the arguments against such a programme structure is that it would be cumbersome to operate. A uniformed police officer might well, in the course of a typical day, be involved on several programmes and so some method of allocating police direct, as well as indirect, costs to different programmes would be required. The administrative effort involved in doing this could well be greater than the benefits and so the inevitable compromise has emerged. The recommended budget format for the police service is to analyse the expenditure over the following divisions of service: police general; regional crime squad; police pensions; police canteens; transport and movable plant; and police training centres. This does represent a move towards a programme structure, but the programmes that are used still fail to provide precise information on the specific activities that are being undertaken. This compromise between a pure line item approach and a pure programme structure for the police budget is a feature of the budget formats adopted for most other local government services.

The annual revenue budget can also be criticized for being incremental in nature. In other words the current year's budget total for a particular item is considered to be the base from which the budget for the coming year will be determined and it is only the changes from this base that are examined in detail. The items that make up the base go largely undisputed. An obvious limitation of incremental budgeting is that expenditure that is no longer required or is at too high a level will not be detected and will therefore continue to be included in the budget. The defects in public sector resource allocation that are caused by short-term planning horizons and line-item and incremental approaches to budgeting have long been recognized. Two of the reforms that have, in their time, received much attention are planning programming budgeting systems (PPBS) and zero-base budgeting (ZBB).[1]

Programme budgeting

PPBS offers a very rational approach to resource allocation. First of all overall objectives have to be determined, then the programmes that might achieve these objectives need to be identified, and finally the costs and benefits of each programme are evaluated so that budget allocations can be made based on the known cost/benefit relationships of different programmes.

The 1960s and early 1970s saw a very serious attempt to implement PPBS into US government budgeting, but by the mid-1970s the attempt had been abandoned. It failed in part because much of the data that were required on outputs were unobtainable. It also failed because it did not take into account the reality of decision making in complex organizations. The loosely defined objectives of many local services, combined with the uncertainty they face, means that political processes and well established negotiation systems tend to dominate decision making. Under such circumstances the rational, orthodox and highly formalized approach to budgeting that PPBS offers is unlikely to find widespread acceptance. Thus, although the philosophy behind PPBS was good, practical difficulties and organizational realities led to its lack of support.[2] One influence that it did have, however, and that still remains, is to have reinforced the advantages of a programme structure. In other words even though programme impacts might not be measurable and the establishment of cost/benefit relationships not possible, the budget might at least show the proposed spending on different activities or programmes.

Zero-base budgeting

After the failure of PPBS another system of budgeting found much prominence, particularly in the USA, and this was ZBB. With incremental budgeting it is simply the increment (or decrement) from the existing base that is examined. With ZBB the whole of the budget request, including the base, is examined. This means that every item in the budget has to be justified as though the particular activity or programme were starting anew. Priorities and preferences might then be re-established in terms of today's requirements and obsolete and unwanted programmes could be isolated so that resources could be deployed elsewhere. As a concept ZBB has therefore much to commend it, but against this must be weighed its practical limitations. To examine thoroughly every item in the budget and every underlying activity or programme would probably be impossible. To overcome the administrative burden of a pure ZBB system a 'decision package' approach was developed. The first requirement of a 'decision package' approach is to identify within each service the various decision units. Decision units must carry out programmes with well defined and measurable objectives and impacts. For each programme carried out by a decision unit, decision packages are then prepared which identify the different levels of activity (and associated costs) that might be undertaken. The lowest level identified will not normally be zero but some minimum level within the base, below which it would be impossible to continue with the programme. Above this minimum level the decision package would identify the levels of service that could be sustained at different levels of funding. The use of decision packages means that the base is being systematically examined but not from zero, and this obviously reduces the workload.

The next stage is to rank the various decision packages in order of priority. The ranking process will almost inevitably be extremely political. Usually the only way to proceed is to make use of a special ranking committee which will examine the decision packages and determine the final rankings.

Even with the decision package approach ZBB is still a bureaucratic and time consuming process and in an organization of any size the number of decision packages may be unmanageable. Commenting on the attempt to implement ZBB in the USA state of Georgia, Anthony (1977, p. 9) points out that 11,000 decision packages were produced. He goes on to state that 'if the Governor set aside four hours every day for two months, he could spend about a minute on each decision package, not enough time to read it, let alone make an analysis of the merits'.

Nevertheless, in spite of the practical limitations of ZBB and in spite of it imposing, like PPBS, a highly rational approach to budgeting on organizations that are essentially complex political groupings, interest in ZBB still remains. When faced with continuous limitations and reductions in their level of spending, organizations might be expected to look for more efficient ways of spreading the impact of those reductions than simply requiring every service to take the same across-the-board cut. Local authorities have found themselves in this situation in recent years and perhaps this helps to explain their increasing willingness to review base estimates. In a survey of local government budgeting practices undertaken in 1983 Pendlebury (1985) found that 48.1 per cent of local authorities claimed to undertake reviews of base estimates for all departments each year. This led him to comment that 'there is clearly an awareness that the base can no longer be thought of as sacrosanct and perhaps the next few years will see increasing involvement with the philosophy, if not the mechanics of ZBB'. In a further study undertaken in 1988, Skousen (1990) replicated the earlier research by Pendlebury and found that the proportion of authorities undertaking reviews of base estimates for all departments every year had increased to 53.9 per cent. This is hardly a dramatic increase and perhaps the reason is that most of the reviews were *ad hoc*, or at least lacking the systematic approach of ZBB, and therefore of limited effectiveness. If this is so it might help to explain why the formal and systematic approach to base budget reviews that ZBB provides is now being increasingly experimented with and applied in local authorities.

One example of such an experiment by the Social Services department of a local authority is reported in Pendlebury (1994). This particular local authority had introduced a system of devolved budgeting which increased the number of budget holders from just a handful of senior staff to over seventy line managers. These new budget holders inherited base budget allocations determined from past histories of spending, with only incremental changes from the base being considered when discussing the budget for the next financial year. Many budget holders felt that a system which enabled historic budget allocations to be challenged and required existing base levels to be justified should be introduced. The result was that for the budget year 1992/93 a system of what was described as zero-based budgeting was attempted. Each budget holder was requested to compile three incremental decision packages for each cost centre under his or her control. The three incremental levels were: current provision; statutory minimum provision; and 90 per cent of current provision. The 90 per cent level was consistent with the basic objective of ZBB of identifying redundant programmes and thereby releasing resources for use elsewhere, but the behavioural reaction to this by budget holders meant that it had to be more or less abandoned. Budget holders obviously felt very threatened by the possibility of a cut of up to 10 per cent in their budget and so devoted much time and effort in devising arguments and strategies to defend the status quo. The consequence was that many assurances that budgets would not be cut had to be given and so the exercise resulted in very little in the way of budget redistributions.

Arguments about the statutory minimum level of service provision also proved to be almost as intractable and so this was also eventually abandoned. However, as Pendlebury (1994) points out, even though this particular project did not in the end turn out to be ZBB, it did have some important benefits. He goes on to state that:

> In particular it forced the pace in terms of carrying out a needs analysis. This would probably have occurred in some form and at some stage without ZBB, but the ZBB project meant that not only needs had to be established but some attempt also had to be made to establish the quality of service that could be offered to meet these needs at different levels of funding. Although attempts to determine the precise relationship between inputs and ouputs often proved to be difficult, it nevertheless did lead to a thorough examination of the relationship between operational decisions and budgetary consequences being undertaken.

It was clear that the budget holder's had felt the ZBB project to be very useful in terms of confirming their 'ownership' of their budgets and in making them aware of the relationship between the actions they take and the impact on their budgets. This particular local authority still felt, even after the problems it had encountered, that ZBB had much to offer and intends to repeat this experiment in a future year.

Budgetary control

One of the more important purposes of a system of budgetary control is to ensure that actual expenditure is in line with budgeted expenditure. Where the actual output or level of activity is different from that budgeted then ideally the budget should be flexed. In reality local government budgeting is concerned almost exclusively with the inputs and so the budget is never flexed. The system is therefore not so much one of budgetary control but one of budgetary compliance. The most important task of the revenue budget in local government is in fixing the level of local taxation.[3] The total revenue that is available from taxation, government grants and other sources is then allocated to services. This allocation represents an authorization to spend. Although over and underspendings could be carried forward to the next year it is clearly undesirable to overspend because of the impact on the tax levels for the next year and it would be illegal (because of the balanced budget constraint imposed on local authorities, under Part VI of the Local Government and Finance Act, 1988) to consistently overspend. The Local Government Finance Act 1988 also imposes a duty on the treasurer of a local authority to report to the members of the authority and the auditor if it appears that the expenditure (actual and proposed) of the authority is likely to exceed its resources for the financial year. Where such a report is made the local authority must consider the report within 21 days and during this period no new agreements which involve the incurring of expenditure may be entered into. There is therefore, a strong pressure to keep spending within the authorizations allocated to each service, even though the level of activity or output may have changed from that envisaged in the budget.

The treasurer or chief financial officer of a local authority plays a key role in both the preparation of budgets and in the subsequent control of spending against budget. The systems of budgetary control used by local authorities varies widely in practice. Pendlebury (1985, p. 13) points out that

> At its most basic the system of budgetary control is little more than a by-

product of the annual financial reporting exercise. As payments are made throughout the year the finance department will record the expenditure against the appropriate line-item headings and then at regular intervals, usually monthly, computer tabulations will be sent to each spending department showing details of the payments made to date.

The limitations of a system that simply produces a mass of computer print-outs which often follow a standard format and therefore fail to reflect the individual requirements of users, have frequently been acknowledged. A number of surveys throughout the 1980s (e.g., Pendlebury, 1985; Audit Commission, 1989; Skousen, 1990) consistently pointed to defects in basic budgetary control information. These included:

- the widespread use of a receipts and payments basis for compiling information on actual spending to date, with the accruals basis being relatively little used and the commitment accounting basis (which shows commitments entered into which will eventually represent a charge against the budget) being rarely encountered.[4]
- the reliance on hard copy printouts for information on actual to date, rather than direct on-line access. Hard-copy printouts are usually prepared monthly and given that there is likely to be a delay of up to two weeks before issue, the information contained clearly lacks timeliness.
- the failure to profile the likely pattern of budget usage throughout the year so as to facilitate the effective analysis of variances between the actual spending at the end of each month and the expected proportion of the budget that would have been spent by the same date.
- the failure to distinguish between controllable and non-controllable information and tailor budgetary control reports to the needs of specific budget holders.
- the lack of concern over outputs and the failure to report on achievement against output targets.

The Audit Commission observed that in spite of these defects, total council spending is almost always well controlled with few cases of overspending, and drew attention to the fact that standards of honesty are high and irregularities are infrequent. The Audit Commission felt that the reason for local government having maintained a strong financial base was because of the existence of: a public service ethic; a strong corps of accountants; a clear budget focus; a wealth of comparable, detailed information; and a tradition of openness and scrutiny. However, it was felt that the changes brought about by the increased use of devolved financial management responsibilities and the competition requirements imposed on a wide range of services might begin to expose deficiencies in financial control.

The Audit Commission felt that if the traditionally strong control of local spending is to be preserved then it is necessary to ensure first of all that financial responsibility is aligned with management responsibility and that front-line managers should be budget holders, but only for items under their control. A second suggestion was that incentives to make economies should be provided in the form of greater freedom over virement and year-end carry forwards. Also, departments should be encouraged to be self reliant and not depend on centrally provided contingencies to meet overspendings, but set up their own provisions for unexpected amounts. This, it is argued, would reduce the need for negotiation between departments and the centre and therefore reduce the opportunity for creative accounting and gamesmanship. A third area that the Audit Commission identified as being needed was to improve information by ensuring that budgetary control reports were well presented, designed to meet the information needs of different levels of management, highlighted significant variances and were up to date. More up-to-date information could be achieved by ensuring that all managers had access to a commitments system and by a quicker turnaround time of budgetary control information through more frequent updating of the main accounts and greater access to on-line information. The Audit Commission point out that in the past when relatively little financial control information was delegated it was possible to overcome the lack of timeliness in budgetary control information by operating on a 'black book' system. In other words the small number of managers with financial control responsibilities would keep their own informal budgetary control records to supplement the centrally prepared, but out of date, information. With the growing trend towards delegated budgetary responsibility, it is increasingly important to provide clear and up to date information to support a much larger number of budget holders. Front-line managers with newly acquired budget responsibilities should not be expected to have to rely on a 'black book' system to ensure budgetary compliance. Finally, the Audit Commission felt that there needed to be much closer links between service department managers and accounting staff, with the treasurer's department providing much more advice to front-line budget holders.

Local government competition

Local authorities have, over the years, undertaken a wide range of trading or commercial activities. Services that are now firmly in the hands of the private sector, such as the provision of gas, electricity and water were, in many part of the country, once provided by local authorities. Other activities such as restaurant and catering services, markets, public transport, airports, theatres, etc., are still provided by local authorities. These are usually referred to as trading services with users being charged a fee which is, in most cases, meant to cover the costs of providing the service.

Trading services are usually provided to members of the public or to other organizations but in addition to these there has also been a long tradition in local government of the in-house provision of activities which support the major services but are of a trading or commercial nature. For example the housing service will require the support of a housing repairs and maintenance activity, the education service will require the support of a school cleaning activity, and so on. Both housing repairs and maintenance and school cleaning could be provided by private sector organizations.

The extent to which the trading services of local authorities are forced to charge prices which reflect consumer preferences is very much dependent on the competition they face. This obviously varies from activity to activity and there will also be examples of subsidies for various reasons such as economic support (e.g. municipal airports) or cultural support (e.g. theatres and concert halls). In general, however, trading services tend to face some level of competition. This was not, until relatively recently, the case with in-house provided support activities. These were not required to be exposed to competition and were simply provided as part of the activities of the major service they were intended to support. However, the Local Government (Planning and Land) Act 1980 changed this by requiring the construction and repairs and maintenance of highways and the construction and repairs and maintenance of houses and other buildings to be organized as separately accountable Direct Labour Organizations (DLOs), which had to tender for their services in open competition with private sector organizations. The DLOs were also required to earn a target rate of return on the current cost value of their capital employed.

The exposure of in-house activities to competition was then extended, with the passing of the Local Government Act 1988, to a range of other activities such as refuse collection, cleaning and catering etc. These activities are to be organized as separately accountable Direct Service Organizations (DSOs). (The term DSO is now generally used to refer to the original activities identified under the 1980 Act, as well as the more recent activities under the 1988 Act, and this is the practice that will be followed in this chapter.)

Direct service organizations

The role of management accounting in providing information for decision making and control in DSOs has changed significantly over the period since the 1980 Local Government (Planning and Land) Act. A large proportion of housing and highways maintenance and construction work has to be won in open competition. It is tenders that win or lose work and successful tendering requires accurate and relevant information on which to base estimates.

The control of costs against the tender price is also important. DSOs are required to make a specified rate of return on capital employed and a persistent failure to achieve the specified rate of return could lead to the DSO being forced to close down. The traditional role of cost accounting in local government has been the production of unit costs. Unit costs are prepared for all services and, as the Audit Commission (1989) points out: 'Local authorities know not only the unit cost of keeping a child in a council home, but can compare each of the elements of the cost of each different type of home.' Although this is clearly a useful facility, it would be inadequate for the needs of DSOs. For example, the managers of buildings maintenance and construction DSOs and highways maintenance and construction DSOs need information on completed jobs and costs, work-in-progress costs, profitable and unprofitable jobs, variances from schedules of rates, labour productivity, idle time, plant and equipment utilization and so on. These earlier, 1980 Act DSOs have therefore been virtually forced to break away from centrally provided financial information for most of their needs, and Pendlebury (1994) reports the experience of one particular local authority in developing more sophisticated management accounting systems. The centralized financial ledgers and budgetary control system suffered from many of the defects described above and were therefore only used to provide the background picture. The major source of relevant management accounting information came from a specifically designed system, which made use of commitment accounting, frequent up-dates of expenditure ledgers (i.e. daily for items drawn from stores), the weekly monitoring of costs against tender price and a monthly monitoring of rates of return. Pendlebury observes that 'the effect of all this is that the management information that is provided from this system is probably as good, if not better, than might be found in many private sector organizations'.

However, Pendlebury also points out that this level of sophistication of management accounting systems was not so evident in the management of the more recent DSOs established under the provision of the Local

Government Act 1988. This Act required that if a local authority wishes to continue with the in-house provision of what are known as 'defined activities', it must ensure that these are exposed to competition. During the Act's progress through Parliament as many as thirty-two potential 'defined activities' were identified but thus far only eight have been put into effect. The relevant Secretary of State has the power under the Act to add to these at some future date. These first eight 'defined activities' were:

- Refuse collection – this covers the collection of household and commercial waste.
- Building cleaning – this includes the cleaning of the interior of any building (except dwellings and residential homes) and the cleaning of windows both inside and outside.
- Other cleaning – this covers street cleaning and the removal of litter, the emptying of litter bins, and the cleaning of traffic signs and street name plates.
- Catering – schools and welfare – this covers the meals and refreshments (including ingredients and preparation) of meals served in schools.
- Other catering – all catering activities except schools and welfare.
- Maintenance of grounds – includes grass cutting, the planting and tending of trees, flowers, plants, hedges, etc., and the control of weeds. This activity is offered for tender in small lots (minimum 20 per cent) to permit small contracting firms to bid for the work.
- Vehicle repair and maintenance – this includes the maintenance (but not accident damage repair) of all motor vehicles, except for police and fire service vehicles.
- Leisure management – this includes all leisure and sports facilities and covers not only leisure centres but also recreational facilities such as tennis courts, bowling greens, etc.

Each of the above activities has to be accounted for separately and, with one exception, has to make a 5 per cent return on the current cost value of capital employed. The one exception is the cleaning of buildings where the requirement is for revenues earned to match the total expenditure incurred, including overhead.

So far, the private sector has been much less successful in winning contracts for the more recently established DSOs of the 1988 Local Government Act, than for the earlier DSOs set up under the 1980 legislation. For example, the Institute of Public Finance (McGuirk, 1993) reports that out of a total of 994 building cleaning contracts awarded under compulsory competitive tendering, 620 had been won by in-house DSOs, 12 by external DSOs and 362 had been awarded to private sector contractors, giving a share of only 36 per cent to the private sector. However, as the private sector becomes more skilled in competing for local authority work it seems likely that the in-house team will have to submit more competitive tenders and will therefore demand increasingly sophisticated information systems to monitor actual spending against tender price.

Central support services

One of the consequences of increased competition has been to challenge the traditional way of charging service departments with the cost of central support services. Central support services will typically consist of the treasurer's department, administration and legal services, personnel and computing. These are usually charged to services on the basis of time spent. These allocated charges, which are outside the control of the manager of a service department or DSO, can have a major impact on financial performance.

A possible alternative to the traditional system is to require central support services to be subject to competition in the same way as DSOs. For many aspects of central support work such as payroll preparation, internal audit and creditor payments this can be done relatively easily. There have been several well publicized cases where this type of central support activity has been voluntarily subjected to competition, or even privatized and in the 1991 'Competing for Quality' consultation paper (Department of the Environment, 1991), the Government signalled its intention to extend competition requirements to a wide range of central support services. These included: corporate and administrative services; legal services; financial services; personnel services; and computing services. However, it was acknowledged that the closeness of many of these activities to the democratic process meant that not everything could be subjected to competition and so it was proposed that proportions, (ranging from 15 per cent for corporate and administrative services, through to 80 per cent for computing) of these services should be exposed to competition. Under the provisions of the Local Government Act, 1992, local authorities can now be required to submit a proportion of their support services to competitive tender.

Even before the extension of competitive requirements to central support services, the problems caused to DSO managers of arbitrarily determined charges for central support was acknowledged and this had led to the widespread use of service level agreements. A service level agreement is a contract to provide a specific service at an agreed quality, frequency and volume. The contract will also specify the basis for charging for this service and the procedure for dealing with complaints and disputes. Making the obvious next step from service level agreements to competing for the underlying activity in the form of competitive tendering, should not present many problems to local authorities.

Devolved financial management

A development that has had a significant impact on the management of local government has been that of devolved financial management. Under the Education Reform Act, 1988, every local education authority was required to devise a formula for allocating the bulk of the total budget for schools to each of its primary and secondary schools. For all secondary schools and for primary schools with over 200 pupils the local education authorities are also required to delegate responsibility for spending the budget allocated to a particular school to the headteacher and governors of that school. This took effect from 1 April 1990 with a requirement for full implementation by 1993.

A further example of devolved financial management can be seen in the provisions of the National Health Services and Community Care Act 1990. Under this Act budgets are to be delegated to case managers who will be responsible for purchasing a package of care for individual users of the service. The package of care can be purchased from the in-house social services team (operating in the same way as a DSO) or from external organizations such as health authorities or voluntary organizations.

Both local management of schools (LMS) and devolved management in community care represent major management challenges. Under LMS management decisions are needed on every aspect of running schools, including staff appointments, dismissals, and the marketing of the school to parents and other members of the community. The governing body of a school has responsibility for controlling the running of the school within the delegated budget and is free from the normal restrictions on virement and year-end carry forwards. The financial information systems that are introduced for schools now have to match these new requirements.

For community care the essential requirement of case managers is for financial information which enables them to estimate the likely cost of a given package of care and then monitor actual costs against estimate on a case by case basis. This represents a significant departure from the traditional form of social services budget preparation and budgetary control and has posed a significant challenge to the financial management systems of local authorities.

Conclusions

The management of local government has changed dramatically in recent years. Compulsory competitive tendering; devolved management in schools, community care and other services; the move from allocated central support service charges to negotiated service level agreements and negotiated charges, have all had an impact. These changes have in turn led to changes in the financial information requirements of local authorities.

Whether the management accounting systems will be able to change to meet these requirements is now the question. Although the ten years or so up to 1988 saw major changes in local government, the traditional budgeting and budgetary control systems appeared in general to have been slow to respond and many of the defects that had been pointed out several years earlier were still very much in evidence. However, there are now clear indications that the more rapid pace of change currently affecting local government is at last having an impact on management accounting practices. The next few years are likely to see an increasingly sophisticated and flexible system of management accounting in use in local government, but with much more emphasis on the decentralized provision of management information.

Notes

1   For a more detailed explanation of the concept, development and application of both PPBS and ZBB see Jones, R. and Pendlebury, M. (1996, Chapters 4 & 5).

2   This does not mean that PPBs is no longer still used. Bellamy and Kluvers (1995) undertook a study of the budgeting practices of municipalities in the state of Victoria, Australia. Their results show that 18 municipalities (out of a total of 122 responding to their survey) claimed to use PPBs as their sole method of budget preparation.

3   See Pendlebury (1985, pp. 27/28) for an analysis of responses to a questionnaire survey of local authority senior financial officers. This revealed that an overwhelming majority of the respondents felt that 'fixing the level of rates and precepts' was the most important reason for preparing an annual revenue budget.

4   Under a system of commitment accounting, expenditure is recorded when orders are issued rather than when an invoice is received. For budgetary control purposes it obviously makes sense to know not only the cash payments and the amounts due to creditors but also the claims

against the budget that have been committed through orders that have been issued.

References

Anthony, R. N. (1977). ZBB – a useful fraud?, *Government Accountants Journal*, Summer.

Audit Commission, (1989). *Better Financial Management*, Management Papers No. 3, Audit Commission.

Bellamy, S. and Kluvers, R. (1995). Program budgeting in Australian local government, *Financial Accountability and Management*, **11**, (1), 39–56.

Department of the Environment (1991). *Competing for Quality – Competition in the Provision of Local Services*.

Jones, R. and Pendlebury, M. (1996). *Public Sector Accounting*, 4th edition, Pitman.

Marshall, A. H. (1974). *Financial Management in Local Government*, London: Allen and Unwin.

McGuirk, T. (1993). *CCT and the Private Sector Vol. 2, A Clean Sweep – An Overview of Building Cleaning in Local Government*, Institute of Public Finance, Croydon.

Pendlebury, M. (1985). *Management Accounting in Local Government*, CIMA Occasional Paper Series, CIMA.

Pendlebury, M. (1994). Management accounting in local government, *Financial Accountability and Management*, **10**, (2), May, 117–29.

Skousen, C. R. (1990). Budgeting practices in local governments in England and Wales, *Financial Accountability and Management*, Autumn, **6**, (3), 191–208.

14

Capital investment appraisal
C. W. Neale and R. H. Pike

In this chapter, Bill Neale and Richard Pike focus on the role of man-agement accounting within the capital budgeting process. They begin by providing an overview of the capital budgeting process starting from the search process and ending with the post-audit process. In particular, they show that capital budgeting involves more than just the appraisal of individual investments.

Having explained capital budgeting within a wider context, the authors stress that it should be viewed within the context of strategic planning. They point out that investment proposals need to be related to the underlying corporate objectives and strategies of the business unit. In the next section, Neale and Pike discuss the principal methods of project evaluation. They describe how the modified internal rate of return can overcome some of the limitations associated with the internal rate of return method of evaluating investments. They also outline the theoretical objections to the payback method and then proceed to examine some of its practical merits.

The problems of risk and how to allow for it in the appraisal process are examined in the following section. The authors show how risk can be assessed by viewing a capital project in isolation, as part of the business and as part of a business whose shares form part of a share-holder's investment portfolio. The final section of the chapter describes the post-audit review of capital projects. In this section, the authors discuss the problems cited by executives responsible for undertaking post-audits and outline some key points to be taken into account when implementing a post-auditing system.

Introduction

What role does the management accountant play in the capital investment process? All too frequently, it seems that the management accountant is the person who puts together the financial paperwork – often long after the decision has, in effect, been taken.

The main aim of this contribution is to help accountants see capital budgeting in a wider context than perhaps they have before, to consider some of the practical developments in recent years, and to encourage accountants to take greater ownership of the whole process.

In a broader macro-economic context, investment decision-making has a profound impact. Economists consider investment expenditure to be probably the major locomotive of economic growth and development. Despite this, investment expenditure in the UK has barely risen in real terms over the past decade or so, which results in continuing difficulty in accommodating upsurges in demand. While weak tax incentives to invest and the allegedly short-term orientation of the financial system may be partially responsible for this, it is at least possible that faulty capital expenditure evaluation is also partly to blame. Academics used to argue that if crude and misleading investment appraisal techniques yielded to more sophisticated DCF methods, firms would accept more productive investments and higher levels of economic activity would follow. However, widespread, if not wholehearted, adoption of DCF methods, has not promoted higher levels of productive investment. One explanation (Pinches, 1982) is that it is misleading to overemphasize the techniques of appraisal; instead, decision-makers should visualize capital budgeting as an integrated, multi-stage process set within the strategy defined by the senior policy-makers of the organization. Critics of UK industrial performance often point to the failure of UK firms (unlike for example, Japanese companies) to evaluate their investment options in a long-term strategic context.

The capital budgeting process

Capital expenditures are normally regarded as investments to acquire fixed or long-lived assets from which a stream of benefits is expected, although the various techniques of appraisal can be applied to any expenditure which promises future benefits. Such expenditures delineate the firm's future operating capability and thus form the basis upon which the firm's future prosperity largely depends. Capital budgeting refers to the whole process of creating, appraising and implementing capital projects. It is therefore far more than a concern with 'correct' appraisal techniques or the correct completion of capital appropriation request forms.

Figure 14.1 is a diagram of the key stages in the capital budgeting process. The process outlined covers the formal steps typically required in organizations. Its primary aim is to ensure that the limited capital resources available are allocated to wealth-creating capital projects which make the best contribution to corporate goals. A second goal should be to see that good investment ideas are not held back and that poor or ill-considered proposals are rejected or further refined.

Stage 1. Determination of the budget

When the investment decision-making body is a sub-unit of a larger group, the budget may be rigidly imposed on it from above. However, for quasi-autonomous investment centres (divisions of larger groups with capital-raising powers) and/or independent units, the amount to be spent on capital projects is a control variable, subject of course to considerations of corporate control and gearing, and to additional demands for funds generated by stages 2 and 3.

Stage 2. The search process

Seeking-out ideas to exploit is arguably the most important part of capital budgeting (and often the first step in the process), since without research and development and exploitation of new products and markets, firms are likely to wither and die. Over time, firms accumulate a 'stock' of project proposals (some of which may have been rejected previously) which are continually refined and re-examined as more information emerges. Evidence tends to suggest that the best *ideas* emerge from an unstructured research process but that the best *projects* emerge from a more highly controlled development process.

Stage 3. Evaluation

All relevant information about a project is exposed to arithmetic analysis using one or several of the available techniques for computing project worth. At this stage, rigorous sensitivity analysis should be conducted to assess the uncertainties surrounding the project and the extent to which the project can underperform before it is no longer viable.

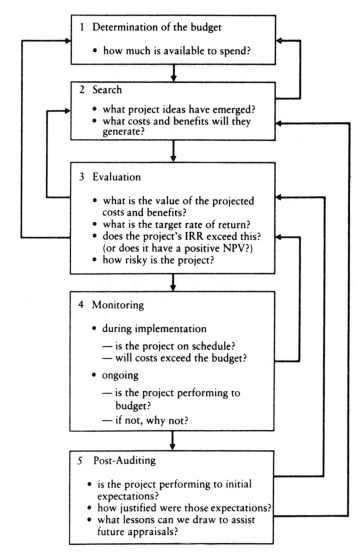

Figure 14.1 *An integrated capital budgeting system*

The preliminary project review conducted at this stage provides management with an early indication of the attractiveness of projects. Those not worth pursuing further are identified at an early stage, thus avoiding unnecessary managerial effort. Those worthy of further investigation are then given the 'go-ahead' to allow the sponsor to coordinate the many activities associated with producing a detailed appropriation request and to prepare for project implementation should approval be granted.

The capital appropriation request forms the basis for the final decision to commit financial and other resources to the project. At this point, the management accountant is usually most heavily involved in coordinating and compiling project-related information, much of which has been provided by other parties both within and outside the organization.

Typical information included in an appropriation request is given below:

- Purpose of project – why it is proposed and how it fits corporation strategy and goals.
- Project classification – e.g. expansion, replacement, modernization, cost saving, quality improvement, research and development, safety and health, legal requirement, etc.
- Finance requested – amount and timing, including net working capital, etc.
- Operating cash flows – amount and timing, together with the main assumptions influencing the accuracy of the cash flow estimates.
- Attractiveness of the proposal – expressed by standard appraisal indicators, such as net present value, DCF rate of return and payback period calculated on after-tax cash flows. (Although some firms request proposals in pre-tax form, the tax adjustments made by central accounting functions are more cognizant of the organization's taxable capacity.)
- Sensitivity of the appraisal indicators – the effect of changes in the main investment inputs. Other approaches to assessing project risk should also be addressed (e.g. best/worst scenarios, estimated range of accuracy of DCF return, etc.).
- Review of alternatives – why they were rejected and their economic attractiveness.
- Implications of not accepting the proposal – some projects which may have little economic merit according to the appraisal indicators may be 'essential' to the continuance of a profitable part of the business or to achieving agreed strategy.

Stage 4. Implementation and monitoring

Setting-up an investment project often becomes the province of engineers and production managers, but close financial control (monitoring) is required to minimize the extent of cost and time overruns, and to provide early warning signals of such difficulties. The term monitoring is applied also to the observation of project performance, once it is 'up-and-running', i.e. producing outputs with definable costs and revenues. Most firms will incorporate the expected impact of a new project into their budgeting procedures, and can observe, very quickly, usually on a monthly basis, how well or badly the project is performing, and then take appropriate remedial action.

Stage 5. Post-auditing

Once a project is established and early teething troubles have been ironed out, it is advisable, usually after about a year, to examine in finer detail its success or otherwise in the light of initial expectation. There are many reasons for doing this, not least being the aim of testing the thoroughness of the original project evaluation in order to improve the quality of future appraisals. This should enhance the likelihood of acceptance of the 'best' projects which should, in turn, enhance corporate profitability. There are, therefore, important feedback loops built into the evaluation stage and also into the search process as shown in Figure 14.1, since an *ex-post* evaluation may reveal new opportunities for exploitation.

Post-auditing is a particularly important component of the capital budgeting system. If, as many executives contend, investment capital is a scarce or expensive commodity, it is vital that maximum benefits are obtained from it, and that potential future errors of misallocation are minimized.

Strategic implications

Until relatively recently, most capital projects were considered very largely in isolation. Sponsors advanced investment ideas as capital proposals to be assessed in terms of their economic attractiveness, with little regard to their impact on broader strategic goals.

Today, within most organizations, certainly larger ones, capital budgeting is viewed as part of a bigger process, the focus moving away from the project in isolation to the project within strategic business units. A business strategy is a set of well co-ordinated action programmes aimed at securing a long-term sustainable advantage. As strategy frequently emerges through a process of backing those parts of the business viewed as 'winners' and eliminating 'losers', capital investments should be viewed within the strategic context. Capital expenditure proposals should be assessed in terms of their impact on longer-term strategy to see if they fit into the overall framework in conjunction with the activities of the business.

A number of useful approaches to analysing the strategic position of business units are available (e.g. the growth-share matrix, business assessment array and directional policy matrix), each of which has investment implications. For example, the business assessment array, developed by General Electric, analyses businesses according to their particular strengths and competitive position on the one hand (e.g. market share and growth, brand loyalty, etc.) and market attractiveness on the other (e.g. size and growth of market, industry profitability, degree of competition, ease of entry, etc.). Figure 14.2 shows that, depending on the perceived location of the business within the matrix, there are clear implications for investment. We could interpret the matrix as shown in Table 14.1.

Business strength

		High	Medium	Low
M a r k e t	**H i g h**	Invest and grow	Invest and grow	Improve and defend
a t t r a c t i v e n e s s	**M e d i u m**	Invest and grow	Improve and defend	Divest
	L o w	Improve and defend	Divest	Divest

Figure 14.2 *Business assessment array*

Investment decision-making therefore is seen as the natural extension of the strategic planning process. A clear understanding of the enterprise and its value drivers (i.e. those key elements of the business which have a major impact on shareholder value) should precede the development of the business strategy, which then gives rise to investment (or disinvestment) implications. Some segments have very little planned capital expenditure, others

Table 14.1

Business position	Investment intention
Highly attractive, fast growing market where we are strong.	Build aggressively – invest and grow.
Attractive, moderate growth industry where we want to build our share, or where it is uncertain whether growth can be sustained.	Build gradually – improve and defend.
Some good positions in an attractive industry.	Build selectively
Few business strengths in an unattractive market.	Divest

concentrate on maintaining existing capacity, while others may be targeted for rapid expansion. But no plan should ever be set in concrete; where an investment idea is outstandingly good, it may mean the business plan needs revision. Alternatively, when a strategic business unit is underperforming, the decision-making team should regularly examine the option to divest.

Investment analysis

While the fit of a project with the business strategy is of fundamental importance, sound analysis of capital investment proposals is still a vital phase within the decision process. Reliable forecasts and estimates and a well-defined project are essential to investment analysis. No matter how sophisticated the appraisal techniques employed, they will be of limited value unless reliable estimates and forecasts are given for markets, likely competitor actions, related new technology, sales volumes and prices, fixed and working capital requirements.

Few management accountants would question the crucial importance of investment decision-making in determining a company's longer-term success or failure. However, surveys of capital budgeting practices suggest that for many organizations, good investment decision-making is not necessarily synonymous with formalized capital budgeting procedures or the application of textbook appraisal techniques, at least in a strict sense.

The obvious danger is that, while we concentrate on project appraisal methods, much of the rest of the capital budgeting process is largely ignored. At the outset, then, let us recognize a few 'home truths' about capital budgeting:

1   Theoretically correct methods may not, in practice, produce optimal investment solutions.
2   Good investment projects do not simply emerge out of the woodwork – they have to be identified, defined and revised.
3   Project risk can rarely be measured in the manner prescribed in textbooks with any great level of accuracy.
4   Non-quantifiable aspects frequently have a significant impact on the decision outcome.
5   Estimates are rarely free from bias.
6   Managers, like politicians, frequently operate to hidden rather than explicit agendas.

In short, the application of formalized investment procedures and sophisticated investment techniques do not automatically deliver better quality investment decisions. We now turn to the application of capital budgeting in practice, where something of a revolution in adopting new methods has occurred in recent years.

A capital budgeting study by Pike (1996), based on the investment practices of the same 100 large UK companies during the 1970s, 1980s and early 1990s analysed capital budgeting trends and considered their relevance to today's business decisions.

Although various investment studies have been conducted over the years, this one has the unique merit of providing reliable comparative data, enabling an assessment of how practices have changed over time. Here, we summarize some of the study's findings, particular attention being paid to investment selection techniques. Following this, we examine the role of the post-completion audit in investment decision-making and control, drawing upon a study by Neale and Holmes (1988), also sponsored by CIMA.

Evaluation techniques

Table 14.2 summarizes the selected capital budgeting practices of 100 large UK companies between 1975 and 1992. Eighty-one per cent of the firms surveyed claimed to use internal rate of return (IRR) in appraising projects, making it the second most popular technique. The net present value (NPV) method is not far behind in corporate usage (74 per cent). Both DCF methods have increased enormously in popularity over the study period.

Table 14.3 reveals that both are now standard techniques for most investment projects, although more companies employ the IRR method on all projects (54 per cent) than the NPV method (33 per cent). The most

Table 14.2 Selected capital budgeting practices 1975–1992

	100 large UK firms			
	1975	1981	1986	1992
	%	%	%	%
Internal rate of return	44	57	75	81
Net present value	32	39	68	74
Average accounting rate of return	51	49	56	50
Payback period	73	81	92	94
Post audit procedure for most major projects	33	46	64	72

likely reason for the rapid uptake in these techniques during the 1980s is the general availability of DCF functions on spreadsheets and other financial software. The IRR method is now no more difficult to compute than the payback method.

Table 14.3 Selected capital budgeting practices

	Frequency of use in 1992 in 100 large UK firms				
	Total	Rarely	Often	Mostly	Always
	%	%	%	%	%
Internal rate of return	81	7	13	7	54
Net present value	74	11	16	14	33
Average accounting rate of return	50	17	13	5	21
Payback period	94	6	12	14	62

The average accounting rate of return (AARR) enjoyed considerable support in 1975, but with very little change in subsequent years, the usage level remains at around 50 per cent.

Modified IRR

While net present value is the capital budgeting technique most preferred by the academic community, practitioners have long favoured a percentage yield-based approach such as the internal rate of return. One of many reasons is that the IRR does not require the specification of a discount rate prior to calculation. The IRR is a sound method for many investment decisions; nevertheless, in some cases, such as the need to choose between alternative projects under conditions of mutual exclusivity or capital rationing, it provides less than satisfactory results. Conflict in ranking projects using IRR and NPV approaches can arise when there exists disparity between projects in terms of project size or life.

The main difference between the two lies in their respective reinvestment assumptions. With the NPV approach, all cash flows are assumed to be reinvested at the firm's cost of capital, reflecting the alternative use of funds; but the IRR approach implicitly assumes a project's annual cash flows can be reinvested at the project's internal rate of return. Thus, a project offering a 34 per cent IRR assumes that interim cash flows are compounded forward at that rate, rather than at the cost of capital. Where the IRR is well above the cost of capital, this assumption is clearly unrealistic.

The modified internal rate of return (MIRR), or terminal rate of return, is increasingly being used in US companies to overcome the above limitation of the IRR and gives a signal consistent with the NPV approach. The MIRR is that rate of return which, when the initial outlay is compared with the terminal value of the project's net cash flows, gives an NPV of zero. This involves a two-stage process:

1 Calculate the terminal value of the project by compounding forward all interim cash flows at the cost of capital to the end of the project.
2 Find that rate or interest which equates the terminal value with the initial cost.

This method will give an answer consistent with net present value, as long as the reinvestment rate is identical to the discount rate that would have been used to find the NPV. However, management can understand it as a rate of return.

Consider a capital proposal costing £32,000 which offers £16,000 annual cash benefits for four years. The project offers an IRR of approximately 35 per cent, well above the firm's required rate of return of 14 per cent. What is the rate of return assuming reinvestment at the 14 per cent cost of capital rather than at 35 per cent.

The MIRR first requires calculation of the terminal values using compound interest at the cost of capital.

Year	Cash flow £	Future value factor @ 14%	Terminal value £
1	16,000	1.4815	23,704
2	16,000	1.2996	20,794
3	16,000	1.1400	18,240
4	16,000	1.0000	16,000
			78,738

The rate of interest which equates the terminal value of £78,738 at the end of year 4 with the initial cost of £32,000 is approximately 25 per cent – some 10 percentage points below the IRR. In this case, it may not affect the decision outcome when considered in isolation because both returns exceed the required rate of return. However, it could be important in project ranking – particularly when the timing of annual cash flows differs appreciably between projects.

Payback

The popularity of payback as an evaluation method continues to grow despite its known drawbacks. Some 94 per cent of firms use this method, approximately two-thirds of which require it to be calculated for all projects.

While academic writers have almost unanimously condemned the use of the payback period as misleading and of little value in reaching investment decisions, it continues to flourish. In this section, we attempt both to explain this phenomenon and also to ascertain whether the payback period does possess certain qualities not so apparent in more sophisticated approaches.

The two main objectives to payback are well known – it ignores all cash flows beyond the payback period and it does not consider the profile of the project's cash flows within the payback period itself.

Although such theoretical shortcomings could fundamentally alter a project's ranking and selection, it would seem that the payback criterion possesses more internal theoretical strength and practical merit than it is sometimes credited with. These are discussed below.

Performance

The payback period can be used to provide a measure of economic performance. When the annual cash receipts from a project are uniform, the payback reciprocal is the internal rate of return for a project of infinite life or a good approximation to this rate for long-lived projects.

The internal rate of return for a project with a very long life, relatively stable annual cash returns and a four-year payback period is conveniently found by calculating the payback reciprocal and expressing it in percentage form:

$$IRR = \frac{1}{4} \times 100 = 25\%$$

However, as the project life falls, so does the IRR. Thus, if the project has only a ten-year life, the IRR falls to approximately 21 per cent. The payback calculation is still useful here because, with the help of annuity discount tables, the IRR is found by locating that rate of interest which gives a payback of four for a ten-year life. In this case, the rate is 21 per cent.

Rationing capital

Payback provides a simple, reasonably efficient measure for ranking projects when constraints prevail, such as the time managers can devote to initial project screening. Only a handful of the investment ideas originally generated may stand up to serious and thorough financial investigation. Payback period serves as a simple, first-level screening device which identifies those projects to go forward for more rigorous investigation.

Many firms resort to payback period when experiencing liquidity constraints. Ranking projects according to their ability to repay quickly, although possessing certain intuitive logic, can lead to sub-optimal solutions. Such a policy may make sense when funds are constrained and better investment ideas are in the pipeline. This could arise, for example, where a major strategic investment is to be made two years hence, when capital rationing conditions prevail. The attractiveness of investment proposals considered during the interim period will be a function more of their ability to 'pay back' rapidly than of their overall profitability.

Uncertainty

Payback is seen as a useful tool in times of high levels of uncertainty and high rates of inflation. Whereas more sophisticated techniques attempt to model the uncertainty surrounding project returns, payback assumes that risk is time-related – the longer the period, the greater the chance of failure. The high levels of inflation and worldwide recession experienced in recent years have rendered the task of forecasting cash flows highly speculative, but for the most part, cash flows exhibit serial correlation, i.e. they are correlated over time. If the operating returns are below the expected level in the early years, this pattern will often persist.

Discounted cash flow, as practised in most firms, ignores this increase in uncertainty over time. Early cash flows, therefore, have an important information content on the degree of accuracy of subsequent cash flows. By concentrating on the early cash flows, payback is based on data in which managers have greater confidence. Should such evaluation provide a different signal from DCF methods, it highlights the need for a more careful consideration of the project's risk characteristics.

Acceptability and communication

Another quality of payback concerns its general acceptability at all management levels. Why do managers feel more 'comfortable' with payback than the DCF? In the first place, its acceptability is a function of its simplicity. The non-quantitative manager is reluctant to rely on the recommendations of 'sophisticated' models when he lacks both the time and expertise to verify such outcomes. Confidence in and commitment to a proposal depend to some degree on how thoroughly the evaluation model is comprehended.

Payback is a particularly useful communication device. It offers a convenient shorthand for the desirability of each investment that is acceptable at all levels of the organization, namely: how quickly will the project recover its initial outlay? Some firms use a project classification system in which the payback period indicates how rapidly proposals should be processed and put into operation.

As the above discussion has sought to convey, while the payback concept may lack the refinements of its more sophisticated evaluation counterparts, it possesses many endearing qualities which make it irresistible to most managers. Herein lies the secret of its resilience.

Risk analysis

Project risk can be assessed by viewing the capital project:

- on its own (stand-alone risk);
- as part of a business (corporate risk); or
- as part of a business whose shares form part of a shareholder's investment portfolio (market risk).

While few firms actually estimate project risk as defined above in statistical terms, a recent study (Pike and Ho, 1991) reveals that at least in a subjective manner, managers in larger UK firms consider all three methods to varying degrees for major products:

Stand-alone risk	79%
Impact on corporate risk	61%
Impact on shareholders' portfolio	26%

Sensitivity analysis is a useful and commonly applied technique which indicates exactly how much the expected NPV or DCF return will change in response to a given change in a single input variable, other things held constant. It is also useful to determine by how much key assumptions can deteriorate before the project ceases to be economically viable.

Scenario analysis is also used by most large firms. This involves three scenarios – the best case, the worst case, and the most likely case. Estimated cash flows under each scenario should be broken down into revenue and cost components. A particular merit of this approach is that it helps identify any skewness in a project's cash flows. Subjective probabilities can be applied to these outcomes to produce an expected NPV or IRR.

The required return on investment

The acid test of financial management is whether the company can achieve a return at least as great as the opportunity cost which the owners incur by investing in the company, i.e. 'the cost of equity'. This generally requires achieving a return of at least that on totally risk-free assets plus some premium for risk. Firms have often applied risk premia on a largely subjective basis, for example by classifying projects into 'low-risk', 'medium-risk' and 'high-risk' categories, with varying discount rates between categories. However, modern portfolio theory (MPT) provides a more coherent guide to determining the cost of equity, based on examining the variability in returns enjoyed by shareholders. The important contribution of MPT is to segregate overall risk incurred by shareholders into two categories:

1 Specific risk – risk specific to the individual company due to factors such as industrial relations problems, news of new contracts, or R&D breakthroughs, etc.
2 Systematic risk – risk due to factors affecting the returns of all companies, e.g. changes in macro-economic parameters like interest rates and exchange rates.

MPT argues that specific risk is irrelevant because investors can diversify it away by forming a well-diversified portfolio of securities. If investors are able to hold such portfolios (and the major and increasingly important investment players, the institutions, certainly do), then the market will only reward investors for bearing that risk due to changes in general economic conditions, as reflected by the behaviour of the stock market in general. However, the returns on different companies vary to different degrees when market conditions change. Some securities are 'aggressive', that is, their returns are more volatile than the market as a whole, while conversely some are 'defensive'. The variability of the returns on a share in relation to the variability of the whole stock market is indicated by its Beta coefficient, which is, in effect, a measure of systematic risk. MPT shows that the rate of return, k_e, which an equity investor should seek is given by the expression:

$$k_e = R_f + \beta [ER_m - R_f]$$

where R_f = the return on a risk-free asset such as three-month Treasury Bills.

ER_m = the return expected on the overall market.

β = the market risk factor for the firm's shares.

This simply tells us that the overall return which a company should offer its shareholders is comprised of an element to compensate them for waiting for their returns plus a risk premium, which is related to the expected risk premium on the overall market by the Beta coefficient. To illustrate this taking the Beta coefficient of 0.71 for Allied Textiles (a company financed entirely by equity capital) from the London Business School's Risk Measurement Service booklet, taking the historical risk premium on the UK market portfolio of some 9 per cent, and using the yield on three-month Treasury Bills of 6.5 per cent as at July 1995, we find a required return of:

$$
\begin{aligned}
k_e &= 6.50\% + 0.71\,[9\%] \\
&= 6.50\% + 6.39\% \\
&= 12.89\%, \text{ say } 13\%
\end{aligned}
$$

The implication is that if shareholders are seeking a return of 13 per cent on their investments, then the cut-off rate applicable to new investment projects of at least a comparable degree of risk as existing activities, should also be 13 per cent (see Pike and Neale [1996] for a fuller exposition of MPT).

Some authorities recommend reducing the risk premium on the market by 1 per cent or so to allow for the effect of gearing on the returns on the market portfolio. Doing this would reduce the required return on Allied Textiles' shares, and by implication, new investment projects to around 12 per cent.

However, few companies are financed solely by equity capital. Most commentators advocate the use of relatively cheap debt capital in order to lower the overall required return. The interest rate on debt capital is normally lower than the return required by shareholders and interest payments can be set against corporation tax. For a tax-paying company borrowing at, say, 10%, tax relief at 33% lowers the effective cost of debt to:

$$10\% \ (1-33\%) = 6.7\%$$

(In practice, delay in payment of tax has the effect of raising the post-tax rate slightly.) Careful use of debt finance, i.e. at levels of gearing below those which invite financial distress will lower the *overall* return which the company should achieve in order to satisfy all its providers of finance.

This return is measured by the weighted average cost of capital (WACC) which is calculated by assessing the costs of the various components of finance weighted according to their contributions to overall capital structure. Generally, market value weights, while more volatile, are preferable to book value weights – investors seek returns on the market values of their holdings, not on their historic costs. A company with a capital structure of 25 per cent debt to total capital involving a cost of 6.7 per cent after tax, and whose shareholders seek a return of 13 per cent would have the following WACC:

$$
\begin{aligned}
\text{WACC} \ = \ & (\text{cost of debt} \times \text{proportion of debt}) + (\text{cost of} \\
& \text{equity} \times \text{proportion of equity}) \\
= \ & (6.7\% \times 25\%) + (13\% \times 75\%) \\
= \ & 1.68\% + 9.75\% = 11.43\%, \text{ say } 11.5\%
\end{aligned}
$$

There are limits to debt financing determined by the value of the company's assets in relation to the book value of outstanding debt and by its expected capacity to maintain ongoing interest payments. Consequently, companies and analysts often suggest the existence of an optimal capital structure. This does, however, seem to vary over time with changes in interest rates and economic conditions, and certainly varies between industries. Consequently, it is common to use target capital structure weights in the calculation of WACC.

The WACC can be used when the new project is not expected to alter the company's capital structure nor to involve moving beyond present risk parameters. If these conditions do not apply, firms may have to 'tailor-make' the discount rate by looking, for example, at Beta coefficients for 'surrogate' firms in other industries and by attempting to assess any additional financing costs and benefits separately from those of the project, as in a lease evaluation.

Use of surrogate companies may be adopted when assessing the divisional hurdle rate – the Betas of divisions are unknown, since they are not traded on the stock market. The central accounting function of a multi-division company may set these divisional target rates, treat projects as financed by equity and then assess separately the value of financing benefits, such as tax relief on debt interest, from an overall corporate perspective. For example, since the central function is more likely to know the expected taxable capacity of the group, it may act to prevent the use of debt financing when group taxable capacity is relatively low.

Some opinion argues however, that financing benefits should be ignored. If a project is only made worthwhile by the inclusion of these benefits, this implies that its cash flow benefits are of marginal value anyhow, and perhaps it should be rejected. This argument may not apply for low risk activities, e.g. lease evaluations. Others argue that attempting to be over-precise about the discount rate is not an effective use of executive resources in a world where all estimates are uncertain.

Some contemporary controversies

It is appropriate to mention several contemporary controversial issues regarding the required return on investment. These concern respectively, the appropriate size of the risk premium, the validity of the MPT itself and the 'stickiness' of investment cut-off rates.

(a) The size of the risk premium

For many years, it was accepted that the return on the market portfolio over and above the return on the risk-free asset, i.e. $[R_m - R_f]$ could be taken at 8–9%. This was based on a series of studies over varying, lengthy time periods in the USA, UK, Holland, Sweden and Japan. This appeared to be one of the parameters of corporate finance underscored by increasingly mobile international investment capital, i.e. in a world capital market where funds are highly mobile, one could expect to find risk premia equalized.

A rather lower risk premium was recorded by Grubb (1993/4), at 6.2 per cent for the period 1960–92. Even so, Grubb suggests that returns to equities in the 1970s and 1980s were exceptional and that under a 'modern scenario' of moderate growth and moderate inflation, a much lower premium on equities in general of only 2 per cent would be reasonable. This view is supported by Wilkie (1994), who, after exhaustive study of past trends in dividend yields and patterns of inflation, argues for a risk premium for longer-term investment of 3 per cent and 2 per cent for the short-term. The jury is still out on this issue, but it is unlikely that many financial directors would contemplate recommending projects with such low allowances for risk.

(b) Doubts about MPT

The cornerstone of MPT is the Capital Asset Pricing Model (CAPM) which posits a stable relationship between the *expected* returns on securities and the *expected* returns on the whole market. The key word here is expected – a model that deals with expectations is very difficult to test and thus verify. Moreover, it is a single-period model and it is doubtful whether a single period required return can be translated into a year-by-year discount rate applicable to an investment project.

Attempts to test the CAPM have also been hampered by the difficulty of specifying the risk-free asset (is there such a thing?), the problem that there is no fully comprehensive market index to act as a benchmark for assessing relative returns (even the FT Actuaries Index only covers a third of all quoted securities) and the omission of other types of capital asset (such as real estate, works of art, antiques, etc.), all of which offer risky returns over time. Empirical testing of the CAPM continues, although the most comprehensive one to date (Fama and French, 1992) is not very supportive. Generally, the historical pattern of returns suggest a far smaller premium for risk than Beta analyses would suggest for individual securities.

Other work is attempting to build an alternative theory to explain the pattern of security returns. Whereas the MPT is a single-factor model with security returns being explained (or not) by the variability of returns on the market, the proposed replacement theory, the Arbitrage Pricing Theory, is a multi-factor model. The problem is that it is difficult to pinpoint the set of factors which jointly explain the pattern of share returns over time, which will hopefully provide a guide for future analysis. Factors which often emerge in this work are a mixture of 'monetary' factors such as the level and growth of the money supply, long-term interest rates and 'real' factors such as world oil prices and the level of industrial production. Whether this work will provide help for industrial decision-makers looking for a coherent guide for selecting investment cut-off rates is very doubtful at this stage.

(c) The 'stickiness' of discount rates

As the UK emerged from the recession of the 1990s, policy-makers were concerned about the slowness of capital investment to recover and increase. Two studies by Wardlow (1994) and Junankar (1994) for the Bank of England and the CBI respectively showed that manufacturing companies have not lowered their cut-off rates despite sharp reductions in inflation and nominal interest rates. Investment appraisals can allow for inflation in two ways – either by discounting cash flows expressed in constant prices at the real rate of required return (i.e. net of inflation) or by discounting cash flows expressed in current prices (i.e. incorporating inflation at the nominal required return – that which incorporates an element for expected inflation). Most firms conduct appraisals in the second way, so that when the rate of inflation falls, thus pulling down interest rates, they 'ought' to lower discount rates accordingly. The two studies found that firms were not in general doing this, suggesting that they were not reviewing their cut-off rates frequently enough or not at all. Alternatively, they may simply be expressing scepticism at the government's longer-term ability to restrain the rate of inflation. Either way, if discount rates are pitched 'excessively' high, it shrinks the pool of worthwhile investment projects.

Post-auditing

The final stage in the capital budgeting decision-making and control sequence is the post-completion audit. UK firms have been considerably more hesitant in appreciating the need to post-audit as compared to their North American counterparts, although there is evidence that this is changing. In a 1985 study, Neale and Holmes (1988) showed that 47 per cent of large quoted UK companies had adopted post-audits, while data collected by Neale in 1990 showed this proportion to have risen to 77 per cent, with about half of these having adopted post-audits between 1986 and 1990.

A post-audit aims to compare the actual performance of a project after say, a year's operation, with the forecast made at the time of approval, and, ideally, also with any revised assessment made at the date of commissioning. The aims of the exercise are twofold. Firstly, post-audits may attempt to encourage more thorough and realistic appraisals of future investment projects and secondly, they may aim to facilitate major overhauls of ongoing projects, perhaps to alter their strategic focus. These two aims differ in an important respect. The first concerns the overall capital budgeting system, seeking to improve its quality and cohesion, while the second concerns the control of existing projects, but with a broader perspective than is normally possible during the regular monitoring procedure when project adjustments are usually of a 'fire-fighting' nature. If these objectives are achieved, then post-auditing may confer substantial benefits on the firm. Among these are the enhanced quality of decision-making and planning which may stem from more carefully and rigorously-researched project proposals, tightening of internal control systems, the ability to modify or even abandon projects on the basis of fuller information, and the identification of key variables on whose outcome the viability of the current and similar future projects may depend.

Problems with post-auditing

There are many possible reasons why UK firms have been slow to adopt post-audits. An insight into these can be obtained by listing some of the problems frequently cited by executives responsible for undertaking post-audits.

The disentanglement problem It may be difficult to separate out the relevant costs and benefits specific to a new project from other company activities, especially where facilities are shared and the new project requires an increase in shared overheads. New techniques of overhead cost allocation may prove helpful in this respect.

Projects may be unique If there is no prospect of repeating a project in the future, there may seem little point in post-auditing, since the lessons learned may not be applicable to any future activity. Nevertheless, useful insights into the capital budgeting system as a whole may still be obtained.

Prohibitive cost To introduce post-audits may involve interference with present management information systems in order to generate flows of suitable data. Since post-auditing every project may be very resource-intensive, firms tend to be selective in their post-audits.

Biased selection By definition, only accepted projects can be post-audited, and among these, often only the underperforming ones are singled out by firms for detailed examination. Because of this biased selection mechanism, the forecasting and evaluation expertise of project analysts may be cast in an unduly bad light – they could have been 'spot on' in evaluating rejected and acceptably performing projects!

Lack of cooperation If the post-audit is conducted in too inquisitorial a fashion, project sponsors are likely to offer grudging cooperation to the review team and be reluctant to accept and act upon their findings. The impartiality of the review team is paramount in this respect – for example, it would be courting resentment to draw post-auditors from other parts of the company which may compete for scarce capital. Similarly, there are obvious dangers if reviews are undertaken solely by project sponsors. There is thus a need to assemble a balanced team of investigators, representing a spread of functional specialisms.

Encourages risk aversion If analysts' predictive and analytical abilities are to be thoroughly scrutinized, then they may be inclined to advance only 'safe' projects where little can go awry and where there is less chance of being 'caught out' by events.

Environmental changes Some projects can be devastated by largely unpredictable swings in market conditions. This can make the post-audit a complex affair as the review team are obliged to adjust analysts' forecasts to allow for the 'moving of the goalposts'.

The conventional wisdom

Studies of investment appraisal, mainly undertaken in North America (e.g. Posey *et al.*, 1985) have generated a 'conventional wisdom' about corporate post-auditing practices. Its main elements are:

1 Larger firms are more likely to post-audit.
2 Few firms post-audit every project, and the selection criterion is usually based on size of outlay.
3 Few projects are post-audited more than once.
4 The commonest time for a first post-audit is about a year after project commissioning.
5 The most effective allocation of post-audit responsibility is to share it between central audit departments and project initiators to avoid conflicts of interest, while utilizing relevant expertise.
6 The threat of post-audit is likely to spur the forecaster to greater accuracy but it can lead to excessive caution, possibly resulting in suppression of potentially worthwhile ventures.

The UK experience

UK research by Neale and Holmes (1988, 1991) broadly confirms these aspects. Among the most important findings generated by survey, interview and consultancy, are the following:

- Firms larger by size, whether measured by capital employed or by turnover, are more likely to post-audit. This suggests a 'sophistication factor', perhaps coupled with a resource effect.
- Firms which are subsidiaries of overseas enterprises are more likely to post-audit, suggesting the importation of more developed parent company control procedures.
- Firms in manufacturing sectors are more likely to post-audit, suggesting that there are particular difficulties in post-auditing service activities, such as measurement of outputs, or that service sector executives do not regard post-auditing as appropriate for their activities. If the latter is true, this suggests too narrow a view of the word 'investment'.
- Despite the differences in adoption rates among different categories of firms, there are no systematic differences in the objectives which they pursue in post-auditing, the benefits they obtain and the problems they encounter.
- Post-audit benefits can be broadly classified into control benefits and decision-making benefits. The first type are found to be greatest when the firm places greatest emphasis on post-auditing as a control device, while the second type are greatest when the main concern is to improve investment decision-making and planning. In other words, the nature and magnitude of post-audit benefits depends upon having clearly specified objectives but realistic expectations from the operation.
- There is no evidence that the adoption of post-audits acts as a deterrent to the flow of new investment ideas.
- One of the major problems cited regarding post-audits is that of environmental turbulence, which many firms use as a reason for not adopting post-audits. However, many of the benefits of post-auditing seem most pronounced under precisely these conditions. This suggests that more astute managers are using post-audits as a device for exploring the complexity of their operating environments. In this respect, post-auditing may have an important role to play in the strategic planning process.

When does post-auditing work best?

Finally, how do these findings help the practising manager? Specifically, what guidelines can we offer to managers who wish to introduce post-audit from scratch or to overhaul an existing system? Here are some key points.

- When introducing and operating post-audit, emphasize the learning objectives and minimize the likelihood of its being viewed as a 'search for the guilty'.
- Clearly specify the aims of a post-audit. Is it to be primarily a project control exercise or does it aim to derive insights into the overall project appraisal system which may benefit the evaluation of future projects?
- When introducing post-audit, start the process with a small project to reveal, as economically as possible, the difficulties which need to be overcome in a major post-audit.
- Include a pre-audit in the project proposal. When the project is submitted for approval, the sponsors should be required to indicate what information is required to undertake a subsequent post-audit, and when would be a suitable time to conduct the post-audit (in the first of a series).
- Be prepared to alter the information system to ensure that the necessary data will be available when required.
- Do not judge project analysts on the basis of a single project. To obtain their willing cooperation, it seems fair to make assessments across a spread of projects.

If all the other components of the capital budgeting system operate properly, i.e. if projects are carefully evaluated, planned and controlled during implementation, then major problem areas will be anticipated and acted upon swiftly and their adverse impact minimized. Indeed, thorough post-auditing may hone the system to such a degree of keenness that further post-audits may seem redundant. However, it is doubtful whether a high proportion of UK firms operate such sophisticated capital budgeting systems that they could afford to dispense with post-audits completely. Even firms with highly-tuned systems find it instructive to study successful ventures and to demonstrate 'ideal' procedures to other staff. Besides, after smoothing the rough edges off a possibly ramshackle system, it seems dangerous to abandon outright the option to post-audit, since even well-oiled human machinery can begin to malfunction through complacency and personnel changes.

Summary

Capital budgeting covers a wide-ranging area, not all aspects of which have been touched upon in this chapter.

Most management accountants are well versed in the detailed application of discounted cash flow techniques, and we have not attempted to cover this ground here. However, we remind accountants that (1) the strong popularity of payback with managers is not entirely without justification, and (2) the modified internal rate of return has some merit because it offers basically the same advice as net present value, but in percentage form.

The main aim of the chapter has been to encourage accountants to view capital budgeting as part of a multi-stage decision process. Five investment stages were discussed: determining the budget, seeking-out and shaping investment projects, evaluation and approval, implementation and monitoring, and post-auditing. Capital budgeting is a crucial dimension of the strategic planning process. This means that capital projects should not be viewed in isolation, but within the strategic context within which they would operate. Finally, we examined post-audit practices, the application of which has increased significantly in recent years, and suggested when post-audits are most appropriate. In our view, post-audits have an important role in helping to ensure that scarce investment capital is used to greatest effect.

References

Fama, E. F. and French, K. R. (1992). The cross-section of expected stock returns, *Journal of Finance*, June.

Grubb, M. (1993). A second generation of low inflation. *Professional Investor*, Dec. 1993/Jan. 1994.

Junankar, S. (1994). Realistic returns: how do manufacturers assess new investment? Confederation of British Industry, London.

Neale, C. W. and Holmes, D. E. A. (1988). Post-completion audits: the costs and benefits. *Management Accounting*, **66**(3).

Neale, C. W. and Holmes, D. E. A. (1991). *Post-Completion Auditing*. London: Pitman.

Pike, R. H. (1996). A longitudinal survey of capital budgeting practices, *Journal of Business Finance and Accounting*, Spring.

Pike, R. H. and Dobbins, R. (1986). *Investment Decisions and Financial Strategy*. Philip Allan.

Pike, R. H. and Ho, S. M. (1991). Risk analysis in capital budgeting contexts: simple or sophisticated? *Accounting and Business Research*, Summer.

Pike, R. H. and Neale, C. W. (1996). *Corporate Finance and Investment: Decisions and Strategies*, 2nd edition. Hemel Hempstead: Prentice Hall.

Pinches, G. (1982). Myopia, capital budgeting and decision-making. *Financial Management*, **11**(3).

Posey, I. A., Roth, H. P. and Dittrich, N. E. (1985). Post-audit practices. *Cost and Management*, May/June.

Risk Measurement Service, London Business School.

Wardlow, A. (1994). Investment appraisal criteria and the impact of low
   inflation, *Bank of England Quarterly Bulletin*, August.
Wilkie, A. D. (1994). The risk premium on ordinary shares. Paper presented to
   the Institute of Actuaries, November.

15

Successfully evaluating and controlling investments in advanced manufacturing technology*

Graham Motteram and John Sizer

Many firms are facing problems associated with the changing manufacturing technology such as how to appraise capital investments in advanced manufacturing technology (AMT), how to compute product costs and how to revise performance measures. The successful evaluation of capital investments is of vital importance because if incorrect judgements are made it is unlikely that the decision can be reversed and therefore adverse business performance is likely to be the outcome.

In this chapter Professor John Sizer and Graham Motteram examine eight major sequential steps involved in successfully evaluating and controlling proposed major investments in AMT. In Appendix 15.1 a case study of a typical AMT investment decision facing many small and medium-sized engineering companies is presented together with the authors' analysis of the case.

Many chief executives and boards of directors are making, or contemplating, major investments in advanced manufacturing technology as part of a world-class manufacturing strategy in order to strengthen or sustain their competitive advantage, both in global and niche market segments. Such decisions are particularly difficult during recessions, but are equally important if companies are to take full advantage of growth markets. The careful evaluation of alternative investments is a crucial first stage in successfully employing AMT and management accountants should make a significant input as part of a structured team approach. Decisions made

*The contents of this chapter represent the personal views of the authors.

will substantially affect a sector of the business's performance when implemented, and if the incorrect judgements are made, it is unlikely the decision process could be reversed, and therefore a damaging negative business performance is likely to be the outcome.

We should recognize at the outset that even in companies employing sophisticated systems of appraisal, capital projects generally tend to over-spend, run late and under-earn. This may partly reflect 'ego trips' of man-agements preparing proposals and/or internal competition for scarce funds. Statements such as the following are not uncommon and must be guarded against:

We will just have to find a way of getting this project through.

Our competitors are going to have one, so we must.

We must have one before our competitors.

Furthermore, many operating managers and accountants have limited experience of evaluating major capital projects; it is not something they do every day. Add the complexities and uncertainties of new technologies, temptations of salesmen and sales literature, shorter product life-cycles, and global competition, and the difficulties and dangers become apparent.

In this chapter we examine eight major sequential steps (Figure 15.1) involved in successfully evaluating and controlling proposed major investments in AMT. In Appendix 15.1 we provide a substantial case study of typical AMT investment decisions facing many small and medium-sized engineering companies. We invite the reader to challenge the appraisal. Our analysis is provided in Appendix 15.2 against which the reader can contrast his/her analysis. Our objective is to give a deeper insight into a typical AMT investment appraisal decision which will allow the reader to more effectively examine and challenge similar submissions in his/her own working environment.

Step 1 – Determination of corporate strategy

The strategic decision to invest in AMT and related management tech-niques, such as just-in-time (JIT), materials requirements planning (MRP I) and manufacturing resource planning (MRP II) should flow from an assessment of corporate strategy; in particular, how to create and sustain competitive advantage in global and/or niche market segments. This must be a board level decision based on hard-nosed strategic analysis rather than detailed investment appraisal. Furthermore, investment in AMT has to be part of a continuous programme of strategic improvement, *not* a

Step 1	Determination of corporate strategy

Step 2	Establishing investment funding implications and prioritizing investment cases

Step 3	Undertake initial investment feasibility study

Step 4	Prepare detailed business case

Step 5	Project authorization

Step 6	Effective control of authorized projects

Step 7	Undertake post implementation review

Step 8	Develop action plans for continuous improvement

Figure 15.1 *Major sequential steps in evaluating and controlling investments in advanced manufacturing technology*

one-off event. The assessment of corporate strategy should lead to the formulation of interlinking products–markets, development, manufacturing and financial strategies. The formulation of a manufacturing strategy will include evaluation of strategic make or buy decisions, and manufacturing organization and methods choice. A full discussion of strategy formulation and manufacturing policies is beyond the scope of this chapter, but it will be recognized that manufacturing investment policy should flow from the assessment of corporate strategy, in particular, manufacturing strategy.

For many large manufacturing companies the analysis will lead the board to conclude, if it is to be internationally competitive, that its strategy must be one of a low-cost producer achieving continuous cost improvements and value improvements to its customers in specific chosen areas of production. For many manufacturing companies this necessitates that investments in AMT should be controlled from the centre, thereby enabling:

1 a global view of manufacturing investment strategy to be maintained;
2 the integration of new technology whilst allowing maximum utilization to be made of existing physical assets and labour skills.

This policy may be best administered by an investment committee of the board.

Step 2 – Establish investment funding available and prioritizing investment cases

Social and environmental pressures are resulting in an increasing proportion of many companies' capital investment programmes being in respect of non-profit adding projects, e.g. improved welfare facilities, safety and environmental expenditure, etc., and for replacement investments. It is important to establish at an early stage the likely scale of investments in AMT required to implement the manufacturing strategy, and whether adequate funding will be available. A capital intensive company should formally have:

1 a detailed two-year investment project profile which is reviewed quarterly;
2 a strategic investment plan in reasonable depth for five years, which is reviewed at least annually; and
3 an outline investment plan to at least a ten-year horizon which is also reviewed annually.

These profiles and plans should be employed by treasury management in preparing short-term cash budgets and forecasts and longer-term financial plans. These provide the basis for determining external funding requirements and determining the company's cost of capital and hurdle rates for capital investment projects. They should take into account any foreign exchange risks.

Once the strategic decisions have been taken, funding availability determined, and investment policy formulated, the evaluation of alternative AMT systems prior to final approval is the key stage. In large companies it is preferable to undertake initial investment feasibility studies on major investments before giving agreement to move to detailed evaluation of alternative systems. Acquisition of individual items of equipment should flow from this evaluation.

Step 3 – Undertake initial investment feasibility study

It is likely that not only will limited funds be available for investment, but so also will be the resources to evaluate and successfully implement projects. Therefore, it is essential that only key important projects are worked upon. It is advisable that prior to any detailed technical and financial work being undertaken, an outline of the proposed investment should be submitted to the investment committee of the board or its equivalent. This should ensure not only that control is exercised via 'top-down' approval in principle, but it also allows the central strategy to be refined by recognition of 'bottom-up' proposals. It will also assist the committee in ranking of projects for detailed evaluation and for building into investment plans.

Step 4 – Prepare detailed business case

Business case preparation on the projects selected for detailed analysis is the crucial stage in the successful evaluation of AMT projects, when realism should not be driven out by 'starry eyed' optimism. The components of the detailed financial evaluation are summarized in Figure 15.2. Close examination and determination of the sensitivities of the assumptions made on each aspect is considered essential. We discuss important aspects of each element.

Investment costs

Investment costs include costs of planning, purchasing, installing and commissioning plant and machinery, and related computer hardware and software. As overspends tend to occur because of these items, it is advisable to test the sensitivity of cash flows and measures of project profitability for variations in both initial spend and time-scales. If alternative manufacturing systems or types of machinery have different initial capital costs/operating costs/maintenance costs structures it may be necessary or

1. Investment costs - including costs of planning, purchasing, installing, commissioning plant and machinery and related computer hardware and software.

2. Running costs

3. Benefits of investment
   – Cost savings
   – Increased flexibility
   – Reductions in working capital
   – Market factored benefits
   – Taxation and investment grants

4. Consequences of not investing

5. Test sensitivity of cash flows, DCF returns or NPVs and payback periods to variations in key assumptions.

Figure 15.2   *Components of financial evaluation of business case*

worthwhile to undertake a life-cycle cost analysis. If the equipment is to be purchased from a foreign supplier, exchange rate risk is an obvious, but frequently overlooked, point. Where major projects are being considered it may be worthwhile undertaking them on a turnkey basis with the selected major supplier. Whilst this may add a little to the investments' costs, resultant implementation may be more successful.

Running costs

It may be sensible at this stage to recognize the need to operate a separate cost centre and build a cost model for the new system. When building the cost model, we would advise:

1 Do not simply accept *manufacturer's cycle times* when evaluating alternative systems, and make sure penalties are built into subsequent contracts for both delivery and technical performance.
2 Do not be over-optimistic about *learning curves*; the greater the complexity the longer the curve.
3 Ensure you will not have problems *feeding* the system and *bottlenecks* out of the system, which would result in under-utilization of capacity levels and higher levels of working capital.
4 Given *high fixed cost/total cost ratio* associated with AMT and therefore, high break-even volume/capacity, recognize the importance of maintaining high levels of capacity utilization, but also accept this may

result in lower utilization of support equipment in order to maintain an even flow through the high cost equipment.
5 Consider the *costs of maintenance*, perhaps in the form of a contract once the guarantee period has expired.
6 Determine if there are any other cost factors which should be taken into account which are peculiar to an individual project proposal, e.g. programming costs.

It is important, therefore, to test the assumptions in your forecast cash flows and profitability measures for these elements of the cost model.

Benefits of investments in AMT

When evaluating the benefits to be derived from investing in AMT systems, you could usefully differentiate between: cost savings, reductions in working capital, and market factor benefits.

Cost savings normally arise from reductions in direct labour, scrap, space requirements, and the benefits of increased flexibility. We would again emphasize, do not simply accept manufacturers' cycle times and efficiencies when estimating direct labour savings; be careful to ensure that subsidiary managements have not made such savings the balancing item to make investment worthwhile. If the reductions will necessitate changes in working practices and/or redundancies, do not be over-optimistic about workforce reactions. Reductions in scrap result from a move towards zero defects, which result in savings in direct material costs and inspection costs. Additional capacity may be created which should generate additional contribution. A reduced space requirement will either reduce occupancy costs or result in benefits from the additional contribution generated by alternative use. Increased flexibility allows merging product lines, reduced diversity of components, simplified and common product designs, reduced engineering overheads, and benefits of designing for manufacturability and customer service. These benefits are difficult to quantify; understanding the factors that drive or determine these costs will provide assistance. Remember, unless the benefits of increased capacity or available space can be utilized as realizable saleable output there is no benefit.

Reductions in working capital are usually a significant benefit arising from investments in AMT systems, particularly if linked to JIT and MRP systems. Reductions should occur in raw materials and bought-in component stocks, and in the length of the work-in-progress cycle. However, it is important to recognize these benefits will only be realized if production lines are balanced. It is easy to be over-optimistic on the timing of working capital savings and therefore sensitivities should be tested. The more complex the system, the greater the step change, therefore the longer the time taken to realize working capital savings.

Market factor benefits. The competitive advantages to be gained in the marketplace are the most difficult benefits to quantify. They are reflected in higher product quality, greater reliability in the hands of the customer and improved customer service. The three key questions are:

1 Will these benefits to customers result in higher contribution ratios, i.e. per cent contribution to sales, or higher volumes at current contribution ratios, or both?
2 Will it be necessary to share benefits with customers in order to maintain competitive advantage or improve market share?
3 What offsetting factors are likely to result from competitors' actions? There may be a gain for a period of time but this may then be partially or fully offset.

The answers will depend partly on the countervailing power and expectations of customers. Major customers are likely to expect and want to share in the benefits! It also depends on the strategies and investment plans of competitors. Hence the importance of competitive benchmarking and continuous monitoring of competitors' plans and actions.

If the system increases capacity, evaluate carefully where the *additional volume* is coming from and the level of contribution (sales revenue less variable product costs) it will generate. If it implies increasing your market share, ask yourselves, who will lose it and how will competitors react? It is all too easy to assume all of the market factor benefits will be retained in the business, and that market share can be increased, which is unlikely to be the case. It is also important to take account of forecast market trends not only in terms of growth, but also recession and product life-cycles, and the impact of these on market share.

Consequences of not investing

The questions posed about market factor benefits also lead into the *consequences of not investing*: possibly rising real costs, falling real selling prices, squeezed contribution ratios, and loss of market share. It is important not to be over-optimistic about the market factor benefits and at the same time over-pessimistic about the consequences of not investing. One risk averse approach is to insist that all claimed market factor benefits and consequences of not investing pass the 3Ms test, i.e. they must be *meaningful, measurable* and *monitorable*.

Taxation and investment grants

Investment projects should be assessed on a post-tax and investment grant basis. In international businesses it is important to recognize that the timing of investment allowances, rates of taxation, and availability of investment grants may vary significantly between countries, and of investment grants within a country. If there are political changes on the horizon and/or taxation policy changes under consideration, you should identify and assess the possible impact of these.

Test sensitivity of cash flows, DCF rates of return, and payback periods

In the preparation of the business case, it is important that key assumptions are identified, and the sensitivity of cash flows and DCF rates of return or net present values, and of simple or discounted payback periods, to these key assumptions are tested, so that the board is presented with a complete picture of the range of possible project outcomes. The board should *not* be presented with a single 'most likely' or, even worse, 'most optimistic' set of cash flow and profitability measures.

Step 5 – Project authorization

The completed business case should be presented to the investment committee of the board, and subsequently for the board of directors for approval. Given the increasing proportion of non-profit adding projects in many companies' capital investment programmes, the board should recognize that this increases the return required from profit adding projects, and therefore increases the gap between its cost of capital and the minimum hurdle rate for profit-adding projects. Faced with a business case that presents a most likely return and range of possible returns derived from the sensitivity analysis, the board will have to exercise judgements. This will require it to formulate its attitude to risk and uncertainty, which should be reflected in different hurdle rates for different project risk categories of profit adding investment projects reflecting both technological and market risks. It will be recognized that there is a point beyond which financial evaluation cannot go and managerial judgement must take over. Sound financial analysis of the business case together with a systematic approach to developing hurdle rates for different project risk categories should minimize the gap to be bridged by such judgements, and ensure management intuition is not overworked.

Step 6 – Effective control of authorized projects

Many major capital projects run late and overspend because of ineffective project management and control. Once a project has been authorized, the implementation time span, recognizing delivery, availability, commissioning and introduction of new technology is a considerable one. It is important that a project implementation manager is formally appointed for all major projects. Using appropriate management tools, he should report to the investment committee on the progress made in implementation compared with project objectives and timetable, hazards encountered and corrective action being taken, and interfaces established both internally and externally to the company. Reporting frequency will be dependent on the nature of the project, and whether implementation is progressing satisfactorily, but for major projects should not be greater than quarterly.

Step 7 – Undertake post implementation review

Managements must learn from their experiences of evaluating and implementing investments in AMT by undertaking realistic *post-completion audits*, and build the lessons into their *investment appraisal* check-list. Why did the project not meet technical specification, run late, overspend, and under-earn? Post-completion reviews should be undertaken by an independent team with technical, operational and financial analysis skills, which is appointed by the investment committee and required to compare project outcomes with the approved business case. A formal post implementation report should be presented to the investment committee and for major projects to the board of directors. It should recognize the key technical and operational, as well as the financial, assumptions upon which the original decision was based.

Step 8 – Develop actions plans for continuous improvement

It is almost inevitable that not all claimed benefits and savings contained in the business case for the new project will be achieved by the time of post-implementation review. On the other hand, benefits and savings not foreseen at the outset of the project may have been realized. Therefore, it is important that ongoing from the review, monitorable action plans are established to ensure they are achieved and that continuous cost improvements are derived from the implementation of the new technology. Furthermore, if the benefits and savings are to be realized and continuous cost improvements sustained, it will be necessary to review the implications for the company's costing and planning and control systems, and to identify the new control information and performance indicators required.

Conclusions

Successfully evaluating and controlling investments in AMT is not easy. However, if the strategic analysis was flawed, the business case analysis was over-optimistic, the project control was ineffective, the post-completion audit non-existent, the implications for costing and planning and control systems were not recognized, and control information for continuous improvement was not identified and generated, a chief executive may find himself in the same situation as the manufacturing director of a medium-sized engineering company who telephoned with the following question:

> We have put in all this advanced manufacturing technology, now we don't know what anything costs and we don't have any relevant control information. Furthermore, we are generating lower profits. Can you help us?

It was too late! Of course, no matter how sophisticated the analysis, some companies will continue to invest in projects that overspend, run late, and under-earn. The eight-step approach advocated for evaluating investments in AMT should assist management accountants in making an effective input into financial evaluations and, therefore, in minimizing the likelihood of this happening in their companies.

You are now invited to consider the case study in Appendix 15.1.

Appendix 15.1   Basic Engineering 1948 Ltd   Financial evaluation of proposed CNC machine investment

Introduction

The purpose of this case study is to provide the reader with a deeper insight into an advanced manufacturing technology investment decision typical of those faced by many small and medium-sized engineering companies. The company's financial appraisal of the decision is presented, which the reader is invited to challenge as to its validity in many aspects, all of which are judgemental, but have to be considered. The reader is also asked to consider other business opportunities which may not have been taken fully into account in the appraisal.

1   Basic Engineering 1948 Ltd is a medium-sized company, founded in 1948 by its current chairman and managing director, and is located in the north east of England. It is engaged in the development and production of high technology engineering products, and has a turnover of approximately £20 million per annum. The company's profitability, although once very high, has been falling over a number of years and has reached what the board of directors consider to be a very unsatisfactory level of £800,000 before interest and tax, an 8 per cent return on net assets employed of £10 million.

2   The equity of the company is owned by the eight directors of the company, as shown in Table A15.1.

Table A15.1

	Age	Relationship to Chairman	Share of equity
Michael Graveyard Chairman and Managing Director	68		45%
Andrew Graveyard Technical Director	64	Brother	15%
Trevor Maintenance Production Director	63	Lifelong friend	10%
Alan Snailswood Company Secretary and Finance Director	59	Founder shareholder	5%
Randy Appleson Marketing Director	40	Son-in-law	3%
Paul Graveyard Non-Executive Chartered Accountant Partner of International Accounting Practice	40	Son	5%
Susan Graveyard Non-executive	58	Wife	12%
Rita Appleson Non-executive	35	Daughter	5%

Since it was founded, the company has raised only limited debt funding from financial institutions; its current debt:equity ratio is 10 per cent.

3   One of the key determinants of the company's profitability, and ultimately its survival, is its international competitiveness in the marketplace. To maintain this, the company must achieve further engineering improvements, both in terms of design and manufacturing. Over the last two decades the company has maintained its competitiveness through the development and utilization of new materials as these have become available, with only minimal expenditure on new manufacturing technology, and more recently through the forging of the close relationships between design and manufacturing methods. Because there has been limited investment in new production plant, the average production plant age is in excess of 17 years. The policy has been one of adapting assets to meet the requirements of new manufacturing technology and methods. It has not to date invested in NC (numerical control) and CNC (computer numerical control) or DNC (direct numerical control) equipment, but relied heavily on a very skilled labour force.

4   In order to regain its competitive edge and move the business forward, the board, initially against the wishes of the chairman, has appointed three new executive managers to form a nucleus of a new policy team under the direction of Randy Appleson, who joined the company three years ago, two years after marrying Rita. The other members of the team are listed in Table A15.2.

Table A15.2

	Age	Background
John Fixit Design Manager	40	Graduate in Mechanical Engineering
Peter Turnkey Manufacturing Engineering Manager	42	Graduate in General Engineering and MBA
Trevor Forward Management Accountant	37	BSc in Finance Management Accountant

All had pursued successful careers within high technology industrial companies and had been recruited with the assistance of an international firm of recruitment consultants recommended by Paul Graveyard.

5   The policy team's objective is to ensure that over the next two decades the company develops and implements engineering and manufacturing strategies which will allow it to improve and sustain its international competitiveness through continuous improvements. As part of the drive for international competitiveness, the manufacturing engineering manager has been seeking to find ways of cost reducing his methods of manufacturing. He has identified a CNC machine, costing £500,000, which he believes will allow substantial savings to be achieved in the manufacture of component A. The machine tool manufacturers have examined the component and claim that current manufacturing times could be reduced by up to 80 per cent with a substantial reduction in shop floor work-in-progress.

6   The Board of Directors is sceptical and has requested the policy team to advise it as to the business case for this proposed investment in CNC machines. The presentation is to be made to the board in two weeks and, to date, the policy team has established the following facts:

6.1   Current sales of component A, which is a mature high technology component, are 1,200 sets per annum at £5,000 per set, and a modest growth is forecast at today's prices over the next five years. The planned standard direct labour time per set is 41.5 hours at a cost rate of £50 per direct labour hour, which covers direct labour and production overheads. There is a single standard direct labour overhead recovery rate for the whole factory.

6.2   To achieve its current production of component A, the company:

- has 20 dedicated machines, fully depreciated, single manned by skilled operators, i.e. one man – one machine interface;
- works a two-shift system with an average of 5 per cent overtime (not planned);
- is subject to considerable machine breakdowns and loss of operating performance;
- incurs £100,000 per annum subcontract costs on a batch-to-batch basis to maintain output through lost performance not covered by the overtime;
- employs ten support staff per shift, including supervision, inspection, progress, and work handling;
- pays: machine operators £16,000 p.a. including benefits, support staff £13,000 p.a. including benefits, overtime at time and a half;
- requires a factory lead time of 20 weeks;
- purchases direct materials at £2,500 per set;

- incurs subcontracted machine maintenance estimated at £50,000 per annum; and
- generates a scrap rate of three per cent.

6.3 Total current operating costs for the company are given in Table A15.3.

Table A15.3

	£m	£m
Direct material		8.0
Variable costs:		
Pay and benefits	3.5	
Subcontract costs	0.5	
Consumables	1.2	
Maintenance – bought out	0.3	
Scrap	0.5	
Fixed costs:		
Pay and benefits	2.5	
Building costs*	0.6	
Depreciation	0.2	
Other overheads	0.7	10.0
Total operating costs:		18.0

*Building costs represent general costs, including rent and rates, building insurance, heat, light and power for premises of 50,000 square feet.

6.4 The introduction of new machine tools would be based on the following:
- three new machines, with installation and commissioning completed six months after order and therefore 50 per cent of the net revenue savings will arise in the first year;
- two shift operations for the three machines manned by two people per shift, one who would be the team leader, additionally there would be one support operator per shift;
- overtime would become planned at 5 per cent but support level would be zero;
- CNC machines would allow operator certification;
- initial special-to-product tooling costs would be £160,000, would have a ten-year life and could be capitalized;
- non-conformance will be minimal;
- consumable materials (£300,000 per annum) will not change significantly;

- machine occupancy time per set would be six and a half hours;
- factory lead time would be reduced to four weeks;
- the company's policy is to depreciate machines for new projects over ten years, and this is the expected operating life of the new machines;
- based on current union agreements, and assuming 75 per cent utilization (metal cutting time) the available hours for the three machines on a two-shift basis will be 8,400 per annum;
- space occupancy will be 5,000 square feet per new cell;
- fixed costs other than depreciated building costs will be recovered on the basis of production hours.

7 In order to undertake a financial evaluation of the proposed investment, Trevor Forward agreed with John Fixit and Peter Turnkey that he should make the following assumptions:
- space is available but needs preparation; therefore there will be no disruption to existing production (cost estimated at £0.2m);
- installation costs will be 10 per cent of the basic cost of the machine, and along with site preparation costs will be capitalized;
- it would not be possible to deploy surplus workforce and redundancy payments would have to be made (estimated £10,000 per person);
- unions will accept the introduction of new technology both in terms of:
  (a) redundancy which may be voluntary across organization, allowing some redeployment; and
  (b) new working practices, e.g. multi-manning and operator certification, product control responsibility;
- premium payment of 10 per cent would be required for multi-skill;
- non-conformance would not fall to zero, therefore 1 per cent conservative estimate should be included;
- to allow direct material purchase to be sensibly phased down on supplier a reduction of 20 per cent should be assumed for year 1 and 80 per cent for year 2;
- purchase of the new machine tools will be in sterling;
- limited maintenance will be required – first year guaranteed, next six months zero, next two years £5,000 per annum, subsequent years £10,000 per annum;

- a team would be required for implementation including proving (cost, £100,000);
- the CNC machine is the most suitable of alternatives evaluated; and
- the machines will have a residual value of £100,000 each at the end of their ten-year operating life, i.e. ten-year life from date of commissioning.

8   Forward has received the following guidance from Alan Snailswood:
- capital allowances 25 per cent reducing balance on capital expenditure, including new special-to-product tooling;
- corporation tax @ 35 per cent;
- minimum required DCF rate of return 15 per cent after tax.

9   Forward has prepared the following financial evaluation, which indicates a perspective.

NPV @ 15%	£2,304
Simple pay back	2 years
Discounted pay back	3 years
DCF rate of return	42%

The evaluation has been agreed by the policy team and forwarded to the board for its approval.

Invitation to reader

The reader is invited to consider the following questions before reading the authors' brief commentary on the case study, in Appendix 15.2. Space does not permit an extensive discussion and detailed sensitivity analysis.

1   Evaluate the capital investment appraisal, including identifying key assumptions, and potential opportunities and hazards if approval to proceed is given.

2   Advise Graveyard whether he should recommend to his board that the project be approved? It would be necessary to raise an additional £2m loan capital from a financial institution at 15 per cent before tax, which would increase the company's gearing ratio to approximately 33.5 per cent.

Financial evaluation of proposed CNC machine investment
Net present value calculation

	1	2	3	4	5	6	7	8
Yer	Capital expenditure	Tax relief on capital allowance @35%	Working capital savings	Net revenue savings	Tax on net revenue savings	Net cash flow	Discounting factors @15%	Present value of net cash flow
	£000	£000	£000	£000	£000	£000	£000	£000
0	(2,010)					(2,010)	1.000	(2,010)
1		176	£185	(102)		259	0.8696	225
2		132	£739	1,077	36	1,984	0.7561	1,500
3		99		1,072	(377)	794	0.6575	522
4		74		1,072	(375)	771	0.5718	441
5		56		1,067	(375)	748	0.4972	372
6		42		1,067	(373)	736	0.4323	318
7		32		1,067	(373)	726	0.3759	273
8		23		1,067	(373)	717	0.3269	234
9		17		1,067	(373)	711	0.2843	202
10		13		1,067	(373)	707	0.2472	175
11	300	10		533	(373)	470	0.2149	101
12		(75)			(187)	(262)	0.1869	(49)
	£(1,710)	£599	£924	£10,054	£(3,516)	£6,351	NPV =	£2,304

Simple payback   2 years
Discounted payback 3 years
DCF rate of return 42%

1. Capital expenditure

	Year 0	Residual value Year 11
	£000	£000
Preparation of site	200	
Cost of NC machines (3 @ £500K)	1,500	(300)
Installation	150	–
New special-to-product tooling	160	–
	£2,010	£(300)

2. Capital allowances

Year	Capital allowances @ 25% reducing balance £000	Corporation tax @ 35% £000
0	502	–
1	377	176
2	283	132
3	212	99
4	159	74
5	119	56
6	90	42
7	67	32
8	50	23
9	38	17
10	28	13
11	(215) (balancing charge)	10
12	–	(75)
	£1,710	£599

3. Working capital savings

£000

Direct material stock reductions

1,200 sets × £2,500 per set $\dfrac{20}{52} - \dfrac{4}{52}$

i.e. 16 weeks stock		£924
First year	(20%)	£185
Second year	(80%)	£739

4. Revenue expenditure – Year 1

£000

Redundancy (see note 3)	540
Implementation team	100
	£640

	Year 1	Year 2	Year 3–4	Year 5–10	Year 11
Revenue savings					
People (Note 1)	402	804	804	804	402
Overtime (Note 2)	31	63	63	63	31
Maintenance (Note 4)	25	50	45	40	20
Material scrap (Note 5)	30	60	60	60	30
Subcontract (Note 6)	50	100	100	100	50
	538	1,077	1,072	1,067	£533
Less					
Revenue expenditure	640	–	–	–	–
Net revenue savings	£1(102)	£1,077	£1,072	£1,067	£533
Tax @ 35%	36	(377)	(375)	(373)	(187)

Notes on revenue expenditure and savings

1. People		£000
Current		
Directs	40 @ £16,000	640
Support	20 @ £13,000	260
		900
Proposed		
Directs	4 @ £16,000	64
10% premium for multi-skill		6
		70
Support 1 per shift (2 @ £13,000)		26
Annual savings		804
Assume ½ first year		402

2. Overtime	£000
Current £900 @ 0.5% × 1.5	68
Plan £70 @ 0.5% × 1.5	5
Annual saving	63
Assume ½ first year	31

3. People redundancy potential	People
Current	60
Proposed	6
Saving potential	54
@ £10,000 per annum	£540,000

4. *Maintenance* £000

		Saving £000
Current cost	50	
Expected cost		
1st half year	–	25
2nd year	–	50
3rd and 4th year	5	45
5th year onwards	10	40

5. *Material scrap* £000

Current (1,200 sets @ £2,500 per set × 3%	90
Expected reduced to 1%	30
Savings	60
50% First year	30

6. *Capacity* Hours

Available hours 2 shifts	8,400	
Expected utilization (6.5 hours × 1,200 sets)	7,800	(93%)
Spare capacity	600	

Subcontracting not necessary

Appendix 15.2   Basic Engineering 1948 Ltd   Financial evaluation of proposed CNC machine investment: authors' commentary

Key assumptions, hazards and opportunities

Assumptions and hazards
Our experience suggests the following key assumptions and hazards need to be recognized with this type of investment.

1 No delay in commissioning the plant. It is a turnkey package from the supplier, and are there penalty clauses if he fails to meet commissioning date?

2 Assumes sales volume constant over life of machines, i.e. 1,200 sets. What research has been made for potential substitute products? Are there any new entrants on the horizon? What developments are taking place in competitor companies?

3 None of the savings arising from the investment will have to be shared with customers. What if competitors have installed new equipment? What would happen in a recession?

4 Inflationary cost increases can be passed on to customers – assumes sequential, i.e. a single rate affecting all elements of the proposal simultaneously not differential inflation, i.e. different rates affecting various elements of the proposal.

5 Existing machines could continue to operate over life of new machines, and relative efficiencies of old and new machines will not change over the life of new machines – unlikely to be the case.

6 Not clear whether all costs of removing existing machines covered.

7 Reduction in working capital cycle: are they over-optimistic regarding extent and timing?

8 What buffer stocks are currently held for the production phase and could these be reduced with a more reliable production response process?

9 Learning curve and training costs – have these been included – first investment in CNC machines.

10 Industrial relations/working practices delaying putting into operation. What if unions won't agree to proposed reduced overtime payments or won't accept changes in working practices?

11 Machines failing to meet technical specifications – unlikely in this case as standard machines. Is it realistic to assume limited maintenance will be required after first year?

12 Any foreign exchange rate risks on the purchase of the new machine tools, even if purchased through a UK agent, and on sale of product?

13 If the special-to-product tooling is capitalized will it last ten years?

14 What are the implications of not investing? Is profitability likely to continue to deteriorate?

15 What alternative machines are available, and what is the technical and financial assessment of these, i.e. should the team have demonstrated the CNC machine as the most suitable alternative available?

Opportunities

The following opportunities should be considered.

1 Space released by existing machines, what opportunities does this create?

2 Can additional sales be found to support spare capacity and would it be possible to introduce a third shift recognizing there are social as well as premium cost factors?
3 Could other production be transferred from existing conventional capacity to new facility – is the facility a flexible one?
4 Are there any grants available from the British Government or the EEC for this type of investment?

Sensitivity analysis
Having identified the key assumptions and hazards, it would be sensible to undertake a sensitivity analysis in respect of:

1 six months delay in commissioning and putting into operation;
2 erosion in real selling prices arising from assumptions 3 and 4;
3 lower sales volume arising from recessions and/or new competitor products;
4 extent of stock reduction (sixteen weeks) and timing (two years);
5 combinations of 1, 2, 3, and 4.

A detailed sensitivity analysis is beyond the scope of this chapter. However, unless commissioning and putting into operation is significantly delayed, and the extent of stock reduction and market factor assumptions excessively optimistic, given the short pay break periods, it is unlikely sensitivity analysis would affect recommendation of the policy team to make the investment, particularly given the consequences of *not* investing.

Should Graveyard advise his board to approve the project?

He would be sensible to recognize that the proposal includes many judgemental factors that cannot be fully quantified in a financial analysis of the investment. These should be fully discussed by the board with the policy team before a decision is taken to proceed. In particular, the detailed business case (step 4) needs to be considered in the context of the company's corporate strategy (step 1) and its future funding scenario (step 2).

There is insufficient information to make a precise decision on the proposed loan, but the 'base case' financial evaluation suggests the loan interest would be adequately covered:

Year	Net revenue savings £000	Interest charge £000	Cover times
0	–	–	–
1	(102)	300	–
2	1,077	300	3.59
3	1,072	300	3.57
4	1,072	300	3.57
5 onwards	1,067	300	3.56

and repaid after three years.

Year	Net cash flow £000	Loan £000	Interest	Tax saving	Net	Cumulative net
0	(2,010)	2,000	–	–	(10)	(10)
1	259		(300)	–	(41)	(51)
2	1,984		(300)	105	1,789	1,738
3	794		(300)	105	599	2,337
4	771		(300)	105	576	2,913
5	748		(300)	105	553	3,466

If the board proceeds (step 5) it is important that steps 6, 7 and 8 follow if the project is to be successfully implemented.

16

Modelling fair transfer prices where no market guidelines exist

Cyril Tomkins and Laurie McAulay

Transfer pricing situations apply where organizations decide to structure themselves into divisions which make decisions independently. A transfer price is then needed where divisions trade with each other. The established transfer price is a cost to the buying division and revenue to the selling division, so that whatever transfer price is set will affect the profitability of each division. In addition, the established transfer price will also significantly influence the buying and selling divisions' input and output decisions and thus the total company profits. The established transfer price should therefore meet the following objectives:

1 It should result in a fair distribution of profits arising from interdivisional trading.

2 It should provide a reliable basis for divisional managers to make sound decisions and thus encourage goal congruence between the division and the whole corporate group. This will happen when the actions which divisional managers take to improve the reported profits of their own division also improve the profit of the corporate group.

Transfer pricing has been one of the most widely debated topics in the management accounting literature and appropriate practical recommendations have not been resolved for all situations. In this chapter Professor Tomkins and Laurie McAulay briefly review the literature and identify those situations where clear practical advice can be given. They also provide guidance on how fair transfer prices might be set where there are no clear market prices to use as guidelines. In particular, the authors present a case for basing transfer prices on long-run variable cost which, they suggest, can be approximated by setting

> *transfer prices to recover full cost. It is stressed, however, that care is needed to avoid assuming that such a long-run perspective is always the most appropriate perspective to adopt and long-run and short-run trade-offs do have to be considered.*
>
> *Having presented a case to recover full costs the authors address the problem of what is a fair profit element to add to full costs to determine the transfer price. Finally, illustrations are presented as to how personal computer modelling techniques can be used to provide a close guide to setting* fair *transfer prices.*

Transfer pricing is one of the most debated topics in management accounting. It has a long history in both professional and academic literature. In his paper reviewing the topic of transfer pricing, Grabski (1985) lists and classifies eighty-one key academic papers in 'Recent transfer pricing literature', i.e. key academic papers on the subject appearing between the previous major review by Abdel-khalik and Lusk (1974) and 1983. Moreover, practice often seems to continue to contradict academic pronouncements on the subject and a number of academics have been quite ready to admit some perplexity with this situation. At first sight, therefore, the task set us by the editor looked daunting. The amount of material on transfer pricing is immense and the appropriate practice has not been fully resolved for all situations met in practice. A full academic review of the literature was not suitable for this type of publication and, given the state of uncertainty in the literature, could we provide any direct practical advice at a level detailed enough to be immediately implementable? We decided that we would attempt to provide just a broad description of the different approaches which have been taken to analyse the transfer pricing problem in order to identify situations where clear practical advice can be given and then try to move the state of the art forward by developing a practical, and very straightforward, modelling approach to providing guidance on fair transfer prices for inter-divisional trading where there are no clear market prices to use as guidelines. This is the very situation in which most disputes about appropriate transfer pricing practices arise.

In pursuing these objectives the chapter will cover a number of issues and readers should be able to understand the following matters at the end of reading it:

1 The main different perspectives for approaching the transfer pricing problem.
2 Why transfer prices should normally be set to recover full cost (more precisely at long-term variable cost) and why that may *not* lead to forgoing large short-term profits.

3   Where care is needed, nevertheless, in balancing short-term and long-term profitability and liquidity.
4   A basic approach to determining a fair profit to add onto the full cost basis in order to set the transfer price.
5   How to deal with risk when applying this approach.
6   How to develop personal computer modelling techniques which are very easy to use, to get a close guide to a fair transfer price to set. These techniques can be used to support a process of negotiation to set transfer prices or help head office decide what is fair.

The approach to be proposed is new. The only paper which we know of which has a similar risk evaluation basis is Monden and Nagao (1989) in their discussion of transfer pricing in the Japanese car industry, but the content of their paper is, otherwise, quite different.

Different perspectives on transfer pricing

What is transfer pricing? A pricing mechanism permits a whole economy to be subdivided into many entities such that each can make decisions on buying and selling for itself. *Transfer* pricing situations apply where large organizations decide to structure themselves into divisions which make decisions independently. A transfer price is then needed where those divisions trade with each other. The transfer price is then basic data for buying and selling decisions and also, by implication, investment decisions. The notion of a fair distribution of profits from inter-divisional trading is central to a satisfactory resolution of the transfer pricing problem in practice and has been largely left aside by academic literature, despite the many articles and books on the topic of transfer pricing itself. Before addressing that issue, however, it is necessary to review, very briefly, the alternate basic approaches to transfer pricing. At the risk of over-simplification, we will reduce this to a consideration of just two generic approaches, although each has a variety of alternative methods within it.

Transfer pricing through economic analysis

Transfer prices based on guidelines from competitive markets
The earliest analysis of transfer pricing problems on a rigorous basis used a theoretical economic approach. Focusing on just short-term considerations, it is clear that profits will be maximized if a firm produces up to the level of output at which marginal cost equals marginal revenue. Beyond that level the cost of an extra unit (marginal cost) will exceed the extra

revenue gained from selling that extra unit (marginal revenue). Also, at levels of output below that level, extra profit could be gained because the extra unit would bring in more revenue than the marginal cost needed to produce it. This approach to transfer pricing therefore sought a transfer price which would induce divisions trading with each other to transfer exactly the optimal amount of output that results in maximum profits for the whole organization. This can be achieved, without undue difficulty, where there is a highly competitive market outside of the organization for the good to be considered for transfer between the two divisions. The appropriate transfer price is the price for that 'intermediate good' in the outside market and the two divisions can be allowed to deal with each other or not – total organizational maximization of profits will be achieved either way. (The substantiation of this position can be found in many references such as Solomons, 1965, Tomkins, 1973 or Drury 1985 to name just a few.)

Difficulties where there are no clear market guidelines

A problem arises where the outside market is not highly competitive or even non-existent. Then economic theory shows that an appropriate transfer price to encourage total organizational optimality is, in the absence of capacity and other constraints, the marginal cost of production at the optimal output level. (Again see Tomkins, Drury, etc.) This is usually interpreted for practical use as the accountant's variable cost per unit. If, however, transfers are made at that price the selling division can make no profit. Indeed, it cannot even cover its fixed costs unless a separate charge is made to recover the fixed costs as a payment for facilities or capacity reserved for the buying division. This obviously amounts to an immediate practical problem; one cannot have a division operating as a profit centre if it is impossible for it to earn a profit.

Extra problems where capacity constraints exist

Where capacity constraints exist, marginal production cost is not the appropriate transfer price (Tomkins, 1973), and those following the general economic approach usually express the appropriate transfer price in this situation as the opportunity cost of the resources used, i.e. their value in their next best use. This statement of a solution is correct in theoretical terms, but is usually of little value in practice. If the group head office knows that the constraint is binding and that it is optimal to produce at maximum capacity, it doesn't seem of much value to devise a transfer price to tell divisions something that is already known. This would seem to be manipulation of divisions rather than motivating them by trusting them to make their own decisions. If, on the other hand, it was the divisions themselves that had discovered that it was optimal to produce right up to the maximum capacity by looking at the relevant costs and revenues in the two divisions involved in transferring the goods, it is crazy to ask them to repeat the calculation by using a transfer price. So there are problems in converting the theory into practice.

As stated above, there is a host of variants on the generic economic model, some of which try to deal with these problems, but there are none which have yet been devised which solve these problems in a completely satisfactory way. It would take considerable space to argue this point thoroughly, addressing all the different models in turn. Consequently, this statement must remain here at the level of a general assertion on the part of the authors, although interested readers might like to consult Abdel-khalik and Lusk (1974) or Grabski (1985). Possibly just a short justification can be made by stating that if any of the economics-based models, including those using mathematical programming techniques, had been of considerable value to practitioners, they would presumably have been in use more widely by now, at least in some industrial sectors. Where there is no clear guide to a transfer price from a highly competitive market, some form of cost-plus transfer price is usually used, i.e. variable product cost plus an element for fixed costs plus a profit charge. On the face of it this conflicts with economic theory which would predict that companies are, therefore, operating at sub-optimal output levels, i.e. not maximizing their profits. A more careful interpretation of the economic theory reveals, however, that practice may, in fact, be approximately consistent with theory.

The accountant's variable cost is not the economist's marginal cost
The practice of transfer pricing above variable cost may be quite consistent with pricing at the economist's marginal cost. The apparent inconsistency may lie in the use of the accountant's variable cost as a surrogate for true marginal cost. To take an obvious example, an economist would argue that marginal cost includes extra wear and tear on plant caused by increases in production. The accountant allows for this through depreciation which is nearly always treated as a fixed cost. Hence, a transfer price which includes an absorption of fixed costs may be a better approximation of true marginal cost than is variable cost. The same argument can be applied to other costs. If some types of costs, e.g. set-up costs, are included within fixed costs and not properly traced to their causal transaction, variable costs in the accounts are being understated if that transaction in turn is a function of output levels, albeit not in the usual proportionate relationship. Hence, the full allocated cost approach may be a better approximation to true marginal cost. Of course, it would be better to establish more accurately what the nature of all the cost functions are and relate them to their specific transactions and thence to changes in output

levels. This is the argument behind activity-based costing. This form of argument leads Kaplan and Atkinson (1989) to suggest that activity-based costing may provide the unifying concept that would enable a practical full-cost system to conform with economic theory. In contrast to Kaplan and Atkinson (1989), however, we do not argue, as they do, that this follows automatically because the transfer price will then approximate *long-run* variable cost. In our view, whether one wishes to price to cover short-run or long-run costs is a conceptually distinct point from using activity-based costing to get a better approximation of short-run marginal costs. We will return to consider this argument after examining the other main alternative approach to transfer pricing.

Transfer pricing by negotiation

Behavioural benefits and the problem of unequal divisional power

The process of arriving at a transfer price by negotiation is usually treated in textbooks as an alternative approach to economic analysis. While divisionalization is sought to provide discretion to act on the basis of local knowledge and to motivate better performance by giving more responsibility to managers of business segments, there is a need for some coordination to ensure that the enterprise as a whole does not miss good opportunities through not seeing how different parts of the business can help each other. If managers are placed in the position where they have to negotiate with each other in order to arrive at acceptable transfer prices, it is felt that they get to understand each other's problems and may plan together to solve them without needing head office to act as coordinator. This approach, then, owes its origins more to behavioural arguments than economic analysis and all that one can say from such a general description of negotiation as this is that this is expected to result in a price which is fair to the two parties concerned. This may be suspect, however, where the two parties have unequal power. The point of bargaining may not be to arrive at a position which is fair to both parties, but to get as much as one can for one's own side. Unequal power can manifest itself in many ways. One division may have many products whereas the other needs to trade in this product to generate a decent profit. Inequality of power to bargain may also arise through access to substitutes or even close relationships with the corporate chief executive. In such situations the word negotiation may become a synonym for an internal corporate battle when, in fact, the prime intention should be to transact with the world outside the group boundaries at a profit. In addition, if negotiation is required over all transactions, it could prove to be very time-consuming and, hence, costly.

Are the approaches based on economic theory and negotiation really separate?

It seems unrealistic to consider the process of negotiation itself as totally separate from economic analysis. Apart from differences in economic power, bargaining depends upon what one has to give up in return for some agreement. Without a knowledge of what the total pot might be (i.e. the maximum profit that could result from combined action), it seems difficult to base one's negotiation strategy on an informed basis. This does not mean that precise knowledge of the economist's cost and revenue curves must be acquired, but there must be some approximate idea of what is at stake. More simply, economic information must provide some basis to the negotiation.

The need for a continuing relationship may affect the negotiation

The nature of the relationship each party is seeking from the other will also influence how negotiations are approached; in particular whether the relationship is to be ongoing for a considerable period of time or merely short-term. This seems to bring the argument in this chapter back to the point where it left the economic analysis and the question of whether transfer prices should take into account the costs of long-term relationships or be guided more by short-term marginal costs.

Should transfer prices recover long-term variable costs?

Pricing for long-run relationships

In our view the answer to the question in the major heading above is usually 'Yes'. Kaplan and Atkinson (1989, p. 609) refer to an executive who stated that he expected to offer products on a long-term basis and that it was not practical to offer products only in the short-term, recovering only short-term costs, and then say to customers later that goods cannot be delivered at that price because it does not cover full cost including the fixed cost commitment. Moreover, Atkinson has pointed out to us in correspondence that the move to fewer and closer relationships between suppliers and their customers (whether external or internal) through JIT arrangements enhances this argument. Hence, it seems entirely appropriate for a purchaser to say to a supplier that it needs a long-term service from the supplier and is prepared to pay for it. The supplier may say that this means that it has to invest in plant or set aside some capacity to ensure delivery and then, at the time the contract is agreed, the full marginal costs should include some of the capital costs. Consequently, it is appropriate for the purchaser to pay for those marginal costs which include more than the traditional definition of accounting variable costs. If, at a later date, the purchaser merely said that it was sorry but it would only pay the current out-of-pocket costs of producing the output, that would, probably, be the end of the long-lasting relationship. Fine, so let us be clear that we agree with Kaplan and Atkinson that this is likely to be a situation widely met in industry and is becoming more widely adopted. Nevertheless, it is not a universal situation.

Does JIT rule everywhere? The case for short-run profit taking

First, even in industries more suitable for using a JIT philosophy, there are still many companies that do not adhere fully to its principles. Also, even in Japan, the majority of industrial companies do not appear to use JIT. Inoue (1988) reports that only 11 per cent of Japanese companies used JIT methods during the mid-1980s (48 per cent still used the job order system in Japan). In the USA and UK the percentage was much lower and, of course, it is growing, but one must beware getting carried away by what is happening in car and similar manufacturing, and electronics. Transfer pricing problems exist to some extent in all other industries and increasingly in the public sector too – at least they do in the UK. In those industries or sectors, long-term relationships may not be so critical to success. Indeed, despite the vast savings which have been achieved by the application of JIT, it is not impossible that this is merely one phase in industrial development, although no doubt a long one. This could be because, after a period of nurturing a few close relationships, the position may become too cosy and efficiency could cease to improve. One might actually expect this if all that remained to compete were a few oligopolistic combinations. At some time in the future, therefore, some entrepreneur might rediscover markets as a spur to efficiency. This might actually be enhanced by advanced flexible manufacturing whereby suppliers can switch quickly to produce modifications to fuel injection systems, electronic ignition or brake mechanisms to suit the requirements of a new customer without needing massive new investment. In some broader sense this is exactly what the UK public sector has been finding out recently. The old cosy single supplier relationships, often within the same organization and supposedly justifiable on the basis of scale economies, have been discovered to be more costly than alternative market arrangements. Also, it must not be forgotten that the very idea of divisionalization itself reflects the felt need to avoid becoming too centralized and tightly coupled.

One does not want to get this argument out of perspective either, which is why we stressed agreement with Kaplan and Atkinson in the sort of industries where long-run close relationships are currently important and will probably remain so for some time. We just wish to beware using the JIT type of argument to provide a universal solution to the transfer pricing problem. It follows that where long-term relationships are less critical, there may be scope for benefits to be derived from purely short-run maximization. Also, even where JIT is currently used and close relationships exist between suppliers and their customers, the authors are aware of a company which is currently quoting supplies to a Japanese company below its full cost. The Japanese may want a close and reliable relationship, but not to the point where it is prepared to pay more than it considers the components in question should cost. The supplier also wants a continuing relationship with the Japanese company, but in order for that to occur it has to survive to see the long-run in times when markets are very depressed and, therefore, it finds it difficult to achieve scale economies. Hence, its survival strategy for the time being is to make a contribution to fixed costs which, to a considerable extent, are sunk. Obviously, this cannot be a permanent solution, but the point is that the long-run consists of a series of short-runs and the path to the long-run may not be smooth. Expressing the matter another way, a decision-maker may have the choice of selling in the short-run just to make a contribution to fixed costs (either for reasons of survival as indicated above or to increase short-term profits when fixed costs are already covered) or may price to cover long-run variable costs. While normal business relationships may be such that the expected value of the latter course of action may be seen to be higher, it is not inevitable and, therefore, the short-term model must not be dismissed from our texts nor, more importantly, should firms completely forget to consider the possibility of short-run/long-run trade-offs. One may, therefore, justify the use of a full-cost-plus approach to transfer pricing on the basis of the need to price to cover long-run marginal costs, but not without a careful assessment of whether that policy is appropriate at the current time for one's own specific competitive situation.

The practicalities of short-run/long-run trade-offs

A summary of the chapter so far

It may be useful to summarize the argument to date in this chapter. First, where there is a well developed and highly competitive market for the 'intermediate good', firms would do well to use the clear market price as their transfer price. In other situations, firms mostly use some variant of full-cost plus a profit percentage and this will be the basis upon which suppliers and purchasers agree to cooperate over the longer term. Only by doing that can the relationship be sustained and, in some parts of industry this long-run relationship is vital, at the current stage of economic and technological development, for driving down costs and competing in world markets for manufactured goods. Sometimes, however, 'short-termism' does make good business sense and so the short-term profit maximization tools must not be discarded as obsolete. If current profits are being given up (e.g. by pricing at full cost and losing a sale even though fixed costs have been recovered on other business), it is necessary to know how great the current sacrifice is in order to decide whether the long-run benefits outweigh them. Moreover, the future longer run benefits may well be more uncertain than the short-run gain.

Careful use of cost-plus transfer prices may closely approximate short-run profit maximization after all

A recent analysis (Tomkins, 1990) has shown, however, that the problems of integrating short-run and long-run thinking may not be as severe as first supposed. In other words, in certain conditions the short-term/long-term trade-off may not be too difficult to make. That analysis assumed that a supplying division pursued a pricing policy to recover both fixed costs and a reasonable profit over a reasonably achievable level of sales, i.e. a level less than the optimal output level to maximize short-term profits. The analysis then showed that, under certain conditions, once the volume of sales was achieved to recover fixed costs and a reasonable profit margin, the remaining profit which could be 'extracted' by marginal cost pricing was a very small proportion of the maximum group contribution earnable by the two divisions together. Hence, it may not matter too much if this short-term profit was lost to the group and one would probably never know what had been lost anyway because the amounts were small enough to be lost in the 'noise' attached to trying to establish revenue and cost schedules in the first place. It follows that divisions may well, therefore, be able to price above short-run variable cost in order to recover long-run variable costs without incurring a huge short-term penalty.

Conditions under which cost-plus prices can be used and short-run profit maximization closely approximated

The statement at the end of the last paragraph may strike the reader as

quite a surprising conclusion and so it is important to spell out the conditions under which this occurs. It occurs where the aggregate target contribution to fixed costs and profits of the supplying division is not too great a
percentage of the maximum contribution earnable by the two divisions
together, or, more broadly, where the supplying division does not bear too
large a proportion of the total fixed costs incurred by the two divisions
together on this product. In fact, making one or two basic assumptions
about the nature of cost and revenue curves, the analysis shows that, if the
supplying division's target contribution is, say, no more than 32 per
cent of the maximum earnable group contribution, pricing at 'full cost' to
recover that contribution (assuming the necessary volume can be sold at
that price) and not varying that price at the margin will mean that the
group will forgo only about 4 per cent of the short-term profits it could
earn. (The proof needs more space than is available here but it can be
consulted in Tomkins, 1990, Table 1.) If the supplying division only bears
about 20 per cent of the fixed costs of both supplying and receiving
divisions, the short-run profit loss is only about 1 per cent! Moreover, if the
supplying division bore a much larger proportion of group fixed costs on
this product, a separate periodic payment could be made in respect of
those fixed costs (this is not a new suggestion) and then the cost-plus transfer price would only need to cover the variable costs plus the target profit
per unit. Then a similar result would hold: the proportion of group short-
run profit lost through refusing to engage in variable cost pricing beyond
the level of output that recovers the aggregate target contribution is very
small.

The argument in this section of the chapter seems to have important
practical implications and *may* go some way towards explaining why it is
that practitioners continue to use full-cost-plus pricing, despite the apparent theoretical advice in the textbooks not to do so. The analysis also
means that following the Kaplan and Atkinson advice to price to recover
long-run variable costs may also not necessitate high short-term sacrifices.
Also, Tomkins (1990) argues that if divisions and companies do wish to
squeeze out a little more profit by marginal trading at a lower transfer
price than that set to recover long-run variable costs, they can do so by
negotiation. Such negotiation is, however, only at the margin and so the
possible damage from bargaining by unequal powers or wasted time is far
less severe. Yet, negotiating at the margin may well still be sufficient collab-
oration to obtain the benefits of interaction between divisions and lead to
a better understanding of each other's situation.

One may conclude that, provided care is exercised and one properly
understands the assumptions of the analysis and the level of reasonable
profit which may be included in the transfer price (see Tomkins, 1990),

companies may not need to worry too much about short-term profits forgone in pricing to recover fixed costs, provided, of course, that one is as efficient as other firms in the industry who are prepared to sell the same product and, hence, one is not in a situation where the major part of the business will be lost through pricing above the full-cost prices of other firms. If the company is less efficient than others it may well have to price at below its own full-cost in order to survive while it tries to become more efficient. That is the position of the company selling to the Japanese as described earlier. It is also consistent with using the outside marketplace as the transfer price where competitive markets exist and we are concerned in this chapter mainly with the situation where such markets do not exist.

It has been argued in this chapter that, in practice, careful and intelligent pricing at full-cost-plus, either with an 'all inclusive price' or by a two part pricing mechanism where fixed costs are paid for separately, may not have large short-term opportunity costs, but that still says nothing about how the full-cost transfer price itself should be fixed. Of course, one can adopt the Kaplan and Atkinson view and say that the price should at least cover long-run variable costs in order to cement long-term relationships and we would agree with this. This is, however, only a first approximation to a desirable price. It says nothing about the level of profit each division should seek. In addition, a price has to be accepted as fair by both parties if a continuing relationship is to flourish. This question has often been referred to, but received hardly an analysis within the transfer pricing literature. An exception was in the paper by Emmanuel and Gee (1982), but the approach to be suggested here is rather different.

Distinguishing between long-run contracting and intra-period marginal negotiation

We can 'hear' the reader saying: 'Surely, you have just spent much space arguing that negotiation is only needed, at most if at all, at the margin. Now you seem to be bringing the possibility of negotiation in again for the establishment of the basic price'. To which our response is: 'Yes, we are, but that is quite different. Negotiation over the basic price level does not need to occur in every period'. We are arguing that at the time two parties are considering whether to begin to do business together on a continuing basis (or at such time intervals at which they review the relationship) they will consider the long-run costs and revenues involved. They will then negotiate a base price level which will hold for several years. This base price level will include a recovery of long-run variable costs incurred by the supplier plus a fair profit. Goods will then be transferred at that price each period, perhaps with an adjustment for inflation and any learning expected to take place within the period of the agreement and, perhaps also subject to agreement to review the base price if market conditions are substantially changed. The supplier/purchaser agreement to trade would stipulate the volume to be taken in each period at the base price and there would be no negotiation within each period about that price. Negotiation within each period would only take place if divisions wished to trade extra volume over and above the standard volume agreed. Thus we are not re-introducing extensive negotiation into every period. Intra-period negotiation is still only needed, if at all, for marginal sales. It is the approach to determining a fair price within this opening, or occasional, negotiation of long-term relationships that now needs to be addressed.

Fair transfer prices through a risk/return analysis

If one is to try to provide guidelines on what is a fair price, one needs, first, to establish a criterion on which fair can be interpreted. There is a very well established mechanism in corporate finance for establishing fair rates of return on investment which says that required rates of return are a positive function of risks faced. Hence, one can say that a transfer price is fair if it provides divisional managers with a return on the transaction commensurate with the risks they face. It follows that, if the outcome of the inter-divisional trading were known with complete certainty (the assumption underlying the economic analysis), divisional managers are not justified to expect more than a risk-free rate of return on those transactions. If, through the possession of some competitive advantage, the two divisions together can earn more than the risk-free rate of return on their combined investment, it would seem fair that they should both benefit equally in the sense of being able to earn the same rate of return, i.e. one above the risk-free rate, on their investment. This would be particularly so if divisional performance were, to a considerable extent, evaluated by means of ROI. Such a conclusion provides the departure point for addressing the situation where divisional risks exist and are unequal between divisions.

It is recognized that there may well be aspects other than risks faced at the time of negotiating or establishing the transfer price which are thought to be relevant for deciding whether the transfer price is fair. For example, a division may have speculated on a development some time ago and feel that it needs some reward for that initiative. There may well be, therefore, additional complexities in some situations beyond those considered in this chapter. On the other hand, we are unaware of any risk modelling approach to transfer pricing like that proposed here and so there seems to be merit in exploring the situation where it is sufficient to consider just fair returns for risks faced when the transfer price is set. The extra problems of taxation across national borders will also be left aside.

We shall also leave aside any consideration of differences between the returns and risks the shareholder faces, which underlies the theory of corporate finance, and those faced by the individual manager. (A discussion of this at some length can be found by anyone interested, in Tomkins, 1991, Chapter 9.) The following analysis simply adopts the position that it is the manager's perceptions of returns and risks which are relevant for considering whether he or she accepts the transfer price as fair. If one can make the divisional manager's risk attitude consistent with that of shareholders, perhaps that is desirable, but it does not affect the basic nature of the modelling approach we wish to propose.

We are now in a position to explain how one might go about establishing a fair transfer price based upon a consideration of each divisional manager's risk perceptions and attitudes. It will be assumed, just for simplicity, that divisional performance is based just upon the absolute level of profit earned and that there is no external market for the good being transferred between divisions. In addition, it will be assumed that cost behaviour is adequately reflected by a conventional formulation in the form:

total costs = fixed costs + output (variable cost per unit)

These are merely simplifying assumptions to keep the modelling simple. The same basic approach as we are proposing can be modelled in as much complexity as desired for practice to take into account activity-based costing ideas and the existence of external imperfect markets.

The basic idea is to calculate not only how both the receiving and supplying divisions' level of profits change as the transfer price is changed, but also how the likely probability distribution of each division's profits change with different transfer prices. If one can then incorporate into one's model an indication of manager's risk attitudes, it should then be possible to show the level of transfer price at which both the supplying and receiving divisional managers think that they have been treated fairly. The basic thinking behind such an approach will now be demonstrated by a relatively simple simulation model. The model uses the 4–5–6 At-Risk package which runs as an add-on to Lotus 1–2–3 and is thence relatively easy to use on a personal computer.

An example of how fair transfer prices may be simulated

Stage one: Identifying the outer bounds of a fair transfer price

Assume that there are two divisions, Division A is supplying goods to Division B. The profits of each division are shown in Table 16.1. It can be seen from the table that when the transfer price is set at £10, Division A is expected to break-even, while Division B would be expected to earn a profit of £75,000. If divisions were evaluated on the basis of the level of absolute profits earned, the manager of Division A is unlikely to be content with such a low transfer price. At the other extreme it can be shown that at a transfer price of £17.50, the situations are reversed: B can only break-even while A earns the whole group profit of £75,000. It follows that a fair transfer price must lie somewhere between £10 and £17.50.

Table 16.1 Calculation of divisional margins

Sales volume	Division A	Division B	Group 10,000
	£	£	£
Sales revenue	100,000	400,000	400,000
Less			
Fixed costs	15,000	25,000	40,000
Variable costs	85,000	200,000	285,000
Cost of transfers	–	100,000	–
Profit	0	75,000	75,000
Margin per cent	0.0%	33.3%	23.1%
Memorandum			
	£		
Final prod price	40		
Transfer price	10		
transfer price inserted as			
@simtable(10,11,12,13,14,15,16,17,18,19)			

Table 16.1 was set up in a format whereby the commercial @Risk simulation package can be used. This is readily available at about £250 and is used in conjunction with Lotus 1–2–3. There are some features of Table 16.1 which are not readily apparent from the hard copy. First, the sales volume figure in Table 16.1 is shown as 10,000. In fact, this is the most likely value which the computer selects from a probability distribution of

sales volumes which was entered into the sales volume cell of the spread-sheet. For the example shown here the sales volume cell contains a prob-ability distribution of sales volume with a specified mean of 10,000 and a standard deviation of the distribution of 700. Similarly, the uncertainty of the cost elements of Table 16.1 were recognized. Hence, costs were also entered in probability distribution form. The full list of probability distri-butions entered into the spreadsheet was:

	Mean	Standard deviation
Sales volume	10,000	700
A: Fixed costs	£15,000	£200
Variable costs per unit	£8.5 per unit	£0.4
B: Fixed costs	£25,000	£200
Variable costs	£20 per unit	£1.5

If it is difficult to express variability of profits in terms of standard devi-ation, the package allows the use of a probability distribution expressed in terms of likelihoods of reaching different levels of output or costs.

In the example in this chapter these distributions were all considered to be independent of each other, but it is quite simple, within @Risk, to create relationships between the different probability distributions if they are expected to have some co-variation.

Also, selling price in the final market was fixed at £40, but the model can easily be re-run by changing that to any other price or, indeed, making the selling price itself a stochastic variable (i.e. one for which a probability dis-tribution is put into the spreadsheet).

With such a spreadsheet and an @Risk package, one can proceed to examine the risks faced by each divisional manager. In other words, one can estimate not just the expected profit as a single figure, but generate the whole probability distribution of likely profit levels. The sort of output one can obtain is shown in Figure 16.1.

From the first simulation of divisional profits at a transfer price of £10, it can be seen in Figure 16.1 that A's expected profit is just £7 with the possibility of profits being as high as about £8,000 or losses as low as approximately £12,000. The standard deviation of that distribution is £4,205 and there is a 51.4 per cent chance of making a loss. In contrast, B expects to get a profit of £75,035 with a standard deviation of £16,665 and there is a one hundred per cent chance of making a profit – indeed it is one hun-dred per cent certain to earn at least £25,000.

It is not sufficient, however, to estimate the uncertainty of profits at just

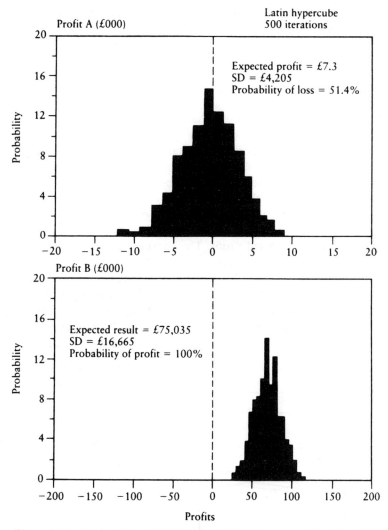

Figure 16.1 *Probabilities of divisional profit levels at a transfer price of £10*

a £10 transfer price; it is clear that A will not accept a transfer price of £10. Consequently, it is necessary to see how each divisional manager's risk and expected profits change as the transfer price is changed and, to do this, Table 16.1 was recalculated at transfer prices from £10 through to £18. The key point, however, is not just to recalculate the profits at each transfer price, but also to calculate the probability of earning profits at different levels at each price. It is only by looking at the likelihood of reaching different profit levels that a manager can begin to consider whether the transfer price is fair.

Stage two: Comparing each division's expected profits and variability of profits at each transfer price

Not only will the divisional profit change as the transfer price is changed, but so will the variability of likely profits through a gearing effect (although the gearing effect is not substantial in the example used in this chapter to illustrate the model). To see this intuitively, imagine that you are a supplying division and your costs are subject to some uncertainty. With a low fixed transfer price, the cost variability could swamp the profits. In contrast with a high transfer price, a given degree of cost variability is less likely to swamp the profitability and the variability will be a far smaller proportion of the expected profit. The converse applies to the receiving division. What the model must provide, therefore, is the expected profit at each transfer price, but also the probability distribution of profits at each price. This was easily achieved using @Risk by means of the @SIMTA-BLE command. This is shown in Table 16.1, but only means that nine simulations will be run, i.e. at transfer prices from £10 through to £18.

The results of these simulations are shown in Figure 16.2. The two solid

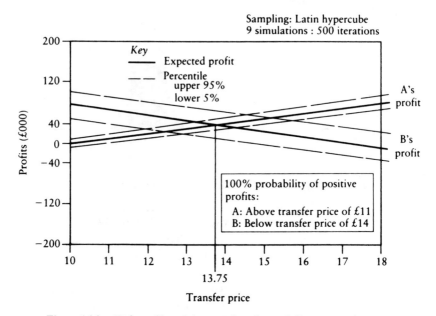

Figure 16.2   *Risk profiles of divisional profits at different transfer prices*

lines show the expected profits of Divisions A and B at each transfer price. The broken lines show the 95 per cent percentiles, on the upper side, and the 5 per cent percentiles on the lower side. (The x per cent percentile indicates the level below which profits are likely to occur only x per cent of the time.)

The results show that each division would be expected to earn the same profit at a transfer price of £13.75. It is not necessary to use @Risk to discover that. A simple manual simulation on a 1–2–3 spreadsheet could determine that in a minute or so. The point to note is that A's risk is far less than B's. The percentile lines are far closer to A's expected profit than they are to B's profit. It is probable, therefore, that a transfer price of £13.75 will not be seen to be fair by B. B will want a lower transfer price.

Suppose next that the divisions were not evaluated by absolute levels of profits, but by profit margins earned on the direct costs incurred in their own divisions (i.e. excluding in B's case the cost of goods acquired from A). A similar simulation exercise was run on margins rather than profits and the results are shown in Figure 16.3. (As a practical modelling point, the reader may be interested to know that @Risk can handle a number of different simulations running at the same time and these simulations were all run simultaneously to save time.) This time each division can earn the same margin at about £12.20 as the transfer price, but again, at that level,

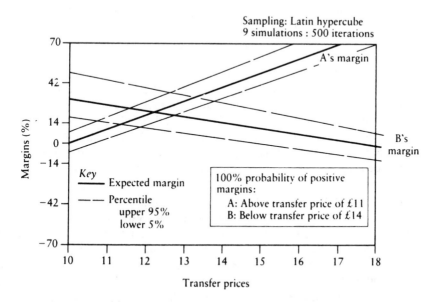

Figure 16.3 *Risk profiles of divisional margins at different transfer prices*

B has a wider (though less marked this time) range of possible outcomes and therefore faces greater risk.

It is proposed that, even if the analysis were to stop at this stage, managers (or head office) would be in a better position to assess where the fair transfer pricing arrangement is than they were just calculating the outer limits of £10 and £17.50. Perhaps this is all that is needed in practice in the form of calculations to make managers more aware of the different risks faced. It is possible, however, to go further in an attempt to be more precise in arriving at a fair transfer price.

Stage three: Homing in on that fair transfer price by incorporating risk attitudes

Earlier in this chapter it was stated that if both managers faced complete certainty they should both expect to make the same return. Now that uncertainty has been introduced into the analysis it is possible to restate that rule as follows: managers of divisions dealing with each other should earn the same returns subject to an adjustment for risk. One way of converting an uncertain profit figure to a certainty equivalent figure is to express the certainty equivalent of the risky profit as equal to the mean (i.e. expected) profit less the standard deviation of the profit distribution times a weighting factor which reflects the decision-maker's attitude towards risk. Thus the certainty equivalent of a division's uncertain profit can be expressed as:

$$RAP = P - B(S)$$

where RAP stands for risk adjusted profit (i.e. the certainty equivalent profit), P represents the expected (mean) level of profits, B is a coefficient to indicate how much importance the decision-maker puts on the riskiness of the situation in making his/her decision and S indicates the riskiness itself in terms of the standard deviation of the profit distribution. (It may be more appropriate to measure risk by S as a percentage of P, but this is left aside here. It is obviously a simple adjustment if practitioners deem it appropriate.)

If one now calculates the RAP for both divisions at each level of transfer price, one could plot them in exactly the same way as we did with the unadjusted profits in Figure 16.1. Where the two functions crossed would be the transfer price at which both divisions could earn the same profits *after allowing for the difference in risk that they face*. This would seem to be one good way of specifying what a *fair* transfer price should be.

Of course, it is difficult to know what number to use for the risk weighting factor B and if one wishes to get managers to accept the transfer price as fair, one may have to allow them to insert their own values of B to reflect their own attitudes towards risk. If, however, this approach were used over some time, it is probable that the company would come to understand what value of B best suited each division. Moreover, one might find that the fair transfer price was not very sensitive to variations in B within reasonable bounds.

To complete the example for this chapter, it was decided to assume that the risk weighting B took on the value of 1.0 first and then another exercise was run with B at 2.0. Rather than produce more graphs, we first took B as equal to 1.0 and calculated the fair transfer prices as defined above. This was done by using the computer to calculate divisional RAPs at each transfer price level and then, instead of plotting them on a graph to find the intersection, we ran two regressions (one for each division) in the form:

$$RAP = a + b\,T$$

where T was the transfer price and a and b were the coefficients derived from the regressions. With two equations and two unknowns it was then easy to solve for the fair transfer price (T) and the prospective RAP facing both divisions at that transfer price. (All regressions in this analysis and R-squares equal to 0.99 indicating that the observations fitted closely to the regression line.) The whole exercise was then repeated with B equal to 2.0.

For good measure, risk adjusted margins (RAMs) were also calculated using the same procedures. The results of these calculations are shown in Table 16.2. A particularly interesting feature of Table 16.2 is that the fair transfer price is relatively insensitive to B. A doubling of the risk attitude coefficient B from 1.0 to 2.0 only changed the fair transfer price by 50p under the absolute profit evaluation and by 30p where margins are the basis of performance measurement. Of course, this is only for the example and simulations in this paper, but the analysis has brought us a long way from the point where we only could say that a fair transfer price was somewhere between £10 and £17.50.

Table 16.2 Risk adjusted profits and risk adjusted margins as determinants of fair transfer prices

Evaluation by absolute profit level			Evaluation by profit margin		
Value of B	RAP £	T £	Value of B	RAM %	T £
1.0	26,960	13.2	1.0	16.3	12.1
2.0	16,573	12.7	2.0	8.6	11.8

372 MANAGEMENT ACCOUNTING HANDBOOK

Summary and conclusions

After explaining the basic alternative approaches to transfer pricing, this chapter has presented a case for basing transfer prices on long-run average costs in accordance with the arguments put forward by Kaplan and Atkinson (1989). It has also, however, argued that care is needed to avoid assuming that such a long-run perspective is always the most appropriate perspective to adopt and short-run and long-run trade-offs do have to be considered. Reference was also made to Tomkins (1990) where it was shown how the short-run costs of taking a longer run view may not be that high in many situations. Finally, the chapter presented a new approach to addressing the problem of what is a fair profit element to add to full costs when determining the transfer price. We believe this is a practical basis for at least providing a better framework for thinking about this complex problem. It may also prove to be valuable for actually specifying what fair transfer prices are. Practical situations will require more complex models than that described here, but the basic approach should still work. Perhaps some practitioner would like to try it out. If so we would like to know how well it works or even help him/ her to work it. Also the modelling described here was easily accomplished on a small lap-top model and so it is quite practical in another sense.

References

Abdel-khalik, A. R. and Lusk, E. J. (1974). Transfer pricing – a synthesis. *The Accounting Review*, January.

Drury, C. (1988). *Management and Cost Accounting*. Van Nostrand Reinhold.

Emmanuel, C. and Gee, K. (1982). Transfer pricing: a fair and neutral procedure. *Accounting and Business Research*, Autumn.

Grabski, S. V. (1985). Transfer pricing in complex organizations: a review and integration of recent empirical and analytical research. *Journal of Accounting Literature*, 4.

Inoue, S. (1988). A comparative study of recent development of cost management problems in USA, UK, Canada and Japan. *The Kagawa University Economic Review*, 61(1), June.

Kaplan, R. and Atkinson, A. (1989). *Advanced Management Accounting*, 2nd edition. R. D. Irwin.

Monden, Y. and Nagao, T. (1989). Full cost-based transfer pricing in the Japanese auto industry: risk sharing and risk spreading behaviour. In *Japanese Management Accounting* (eds Y. Monden, and M. Sakurai). Productivity Press.

Solomons, D. (1965). *Divisional Performance: Measurement and Control*. R. D. Irwin.

Tomkins, C. (1973). *Financial Planning in Divisionalised Companies*. Haymarket Press.

Tomkins, C. (1990). Making sense of cost-plus transfer prices where there are imperfect intermediate good markets by a 'pragmatic – analytical' perspective. *Management Accounting Research*, 1(3) 199–216.

Tomkins, C. (1991). *Corporate Resource Allocation – Financial Strategic and Organisational Perspectives*. Blackwell.

Surveys of management accounting practice

Colin Drury and David Dugdale

In this chapter Professor Colin Drury and Dr David Dugdale examine the gap between the theory and practice of management accounting. They review some of the published empirical studies of management accounting practice and discuss the differences observed between theory and practice. The implications arising from gaps between theory and practice for the future education of management accountants are considered in the concluding section of the chapter.

In recent years a belief has emerged that there is a wide gap between the theory and practice of management accounting. For example, Scapens (1991) argued that there is a considerable difference between the theory of management accounting as portrayed in current textbooks and management accounting practice, while several writers (for example Otley, 1985; Choudhury, 1986; Edwards and Emmanuel, 1990) have drawn attention to the fact that management accounting research has had very little impact on practice. The perceived gap between management accounting theory, as portrayed in textbooks, and management accounting practice, however, appears to be based on anecdotal evidence and impressions gained through informal contacts between academics and practitioners, rather than from in-depth company studies or surveys of management accounting practice.

In this chapter we shall, therefore, review some of the published empirical studies of management accounting practice. In addition we shall report on the findings of research which we have undertaken into the management accounting practices of UK manufacturing companies. These findings are based on twenty in-depth interviews undertaken between 1988 and 1990 and over 300 replies to a questionnaire survey which was completed in 1992. In addition we shall comment on differences between theory and practice and consider the possible implications of these differences for the education of management accountants.

Analysis of cost behaviour

'Traditional' theory has emphasized the importance of dividing costs into 'fixed' and 'variable' components – where 'fixed' means 'fixed in relation to volume of output/sales' and 'variable' means 'variable in relation to output/ sales'. The argument is based on the proposition that financial advice to decision-makers should be based on 'relevant' cash flows and, for certain classes of decision, fixed costs (once identified) are irelevant and can be ignored. This argument emphasizes *revenues* and *avoidable costs* and, in the short-term, avoidable costs can often be approximated by the accountant's *variable* costs. A substantial body of theory has been developed around these ideas with the difference between revenue and variable cost being termed *contribution* and the analysis typically being recommended for product mix, pricing and make or buy decisions.

It would seem however, that practitioners do not share this enthusiasm for cost analysis. Coates *et al.* (1983) surveyed a relatively small sample of companies finding that 'little formal analysis of cost behaviour was undertaken' and they quoted attitudes which varied from 'in these days all costs except the bought out variables are fixed' to 'cost behaviour is not simply a matter of fixed and variable, it is much more complex than that, and one cannot afford the resources to carry out detailed cost behaviour studies.'

It is unlikely that these attitudes would be representative today. The increasing use of microcomputers has made financial analysis easier and, as reported by Kirwan (1986) there is an increasing use of spreadsheets and financial modelling for forecasting financial outcomes. Such analysis can hardly be attempted without the division of costs into 'fixed' and 'variable' components and we would suggest that, for budgeting and forecasting (up to, say, one year ahead), fixed/variable analysis *is* important. It would seem, though, that practitioners see only limited value in the traditional analysis for decision-making and control. (For example, in later sections we discuss the widespread use of 'full' costs for pricing decisions, the prevalence of 'full' cost allocation in divisionalized companies and the limited use of 'flexible' budgets.)

Whilst, in 1983, some practitioners might have seen detailed cost analysis as 'too expensive' many companies are now implementing 'activity-based costing' (ABC), a technique which *does* purport to recognize the complexity of cost behaviour and to provide a means of analysing it. Some companies obviously *do* feel that it is worthwhile to scrutinize cost behaviour in considerable detail in order to build up 'accurate' activity-based costs. According to the advocates of ABC such costs provide an appropriate input to pricing, product mix and make/buy decisions. However, it would be a mistake to assume that all companies have accepted the need for ABC style analysis. A UK survey by Innes and Mitchell (1995) reported that 20 per cent of the responding organization had implemented ABC. A further 27 per cent were considering implementing ABC.

Costing systems

As a consequence of the emphasis given to fixed/variable cost analysis, 'theory' often recommends that costing systems should be based on marginal or variable costs. It is argued that such systems provide more valuable information than systems based on absorbed costs because, firstly, profit is more closely linked with the level of sales and, secondly, because the identification of variable costs is itself valuable to management. However, Puxty and Lyall (1989) report that 70 per cent of their respondents based standards on absorption costing and this finding is supported by our own interviews where only one of the 20 companies visited operated a marginal costing system. This evidence provides UK support for Johnson and Kaplan's (1987) contention that, for several decades, costing systems have primarily served the requirements of financial reporting by providing a basis for stock valuation. Our evidence indicates that most companies generate profit reports frequently (typically monthly) and meeting this requirement simply and economically is an important factor in the design of costing systems. Many companies prefer their profit reports for management to be consistent with reported profits and, given the SSAP9 requirement that stock be valued at *full* production cost, this provides a rationale for the prevalence of 'absorption' costing systems. 'Absorption' costing implies recovery of overhead against an appropriate base and Kaplan (1987) has argued that one of the problems in traditional costing systems is the prevalence of labour hours/cost as a base for overhead recovery – given the steadily reducing proportion of 'direct' labour as a percentage of total costs. In practice overhead recovery was often based on labour hours, giving some support to Kaplan's criticism; *however*, a number of companies employed overhead recovery bases other than labour. Material value, machine hours and engineering hours were all relatively common bases and, in process industries, rates per kilogram, tonne and litre could be observed.

The companies which had introduced significant numbers of numerically controlled machines seemed to be most concerned that labour hour based overhead recovery rates were inadequate. Some of these companies had replaced labour as a recovery base with machine hours and others intended to do so. Some practitioners thought that switching to machine hours would mean that labour efficiency could no longer be measured and, whilst in theory this is not necessarily true, the common practice of quoting labour and overhead rates as a single (composite) rate may have encouraged this view.

While Coates *et al.* (1983) reported that 'blanket' (i.e. single or plant wide) overhead rates were prevalent this finding was not confirmed by our studies. Several companies employed five or more rates and Drury *et al.* (1993) report only 26 per cent of companies surveyed employing blanket overhead recovery rates.

While most of the twenty companies visited had, or intended to have, computer systems which would integrate manufacturing, costing and financial systems a survey by Price Waterhouse (1991) of 677 companies indicated that '32 per cent of respondents reported that their financial stock valuation and manufacturing stock recording systems were not integrated and 50 per cent of product cost roll-up systems were stand-alone.' (The term 'roll-up' has become a commonly used expression meaning the accumulation of cost (material, labour and overhead) for a particular product. It implies working methodically through the product bill of materials 'rolling-up' costs from lower levels until the total cost of the 'top level' product has been accumulated.) This finding suggests that many companies are still striving to reap the benefits which technology ought to bring. As the authors of the Price Waterhouse survey point out, for these companies, the logical first step (before attempting to implement some of the 'modern' techniques currently recommended) is to 'put the building blocks in place.'

Standard costing and variance analysis

A number of reasons are advanced in order to justify 'standard' costing as an important technique:

- forces critical review of existing operations;
- provides a basis for planning;
- allows identification of variances between standard and actual results and so facilitates exception reporting;
- simplifies accounting because all stock is valued at standard costs;
- provides a basis for performance evaluation.

Few empirical surveys have been undertaken but those of Puxty and Lyall (1989) and Drury *et al.* (1993) indicate that many companies *do* employ standard costing systems. In both cases some 75 per cent of respondents reported that standard costing systems were employed. Detailed analysis of twenty companies was not quite so convincing in that a number of these companies place considerable emphasis on actual costs. (A number of companies employed 'hybrid' systems, part standard and part 'actual' with, for example, an average costing system for materials but a standard costing system for labour.) Examination of costing systems in these companies revealed discrepancies between textbook 'theory' and practice. For example, material standards were often based on latest prices (not projected costs) – defended on the basis that they were simple to administer, understandable and auditable. And material and labour cost standards often *excluded* related costs such as carriage/duty and labour 'fringe' benefits – defended as permitting easy comparison with invoice prices (for materials) and on the basis of administrative simplicity (for labour).

The logical extension of a standard costing system – variance analysis – also occupies an important place in management accounting theory. Control of operations is seen as a key element of management accounting and, in principle, this involves the comparison of actual results with a pre-set standard so as to determine whether corrective action need be taken. Textbooks develop the subject in considerable depth, not only identifying total material, labour and overhead variances but also analysing these into material price, mix and yield variances; labour rate and efficiency variances; overhead spend, capacity and efficiency variances, etc.

Analysis in practice seems to be rather simpler than that portrayed in the textbooks. Puxty and Lyall (1989) summarize their findings:

> first, total variances are not necessarily the most commonly found: and in the case of materials variance, price variance is more common than total variance. Second, labour variances are less frequently used than material variances ... Third, variable overhead variance is the least commonly reported.

These results are broadly supported by those of Drury *et al.* (1993) who found that over 90 per cent of respondents calculated material price variance, 60 to 70 per cent reported labour variances and about 35 per cent reported variable overhead variances.

In-depth interviews in twenty companies again supported the findings of Puxty and Lyall and Drury *et al.* with variance analysis often being quite unsophisticated. 'Variable' overhead was not usually separately identified and therefore overhead variances contained both fixed and variable cost elements. Despite this deficiency, overhead expenditure variances (by cost centre and expense type) were reported by all twenty companies and treated as important controls with variances between budget and actual expenditure being routinely investigated. Overhead 'volume' variances were not so important and very few companies identified the overhead 'efficiency' and 'capacity' variances as subdivisions of the 'volume' variance. Drury *et al.* broadly confirm these findings with 90 per cent of respondents identifying overhead expenditure variances but only 20 per cent of respondents calculating efficiency and capacity variances.

Not every company identified labour variances and several combined 'labour' with 'overhead' – quoting composite variances. (These companies still *accounted* for labour, they simply chose to report labour/overhead variances together.) These companies might calculate the 'efficiency' variance referred to above – effectively identifying labour efficiency/inefficiency and valuing it at the total of labour and overhead cost. (One manager noted that the practice made an allowance for opportunity cost in the costing of labour inefficiency.)

Of the companies which did identify a separate labour variance a surprising number did not analyse this variance into 'wage rate' and 'efficiency' elements. However, the fact that 'efficiency' variance was actually partly due to variation in wage rate did not prevent the variance being treated as an important control measure!

Material price variances were generally treated as very important. Puxty and Lyall note that material price variances are more common than total material variances – but this is not really surprising, material price variance is usually extracted on receipt of material while a usage variance (if calculated at all) is extracted when production takes place. As the constituent variances refer to different points in time a meaningful total variance cannot be calculated.

Whilst this discussion might indicate a lack of sophistication, in two respects practice is, arguably, ahead of theory. Firstly a number of companies analysed the material price variance into subcomponents. In particular, five companies (from eight which identified 'standards' for material) calculated that element of the price variance which was due to variation in exchange rates. This 'material price variance due to exchange rates' is not mentioned in the standard texts. And secondly, some companies were aware of the importance of 'structure' (revision) variances in the valuation of stock. These variances arise if the composition of a (relatively complex) product is changed (e.g. by an engineering change order). Material cost might be debited to work-in-process according to the new product structure while work-in-process continues to be credited (when product is completed) with a product cost based on the original bill of materials.

These last points may be significant in indicating that the imminent demise of traditional standard costing and variance analysis can be overstated. In many companies the policy of monthly profit reporting and the attendant problem of stock valuation is not trivial and standard costing systems might be justified on the basis of administrative efficiency alone.

Budgeting

Budgeting is recommended as an important technique which helps management in at least six ways:

- by forcing managers to *plan* ahead and reduce the number of *ad hoc* decisions;
- by aiding *communication* as top management set out objectives and lower management indicate the problems and opportunities they perceive;
- by aiding *coordination* as separate functional departments provide inputs which have to be reconciled during the budget process;
- by setting clearly defined targets which (if set at an appropriate level of difficulty and accepted by managers) aid *motivation*;
- by providing standards and plans which can be employed as part of the *control* process;
- by providing a yardstick against which managers can be *evaluated*.

The advantages claimed for budgets provide an apparently overwhelming case for employing them and, despite the well-documented dysfunctional behavioural consequences which budgets tend to generate, most companies do set budgets. Puxty and Lyall reported 94.3 per cent of respondent companies operated budgeting systems. Most of these companies compared actual results with the predetermined budget on a period by period basis.

Puxty and Lyall did, however, report that only 20 per cent of their respondents used 'flexible' budgets and noted that, given the advantages claimed for flexible budgets, this seemed to be a remarkably low proportion. Our own evidence concerning the use of flexible budgets is somewhat equivocal. Interviews in twenty companies gave clear support for the findings of Puxty and Lyall, with only four companies differentiating fixed and variable overhead as part of the formal costing system and no company 'flexing' the budget on a routine basis. However, the results of Drury *et al.* run somewhat counter to these findings with 42 per cent of respondents claiming the use of flexible budgets. It is possible that this apparent discrepancy can be explained by considering what respondents might mean when answering 'yes' to the question 'is flexible budgeting employed?'

Whilst careful scrutiny of company systems might reveal that flexible budgets are not formally and routinely prepared the *ideas* of flexible budgeting might still be employed. In particular, overhead expenditure variances (which often contain both fixed and variable overhead) might be 'explained' by reference to the level of activity achieved. The extent of application of flexible budgeting and its usefulness would appear to be a fruitful area for future research.

Pricing

'Traditional' management accounting has, usually, favoured the use of 'marginal' or 'variable' costs as a basis for pricing decisions. This theoretical approach is justified by the familiar argument that only 'relevant' costs should be considered in decision-making and, as 'fixed' costs will be unaffected by the changes in output which might result from changing prices, they should be ignored. This reasoning leads to the view that, *provided sufficient capacity is available*, any price which would generate a positive contribution (i.e. surplus over variable cost) could be considered, and such a practice is sometimes referred to as 'marginal cost based pricing.' However, surveys of practice have consistently found that pricing decisions are *not* usually based on marginal costs. Where costs are an important input to the pricing decision they are usually 'marked-up' to ensure adequate contribution to fixed costs and profit and, often, 'full' cost (*including* fixed overhead) is used as the base to be marked up. Mills (1988) reports that previous studies (e.g. Skinner, 1970; Atkin and Skinner, 1975; Govindarajan and Anthony, 1983) 'have shown somewhere between 63 and 83 per cent of firms allocating overhead to product when making the pricing decision.' Mills's own survey of 52 manufacturing and 42 service companies supports these findings with 71 per cent of manufacturing and 65 per cent of service companies using full/absorption costing as a basis for pricing. Govindarajan and Anthony provide more detail in their survey reporting that 41 per cent of 501 firms surveyed used *total manufacturing* cost while 33 per cent used *total* cost as a basis for mark-up.

Rationales for practice are fairly easy to find. First, *so long as the volumes on which 'fixed' costs have been apportioned and absorbed are reasonably accurate*, the cost-plus approach should ensure that profit is generated. And, second, it is argued that, 'full' costs may provide an approximation to *long-run* marginal costs. This point is central to the development of activity-based costing and recently, Kaplan (1987) attacked the use of marginal costs by answering the rhetorical question 'Shouldn't I take that order if it covers my short run variable cost?' He responded: 'If you promise me you will just accept this order one time, this month, and you will never do it again, take the order. But you have to keep your promise because once you get in the habit of taking incremental business, the incremental costs are much higher than you think. Over time, you are going to add more overhead people; you are going to expand support departments somewhere.'

And Kaplan uses the argument that, in the medium/long term, costs are often driven by complexity (not volume) and, as product pricing and strategy decisions often do have medium/long-term implications, the appropriate cost for use in such decisions is an 'activity-based cost' – which takes overhead cost into account in a reasonably sophisticated manner. It is possible to partly account for the widespread interest in ABC because it addresses a clear business need – to provide more 'accurate' full product costs on which pricing strategies can be based.

However, the enthusiasm for variants of full cost pricing can be overstated. The evidence of Drury *et al.* indicates that cost information is used in a very flexible manner as an input to the pricing decision and examples of the (sensible) use of marginal costs in pricing decisions can readily be identified:

> A wire manufacturer found that potential customers purchased from foreign competitors – at very competitive prices. However, during recessions, the manufacturer was prepared to match this competition on a marginal cost pricing basis. These UK customers were prepared to switch to a UK supplier – but only if the price was competitive.
>
> A drinks manufacturer quoted very competitive prices to British Rail. The British Rail buffet was regarded as a 'shop-window' – with, relatively little choice and a captive market. And BR could be relied on not to ruin the general market by reducing retail prices!

This discussion suggests that, where a company has some discretion in setting prices, costs *are* a very important input to the pricing decision and both 'marginal' costs and 'full' costs (whether based on 'traditional' or 'ABC' analysis) have important roles to play.

Investment appraisal

As Pike and Neale say, in Chapter 14, 'academics used to argue that if crude and misleading investment appraisal techniques (such as 'payback' or 'accounting rate of return') yielded to more sophisticated DCF methods, firms would accept more productive investments and higher levels of economic activity would follow.' This argument was based on the indisputable fact that early project cash flows are more valuable than later flows – because the early cash flows can be invested to earn a return. Two DCF techniques have, traditionally been described, based on either the 'net present value' of a project or the project's 'internal rate of return.' Theory has recommended the use of 'net present value' (NPV) in preference to 'internal rate of return' (IRR) because:

- calculation of IRR is more complex than NPV;
- if cash flows reverse there may be multiple IRRs;
- IRR is inappropriate if projects are mutually exclusive;
- the reinvestment assumption implicit in the IRR calculation is less 'sound' than that implicit in the calculation of NPV.

These arguments might lead one to expect the widespread use of net present value at the expense of other techniques. However, as Pike and Neale point out, surveys consistently reveal that *all* the techniques of investment appraisal are widely used with 'net present value', typically, used least! The survey by Drury *et al.* again supports previous findings with payback and discounted payback being the favoured techniques whilst, of the discounting methods, 'internal rate of return' continues to be preferred to 'net present value.' Dugdale (1991) provides an analysis of the reasons for widespread use of all the techniques and research has tended to move away from attempting to demonstrate that one technique is 'better' than another, concentrating, instead, on analysing *why* practitioners prefer certain techniques. Instead of trying to show why techniques should be rejected attempts have been made to improve the manner in which favoured techniques are applied. Thus theory would recommend 'discounted payback' in preference to 'payback' and Pike and Neale discuss the 'modified internal rate of return' (MIRR) which generates an 'internal rate of return' consistent with the reinvestment assumption implicit in the NPV calculation.

There has also been a tendency to recognize the limitations of financial analysis in the decision-making process and to accept that appraisal techniques have only a relatively small part to play in investment decisions. As Pike and Neale note, investment decisions are the outcome of a complex process in which strategic considerations can have an important role, together with the need to 'search' for suitable opportunities before any evaluation can be carried out.

These conclusions echo those of earlier researchers such as Haynes and Solomon (1962) who identified five managerial functions in the process of investment decision-making and King (1975) who rejected the implicit assumption of 'theory' (that all projects could be defined and choice exercised on the basis of their economic worth). Hastie (1974) emphasized the importance of 'asking the appropriate strategic questions' rather than concentrating on the refinement of capital expenditure analyses and other researchers (for example, Ackerman, 1970 and Scapens *et al.*, 1982) have concluded that, in practice, 'strategic' considerations often override financial analysis in investment decision-making. A more detailed review of these 'non-financial' considerations can be found in a paper by Dugdale and Jones (1991).

Divisional performance measurement

Surveys in a variety of countries (see for example, Scapens *et al.*, 1982 for a comparison of UK and US companies, Reece and Cool, 1978 for US companies and Skinner, 1990 for a comparison of Australian and New Zealand companies) indicate that the vast majority of companies have adopted divisionalized organization structures and the manner in which such divisions are controlled and evaluated is therefore of considerable practical importance. The conventional wisdom, as reflected in most of the management accounting literature, suggests that divisional performance ought to be evaluated using residual income rather than return on investment (ROI). ROI, being a ratio rather than an absolute measure of divisional profitability, can encourage managers to make sub-optimal decisions. For example, a manager who is currently earning a 30 per cent return might be reluctant to accept a project earning only a 25 per cent return as this would dilute the division's rate of return. However, if the company (and the divisions) cost of capital is 15 per cent, the project is profitable and ought to be accepted. The residual income approach encourages the 'correct' decision by deducting from the profits earned by the division an interest charge computed on its capital employed. A project with a 25 per cent return would be acceptable to the divisional manager if performance is evaluated on the basis of residual income since 25 per cent return could be added to profits while deducting only a 15 per cent cost of capital.

However, despite the theoretical recommendation, surveys indicate a strong preference for return on investment (ROI). For example, the survey undertaken by Drury *et al.* (1993) indicates that approximately 20 per cent of the companies used residual income, 60 per cent used ROI, 50 per cent used target profit and 45 per cent used target cash flow. These findings suggest that corporate management do not rely exclusively on a single accounting measure, instead, a range of available techniques is used to give a general picture of divisional performance. The management accounting literature advocates that it is appropriate to measure divisional performance using profit before interest and taxes and/or cash flows in only certain situations, such as where divisions are unable to influence their capital asset base. In such situations divisions can be motivated to earn the best profit/cash flows by using the capital assets at their disposal.

Why is there a great preference for ROI rather than residual income? Skinner (1990) found evidence to suggest that firms prefer to use ROI because, being a ratio, it can be used for inter-division and inter-firm comparisons. ROI for a division can be compared with the return from other divisions within the group or with whole companies outside the group whereas absolute monetary measures such as profit, cash flow or residual income are not appropriate in making such comparisons. A second possible reason for the preference for ROI is that 'outsiders' tend to use ROI as a measure of a company's overall performance. Corporate managers therefore want their divisional managers to focus on ROI so that their performance measure is congruent with 'outsiders' measure of company overall economic performance.

The management accounting literature distinguishes between the economic performance of a division and the performance of its manager. The literature advocates that costs should not be allocated when evaluating the division's *managerial* performance but full allocations may be appropriate for evaluating the division's *economic* performance. However, none of the respondents in the survey undertaken by Skinner (1990) found it practicable to distinguish between managerial and economic performance. Nearly all the respondents used net profitability (after cost allocations) as a measure to control divisional performance and most of the respondents indicated that divisional net profitability was also used for strategic decision-making such as increasing the size of a division or closing one down. Skinner suggests that fully allocated cost is a good estimate of long-run incremental cost and profitability which can be used for long-run decision-making. For *cost control* purposes the literature advocates that divisional managers should be evaluated strictly on the basis of costs and revenues directly traceable to them. Thus all allocations of indirect costs, such as central service and central administration costs which are not controllable by divisional managers, ought not to be allocated to divisions for *managerial* performance evaluation purposes. Such costs can only be controlled where they are incurred, which means that they can be controlled only by central service managers and central management.

Despite the many theoretical arguments against allocations for cost control and managerial performance evaluation the evidence indicates that allocations are widely used for these purposes (see Reece and Cool, 1978, Fremgen and Liao, 1981; Ramadan, 1989; and Skinner, 1990). The UK study by Drury *et al.* (1993) supports the evidence of previous studies indicating that just over 50 per cent of the companies measure divisional *managerial* performance after allocating corporate costs.

In the Fremgen and Liao survey respondents were asked why they allocated indirect costs. The most important performance evaluation reason was to 'remind profit centre managers that indirect costs exist and that profit centre earnings must be adequate to cover some share of these costs.' A further reason cited by Fremgen and Liao (1981) and Skinner (1990) is that it encourages divisional managers to put pressure on service department managers or general managers to do a better job of controlling central costs. Skinner also found considerable support for the view that the allocation of central costs can lead general management to question whether it would be better if an existing central service were to be supplied (wholly or partially) either from outside the company or within each division.

Transfer pricing

Transfer pricing has received considerable attention in the management accounting literature. In Chapter 16 of this handbook, Tomkins and McAulay provide a brief review of the literature. You will have noted from Chapter 16 that the literature advocates two basic approaches to transfer pricing. First, where there is a highly competitive market outside the organization for the transferred product the appropriate transfer price is the price for that 'intermediate product' in the outside market. Second, where the outside market is not highly competitive or even non-existent, theory shows that, in the absence of capacity and other constraints, the transfer price which would encourage total organizational optimality is the marginal cost of production at the optimal output level. This is usually interpreted for practical use as the accountant's variable cost per unit. Tomkins and McAulay point out that if transfers are made at variable cost the selling division can make no profit and to overcome this problem it has been suggested that the buying division should pay the selling division an annual lump sum payment to reimburse the fixed capacity costs associated with meeting the buying division's requirements. This payment should provide a contribution towards fixed costs and profit.

The process of arriving at a transfer price by negotiation is presented in textbooks as an alternative approach to setting transfer prices based on economic analysis. Tomkins and McAulay, however, point out that it is somewhat unrealistic to consider the process of negotiation itself as totally separate from economic analysis. Economic information must provide some input to the negotiation process and it is claimed that if managers negotiate with each other to arrive at acceptable transfer prices they are motivated to coordinate their activities and to make decisions which will maximize company profits.

Table 17.1 reports the results of the survey by Drury *et al.* (1993) of transfer pricing methods used by 195 UK companies. The survey indicates that market-based transfer prices are widely used whereas unit variable/marginal cost transfer prices are rarely used. Where cost-based methods are used full cost or cost-plus transfer prices are more widely used than unit variable cost transfer prices. In Chapter 16 Tomkins and McAulay suggest that unit full cost may actually be a better approximation than unit variable cost to 'true' marginal cost and this would imply that full cost transfer prices may not be inconsistent with the marginal cost approach advocated in the management accounting literature. The justification for equating full unit cost with the economist's marginal cost and the arguments for setting transfer prices based on full cost in situations where the outside market is not highly competitive is described in detail in Chapter 16. The discussion will not therefore be repeated here.

Table 17.1 Transfer pricing methods used by UK companies

	Never %	Rarely %	Extent of use Sometimes %	Often %	Always %
Unit variable cost	82	12	4	1	1
Unit full cost	58	8	13	11	10
Unit variable cost plus fixed markup	69	13	6	6	6
Unit full cost plus markup	48	7	18	15	12
Market price/adjusted market price	48	5	14	21	12
Negotiated transfer prices	30	11	29	19	11
Lump sum payment plus a cost per unit transferred	91	4	4	1	

The application of quantitative techniques

The evidence from several UK studies indicates that the various mathematical/statistical quantitative techniques advanced in the management accounting literature tend not to be used in practice. In a study of the management accounting practices of a small sample of fourteen companies Coates *et al.* (1983) observed a general lack of 'sophisticated' mathematical techniques. They found no evidence of linear programming or other mathematical techniques for budget setting, transfer pricing or decision-making. In another study Gregory and Piper (1983) found little evidence to indicate that mathematical models were used for stock control purposes. A number of studies have been published in the USA describing the use of various quantitative techniques in US industry. However, the evidence indicates that, whilst some US companies do use quantitative techniques for long-range planning and operations management, there are a large number of companies which do not make extensive use of such techniques.

It could be argued that since many of the quantitative techniques were not advanced in textbooks prior to the mid-1970s there may be a lag in these techniques being implemented in practice. However, the most recent study by Drury *et al.* (see Table 17.2) is consistent with the US findings and indicates that, whilst some UK companies do use quantitative techniques, the majority do not make extensive use of such techniques.

Table 17.2 Quantitative techniques used by UK companies

		Extent of use		
	Never %	Rarely %	Sometimes %	Often %	Always %
Multiple regression techniques for cost and sales estimation	64	23	11	2	–
Linear programming techniques	63	19	13	4	1
Inventory models	33	14	29	19	5
Statistical probability analysis to estimate payoffs from alternatives	49	24	20	7	–
Learning curves for cost estimation	36	26	21	14	3

It would seem reasonable to expect that quantitative methods advocated in the literature would be more widely used if they offered real benefits to practitioners. Scapens (1991) suggests that in a competitive economy new techniques of management accounting will be implemented quite quickly if they assist decision-makers to maximize their profits. He therefore sought to explain the gap between theory and practice by questioning the basis of theory. Scapens concluded that the quantitative models required too much information, some of which was extremely difficult to obtain, for their implementation and the models presented in textbooks ignored the costs of providing such information. It is therefore possible that the benefits from using complex techniques do not outweigh the cost of obtaining information. Furthermore, when one moves away from simplistic textbook situations to complex real-world situations it may not be possible to obtain the information which is required as an input into the models. Scapens therefore argues that the use of simple techniques in practice may be an optimal response to the decision-making situation and not an irrational rejection of textbook models.

Conclusion

Survey evidence suggests that the conventional wisdom of management accounting as portrayed in textbooks is frequently not applied in practice. Scapens (1991) has suggested the following reasons as to why there might be a gap between theory and practice:

- delay in theoretical developments being applied in practice;
- poor communication between theorists and practitioners;
- theory fails to address the reality faced by practitioners.

Of these possibilities the first two do not offer plausible explanations. Many of the concepts and techniques have been advocated in textbooks since the 1970s and one would have expected them to have been widely adopted in practice if they offered real benefits. Also the conventional wisdom of management accounting forms a large part of the examination syllabi of the professional accountancy bodies and, if the theoretical techniques offered real benefits, there would be evidence to indicate that younger practitioners were implementing them. Whilst some academics may be poor communicators this cannot be true of all and, given that the conventional wisdom has formed part of the examination syllabi for many years, it is unlikely that a gap exists because of a lack of understanding or misunderstanding of theory.

Of the three explanations put forward the last seems the most plausible – that theory fails to address the reality faced by practitioners. To overcome this situation it could be argued that future generations of textbooks should be based on the construction of theory through the observation of practice and the abstraction of assumed principles from such observations. In other words there should be a change of emphasis from normative theory (what ought to be) to positive theory (what is). We believe that focusing entirely on positive theory would be a mistake since it would be dependent on existing practice, and would not seek to change it (see also Lee, 1989). In other words theory and practice would reinforce one another, habits of thought would not be altered and progress would not be made.

At the other extreme conventional wisdom should not be based solely on normative theories and ignore current management accounting practice. In our opinion conventional wisdom should describe both theory and practice. Theory should represent the desired state and practice should represent the current state. The desired state should not necessarily be seen as representing the set of techniques which *ought* to be used in practice. Instead, the desired state should represent a constantly updated stock of concepts and techniques which are available to practitioners and which should be considered alongside existing techniques used in practice. In evaluating the alternatives, future generations of textbooks should identify possible implementation problems and draw attention to the costs and benefits in actual applications. The choice of appropriate accounting techniques should thus be seen as situation specific. In order to adopt such an approach Scapens (1991) has indicated that there is a need for researchers to investigate the nature of existing management accounting practice in order to lead to a better understanding of the situation and contexts in which particular theoretical techniques may be appropriate in practice.

It is important that practitioners have a sound understanding of theory. If theory is ignored, or not understood, accounting systems will be implemented on the basis of ignorance, and fail to consider the alternatives available. Consequently there would be a tendency to perpetuate existing practices rather than select the optimal alternative. Furthermore, an understanding of theory enables practitioners to be aware of the conceptual weaknesses of the techniques which they use in practice and thus seek to avoid the pitfalls when interpreting the information generated by these techniques.

If conventional wisdom is to place greater emphasis on providing an understanding of the nature of existing management accounting practice and identify situations in which particular techniques are appropriate or inappropriate it is necessary for practitioners to cooperate with academic accountants. Academics can only undertake empirical research by obtaining access to organizations. In the past many practitioners have been reluctant to cooperate but this is now beginning to change. Academics have been criticized because of their failure to relate theory to practice and practitioners have been critized because of their failure to adapt to the changing manufacturing and competitive environment. Faced with these criticisms academics and practitioners ought now to become more aware of the mutual benefits which can be obtained from closer cooperation.

References

Ackerman, R. W. (1970). Influence of integration and diversity on the investment process. *Administrative Science Quarterly*, September, 341–52.

Atkin, R. and Skinner, R. (1975). How British industry prices. Industrial Market Research Ltd.

Choudhury, N. (1986). In search of relevance in management accounting research. *Accounting and Business Research*, Winter, 21–36.

Coates, J. B. and Longden, S. G. (1987). Management Accounting in New and High Technology Growth Companies – *CIMA Report*, London: CIMA.

Coates, J. B., Smith, J. E., Stacey, R. J. (1983). Results of a preliminary survey into the structure of divisionalised companies, divisionalised performance appraisal and the associated role of management accounting. In *Management Accounting Research and Practice* (eds. D. J. Cooper, R. W. Scapens, and J. A. Arnold). CIMA.

Drury, C., Braund, S. and Tayles, M. (1993). A survey of management accounting practices in UK companies. *ACCA Research Paper*. Chartered Association of Certified Accountants.

Dugdale, D. (1991). Is there a 'correct' method of investment appraisal? *Management Accounting*, May, 46–50.

Dugdale, D. and Jones, T. C. (1991). Discordant voice – 'accountants' views of investment appraisal. *Management Accounting*, November, 54–56, 59.

Edwards, K. A. and Emmanuel, C. R. (1990). Diverging views on the boundaries of management accounting? *Managing Accounting Research*, March, 551–63.

Fremgen, J. M. and Liao, S. S. (1981). The allocation of corporate indirect costs. New York, *National Association of Accountants*.

Govindarajan, W. and Anthony, R. N. (1983). How firms use cost data in pricing decisions. *Management Accounting (USA)*, July, 30–36.

Gregory, G. and Piper J. A. (1983). A study of the raw material reorder decisions in small batch manufacturing companies. In *Management Accounting Research and Practice* (eds D. J. Cooper, R. W. Scapens and J. A. Arnold). Chartered Institute of Management of Accountants.

Hastie, K. L. (1974). One businessman's view of capital budgeting. *Financial Management*, Winter, 36–44.

Haynes, W. W. and Solomon, M. B. (1962). A misplaced emphasis in capital budgeting. *Quarterly Review of Economics and Business*. February, 39–45.

Innes, J. and Mitchell, F. (1989). Management Accounting: The Challenge of Technical Innovation – *CIMA Report*. London: CIMA.

Innes, J. and Mitchell, F. (1995). A survey of activity-base costing in the UK's largest companies, *Management Accounting Review* 6(2), 137–54.

Johnson, H. T. and Kaplan, R. S. (1987). Relevance lost, the rise and fall of management accounting. Boston: Harvard Business School Press.

Kaplan, R. S. (1987). Regaining relevance. In *Cost Accounting, Robotics and the New Manufacturing Environment* (eds R. Cappetini and D. Clancy). American Accounting Association.

King, P. (1975). Is the emphasis of capital budgeting theory misplaced? *Journal of Business Finance and Accounting*, Spring, 69–82.

Kirwan, M. (1986). Management accounting in practice – a consultant's view. In *Research and Current Issues in Management Accounting* (eds M. Bromwich and A. G. Hopwood). London: Pitman.

Lee, T. (1989). Education, practice and research in accounting. *Accounting and Business Research*, Summer, 237–53.

Mills, R. W. (1988). Pricing decisions in UK manufacturing and service companies. *Management Accounting*, November, 38–9.

Molyneux, N. and Davies, R. (1988). Machiavelli and the art of cost management. Leading Edge, Spring, 19–20.

Otley, D. T. (1985). Developments in management accounting research. *The British Accounting Review*, **17**, 3–23.

Price Waterhouse Survey. (1991). Paper by J. Bright, R. E. Davies, C. A. Downes and R. C. Sweeting. UK national survey of manufacturing costing techniques and practices. Presented to the Management Accounting Research Group. London School of Economics, April 1991.

Puxty, A. G. and Lyall, D. (1989). A survey of standard costing and budgeting practices in the UK. London: CIMA.

Ramadan, S. (1989). The rationale for cost allocation: a study of UK companies. *Accounting and Business Research*, Winter, 31–7.

Reece, J. S. and Cool, W. R. (1978). Measuring investment centre performance. *Harvard Business Review*, 29–49.

Scapens, R. W. (1991). *Management Accounting: A Review of Recent Developments*. Macmillan.

Scapens, R. W., Sale, J. T. and Tikkas, P. A. (1982). Financial control of divisional capital investment. London: CIMA.

Skinner, R. C. (1970). The determination of selling prices. *Journal of Industrial Economics*, July, 201–17.

Skinner, R. C. (1990). The role of profitability in divisional decision making and performance. *Accounting and Business Research*, Spring, 135–41.

Index